FAMILIES OF STUDENTS WITH DISABILITIES

Consultation and Advocacy

Dr. Sandra Alper
University of Missouri—Columbia

Dr. Patrick J. Schloss
University of Missouri—Columbia

Dr. Cynthia N. Schloss
Director, Missouri Protection
and Advocacy Services

Allyn and Bacon
Boston • London • Toronto • Sydney • Tokyo • Singapore

To our children—Seth, Patrick, Rebecca, and Tarah

Senior Editor: Raymond Short
Series Editorial Assistant: Christina Shaw
Production Administrator: Marjorie Payne
Editorial Production Service: Chestnut Hill Enterprises, Inc.
Cover Administrator: Linda Dickinson
Cover Designer: Suzanne Harbison
Composition Buyer: Linda Cox
Manufacturing Buyer: Louise Richardson

Copyright © 1994 by Allyn and Bacon
A Division of Simon & Schuster, Inc.
160 Gould Street
Needham Heights, MA 02194

Library of Congress Cataloging-in-Publication Data

Families of students with disabilities : consultation and advocacy /
  Sandra K. Alper, Patrick J. Schloss, Cynthia N. Schloss.
    p. cm.
  Includes bibliographical references and index.
  ISBN 0-205-14038-6
    1. Handicapped children—United States—Family relationships.
  2. Handicapped children—Education—United States. I. Alper,
Sandra K. II. Schloss, Patrick J. III. Schloss, Cynthia N.
  HV904.F36 1994
  362.4'083—dc20   93-6854
                                          CIP

Printed in the United States of America

10 9 8 7 6 5 4 3 2 1   99 98 97 96 95 94 93

Contents

Preface

Children with disabilities make an indelible impression on their families—and their families on them—from the first moment and forever after. This truth seems so self-evident as to be simplistic. Yet, the history of the field of special education is focused almost exclusively on the study of the child. Our textbooks and professional journals are filled with descriptive and empirical studies in which students with disabilities are counted, described, assessed, trained, and evaluated. Parents of these children have received much less attention in the professional literature. Brothers, sisters, grandparents, aunts, uncles, and cousins of children with disabilities are rarely discussed.

Special education teachers and other professionals who work directly with students with disabilities understand the significant impact on the family has on the child. They know how much of the student's progress in school is directly influenced by what happens or does not happen at home. Counselors and others who work directly with the parents of these students understand that a child with a disability affects the parents personally, economically, socially, and in many other ways, every day for their entire lives. We are only beginning to learn about other family members and their reciprocal interactions with the child with a disability.

Why has the field of special education focused for so long only on the student with disabilities? Part of the answer may lie in the professional disciplines that were precursors to special education. Persons with disabilities were, for many years, considered to be clinically sick (Szasz, 1972). Persons who were mentally retarded or who experienced any type of physical or sensory disability were usually treated by physicians. Thus, the medical model, in which the focus is on treating the pathology assumed to exist within the individual, significantly shaped the field of special education. Parents and siblings were considered to have no greater role in the "treatment" of mental retardation or learning disabilities than they would in conditions such as tuberculosis or polio.

Another part of the answer to the question of why families of students with disabilities have been overlooked for so long lies in the age of our field. Special education as a formal discipline is relatively new. Only since 1975 have we had a federal mandate, the Education of All Handicapped Children Act (Public Law 94-142), to educate these students. It is only recently that the first generation of special education students has passed through the school system and graduated.

Many of these special education graduates and their families are facing a dismal reality. The "appropriate" education legally mandated by Public Law 94-142, The Education for All Handicapped Children Act of 1975, has not prepared persons with disabilities to live and work in their home communities. In many cases, the only post-school options available are sheltered, segregated environments that often result in dependence, little movement into less restrictive settings, and segregation from persons without disabilities and from community facilities. If the goal of education is to prepare people to be full participants in their communities and to lead productive, independent lives, then special education has failed many persons with disabilities. The U.S. Commission on Civil Rights (1983) reported that between 50 and 80 percent of all people with disabilities are unemployed.

While special education programs have focused on functional academics, social and communication skills, and skills needed for successful day to day functioning both in and outside school, relatively little emphasis has been placed on family participation in these programs. Yet, the literature emphasizes the importance of family involvement (McLoughlin, 1993; Turnbull & Turnbull, 1990). Public Law 94-142 protects the rights of parents, as well as the rights of their children with disabilities. The role of parents and other family members as active participants in special education programs is particularly critical as students with disabilities grow older. There are no federal laws mandating education or rehabilitation services to persons over 21 years of age, the age at which eligibility for special education services ends.

The reasons for minimal participation by families in special education programs vary. Meyers and Blacher (1987), in a review of published reports on parental participation, found several explanations. These included apathy, lack of information, and intimidation by school personnel. Brantlinger (1987) reported that parents of children with mild learning and behavioral problems lack information essential to making informed decisions. Goodall and Bruder (1986) pointed out that even parents who want to be effective participants in their child's special education program have few clear guidelines as to their roles.

In one of the few published surveys of parents of young adults with disabilities, Hill, et al. (1987) reported that only 12 percent of parents in their study preferred a competitive job for their son or daughter after graduation. This finding may underscore the need for more communication with parents concerning the capabilities of their children. In another survey of 48 parents of young adults with physical and intellectual disabilities, Brotherson et al. (1988) noted that parents perceived a lack of support from professionals in planning for their child's future.

These parents cited insensitive professionals who offered little help, who were not knowledgeable about options available, and who did not speak in terms that the parents could understand.

Cumulatively, these results have serious implications for special education teachers and other professionals working with students with disabilities and their families. These professionals need more information relative to parents' needs and participation. Identification of the needs and concerns of family members of persons with disabilities should lead to the design of programs that facilitate family participation in all phases of the schooling process, and teachers and parents working together should lead to more effective outcomes for students with disabilities as they go through school and prepare to live, work, and recreate in the community as adults.

Advocacy means to plead on behalf of the rights of oneself or another. It is our position that advocacy, and particularly self-advocacy, can enable parents and other family members to participate fully in the education of their children. Further, we maintain that even when advocacy efforts have been strong, they often focused on parents and ignored other family members (e.g., brothers, sisters, grandparents, aunts, and uncles). What impact does a child with disabilities have on these family members? What is their impact on the child?

In this text, we address family dynamics, roles of parents, and counseling and communication techniques. We also focus on the concept of advocacy. We emphasize empowering professionals and parents with advocacy techniques so they can better access resources that can help students with disabilities become full and respected participants in their school, neighborhood, and community. In addition, we will address siblings, grandparents, and other often overlooked family members of persons who have disabilities. Reviews and discussions of the social and legal foundations of the advocacy movement on behalf of persons with disabilities, working in partnership with families of persons with disabilities, and ethical and moral issues and dilemmas facing professionals will also be included in our discussions.

Our primary goal in this book is to enable teachers and other professionals to assist parents and other family members in becoming full partners in the educational process by teaching advocacy techniques. The text is intended for preservice students preparing to become special education teachers, counselors, therapists, and program administrators.

CONTENT

This book is unique in its focus on advocacy, self-empowerment, and *all* members of traditional, as well as nontraditional, families of persons with disabilities. Special attention is given to the following topics:

- Counseling and communication techniques with traditional and nontraditional families

- The needs and special interests of members of the family with a child with disabilities
- Empowering teachers and families with self-advocacy skills so they can better access resources that can assist persons with disabilities
- Reviews and discussions of the social and legal foundations of the advocacy movement on behalf of persons with disabilities
- An across-the-lifespan approach to working in partnership with families of persons who experience disabilities
- Ethical and moral issues faced by professionals

As is evident from the preceding discussion, the critical feature of *Families of Students with Disabilities: Consultation and Advocacy* is its focus on enabling teachers to assist parents in becoming full partners in the educational process by teaching self-advocacy techniques. This text integrates advocacy concepts and techniques into a comprehensive text on working with families of individuals with disabilities. This text is suitable for graduate and undergraduate level coursework.

In addition to addressing this content, *Families of Students with Disabilities: Consultation and Advocacy* has a number of other unique features. First, the text is written from a practical perspective. Methods discussed involve parents and other family members in school activities so they can act as effective advocates. By describing specific techniques and activities for working with family members and providing case studies and examples, the reader is equipped to be of specific service to parents or to direct them to other professionals within and without the school setting.

Second, the text offers a comprehensive treatment of the subject matter. Presenting recent information appearing in the periodical literature, we cover an array of services and programs based on local community resources. Writing from the areas of special education, rehabilitation, social work, mental health, and psychology are integrated and directed at the needs of educators.

ORGANIZATION

Families of Students with Disabilities: Consultation and Advocacy includes two major sections. The first section describes historical, social, and legislative foundations for empowerment of families with disabled members. This section focuses on the unique characteristics and needs of these families. It addresses the social context in which they function. Finally, litigative, legislative, and political issues will be addressed.

The second section addresses methods and models of advocacy. Chapters emphasize strategies for working with individual family members as well as small groups and agencies. Special attention is focused on interpersonal skills and problem solving in the consultation and advocacy relationships. Ethical considerations are addressed. In the final chapter resources for advocates are described.

ACKNOWLEDGMENTS

We owe many thanks to the people who have made the completion of this text possible. First, our reviewers, Vicki D. Stayton, Western Kentucky University, Department of Teacher Education, and Timothy E. Heron, The Ohio State University, Department of Educational Services and Research, for their valuable suggestions. Ray Short, our editor at Allyn and Bacon, has provided encouragement from the outset of this project through the final production. His leadership has ensured that the product is responsive to the needs of those who work with persons with disabilities and their families.

We would also like to express our appreciation to Christine Shaw, Editorial Assistant at Allyn and Bacon, for her assistance. Appreciation is also expressed to Betty Peterson and Donna Hale for their outstanding clerical assistance.

Finally, we would like to acknowledge the extraordinarily fine work of our contributing authors. Their dedication and sensitivity to the many issues faced by persons with disabilities and their families are reflected throughout the text.

S. A.
P. J. S.
C. N. S.

REFERENCES

Brantlinger, E. (1987). Making decisions about special education placement: Do low income parents have the information they need? *Journal of Learning Disabilities, 20* (2), 94–101.

Brotherson, M. J., Turnbull, A. P., Bronick, G. J., Houghton, J., Roeder-Gordon, C., Summers, J. A., & Turnbull, H. R. (1988). Transition into adulthood: Parental planning for sons and daughters with disabilities. *Education and Training in Mental Retardation, 23* (3), 165–174.

Goodall, P., & Bruder, M. (1986). Parents and the transition process. *The Exceptional Parent, 53* (1), 22–28.

Hill, J., Seyfarth, J., Banks, P., Wehman, P., & Orelove, F. (1987). Parent attitudes about working conditions of their adult mentally retarded sons and daughters. *Exceptional Children, 54* (1), 9–23.

McLoughlin, J. A. (1993). The families of children with disabilities. In A. E. Blackhurst and W. H. Berdine (Eds.), *An introduction to special education* (3rd ed.). New York: Harper-Collins.

Meyers, C. E., & Blacher, J. (1987). Parents' perceptions of schooling for severely handicapped children: Home and family variables. *Exceptional Children, 53* (5), 441–449.

Szasz, T. (1972). *The Manufacture of Madness.* New York: Dell.

Turnbull, A. P., & Turnbull, H. R. (1990). *Families, professionals, and exceptionality: A special partnership.* Columbus, OH: Merrill.

U. S. Commission on Civil Rights. (1983). *Accommodating the spectrum of disabilities.* Washington, DC: Author.

1

INTRODUCTION AND BACKGROUND

The Roles of Parents

Sandra Alper

Department of Special Education, University of Missouri-Columbia

Chapter Objectives

After completing this chapter you will be able to:

1. Describe the major historical roles played by parents of children with disabilities including: (a) the cause of the problem, (b) patients, (c) passive recipients of professionals' advice, (d) service providers, (e) teachers, (f) political activists, and (g) family members

2. Explain why the field of special education has focused on mothers of children with disabilities and placed much less emphasis on other family members

3. Describe the dynamic and reciprocal impact made on students with disabilities by their fathers, sisters, brothers, aunts, uncles, and grandparents

4. Discuss the results of follow-up studies of students with disabilities who graduated from special education

5. Explain why parents of students with disabilities are demanding state of the art special education services

6. Describe the growth of the national advocacy movement on behalf of students with disabilities and their families

7. Explain the need for professionals to be skilled in teaching self-advocacy techniques to students with disabilities and their families

Key Terms and Phrases

adult service system	family subsystem
ARC	family systems theory
best practices	functional skills
emotional reactions to birth of	Public Law 94-142
child with disability	right to education
empirical validation	state protection and advocacy
eugenics movement	agency
family members	transition

THE ROLE OF PARENTS

Two recent developments have expanded our perspective on families of students with disabilities. First, educators and other professionals now realize the reciprocal impact all family members have on one another. Every member of a family with a child who has disabilities influences every other family member. Second, recent changes in the demographics of the American family have resulted in family members other than parents assuming responsibility for the care of children with disabilities. Historical accounts of families of students with disabilities are incomplete because they focus almost exclusively on the roles of parents and exclude other family members. Historical perspectives of society's treatment of persons with disabilities and their family members are important, however, because they help us better understand the need for the advocacy movement. History also increases our understanding of how current policies and procedures affect students with disabilities and their families.

Parents have been cast into a number of different roles throughout history. Two noted authorities on families of students with disabilities, Turnbull and Turnbull (1986; 1990), identified the following roles: (a) parents as the cause of the problem, (b) parents as emotionally disturbed, (c) parents as implementors of professionals' advice and decisions, (d) parents as independent service developers and providers, (e) parents as teachers, (f) parents as political activists, and (g) parents as family members. Turnbull and Turnbull (1986; 1990) have presented an in-depth discussion of each of these roles. As these authors noted, parental roles are not separate and distinct from one another, nor do they fall into distinct chronological periods. Rather, they often overlap and share common elements. Parents often find themselves playing multiple roles. Parental roles discussed by the Turnbulls are reviewed below.

Parents as the Cause of the Problem

Turnbull and Turnbull (1990) discussed why proponents of the **eugenics movement** (1880–1930) assumed parents to be the underlying source of the child's physical, emotional, or intellectual disability. A primary goal of this movement was to remove human flaws by regulating human reproduction. The eugenics movement was fueled by a number of factors. First, after studying the Kallilak family, Goddard (1912) convincingly argued that mental retardation, or "feeblemindedness," was hereditary. Second, there was renewed interest in applying Mendelian laws of plant genetics to human beings. Gould (1984) related that proponents of eugenics even cited the preface to the Ten Commandments as evidence of their cause:

> . . . *for I, the Lord thy God, am a jealous God, visiting the iniquity of the fathers upon the children unto the third and fourth generation of them that hate me. (Exodus 20:5)*

National immigration quotas were set to prevent anyone deemed mentally impaired based on results of early versions of intelligence tests from entering our country and "polluting" the gene pool (Gould, 1984). Laws were passed that made marriage illegal for persons thought to have mental disabilities and institutionalization increased (Turnbull & Turnbull, 1990). Compulsory sterilization of people who were thought to be mentally unfit became common, aided by the political popularity of eugenics and the perfection of simple vasectomy and salpingectomy (tying of Fallopian tubes) operations (Gould, 1984). More than 30 states had legalized compulsory sterilization by the 1930s. According to Gould (1984), the eugenics movement reached its peak of respectability in 1927 when Supreme Court Justice Oliver Wendell Holmes, in his decision to uphold Virginia's forced sterilization laws, stated the quintessence of the eugenics principle in *Buck vs. Bell:*

> *It is better for all the world, if instead of waiting to execute degenerate offspring for crime, or to let them starve for their imbecility, society can prevent those who are manifestly unfit from continuing their kind. The principle that sustains compulsory vaccination is broad enough to cover cutting the Fallopian tubes. Three generations of imbeciles are enough. (cited in Gould, 1984, p. 15)*

According to Turnbull and Turnbull (1986), the belief that parents were the root cause of the child's disability outlived the eugenics movement. They described how parents' psychological characteristics and child care practices were often blamed for their child's disabilities during the 1950s and 1960s. This view was particularly evident in the work of Bruno Bettleheim (1967), who argued that children with autism withdrew from reality because their mothers were cold and rigid. Bettleheim concluded that as part of their "therapy," children with autism should be hospitalized with no parental contact for long periods of time (Turnbull & Turnbull, 1990). More recent definitions of autism (see Johnson & Koegel, 1982) emphasize that there is no relationship between parental attitudes and autism.

Turnbull and Turnbull (1990) noted that some disabilities are genetically passed on to the child by the parents. Conditions such as phenylketonuria, Tay Sachs disease, and Down syndrome are all associated with some type of genetic anomaly. But, predicting before pregnancy whether or not a parent will pass on to the child some genetically linked disability is often difficult, if not impossible. And in the vast majority of children with disabilities, no genetic cause can be identified.

There are cases in which the disability of a child can be directly associated with some action taken by the parent. For example, fetal alcohol syndrome (FAS) is associated with the mother's intake of alcohol during pregnancy. Babies born to mothers who abused drugs during pregnancy often have a host of developmental disabilities. Yet, blaming the parents when children are born with these conditions seldom leads to productive parent-professional interactions (Turnbull & Turnbull, 1986).

Sometimes, tracing the cause of a disability to some factor related to the parents may prove helpful relative to diagnosis and prevention of similar cases in the future. But as Turnbull and Turnbull (1986) pointed out, the attitude that parents do the best they can under difficult circumstances is, perhaps, most conducive to good working relationships.

Parents as Patients

Parents' reactions to the birth of a child with disabilities vary widely. Factors such as religion, socioeconomic status, level of education, personal goals, family support, severity of the child's disability, how the diagnosis is conveyed, amount of accurate information available to parents relative to prognosis, and available resources can all affect how each parent responds (see Chapter 3).

A variety of models of the emotional stages parents of children with disabilities may pass through have been offered (Faerstein, 1981; Farber, 1960; Kubler-Ross, 1969). While somewhat speculative, three to seven stages are usually identified (Blacher, 1984). Generally, these stages are described as: (a) feelings of shock and disbelief; (b) denial; (c) anger and guilt or depression; and (d) a shift from self-absorption to concentrating on how to deal with the child's needs. Whether all these stages are experienced by all parents is still controversial, as is the exact sequence of stages (Blacher, 1984).

While many professionals are increasingly aware of these emotional reactions, not all are sensitive to the idea that feelings such as guilt, chronic sorrow, anger, and hostility may be normal coping responses to extremely difficult circumstances. Roos (1977) was one of the first parents to charge that many professionals view parents of children who are mentally retarded as emotionally disturbed people who are in need of counseling. All too often, according to Roos, the objectives of counseling are limited to enabling parents to accept their child's disability and alleviating depression. Depression and chronic sorrow, however, have been described as normal responses in parents of a child with disabilities (Blacher, 1984;

Turnbull & Turnbull, 1986). While some parents may seek professional counseling in order to cope with their feelings, they also need factual information about their child's disability and how to obtain needed services.

Parents as Implementors of Professional Advice

The field of special education was long dominated by the medical profession. Prior to the 1960s and 1970s when behavioral psychologists discovered that persons with even severe intellectual disabilities were capable of learning, many children with disabilities were placed in institutions shortly after birth. Many of these facilities were administered by staff from the medical profession. When children with disabilities gained access to public schools after the passage of **Public Law 94-142,** psychologists, educators, physical and occupational therapists, speech clinicians, and rehabilitation personnel all joined in assuming some responsibility for developing and implementing the students' programs.

A widely held assumption during the 1970s was that parents should conscientiously implement decisions made by the professionals (Turnbull & Turnbull, 1990). If a child was not making satisfactory progress in the special education program, it was often assumed that the parents were not assuming their responsibility for implementing the program at home.

Roos (1977) described the "myth of professional omnipotence," or the assumption that professionals, by virtue of their specialized training and technical expertise, have the ability to make wise decisions about other people's lives. Even when multidisciplinary teams develop sophisticated, individualized education programs for a child with disabilities, parents may be excluded from the decision-making process. They may be expected to passively accept the educational program with gratitude.

The problem with casting parents in the role of passive recipients of professionals' decisions is that the needs and priorities of the family may differ from those of professionals. For example, a teacher may place high priority on functional reading, while the parents' prime concern is teaching the child to sleep through the night. Teachers of older students with disabilities may place first priority on vocational training and job placement, when in fact, the student's work schedule interferes with the family's long planned and needed vacation. Teachers of a child with severe disabilities may emphasize toilet training and expect the parents to carry out the program at home during evenings and weekends. But if the child is heavy and has to be carried to and from the bathroom frequently, the parents may simply not have enough physical strength and energy to consistently implement toilet training at home.

The unfortunate outcome of assuming parents should be appreciative and obedient recipients of professionals' advice is that open and direct parent-professional communication about the relative priorities of family members and professionals will not occur. Instead, parents and educators may blame each other whenever a problem arises (Turnbull & Turnbull, 1990).

Parents as Service Providers

Out of necessity, parents had to assume the role of service providers due to the lack of public educational services for students with disabilities prior to the 1960s (Turnbull & Turnbull, 1986). Parents of children with disabilities banded together and formed informal and formal groups on local and state levels. These parent groups served as a mechanism through which parents could give each other mutual support and share information. Some parents even started their own schools and conducted fund raising activities to support them (Turnbull & Turnbull, 1990).

Today, there are national organizations formed primarily by parents of children with a wide array of disabilities (see Chapter 13). These organizations have multiple functions, including advocacy, political lobbying, raising funds, promoting aware-ness, stimulating research, and providing services. The Association for Retarded Citizens **(ARC)** is one example (Roos, 1977).

Turnbull and Turnbull (1990) observed that many significant developments in the field of special education occurred because of parent rather than professional initiative. Parents initiated and supported efforts, often at great personal expense, that won the legal right to a free and appropriate public education in the least restrictive environment, better conditions in residential facilities, and integrated vocational, residential, and recreational services in the community.

Parents as Teachers

Turnbull and Turnbull (1990) explained why great emphasis was placed on the role of parents as teachers and members of the multidisciplinary team, particularly in the 1970s. First, the influence of early environmental experiences in the home on how much knowledge children acquired was heavily emphasized. Head Start and other compensatory programs were funded by the government. The purpose of these programs was to prepare children from home environments thought to be "deprived" or unstimulating for the demands of the public schools.

Second, Turnbull and Turnbull (1990) noted that the relationship between parental teaching and improved student performance was documented by research data. Since parents were now viewed as capable of assisting their children in learning cognitive and social skills so important for success in school, they were expected to teach (Benson & Turnbull, 1986).

As Turnbull and Turnbull (1986) pointed out, the term "parents" during this time usually included only the mother. Very few published reports during the 1970s even mentioned the influence of the father or siblings on the progress of the child with disabilities.

Third, training materials based on behavioral principles were designed for parents (see Bricker & Bricker, 1976). The purpose of these materials was to train parents to teach their own children. Some parent training programs were set up in schools. In other cases, special education teachers went into the home to observe parents working with their children and offer suggestions for teaching new skills and dealing with problem behaviors.

Parents as Political Advocates

The development of parent organizations such as the ARC has been described in detail (Roos, 1970; 1975). These groups evolved from small, local support groups of parents to national professional organizations. The primary function of many parent organizations has changed from providing direct services to advocating for political, legal, economic, and social change (Roos, 1975).

The *Pennsylvania Association for Retarded Children* v. *Commonwealth of Pennsylvania* (1972), referred to as the PARC case, is perhaps the most frequently cited example of parent advocacy. Prior to 1972, students labeled mildly retarded were eligible for services from the public schools in Pennsylvania. Students with moderate to severe mental retardation, however, could be denied access to public educational services if they were judged to be unable to benefit from schooling. Parents of these students and the Pennsylvania Association for Retarded Children sued the state to obtain the right to education for all students with mental retardation. The court decreed that all students with mental retardation, even those with severe and profound levels of retardation, were guaranteed the right to a free public educational program in the State of Pennsylvania.

Right to education suits were filed soon after in many other states (Turnbull & Turnbull, 1990). Many of these cases sought the right to education for students with a wide range of disabilities. Parent organizations served as a powerful lobby in the passage of the federal right to education law, Public Law 94-142, The Right to Education for All Handicapped Children Act of 1975. This law has been amended three times since 1975 (P.L. 98-199, P.L. 99-457, and P.L. 101-476). Another landmark piece of legislation, P.L. 101-336, the Americans with Disabilities Act (ADA), was passed in 1990. This act guarantees a broad spectrum of legal rights in the workplace and community for all persons with disabilities. (See Chapter 2.)

These feats demonstrate that parents can be potent agents of social change on behalf of persons with disabilities and their families. Legal victories such as these challenge the myth that persons with disabilities and their families must rely on the kindness and generosity of those with political and economic power (Roos, 1975).

Parents as Family Members

Professionals are becoming more aware of the necessity to consider the needs and roles played by all members of the family with a child with disabilities. Increased emphasis has been placed on family systems theory, as a result. A basic assumption of family systems theory is that the family is a dynamic social system whose members are mutually interrelated (Goldenberg & Goldenberg, 1980; Turnbull, Brotherson, & Summers, 1985). All family members are influenced by any one experience.

Turnbull and Turnbull (1986) and their colleagues (Turnbull, Brotherson, & Summers, 1985; Benson & Turnbull, 1986) reviewed special education research on the impact of a person with disabilities on family members and family systems theory literature from sociology. These authors proposed four major elements that serve as a framework for understanding the family: (a) family resources; (b) inter-actions that occur among family members on a day to day basis; (c) different needs the family must address; and (d) changes that occur over time that affect family members. Their work should prove instrumental in understanding and serving the needs of the entire family that includes a loved one with disabilities.

We have moved from a time when parents were virtually blamed for their child's disability to a point at which we value the family's participation in develop-ing and implementing educational programs. Professionals no longer assume that parents have to be trained before they can contribute to their child's education. Today, we realize that family members have much to offer professionals. They often have unique insights gleaned from their day to day experiences living with the student who has disabilities.

THE NEED FOR CONSULTATION AND ADVOCACY

Since the passage of PL 94-142 in 1975, educators have focused on informing parents of their legal rights, assisting them in gaining access to public education for their son or daughter with disabilities, and developing individualized educational programs for each student labeled with a disability. One result of these efforts was that during the 1986–1987 school year, more than 4,400,000 children were receiving special education services (U.S. Department of Education, 1988).

Parents have accumulated information about their legal rights and gained more experience with school personnel as their children with disabilities have matricu-lated through special education. This has resulted in a new need. Today, more and more parents are not satisfied simply to have a special education program for their son or daughter. Instead, many are demanding their legal right to an *appropriate education in the least restrictive environment*. Stated another way, many parents are demanding state-of-the-art services. Professionals are increasingly required to assist parents in advocating for these services. There are several events that culminated in parental demands for high-quality and effective special education programs. These are discussed below.

Follow-up Studies

Follow-up studies of special education graduates have raised questions about how well prepared students with disabilities are for life after graduation. Several studies have indicated that large numbers of special education graduates have not acquired the skills to live, work, and recreate in the community (Hasazi, Preskill, Gordon & Collins, 1982; Mithaug, Horiuchi, & Fanning, 1985; Wehman, Kregel, & Seyfarth, 1985). Instead, many have remained unemployed. Services available to these individuals are often sheltered and segregated from age peers without disabilities and from community facilities (Rusch, Mithaug, & Flexer, 1986).

Many parents and educators agree that if the goal of education is to prepare students with disabilities for life after graduation, then curriculum modifications are needed (Falvey, 1989). Consequently, special education curricula increasingly emphasize functional skills (for example, balancing a checkbook, using public transportation, preparing meals, and so on) needed in order to function in a variety of settings outside of school. Vocational training that will enable the student to obtain and keep a job is also emphasized, particularly as the student grows older. In addition, parents are demanding increased planning to make the transition from school to adult life easier for themselves and their children.

Adult Service System

A second reason that parents demand high-quality special education services is related to the first. While the first generation of special education graduates is growing older, parents have become increasingly aware of the needs of their adult children with disabilities. We have emphasized that there is no federally mandated guarantee of rehabilitation services for persons over the age of 21 who have disabilities. In addition, the adult service system is fragmented. Services needed by adults with disabilities are often spread among many different agencies including vocational rehabilitation, state departments of mental health, social security, and a host of other city, county, and/or state funded agencies. Learning what each separate agency can provide and then accessing those services can be a long and frustrating task for parents. That is why more and more parents are asking for information and help in obtaining these services from special education profession-als long *before* their child reaches the age of 21. After graduation, it is critical that family members know how to advocate for the right of their adult children as they navigate a fragmented and overtaxed **adult service system.**

Indicators of Program Quality

Third, more knowledge is now available relative to quality indicators of special education programs (Falvey, 1989; Meyer, Eichinger, & Park-Lee, 1987; Wilcox & Bellamy, 1983). Educators and psychologists have been able to determine what specific types of learning problems students with disabilities are likely to encounter in school. These students often experience difficulty in attending to the relevant features of a problem. They may have difficulty in remembering information recently presented. Often, they have difficulty in transferring information learned in one setting to another setting. Slow learning rates are common. They may be significantly behind their chronological age peers in reading and math skills. In addition to their academic problems, many of these students have social skill deficits and inappropriate behaviors.

A body of instructional technology, or **best practices,** has been empirically documented as effective in teaching these students. The term best practices includes techniques such as operationally defining the behaviors to be changed, ongoing assessment of students' observable strengths and weaknesses, direct and systematic instruction, reinforcement strategies, modeling, shaping, systematic prompting strategies, collecting data with which to monitor student progress and make educational decisions, opportunities to practice skills in the settings in which they naturally occur, and opportunities to interact with chronological age peers without disabilities.

These instructional strategies have been empirically validated. They have been documented to be effective with a wide range of persons. In addition, these instructional strategies can be implemented in a wide array of settings, both inside and outside the classroom.

Increasingly, parents have been trained to "know what to look for" as they observe their child's educational program. The Center on Human Policy, located at Syracuse University, has developed an exemplary program for training parents how to evaluate the quality of their child's special education program.

Expanded Knowledge Base about Families

Professionals who work with students with disabilities are called upon increasingly to advocate and train others in self-advocacy as knowledge about the families of these students increases. Two areas of expanded information were previously mentioned in the section on historical perspectives on parental roles, but merit attention here, as well. First, we have learned that students with disabilities have family members in addition to parents. They may have brothers and sisters, aunts and uncles, or grandpas and grandmas.

Recent work in **family systems theory** has made clear that these individuals have a significant impact on the family member with disabilities, and he or she on them. Some researchers view the family as a set of subsystems (the spouse subsystem, the sibling subsystem, and the parent-child subsystem) that reciprocally influence one another (Stoneman & Brady, 1984). It is important to remember that the parents are not the only family members who may be able to help the student with disabilities. Hofius (1990) described how the brothers and sisters of children with disabilities can serve as effective peer tutors. Strully and Strully's (1989) work has shown how the entire family can be effective advocates for children with disabilities in integrated settings. Finally, we should point out that sometimes a family member without a disability is in need of an advocate. Teachers may, for example, turn an episode of teasing a child about his or her sibling with a disability into a lesson on understanding individual differences.

A second area in which we are learning more about families of children with disabilities concerns nontraditional families, the topic of Chapter five. The term nontraditional, as used here, is applied to any family constellation other than one involving two adults who are married and biological parents of one or more children. Single parent families, adoptive families, families with multiple care providers, and reunited families are included. Because of the day to day child care, economic, and other demands placed on these families, they may have a limited amount of time to invest in obtaining quality services for their children. Self-advocacy skills are critical.

Growth of the National Advocacy System

The final factor related to the need for teachers and other professionals to be knowledgeable and skilled in advocacy techniques is the growth of the national protection and advocacy movement. Originally mandated by the *Developmental Disabilities Act of 1972,* every state must have a designated advocacy agency. These agencies have primary responsibility for advocating and protecting the legal rights of three groups of citizens: (a) persons with developmental disabilities, (b) persons who have currently or in the past experienced mental illness, and (c) persons who are eligible for services from vocational rehabilitation.

These state protection and advocacy agencies work closely with persons with disabilities and their family members. They have played a significant role in informing and training these individuals about their legal rights. In addition, they assist in remedying situations in which persons with disabilities are not receiving legally mandated services (an education in the least restrictive environment, for example).

One result of the national advocacy movement is that students with disabilities and their families have become informed consumers of special education services. They are more knowledgeable about what constitutes an effective educational program, their rights under the law, and how to obtain them. And, they expect special education teachers and other professionals to be informed and skilled advocates as well. The largest number of students served by special education are those with mild to moderate disabilities. The special education teacher is often the first person consulted regarding information or services needed by these students and their families. This is true even when the need is outside the area of special education.

SUMMARY

We have reviewed several roles played by parents of students with disabilities throughout history. It should be clear that parents are often called upon to play several different roles at the same time. It is not enough to consider the needs of only the parents of students with disabilities. Rather, we now recognize that students with disabilities are significantly affected by brothers, sisters, aunts, uncles, and grandparents as well as by their parents. At the same time, these children have a significant and reciprocal impact on other members of the family. And so the family must be viewed as a dynamic group of individuals who mutually influence one another in many different ways as they all grow and mature.

Emphasis has been placed on the issue that as we learn more about students with disabilities and their families, the role of special educators and other professionals who work with these individuals expands. In addition to providing instruction to the special education student, the teacher is called upon to perform many other duties including consulting with family members. As the first generation of special education graduates move into adulthood, parents have become more knowledgeable about the field of special education. They expect and demand quality educational services for their children with disabilities, as well as other rights guaranteed to them by law. This means that special educators also have to serve as advocates for their students and families. In addition, they have to train families in self-advocacy strategies.

What are the historical antecedents of the advocacy movement? What events and cultural influences led up to the passage of laws that protect the rights of persons with disabilities? What laws currently support family advocacy? The next chapter provides answers to these questions. First the conditions under which humans lived and how they influenced attitudes and treatment of persons with disabilities during four major periods of history will be reviewed. Then, the legal rights currently guaranteed to individuals with disabilities and their families are reviewed. Finally, three major laws that prescribe services to persons with disabilities and their families will be detailed.

The Roles of Parents

1. Historically, discussions of families of children with disabilities have emphasized the roles of the parents and placed much less emphasis on other family members such as brothers, sisters, grandparents, aunts, and uncles.

2. Parents of children with disabilities play a number of different roles, often at the same time.

3. The eugenics movement was intended to remove defective genes believed to be associated with human flaws through controlling human reproduction. Disabilities were thought to be transmitted from parent to child by heredity.

4. We now know that in the vast majority of students with disabilities, there is no known genetic cause.

5. Parents' psychological characteristics were often blamed for disabilities like autism. Current definitions of autism emphasize that there is no causal relationship between the child's psychological environment and the onset of autism.

6. Parents often experience a variety of emotional reactions to the birth of a child with disabilities. These often include emotions like denial, anger, and grief. Because of these emotional reactions, some have characterized parents as in need of therapy and counseling.

7. A widely held assumption in the 1970s was that parents should enroll their child in special education and then passively accept all decisions made by professionals.

8. Today, parents are regarded as team members who participate on an equal level with professionals in decisions about their children.

9. Due to the lack of a legally mandated public education for children with disabilities before 1975, many parents banded together and started their own educational programs.

10. Today, there are national organizations that were originally formed by parents and other family members of students with disabilities. These organizations have multiple functions including advocacy, political lobbying, fund raising, and stimulating research.

11. There is a wealth of data indicating that parents can be effective teachers of their children with disabilities.

12. There is no reason to assume that all parents can or should participate in their child's educational program to the same degree.

13. Parent-initiated efforts have won several victories in the courts including the right to a free and appropriate education for all students with disabilities.

14. We have moved from a time when parents were viewed as the cause of their child's disability to the point at which we value the entire family's participation in developing and implementing educational programs. We have also learned to appreciate the many demands and needs of all family members.

The Need for Consultation and Advocacy

15. Parents have accumulated more information and experience with special education services. Today, many parents are no longer satisfied to have a program for their son or daughter; they demand state-of-the-art services.

16. In addition to functional school programs, parents are demanding services that will enable their children to make the transition from school to living and working in the community as an adult.

17. Increasingly, parents have been trained to identify and demand effective instructional practices. These include functional skills training in natural settings and opportunities to interact with persons without disabilities.

18. Professionals are increasingly called upon to advocate and train others in self-advocacy. Self-advocacy skills are critical for all members of a family with a loved one with disabilities.

19. The *Developmental Disabilities Act of 1972* required every state to have a designated advocacy agency. These agencies have primary responsibility for protecting the legal rights of citizens with developmental disabilities, mental illness, and/or who are eligible for vocational rehabilitation services.

REFERENCES

The Association for Persons with Severe Handicaps (1989). *Program quality indicators checklist.* Seattle, WA: Author.

Benson, H. A., & Turnbull, A. P. (1986). "Approaching families from an individualized perspective," in R. H. Horner, L. H. Meyer, & H. D. Fredericks (Eds.), *Education of learners with severe handicaps: Exemplary service strategies.* Baltimore: Paul H. Brookes.

Bettleheim, B. (1967). *The empty fortress: Infantile autism and the birth of the self.* London: Collier-MacMillan.

Blacher, J. (Ed.) (1984). *Severely handicapped young children and their families: Research in review.* New York: Academic Press.

Brantlinger, E. (1987). "Making decisions about special education placement: Do low income parents have the information they need?" *Journal of Learning Disabilities, 20*(2), 94–101.

Bricker, W. A., & Bricker, D. D. (1976). "The infants, toddler, and preschool research and intervention project," in T. D. Tjossem (Ed.), *Intervention strategies for high risk infants and young children.* Baltimore: University Park Press (pp. 545–572).

Brotherson, M. J., Turnbull, A. P., Bronick, G. J., Houghton, J., Roeder-Gordon, C., Summers, J. A., & Turnbull, H. R. (1988). "Transition into adulthood: Parental planning for sons and daughters with disabilities." *Education and Training in Mental Retardation, 23*(3), 165–174.

Faerstein, L. M. (1981). "Stress and coping in families of learning disabled children: A literature review." *Journal of Learning Disabilities, 14,* 420–423.

Falvey, M. (1989). *Community-based curriculum. Instructional strategies for students with severe handicaps.* Baltimore: Paul H. Brookes.

Farber, B. (1960). "Family organization and crisis: Maintenance of integration in families with a severely retarded child." Monographs of the Society for Research in Child Development, *25*(1).

Goddard,, H. H. (1912). *The Kallikak family: A study in the heredity of feeblemindedness.* New York: Macmillan.

Goldenberg, I., & Goldenberg H. (1980). *Family therapy: An overview.* Monterey, CA: Brooks/Cole Publishing Co.

Goodall, P., & Bruder, M. (1986). "Parents and the transition process." *The Exceptional Parent, 53*(1), 22–28.

Gould, S.J. (1984). "Carrie Buck's daughter." *Natural History, 93*(7), 14–18.

Hasazi, A., Preskill, H., Gordon, L., & Collins, C. (1982). *Factors associated with the employment status of handicapped youth*. Paper presented at the Educational Research Association, New York, NY.

Hill, J., Seyfarth, J., Banks, P., Wehman, P., & Orelove, F. (1987). "Parent attitudes about working conditions of their adult mentally retarded sons and daughters." *Exceptional Children, 54*(1), 9–23.

Hofius, D. (1990). "Training nonhandicapped children to serve as peer tutors for their brothers and sisters with disabilities." Unpublished manuscript. Columbia, MO: University of Missouri-Columbia, Department of Special Education.

Johnson, J., & Koegel, R. (1982). "Behavioral assessment and curriculum development," in R. Koegel, A. Rincover, & A. Egel (Eds.), *Educating and understanding autistic children*. San Diego: College-Hill Press (pp.1–32).

Kubler-Ross, E. (1969). *Death and dying*. New York: MacMillan.

McLoughlin, J. A. (in press). "The families of children with disabilities," in A. E. Blackhurst and W. H. Berdine (Eds.), *An introduction to special education* (3rd ed.). New York: Harper-Collins.

Meyer, L. H., Eichinger, J., & Park-Lee, S. (1987). "A validation of program quality indicators in educational services for students with severe disabilities." *Journal of the Association for Persons with Severe Handicaps, 12*(4), 251–263.

Meyers, C. E., & Blacher, J. (1987). "A validation of program quality indicators in educational services for students with severe disabilities." *Journal of the Association for Persons with Severe Handicaps, 12*(4), 251–263.

Mithaug, E. E., Horiuchi, C. N., & Fanning, P. M. (1985). "A report on the Colorado statewide follow-up survey of special education students." *Exceptional Children, 51*(5), 397–404.

Roos, P. (1970). "Parents organizations," in J. Wortis (Ed.), *Mental retardation: An annual review* (Vol. 3). New York: Grune and Stratton.

Roos, P. (1975). "Parents and families of the mentally retarded," in J. M. Kauffman & J. S. Payne (Eds.), *Mental retardation: Introduction and personal perspectives*. New York: Charles E. Merrill.

Roos, P. (1977). "A parent's view of what public education should accomplish," in E. Sontag, J. Smith, & N. Certo (Eds.), *Educational programming for the severely and profoundly handicapped*. Reston, VA: The Council for Exceptional Children.

Rusch, F. R., Mithaug, D. E., & Flexer, R. W. (1986). "Obstacles to competitive employment and traditional program options for overcoming them," in F. R. Rusch (Ed.), *Competitive employment issues and strategies*. Baltimore: Paul H. Brookes Publishing Co.

Snell, M. (1987). *Systematic instruction of persons with severe handicaps*. Columbus, OH: Merrill.

Stoneman, Z., & Brady, G. H. (1984). "Research with families of severely handicapped children: Theoretical and methodological considerations," in J. Blacher (Ed.), *Severely handicapped young children and their families:* Research in review. Orlando: Academic Press (pp. 179–214).

Strully, J. L., & Strully, C. F. (1989). "Family support to promote integration," In Stainback, S., Stainback, W., & Forest, M. (Eds.), *Educating all students in the mainstream of education*. Baltimore: Paul H. Brookes (pp. 213–219).

Szasz, T. (1970). *The Manufacture of Madness*. New York: Dell.

Turnbull, A. P., Brotherson, M. J., & Summers, J. A. (1985). The impact of deinstitutionalization on families: "A family systems approach," in R. H. Bruininks (Ed.), *Living and learning in the least restrictive environment*. Baltimore: Paul H. Brookes Publishing Co. (pp. 115–152).

Turnbull, A. P., & Turnbull, H. R. (1986). *Families, professionals, and exceptionality: A special partnership*. Columbus, OH: Merrill.

Turnbull, A. P., & Turnbull, H. R. (1990). *Families, professionals and exceptionality. A special partnership*. (2nd ed.). Columbus, OH: Merrill.

U. S. Commission on Civil Rights (1983). *Accommodating the spectrum of disabilities*. Washington, DC: Author.

U. S. Department of Education (1988). *Tenth Annual Report to Congress on the Implementation of the Education of the Handicapped Act.* Washington, DC: Author.

Wehman, P., Kregel, J., & Seyfarth, J. (1985). "A follow-up of mentally retarded graduates vocational and independent living skills." *Virginia Rehabilitation Counseling Bulletin, 29*(2), 90–99.

Wilcox, B., & Bellamy, G. T. (1983). *Design of secondary programs for students with severe handicaps.* Baltimore: Paul H. Brookes.

2

HISTORICAL AND LEGAL FOUNDATIONS FOR PARENT ADVOCACY

Patrick J. Schloss

Department of Special Education, University of Missouri-Columbia

Chapter Objectives

After completing this chapter you will be able to:

1. Identify four major historical trends leading to the current services provided to students with developmental delays and their families

2. Define social support advocacy, identify situations in which social support advocacy may be used, and describe how social support is implemented

3. Define interpersonal advocacy, identify situations in which interpersonal advocacy may be used, and describe how interpersonal advocacy is implemented

4. Define legal advocacy, identify situations in which legal advocacy may be used, and describe how legal advocacy is implemented

5. Enumerate rights accorded to individuals with disabilities under the Constitution of the United States as well as major legislation and litigation

6. Identify four events that may result in the abrogation of rights for individuals with disabilities and discuss methods for reinstating these rights

7. Explain the relationship between litigation and legislation in defining rights and assuring services for individuals with disabilities

8. Enumerate services available to individuals with disabilities under the United States Constitution as well as major legislation and litigation

Key Terms and Phrases

The Americans with Disabilities
  Act of 1990
Armstrong v. *Kline*
*Board of Education Hendrick
  Hudson Central School District*
  v. *Rowley*
Brown v. *Board of Education of
  Topeka, Kansas*
confidentiality
consent agreement
Diana v. *(California) State
  Board of Education*
Education of the Handicapped
  Act Amendments of 1986
The Education for All
  Handicapped Children Act
  of 1975
evaluation
Family Educational Rights and
  Privacy Act
family service plan
independent review of evaluation
individualized education
  program

Individuals with Disabilities
  Education Act of 1990
interpersonal advocacy
least restrictive environment
legal advocacy
mediation and resolution of
  differences
Mills v. *Board of Education of
  the District of Columbia*
multidisciplinary team
notice
PARC, Bowman et al. v.
  Commonwealth of Pennsylvania
science
Section 504 of the Rehabilitation
  Act of 1973
service
Smith v. *Robinson*
social support advocacy
stare decisis
superstition
threat to survival
Wyatt v. *Aderholt*

HISTORY OF SERVICES AND RIGHTS

Recorded history has chronologued substantial shifts in societal perceptions of individuals' disabilities. Hewett and Forness (1977) provided one of the most articulate treatments of social patterns. They suggested that cultural values associated with disabilities have been influenced by the conditions under which humans have lived. Four major determinants included: **threat to survival** from primitive conditions of the physical environment; **superstition** resulting from the unexplainable appearance and behavior of people with disabilities; **science,** which is directly opposed to superstition and relies on natural and lawful objective study of the individual; and **service** as an effort to counter threats to survival imposed on individuals with cognitive, sensory, and physical disadvantage.

Hewett and Forness (1977) emphasize that trends in the treatment of individuals with disabilities do not follow an orderly progression from mythical to scientific, harsh to benevolent, diffused to focused, and so on. Rather, they offer a "swinging-pendulum" analogy in which the movement of the pendulum is a function of physical conditions, irrational beliefs, rational beliefs, social conditions, economic conditions, religion, and law. They further emphasize that throughout history, prominent spokespersons have been able to shift the pendulum based on persuasive action. John Kennedy, Martin Luther King Jr., and Mother Teresa, for example, have exerted such influence in recent decades.

In the following sections we will describe hallmarks of the four major periods. It is important to note that elements in each period influence our current cultural values. The reader will be left to judge the extent to which this influence occurs in contemporary society. He or she is also encouraged to consider (and hopefully alter) the direction of the next swing of the pendulum. Later in the chapter we will outline existing rights of individuals with disabilities and their families. Finally we will provide a detailed analysis of major laws that prescribe services available to individuals with disabilities and their families.

Threat to Survival

The threat to survival has been a major cultural determinant to the treatment of individuals with disabilities. The harsh physical environment of primitive times placed a premium on physical speed, agility, strength, and, to a minor extent, cleverness. Those unable to escape danger, forage for food, and avoid exposure to the elements were quickly killed. In the family unit, the burden for such survival rested with the most capable adult members. Consequently, little value in the family unit was given to females and even less value was given to individuals with disabilities. In some cases, sustaining the life of a "noncontributor" may have been judged to be unethical.

The "survival of the fittest doctrine" continued through Greek and Roman periods. Spartans, for example, practiced ruthless eugenics to eliminate individuals with disabilities who would pose an unneeded burden on the family and society. Romans practiced infanticide by allowing the father to dispose of any defective child or female. Plato advocated eugenics in his *Republic* stating that children of inferior parents and children who were defective should be secretly removed from society. Plato also supported the identification of more capable children for special nurturing. The most knowledgeable and capable would become the leaders of the state (Hewett & Forness, 1977).

Vestiges of the survival determinant exist today. Discussions about euthanasia, abortion, and institutionalization often reference the extent to which providing necessary services would undermine the welfare of the general population. In a recent Supreme Court case, *Cruzan* v. *Webster and the State of Missouri,* a major argument was the cost of sustained treatment in perpetuating the life of a young woman in a persistent vegetative state. Also commonly debated is the cost of mental health and educational services to individuals with disabilities. Administrators frequently argue that funds devoted to individuals with special needs detract from the ability to provide services to more capable students.

Superstition

We continuously seek to find explanations for events not readily understood. Physical phenomena have been explained by the presence of gods or other mythical beings reacting to desirable and undesirable behavior of society. Floods, plagues, and other natural disasters have been attributed to the retaliation of mythical beings as a show of displeasure with the actions of society. Similarly, throughout history, humans have superstitiously attributed individual differences to the intervention of mythological phenomena.

Early Chinese, Egyptian, Greek, and Hebrew cultures attributed disabilities to demonic intervention. Amulets, charms, and talismans were used to ward off spirits that would be manifest in irrational behavior. Early Babylonians developed magic potions for eliminating evils that produced cognitive, sensory, and physical disorders.

The Middle Ages saw people who were mentally ill and disabled being treated as demonically possessed. Treatments generally involved exorcism or attempts to purge the soul of demonic spirits. Exorcisms could be benign and passive such as laying on of hands and praying. They may have also been highly ritualistic including incantations, scripture recital, and chanting. Finally, they could have been punitive and destructive including floggings, burning, starving, and other torturous activities. As a related example, the influence of superstition in the middle ages led many to consider blindness to be retribution for sexual sins. This belief led to the barring of people with visual impairments from religious organizations.

The association of disability with divine intercession resulted in clergy becoming a principal treatment agent. St. Gregory of Tours, for example, emphasized the importance of heavenly interventioon to the exclusion of earthly attempts at cures. Prayer and religious ceremonies were held in attempts to remedy mental disorders. At other times, individuals with disabilities were tortured or killed in attempts to exorcise demons that produced the deranged behavior. Also common was the practice of abandoning children with disabilities to priests or other clergy. Monasteries that provided benevolent asylum for individuals with disabilities became the forerunners to contemporary in-patient care facilities.

Superstition continues to serve as a foundation for select rehabilitation and treatment practices in modern society. Certain mineral springs throughout the world attract disabled individuals because of their presumed curative powers. Pseudoreligious healing ceremonies are still conducted to invoke divine intercession for persons with disabilities.

Many individual still believe that heterosexual conduct between people with disabilities assures the perpetuation of disabilities to subsequent generations. Residents of mental health facilities and group homes are often segregated by sex and natural heterosexual and social interactions are prevented. In extreme cases, members of society advocate sterilization. While these beliefs may be true for some disorders or in certain social contexts, the generalization to all individuals with disabilities is not founded in fact and results from superstitious beliefs.

Similarly, society often associates cognitive deficits with violent and unlawful behavior. Communities have opposed the formation of group homes because the presence of people with disabilities will jeopardize the safety of the neighborhood. Further, advocates of institutionalization sometimes cite the need to protect society from people with cognitive deficits. Clearly, broad generalizations about the propensity toward criminal conduct among individuals with disabilities can only be founded in superstitious belief.

Service

Throughout history, and particularly in recent centuries, there have been advocates for the benevolent treatment of people with disabilities. While supporting the use of eugenics, Plato also encouraged families to serve disabled members. As reported in Coleman (1972), "If anyone is insane . . . let the relatives of such a person watch over him in the best manner they know of and if they are negligent, let them pay a fine." (p. 28) Affluent Romans provided for "natural fools" or individuals with cognitive disabilities in their homes. They served as objects of curiosity and entertainment at social gatherings. Romans also provided aid to blind veterans.

In the Middle Ages, Christian influence provided comfort to individuals with disabilities. Middle Eastern, Oriental, and European societies encouraged the training of people with sensory impairments. St. Mary of Bethlehem (Bedlam) was founded in London in the Mid-1500s and, in the 1600s, mental health facilities were established throughout the country. Some of the more notable centers included York Retreat in England and the Pennsylvania Hospital in America.

In the nineteenth century, the French founded agrarian work colonies for people with disabilities. The most visible crusader in the United States was Dorothea Dix. She advocated for the establishment of humane treatment facilities devoid of mechanical restraint and physical abuse. Dix, a retired schoolteacher, is held responsible for establishing 32 treatment facilities. Services for individuals with visual impairment were substantially aided through the invention of an embossed communication system by Louis Braille. Systematic procedures for teaching cognitively impaired individuals were popularized by Jean-Marc-Gaspard Itard in his work with a feral child found in the woods of Aveyron, France.

The work of professionals including Edouard Seguin, Sigmund Freud, B. F. Skinner, and Alfred Binet provided optimism for the efficacy of educational and rehabilitation services for individuals with disabilities. Due, in part, to the work of these scholars, service provisions shifted from passive custodial efforts, to direct therapeutic and educational services. Goals of intervention progressed from maintenance in a segregated setting to the development of skills and insights that lead to the full or partial integration into mainstream society.

Most recently, the United States and other industrialized nations have developed comprehensive service delivery systems for all people with disabilities. Current laws and practice in the United States emphasize broad-based services to individuals ages 3–21. However, there is growing interest in extending social services from birth to death (Cleland & Swartz, 1982).

Science

The history of science as related to human exceptionality can be divided into periods of pseudoscience and empirical science. Early efforts are best described as pseudoscience because superstitious beliefs exerted an undue influence over the practice of objective scientific method.

Archaeological evidence indicates that Stone Age cavemen practiced a form of psychosurgery referred to as *trephining*. This procedure was conducted to permit the departure of evil spirits from the brain. The spirits were thought to be responsible for headaches, convulsions, and irrational behavior. In fact, the procedure may have relieved pressure and effected a cure for some patients.

The Greek scholar, Hippocrates, articulated the need to develop a scientific understanding of people with disabilities. In reaction to the superstitious beliefs of this time, he argued, "If you cut open the head, you will find the brain humid, full of sweat, and smelling badly, and in this way you may see that it is not a god which injures the body but disease." (Zilboorg & Henry, 1941, pp. 43–44).

In Rome, Aretaeus may have been the first to develop a system of nosology used in studying cognitive defects. Asclepiades developed treatment regimens that included hydrotherapy, massage, vegetarian diet, physical activity, and sunshine. Conversely, Celsus advocated a more harsh treatment regimen including keeping individuals with disabilities in darkness, shaving their heads, anointing with oils, administering drugs, and drawing blood. Finally, Soranus suggested the treatment of people with mental illness through placement in a sensory neutral setting free of criticism or attention to faults. He also prescribed a form of relaxation and psychotherapy.

More unusual forms of treatment emerged in the seventeenth and eighteenth centuries. In one example, mental illness was attributed to disorders of bodily fluids. This explanation led to the practice of bloodletting. The use of a twirling stool in which the patient was spun into unconsciousness was also common. Finally, historical accounts report the practice of partial drowning in an attempt to alter the motion of liquids in the brain.

The most notable scientific contribution of the nineteenth century was Itard's treatment of the feral child, Victor. His careful analysis of educational provisions and behavioral outcomes may have been the precursor to modern case study technique. The most direct outcome was evident in the work of his student, Seguin, whose book *Idiocy and Its Treatment by the Physiological Method* won acclaim from the French Academy of Science. This description subsequently became influential in the work of Dr. Maria Montessori (Hewett & Forness, 1977).

The case study tradition was sustained through the work of Anne Sullivan, a graduate of Perkins Institute who was visually impaired. She was commissioned to "tutor" Helen Keller, the seemingly uneducable deaf blind child. The association of tactile symbols with physical experiences resulted in a major educational breakthrough for Helen. Subsequent achievement brought Helen to the point of near normality. Helen Keller later graduated from Radcliffe College and wrote several books describing her work with Anne Sullivan. *The Miracle Worker,* a Broadway play and feature movie, popularized the story.

The twentieth century included the most dramatic advances in science for individuals with disabilities. Early work included advances in mental measurement by Terman, Simon, and Binet. Sigmund Freud advanced the case study method. Contemporary researchers including Thorndike, Watson, Pavlov, Skinner, Bandura, and others have advanced a learning theory base for the understanding and treatment of learning and behavior problems. Genetic research offered the promise of anticipating, preventing, and treating genetic defects. Additional medical research isolated the cause of disorders such as phenoketonuria, hydrocephalus, and maternal rubella. Effective preventative and treatment measures soon followed.

We are currently riding the wave of immense proliferation in the empirical understanding of the environmental, biological, and social aspects of disability. It is likely that growth in broad-based research will continue as new and promising approaches for the prevention and treatment of disabilities are detected.

Historical trends identified as *survival, superstition, service,* and *science* clearly influence our current understanding of individuals with disabilities. Current emphasis is on service and science. However, we cannot discount the continuing influence of superstition and survival orientations. Parents and practitioners must aggressively pursue effective programs and procedures. They must avoid those based on superstition and unfounded survival notions. The following section of this chapter will discuss social and legal foundations through which this advocacy can occur.

CONTEMPORARY PARENT AND PROFESSIONAL ADVOCACY

As emphasized above, professionals and parents must endeavor to advocate for the most effective services for students with disabilities. In doing so, they may prevent the pendulum from shifting back to less effective superstition and survival orientations.

Advocacy must focus on an enhanced range of services and an enhanced quality of services. The range of services is judged by evaluating the relationship between student needs and professional effort. The quality of services is judged by determining the extent to which an empirical foundation exists for the practice. It is also judged by determining the extent to which the effectiveness of the practice is assessed with the individual student.

Current litigation and legislation provide a strong foundation from which advocacy rights for individuals with disabilities and their families can be established. Unfortunately, the litigative and legislative processes are often adversarial and may produce negative effects. The most obvious and common of these effects involves jeopardizing working relationships between the advocate and administrator, parent and teacher, or other individuals whose cooperation is important to the well-being of the student. While a major aim of this chapter is to outline a legal basis for parent involvement and advocacy, it is also important that these rights be addressed within a broader and less adversarial perspective.

Advocacy strategies useful in achieving the objective of comprehensive and validated services for an individual student can range from being highly informal and laissez-faire to extremely prescriptive and adversarial. For the purpose of clarity, these strategies can be conceptualized as involving *social support advocacy, interpersonal advocacy,* and *legal advocacy.* As emphasized above, we advocate exhausting all efforts at social support and interpersonal levels prior to engaging in legal advocacy. We will discuss each level of advocacy prior to highlighting the major role of litigation and legislation in the advocacy process.

Social Support Advocacy

Social support advocacy involves general actions that improve the quality of life for all members of society regardless of disability. It enhances accessibility and quality of services for students without specific reference to the immediate needs of an individual. Parent groups who are generally concerned with the quality of teacher education in the state may lobby for increased appropriations to higher education. They recognize that this effort will generally improve the quality of services for all individuals with disabilities, though no one student is identified as a principal beneficiary. Similarly, the parent who runs for the school board so that she may have an impact on diverse educational practices in the school district is practicing social support advocacy.

It is important to note that social support advocacy need not be a formal activity as those cited above. Any activity that enhances public responsiveness to the needs of individuals with disabilities satisfies our definition. Casual comments about the value of a particular agency for individuals with disabilities, contributing funds to the United Way and specific agencies, or voting for specific representatives who have a particularly strong record of support for social services all constitute social support advocacy.

The overall goal of social support advocacy is to reduce the need for more intrusive advocacy approaches. A perfect world in which general social support efforts were sufficient to open needed services would not require specific attention to the individual needs of a given student—they would be anticipated by society and routinely provided. In many ways social support advocacy can achieve this level of effectiveness. Few members of society, for example, question the value of education for a majority of students. Specific advocacy is not required to gain access into educational programs for the vast majority of students. Similarly, post-secondary education is routinely available for students throughout this country. While differences may exist regarding eligibility criteria and economic support, few would question the appropriateness of readily available technical schools, community colleges, and universities.

Social support advocacy may not be sufficient in addressing individual needs of some students. Because of the relatively low incidence of severe disabilities, little overall attention may be given by a school district to the needs of one or two individuals with these extreme needs. Also, the interests of some students and their families may run counter to the general social standard. Schools may generally desire that all students be well-mannered. They may not tolerate aggressive students who pose a physical threat to the general population. Finally, while appropriate levels of concern exist, the local social support system may not have adequate resources with which to address the needs of an individual student. In each of these cases, the next level of advocacy may be required.

Interpersonal Advocacy

This form of advocacy involves the direct interactions of the student, family members, or others, with those concerned for services and rights. Unlike social support advocacy, the focus is on the specific needs of an individual and specific steps that can be taken to meet these needs. Interpersonal advocacy usually results from recognized limitations in the general social system. Its goal is to encourage the service provider to make special accommodations not currently available for the general population.

Interpersonal advocacy can include ongoing informal interactions between the advocate and provider. It may also include occasional formal interactions. The parent who spends a few minutes each week with the teacher talking about the child's progress as well as expectations for future educational efforts is practicing interpersonal advocacy on an informal and ongoing basis.

While not the most provocative or dramatic advocacy approach, this strategy may be the most effective over time. Frequent informal interactions ensure that strong lines of communication exist by which both the provider and advocate can exchange views. These interactions generally result in good faith efforts to accommodate each other's interests on behalf of the student. These frequent interactions are also effective in identifying and addressing minor problems before they grow into major problems.

Parent-teacher meetings, IEP staffings, or other interactions in which educational and rehabilitation plans are developed allow family members to advocate for specific opportunities in a more formal forum (Turnbull, Strickland, & Brantley, 1982). The advantage to these forums is that the service provider and family member are often more attentive to specific requests. In the case of IEP staffings, family member and teacher requests must conform to due process provisions that will be discussed later. Consequently, there is an assurance that all requests will be considered. Both parties recognize that failure to address a specific request may result in a formal and binding solution. The disadvantage is that the more formal the nature of the interaction, the more likely it is that service providers will assume a defensive posture protecting the agency from subsequent recourse as opposed to focusing attention on the specific needs of the student. There is also a risk that competitive urges of advocates may result in greater concern for upholding initial positions as opposed to modifying positions as new information is obtained.

As with social support advocacy, interpersonal advocacy may not be sufficient to assure rights and services for all students. While more adversarial approaches should be viewed as methods of last resort, not all providers operate in good faith. In these cases, the "power" of interpersonal interactions may be insufficient to motivate a school district, rehabilitation agency, or other provider to extend services or rights to an individual student. Even when operating in good faith, legitimate differences exist between advocates and providers in judging the appropriateness of services. In these cases, a more formal process based directly on the due process provisions of law may be required (Crosson, 1977).

Legal Advocacy

Legal advocacy involves applying the due process provisions of federal and state mandates to ensure appropriate services for the individual who is disabled. In most cases, survival (economic) and superstition concerns are seldom influential in the ultimate judicial decision. As with interpersonal advocacy, legal advocacy is concerned with specific service needs or rights of an individual student. Also similar to interpersonal advocacy, legal advocacy results from recognized limitations in the general social system designed to provide for all students. Finally, legal advocacy shares a common goal with interpersonal advocacy of encouraging service providers to make special accommodations for an individual student. Given these common features, it is important to highlight that all good legal advocacy is initiated through interpersonal advocacy. When these less formal approaches become ineffective, the more adversarial legal approach may be adopted.

Legal advocacy differs only in that it recognizes and follows the due process provisions of the law. Specific due process provisions will be discussed in subsequent sections of this chapter. In general, however, legal advocacy begins with a formal and written request for staffing by a parent/advocate to the superintendent of schools (Rothstein, 1990). At that time, specific issues that the parent/advocate seeks to have addressed are identified. Four outcomes of the meeting may include: the parent/advocate convinces school personnel of the appropriateness of their position and the service plan is altered to the satisfaction of the parent/advocate; school personnel convince the parents of the appropriateness of their positions and the service plan is maintained with the parent's/advocate's approval; school personnel and the parent/advocate arrive at a mutually satisfying compromise; and neither side will yield to the satisfaction of the other. In the latter case, the next level of legal advocacy is pursued.

This higher level involves the parent/advocate requesting in writing a due process hearing. Parent/advocate and school personnel formally present their positions to an impartial hearing officer or hearing panel. School personnel and parent/advocates are generally represented by counsel and may present testimony of expert witnesses. The judgment of the hearing officer is binding upon the parent/advocate and school unless either side appeals the ruling to a higher authority. In most states, this involves submitting a written transcript of the hearing to a state board of education hearing panel for final adjudication.

It is important to note that the three general approaches to advocacy are cumulative in nature and legal advocacy is viewed to be a method of last resort. Most advocacy begins at the social support level. Parents and others concerned for the general well being of all students in the school system become active in school support and governance. They seek to ensure that the general needs of all students facing any possible contingency are met. The same parents advocate for the individual needs of a learner when the general support system is not effective. Interpersonal advocacy progresses along the continuum from frequent informal interactions to infrequent formal discussions. When these approaches result in an impasse, the parent/advocate may resort to the method of last resort—legal advocacy.

Figure 2-1 illustrates the relationship between advocacy methods. The goal of the advocate is to accomplish the desired service provision outcome using a method at the lowest level of the hierarchy. When administrators or others can be influenced through social support advocacy, interpersonal and legal advocacy should be avoided. When this is not possible, interpersonal advocacy should be employed. Legal advocacy should be reserved for the point at which essential rights and service needs are not available due to the lack of good faith efforts on the part of the school or the inability of the parent/advocate to arrive at a compromise when differences in judgment exist.

ADVOCACY OUTCOMES

As we have emphasized, the goal of advocacy work by families of individuals with developmental disabilities is to improve the quality of life for their children and youth. Two general advocacy outcomes may serve this function. The first is advocacy that ensures the human rights of the family and individual with disabilities. These rights are confirmed under the United States Constitution and further delineated by recent legislation such as Section 504 of the Rehabilitation Act of 1973, The Freedom of Information Act, and The Education for All Handicapped Children Act, and The American Disabilities Act. The second is advocacy that ensures effective services that may remediate or compensate for disabilities. These services are also identified in the preceding legislation.

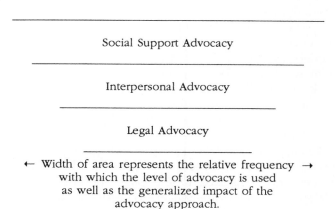

Social Support Advocacy

Interpersonal Advocacy

Legal Advocacy

← Width of area represents the relative frequency →
with which the level of advocacy is used
as well as the generalized impact of the
advocacy approach.

FIGURE 2-1 • Relationship Between Advocacy Methods

Rights of Individuals with Disabilities

The historical overview early in this chapter identified numerous examples of people with disabilities being denied even basic human rights. These included freedom from harsh treatment, freedom of segregation, protection from public scorn and prejudicial treatment, access to public facilities and services, access to full employment, and liberty of thought and action. Further, some persons with disabilities have been denied due process as guaranteed by the U.S. Constitution. The authors also define due process as a sincere disposition of fairness between people, and more particularly, between the individual with disabilities and government providers. In short, families of individuals with disabilities have been required to overcome, on behalf of their children and youth, a history of substandard citizenship in which rights to full political, economic, and social participation in American life were denied.

Not all groups of individuals with disabilities shared equally in the hardships imposed by society. The most disadvantaged included individuals least able to self-advocate and whose families were in the least tenable position to influence public opinion. This often included individuals with cognitive deficits and mental illness. Because many of these disabilities have no objective and easily understood origin, society has been inclined to view them suspiciously and seek reasons that the denial of rights is justified.

Groups with more objective and easily understood disabilities have been more effective in advocating for rights. Individuals with visual impairment, for example, have represented one of the stronger lobbies for federal and state action. Individuals with physical disabilities have also fared well in the political and judicial process.

Policies and laws supporting the rights of individuals with disabilities are generally motivated by the extent of medical knowledge of the cause and treatment of the disorder. In the absence of this knowledge, superstitious and survival of the fittest attitudes are likely to prevail.

Further, government impact is influenced largely by the extent to which influential community members acknowledge responsibility for services. Again, disorders based on objective diagnoses (such as sensory and physical impairments) are more likely to be supported by public awareness of the innocence of the individual. Poorly understood disorders (Aids is a recent example) often generate superstitious beliefs attributing cause to the individual and his or her family. In these cases, social deprivation suffered by the individual may be considered to be a just outcome.

Finally, awareness by the legal profession of the social and political implications of disability influences the extent to which extrafamilial advocacy occurs. Attorneys not sensitized to the plight of institutionalized people with severe developmental delays are unlikely to pursue litigation on behalf of this group. Their attention is more likely to focus on issues affecting more verbal, visible, and affluent members of society.

Despite these impediments, the United States Constitution accords specific rights to all members of society regardless of race, religion, creed, or disability.

Current legislation further defines these rights and stipulates the manner in which they are assured. We are confident that at least partial attainment of rights for the general population of individuals with disabilities has been obtained. These rights are supported by the work of numerous professional and advocacy groups including: The Association for Persons with Severe Handicaps, American Association on Mental Retardation, The Association for Retarded Citizens, Association for Children with Learning Disabilities, Alexander Graham Bell Association, Council for Exceptional Children, National Association for State Directors of Special Education, American Psychological Association, and others.

Table 2-1 illustrates many of the rights accorded to individuals with disabilities. A long history of state and federal litigation provides precedence through which these rights are sustained. Supporting legislation includes: Family Educational Rights and Privacy Act, The Education for All Handicapped Children Act of 1975, Education of the Handicapped Act Amendments of 1986, Section 504 of the Rehabilitation Act of 1973, and The Americans with Disabilities Act of 1990.

While the rights of the general population may be upheld through the work of the courts and advocacy groups, not all individuals experience the full benefit of these advances. Four events typically result in an individual's being denied the rights accorded through state and federal mandate. These include:

- The presence of a condition or circumstance for which there are no legal precedents
- The restriction of liberty for isolated individuals unable to self advocate and for whom there are no advocates
- The abrogation of rights for an individual due to the lack of information on the part of service providers, families, and other advocates
- The abrogation of rights for an individual due to the lack of good faith efforts on the part of administrators and/or services providers

Each of these problems requires distinct strategies that are discussed in the following paragraphs.

Denial of Rights Due to Limited Legal Precedence

As society matures and we become increasingly attentive to the legal rights of individuals with disabilities, more and more unique cases emerge. Original efforts focused on the most basic of rights, including access to educational opportunities for all citizens (*Brown* v. *The Board of Education,* 1954). Later efforts focused on the rights of individuals who are institutionalized (*PARC et al.* v. *Commonwealth of Pennsylvania,* 1971). Even more recent cases have addressed the specific nature of services (*Board of Education of the Hendrick Hudson Central School District* v. *Amy Rowley,* 1982). We are currently on the threshold of a new era of litigation addressing issues of concern to people with the most severe disabilities. As increasingly refined and focused questions arise pertaining to the rights of individuals with disabilities, families and advocates will need to seek legal recourse. The

TABLE 2-1 • Rights of Individuals with Disabilities and Their Families

Right to vote	Unless convicted as a felon or adjudged incompetent
Right to marry	Unless adjudged incapable of entering into a marriage contract, or if the marriage gives rise to an incestuous relationship
Right to sue	Action may be initiated by guardian if individual is judged to be incompetent
Right to contract	May not be enforceable if individual is judged to be incompetent and the contract was enforced without the consent of the person's guardian
Right to transportation	Public transportation vehicles and facilities must be accessible to individuals with disabilities. Individuals able to pass knowledge, vision, and driving test are eligible to receive a drivers license regardless of disability.
Right to access	Buildings constructed or financed with federal funds after August 12, 1968 must be accessible to individuals with disabilities.
Right to confidentiality	Individuals with disabilities and their families must be aware of and agree to the distribution of personnel records. They must also have access to records.
Right to protection from discrimination in employment	Companies employing over 15 workers (after 1992) may not discriminate in recruitment, hiring, promotion, authorizing transfers, awarding tenure, reinstating following layoff, establishing salary or other compensation, establishing job assignment, classification, and description, determining seniority, awarding leaves of absence and sick leave, providing fringe benefits including training and support for training, providing access to employment sponsored social and recreational activities, or any other privilege and condition of employment.
Right to freedom from discrimination in housing practices	Individuals selling or renting housing are prohibited from discriminating in advertising, accommodating, or providing housing to individuals with disabilities. This provision also ensures the rights of agencies to form group homes in neighborhoods. Zoning, deed restrictions, covenants, and other land use regulations must conform to the rights of individuals with disabilities. Also, multifamily dwellings (four or more units) first occupied after March, 1991 must provide accessible common areas.
Right not to be involuntarily confined to an institution	Admission to mental health and developmental centers must be voluntary unless minimum legal standards are met. The first standard is evidence of informed consent for individuals judged capable of making the decision. When judged not capable, a judicial review of the appropriateness of placement must occur. The second standard involves a determination that the individual is not able to care for his or her self in a less restrictive community setting even with the help of others. The third standard is that the individual is judged not to be dangerous to self or others without protections provided through residential care.

TABLE 2-1 • *Continued*

Right to reasonable and safe confinement when institutionalized	This standard includes freedom from unreasonable body restraint, seclusion, and aversive behavior modification practices. Also, the assurance that basic health care needs are provided. Clothing, food, and personal care needs are addressed. Finally, sanitary living conditions are provided.
Right to refuse treatment while in residential care	Unless the individual is judged to be dangerous without the provision of an effective treatment, the individual has the right to refuse prescribed medicine or services.
Right to refuse participation in non-therapeutic labor in residential settings	Persons served in residential placement can not be required to engage in labor for the economic benefit of the facility or state.
Right to be treated with dignity	Individuals served in mental health and developmental centers or other educational and rehabilitation settings may not be neglected, verbally harassed, or physically abused. In many states abuse is a criminal offense.
Right to privacy	Residents of mental health and developmental centers and participants of educational or rehabilitation programs may have free access to records. They may also protect those records from being viewed by unauthorized individuals.
Right to visitation while in residential care	Individuals with disabilities have the right to private visits from family members, physician, attorney, clergy member, or advocate.
Right to refuse participation in experimental research	Residents of mental health and developmental centers, educational or rehabilitation settings must provide informed consent prior to being included in experimental studies.
Right to due process when suspicion of rights violations occur	Residents of mental health and developmental centers must receive an impartial investigation and review whenever violations of rights are claimed by the individual or suggested by others. Due process provisions must also ensure that family members can challenge educational placement and service decisions.
Right to maintain reasonable personal possessions	Residents of mental health and developmental centers must be allowed to possess and wear their own clothes, keep and spend reasonable sums of their own money, utilize personal possessions, and access newspapers, magazines, radios, or televisions.
Right to qualified service providers	Paraprofessional and professional staff members must be qualified to provide services required by individuals in mental health and developmental centers, as well as educational and rehabilitation programs. Sufficient numbers of staff must be available to effectively provide required services.
Right to least restrictive placement	The degree of segregation and restriction within a mental health facility, developmental disabilities center, educational program, and rehabilitation program must be no greater than warranted by the personal needs of the individual.

outcomes of these cases will provide a foundation for the continuous refinement of rights for individuals with disabilities.

Denial of Rights Due to Isolated and Low Incidence Conditions

Initial litigation and legislation focused on the legal rights of broad populations. Current legislation addresses individuals with specific handicapping conditions identified under P.L. 94-142. Parents and advocates will increasingly focus on the rights of individuals not specifically identified in the law. Recent attention, for example, has focused on individuals with attention deficits disorders, dual sensory impairments, and fragile health conditions (Hallahan & Kauffman, 1991). Of special concern in coming years will be individuals who are generally not effective self-advocates. This may include individuals with multiple disabilities and severe cognitive/language limitations (Cartwright, Cartwright, & Ward, 1989). Also a priority will be individuals continuing to reside in state facilities with limited family involvement.

Denial of Rights Due to Limited Knowledge of Service Providers

Professionals are increasingly aware of rights accorded to individuals with disabilities. P. L. 94-142, for example, provides for the allocation of federal funds for the continuing education of special education personnel, regular education personnel, related service providers, and administrators. Many states require that all individuals obtaining teaching and administrative certificates demonstrate minimum competence in knowledge of the legal implications of disabilities. Despite these provisions, individuals with disabilities may be denied rights because of educational and rehabilitation personnels' lack of knowledge. As emphasized above, litigation and legislation continues to proliferate and there is no assurance that all service providers are kept informed as changes occur. Consequently, it is increasingly important that families remain aware of changes related to their child's legal rights. Participation in parent groups such as The Association for Retarded Citizens, Association for Children with Learning Disabilities, and others may aid in accomplishing this objective.

Denial of Rights Due to the Lack of Good Faith Efforts on the Part of Professionals

Unfortunately, not all professionals work toward the best interests of individuals with disabilities. Budget constraints, difficulty in employing qualified personnel, and adverse public opinion may result in administrators or others ignoring and violating individual rights. While on the surface, these acts appear to be inexcusable, in reality, few professionals actually acknowledge that they are not making a good faith effort. Rather, they attribute the failure to accord rights to factors out of their control. Whether or not these factors are actually out of their control is open to debate.

Substantial negotiation and advocacy is often required to encourage the responsible individual or agency to amend their practices. This may require formal proceedings that take advantage of due process provisions of law. As highlighted above, advocacy organizations may be effective allies in ensuring the rights of individuals with disabilities.

Services for Individuals with Disabilities

Beyond assuring certain rights, a second advocacy outcome is the provision of services for individuals with disabilities. As is suggested in our historical overview, the services provided to individuals with disabilities has expanded greatly in recent years.

Meyen (1982) has provided a comprehensive comparison of service options in the 1950s and 1980s. He suggested that most programs in the 1950s included the exclusive use of self-contained special classes predominantly for individuals with mental retardation and emotional disturbance. Resource rooms, consultation services, or itinerant teachers were not available. Gifted students were accommodated only through special instructional grouping or accelerated promotion. Special classes may have existed for individuals with orthopedic impairments but classes were generally not provided for individuals with severe developmental delays. Students with visual and hearing impairments were served on a limited basis through cooperative programs involving several districts, but segregated state residential facilities were the predominant treatment setting for individuals with sensory impairments and severe disabilities.

Speech clinicians had heavy case loads devoted primarily to initial screening and remediation of articulation problems. School psychologists were principally responsible for placement decisions and family members had little involvement. Most special education classes were located in primary school buildings with few secondary programs available and most instructional materials were teacher made. Students were seldom "declassified" and returned to regular classes once they had progressed through special programs. A disproportionate number of children served in special classes were minority group representatives. Finally, educational and rehabilitation services outside of school settings were virtually nonexistent with mental health and developmental centers serving as long-term custodial placements as opposed to transitional therapeutic environments.

Meyen (1982) goes on to identify differences that may be found in current educational settings. He suggests that the number of individuals with disabilities served in special programs of all types has more than doubled. Individuals with severe disabilities comprise a substantially larger portion of the case load. Those with mild to moderate disabilities are much less likely to be segregated into separate classes or facilities. Resource, consultation, and itinerant programs are used to a greater extent and professionals have increased use of commercial materials including specialized diagnostic instruments, curricula, and learning aids. Options for gifted and talented students exist in many school districts.

Speech and language therapists are increasingly attentive to the full communication needs of special students. They are likely to develop alternative and augmentative communication approaches. They are also increasingly focused on pragmatic language skills. Along with students who are speech and language impaired, students with specific learning disabilities have emerged as the largest group of individuals for whom special services are provided.

Individualized education programs are developed for all students with disabilities. Testing that leads to special education services is increasingly sensitive to cultural effects. This is expected to reduce the relative number of minority students inappropriately served. Parents are active participants in decision-making and implementation of educational programs. Few individuals are still served in residential facilities with a major increase in the use of group home placements and community based services. Services are provided from preschool to adulthood with active cooperation between family members, educational, mental health, rehabilitation, and social service agencies. Instructional, medical and rehabilitation technology has been effective in accommodating many sensory and physical impairments.

As has been emphasized in this text, and by others (see Cartwright, Cartwright, & Ward, 1989), the major impetus for these changes has come from families of individuals with disabilities. The advocacy movement, spearheaded by the interests of politically astute parents, has yielded substantial legislation expanding service options throughout the age and disability range. Table 2-2 illustrates the services mandated under Section 504 of the Rehabilitation Act of 1973, The Education for All Handicapped Children Act and its amendments, and The Americans with Disabilities Act. The following section will provide specific details pertaining to these legislative landmarks.

Influential Litigation

The basic rights of individuals with disabilities are established in the United States Constitution. Specifically, the Fourteenth Amendment provides that no state shall "deprive any person of life, liberty, or property, without due process of law nor deny equal protection of the laws." Interestingly, education is not addressed in the constitution. The Tenth Amendment, however, indicates that "powers not delegated to the United States by the Constitution, nor prohibited by it to the States, are reserved to the states. . . ." As a consequence, education is mandated through state statute or individual state constitutions.

Given provisions of the Fourteenth Amendment, the Tenth Amendment, and state mandates for educational services, all students in the United States are guaranteed equal access to education. Further, they are assured due process prior

TABLE 2-2 • Services Provision Requirements for Individuals with Disabilities and Their Families

Right to recreation	All public parks and recreational facilities constructed with federal funds after 1976 must be accessible. Individuals served in residential facilities must be provided recreational programs.
Right to education	Free and appropriate public education must be provided to all individuals ages 3–21. Education must include necessary related services, an individualized education program, and family consent for evaluation and placement.
Right to the development of an individualized education program	Individuals with disabilities served in public school programs must receive the written document describing their current educational levels, annual goals and short term objectives, specific services to be provided and specific service providers, anticipated date for initiating and completing services, criterion for the success of the program, and extent to which services are provided in the least restrictive environment. Family members must be invited to participate in the development of the written program. To the extent possible, the individual with disabilities may also be asked to participate.
Right to vocational rehabilitation	All individuals having a reasonable chance to obtain and hold employment are eligible for specific vocational rehabilitation services. These include: vocational evaluation; career guidance, employment counseling, employment placement; medical, surgical, and psychiatric care related to employment; provision of prosthetic devices; vocational training; basic living expenses and transportation related to medical treatment or vocational training; work related equipment, uniforms, and licenses; and rehabilitation engineering to accommodate work demands. These benefits must be summarized in an annual individualized written rehabilitation plan.
Right to summer school	Individuals ages 3–21 who are likely to regress substantially must be provided an extended school program at public expense.
Right to assessment in native language	Hispanic, Asian, and other individuals for whom English is a second language must be assessed in the native language.
Right to social support	Individuals with disabilities are eligible to receive Supplemental Security Income, Medicare, and Medicaid.
Right to an educational program while in residential care	All institutionalized people have the right to treatment and habilitation required to develop or maintain skills that will lead to discharge from the facility.

to denying equal educational opportunities. Unfortunately, the preceding documents fail to stipulate precisely what constitutes equal access to education and precisely what constitutes due process prior to the denial of services. Greater specificity occurs through case law and statutes. The present section will address case law while the following section will cover federal Statutes.

It should be clear from this discussion that court cases and legislation do little to expand constitutional rights. They do, however, clarify and operationalize these rights. Specifically, the United States Constitution provides for equal treatment of all Americans. Subsequent legislation simply clarifies the specific rights that are accorded under the Constitution.

Case law establishes rights and practices before sufficient legislation is available to cover all contingencies not anticipated in drafting the constitution. This is accomplished through the concept of **stare decisis.** This philosophy emphasizes that courts base decisions on previous legal precedents. Departure from findings of previous cases can only occur if the current judicial decision notes that relevant facets are different from those in previous cases, that judicial error occurred in previous cases, or that relevant conditions have changed since the earlier cases were tried.

Knowledge of previous judicial decisions, therefore, provides strong grounds for future practice. The higher the court of standing, the more confidence can be placed on the ruling. The federal and most state judicial systems include three levels. Within the federal court system, the highest and most influential court is the United States Supreme Court, the next highest court is the United States Court of Appeals, finally, the lowest and least influential level is the the United States District Court. Within most state judicial systems, the highest level is the State Supreme Court, followed by the State Court of Appeals, and the State Trial Court.

Cases are generally tried initially in the United States District Court or the State Trial Court, depending on jurisdiction. The outcome of a case can be appealed to the Federal or State Court of Appeals and finally the Federal or State Supreme Court. The ruling of a state court is binding only on the specific state. State court rulings, however, may be used as nonbinding precedents in other states. Also, a ruling of a State Supreme Court can be appealed to the United State Supreme Court through a *petition for certiorari.*

Because of the concept of stare decisis, most judicial opinions in the federal court system and a majority of opinions within the state system are published. Access to these opinions through law libraries allows family members, advocates, attorneys, and professionals to know requirements relating to access to education and due process under case law. We have abstracted what may be described as the most influential judicial decisions bearing on rights and services for individuals with disabilities. As would be expected, most of the cases were eventually tried within the federal court system and most were appealed to the United States Supreme Court or the United States Court of Appeals. It is important to note that the findings of a majority of these cases have subsequently been subsumed in provisions of federal and state legislation. The section that follows will discuss the provisions of key cases affecting rights and services provided to individuals with disabilities.

Brown v. Board of Education of Topeka, Kansas, 347 U.S. 483 (1954)

The United States Supreme Court established that the Fourteenth Amendment to the United States Constitution extends to the free access of African-American students to public schools. The court ruled that it is unlawful to discriminate against these students for reasons unrelated to the specific educational procedures and goals. Highlighting the court's opinion, Chief Justice Warren wrote: "In these days it is doubtful that any child may reasonably be expected to succeed in life if he is denied the opportunity of an education. Such an opportunity, where the state has undertaken to provide it, is a right which must be made available to all." This ruling serves as a foundation for prohibiting the exclusion of all children, including those with disabilities. This outcome was emphasized by opening arguments of the plaintiff's attorney, John W. Davis:

> *May it please the Court, I think if the appellants' construction of the Four-teenth Amendment should prevail here, there is no doubt in my mind that it would catch the Indian within its grasp just as much as the Negro. If it should prevail, I am unable to see why a state would have any further right to segregate on the ground of sex or on the ground of age or on the ground of mental capacity.*

Diana v. (California) State Board of Education, C-70 37 PFR (1970)

This California *class action suit* brought on behalf of nine Mexican-American adolescents produced a **consent agreement** that affirmed the right of the students to be tested in their native language. The court recognized that a disproportionate number of minority students were placed in special classes as a consequence of testing in English for students for whom English was a second language. The court concluded that testing must be done in the native language even if an interpreter is required. This finding has been extended to all cultural minorities. It has also been generalized to ensure that interpreters and/or alternative communication methods be used with individuals with hearing impairment, visual impairment, and physical disabilities.

Wyatt v. Aderholt, 334 F. Supp. 1341 (1971)

The Federal District Court ruled in *Wyatt* v. *Aderholt* that institutionalized children and youths with mental retardation are guaranteed necessary and appropriate services. The court stipulated that institutions must provide individual treatment plans and educational services, and that persons who are institutionalized must be protected from involuntary servitude, must be provided a humane psychological environment, and must be ensured services in the least restrictive setting necessary for habilitation.

PARC, Bowman et al. v. Commonwealth of Pennsylvania, 334 F. Supp. 279 (1971)

Parc et al. in Federal District Court extended the provisions of *Wyatt* v. *Aderholt* (1971) by requiring access to education and due process for students with mental retardation. The consent decree stipulated that all students be provided educational programs commensurate with their educational characteristics. The court directed that educational services be provided in regular public school classes when appropriate to the student's educational characteristics. The consent degree also required periodic (at least every two years) **evaluations** of students. This is also the first case to specify *due process* protection for individuals with disabilities and their families. Due process safeguards include requiring that districts obtain parental permission prior to conducting a case study evaluation and prior to changing educational placements.

Mills v. *Board of Education of the District of Columbia,* 348 F. Supp. 866 (1972)

The Mills class action suit brought to a United States Federal District Court further extended provisions for the right to education from individuals with mental retardation to all children and youths with disabilities. Highlighted in the court's ruling was the student's constitutional right to due process and least restrictive educational placement.

Armstrong v. *Kline,* 476 F. Supp. 583 (1979)

The federal district court ruled in *Armstrong* v. *Kline* that an individual with severe disabilities demonstrates a substantial loss of educational progress during inactive summer months. An excessive portion of the subsequent school year is then required to recover skills. The terms *regression* and *recoupment* were coined to describe the criteria for establishing the requirement for *extended school year* (summer school program). Individuals who are expected to regress during summer months to the extent that a substantial portion of the coming year will be spent in recoupment must be provided an extended year program. A limited amount of research evidence supports the importance of extended school programs for this population (see Barton, Johnson & Brulle, 1986). However, specific criteria for regression and recoupment based on objective tests or observational data are not currently available.

Board of Education of the Hendrick Hudson Central School District v. *Amy Rowley,* 458 U.S. 176 (1982)

The Rowley case was originally brought to the Federal District Court, appealed to the Second Circuit Court of Appeals, and eventually settled in The United States

Supreme Court. The lower courts ruled that a sign language interpreter must be provided under the provisions of a "free and appropriate public education" for a student with hearing impairment. The student was already making above average progress with alternate, but less expensive, support services. These included extensive and effective training in speech reading, and use of an FM hearing aid that amplified the teacher's or other students' voices spoken into a wireless receiver. The Supreme Court overturned the ruling, indicating that the Constitution does not establish a right to educational programs exceeding those required for average progress. Provision of an interpreter, while enhancing progress, is therefore not required. This ruling is interpreted to limit the rights to educational services to those activities "reasonably calculated to enable the child . . . to receive educational benefits." The court concluded that there is no one test of "reasonable benefit." However, it stipulated that "The achievement of passing marks and advancement from grade to grade will be one important factor."

Smith v. *Robinson* 468 U.S. 992 (1984)

Justice Blackmun, in delivering the opinion of the Supreme Court, indicated that the cost of attorneys' fees resulting from families' successful efforts to ensure rights under law must be reimbursed by school districts. This provision ensures that the due process provisions of federal law are available to all individuals regardless of the ability to employ council (Wolf, 1985). This opinion was subsequently accommodated through the Handicapped Children's Protection Act of 1986 that authorized reimbursement of legal fees and expenses to families winning court actions against public schools.

Influential Legislation

The United States Constitution provides a vague yet emphatic foundation from which educational services are mandated. Case law noted above provides greater clarity regarding the specific services and safeguards afforded to individuals with disabilities and their families. Unfortunately, case law frequently leads to uneven application of rights and services. *Brown* v. *The Board of Education* (1954) in and of itself did little to expand educational options for students with disabilities. While the ruling provided clear precedence from which families would prevail in litigation efforts, the vast majority of families (and school administrators) were unaware of the specific implications for special education programs.

Even subsequent cases that added increased clarity such as *Mills* v. *The Board of Education* did not automatically enhance access to educational services and due process. Again, lack of public and professional information had a detrimental effect. A second, and possibly more influential, detriment was that precedence of case law carries no fiscal support for enhanced services. Without fiscal support schools would have to expand services without increased revenue. In many conservative school districts, administrators would rather risk being sued than deficit-spend to provide broader services.

Further, case law provides no expedient recourse for failure to provide services. Failure to accord due process under case law is adjudicated only through subsequent trials that must be initiated by family members. While the outcome may be certain due to the confidence of legal precedence, the process may be so time consuming and fiscally and emotionally burdensome as to dissuade family members.

Statutory law or legislation promulgated by the United States Congress resolves these difficulties in several related ways. First, federal statutory law provides a uniform set of standards across states and individual educational agencies. As opposed to legal precedence through the state judicial system, the same requirements under law that apply in one part of the country apply in another. Families residing in a "service rich" state can be assured that the same services would be available upon moving to another state.

Second, statutory law provides a clear and comprehensive mandate for the provision of services. Legislative mandates generally encompass all elements of related judicial findings. In this way, family members and professionals are not required to study isolated case law to establish comprehensive requirements for the provision of services. They are also not bound to provide relative weight to provisions of various judicial findings based on the level and standing of the court.

Third, statutory law may include fiscal provisions that underwrite excess costs incurred as a consequence of its provisions. Federal mandates that stipulate expanded services may also include fiscal support to offset at least a portion of the additional expense to the state or local educational agency.

Finally, statutory law may include specific due process provisions that provide speedy and effective remedies when rights are denied under the mandate. In some cases, these provisions avoid local, state, and federal court systems by stipulating informal arbitration and review procedures. In others, the mandate may specify that attorney fees are due to the family when they prevail in efforts to ensure access to services.

Three major laws and their amendments that have direct and emphatic implications for the rights of students with disabilities and their families will be reviewed here. They include: The Rehabilitation Act of 1973 (Public Law 93-112, 1973) and its amendment in the Rehabilitation Act Amendments of 1986 (Public Law 99-955), the Education for All Handicapped Children's Act of 1975 (Public Law 94-142, 1975), its early amendment (Public Law 99-457, 1986), its most recent amendment (Public Law 101-476, referred to as the Individuals with Disabilities Education Act), and the Americans with Disabilities Act of 1990 (Public Law 101-336).

The Rehabilitation Act of 1973

Crosson (1977) provides a general overview of the major provisions of the Rehabilitation Act of 1973. She states that the general purposes of the Act are to:

> 1. *Develop and implement comprehensive and continuing state plans for meeting the current and future needs for providing vocational rehabili-*

tation services to handicapped individuals and to provide such services for the benefit of such individuals, serving first those with the most severe handicaps, so that they may prepare for and engage in gainful employment; and

2. *Devise methods of providing rehabilitation services to meet the current and future needs of handicapped individuals for whom a vocational goal is not possible or feasible so that they may improve their ability to live with greater independence and self sufficiency. (p. 18)*

Section 504 of the Rehabilitation Act includes a major civil rights statement on behalf of people with disabilities. Section 504 prohibits discrimination on the basis of physical, cognitive, or sensory disability. It poignantly states:

No otherwise qualified handicapped individual in the United States shall, solely by reason of his handicap, be excluded from the participation in, be denied the benefits of, or be subjected to discrimination under any program or activity receiving federal financial assistance. (29 U.S.C. 794)

Under Section 504, a state agency that fails to provide equal access to individuals who are otherwise qualified but possess certain disabilities may suffer the loss of federal education and rehabilitation funds. The most generally apparent outcome of this legislation is evidenced in the architectural design of buildings constructed (at least in part) with federal funds. One will notice ramps in place of stairs, elevators, curb cuts, braille noting location and access information, wide doorways, grab bars, and so on. Mass transit systems include special units for individuals who use wheel chairs. More subtly, universities staff special academic resource centers for individuals with sensory impairment, learning disabilities, or other disabilities. Finally, public schools are unable to exclude individuals with behavior disorders through expulsion.

The Rehabilitation Act of 1973 also confirms affirmative action requirements on behalf of individuals with disabilities. Service agencies, contractors, or other businesses in the private or public sector that receive over 2,500 dollars annually from the federal government (such as the Department of Defense, Health Education and Human Services, Natural Resources, and so on) must participate in an extensive affirmative action effort. This effort must ensure that individuals with disabilities are provided equal opportunities for employment when otherwise qualified.

Rehabilitation Act Amendments of 1986

The major departure in this amendment of the Rehabilitation Act of 1973 involves the provision of transitional services for youths with severe disabilities. All students must be provided a transition plan within two years of graduation. The transition plan must stipulate goals that enhance adjustment to community adult settings including recreation, work, transportation, independent living, and so on. Participants in transition plan development may include traditional school based professionals including representatives of vocational rehabilitation, social services, and other community based agencies.

The Education for All Handicapped Children Act of 1975

By far the *Education for All Handicapped Children Act of 1975,* or Public Law 94-142, represents the most comprehensive legislative act ever initiated on behalf of individuals with disabilities. The major provision of the law is that a *free and appropriate public education* be provided for all children with disabilities and youths residing in the United States. The free and appropriate provision ensures that special education and related services be provided "at public expense, under public supervision and direction, and without charge" (United States Office of Education, 1977a, p. 42478). The provision stands regardless of whether the student is served in a public or private school setting.

One of the more elusive issues associated with the law is what constitutes an appropriate education. This issue was clarified in *Board of Education of the Hendrick Hudson Central School District* v. *Amy Rowley,* 458 U.S. 176 (1982). Critical features highlighted in the case include: individualized instruction specifically designed for the student and based on an appraisal of his or her characteristics; related services needed to provide a comprehensive educational program; multidisciplinary and family participation in the development of an individualized educational program; good faith efforts in implementing the program; and an annual review of progress toward goals identified in the program.

School districts must engage in *child find* activities to ensure that all eligible students are identified. Schools' responsibility to identify exceptional individuals begins at birth (though services are not required until later) and continues throughout school years. Eligible students under the law include 3–21-year-olds identified as falling within categories appearing in Table 2-3.

TABLE 2-3 • Students Eligible for Special Education Services under Public Law 94-142 and 101-476

Autistic	Mentally Retarded
Deaf	Multi-handicapped
Deaf-Blind	Orthopedically Impaired
Emotionally Disturbed	Speech/Language Impaired
Hard of Hearing	Traumatic Brain Injured
Health Impaired	Visually Handicapped
Learning Disabled	

A focal point in the law is the requirement for all handicapped students to be provided an individualized education program. This program must be developed and approved by a multidisciplinary team that may include the student's special and regular education teachers, building administrator, school psychologist, social worker, physical and/or occupational therapist, speech therapist, counselor, and vocational rehabilitation professional. Family members must be invited to participate in the planning process. When appropriate, the student may also be invited to join the multidisciplinary team. The individualized education program must include the following elements:

Assessment outcomes reporting the student's current educational levels
Annual goals developed on the basis of the assessment data
Short term objectives that comprise the annual goals
Specific educational and related services to be provided
Specific educational programs to be implemented
Time at which specific services are to be initiated
Anticipated date at which goals will be accomplished
Instruments and procedures used to monitor progress toward goals
Extent to which instruction will occur in regular education settings

A critical provision of the law is that educational programs be provided in the **least restrictive environment** appropriate to the characteristics of the student. The law emphasizes that a variety of service settings be available to the student. These should range from most integrated in relationship to peers who are not disabled to least integrated. The continuum may include: regular class only, regular class with consultative assistance to the regular teacher, intermittent instruction through an itinerant specialist, resource instruction, part time self-contained class, full time self-contained class, segregated day school, and residential school. Once placed, the multidisciplinary team must be vigilant for changes in learning and behavioral characteristics that would allow for movement to less restrictive (more integrated) settings. Movement to more restrictive settings may occur if the current placement is demonstrated not to be sufficiently structured to promote reasonable success for the learner.

Public Law 94-142 also ensures that testing be conducted in the student's native language and that assessment results be interpreted with reference to characteristics found in the student's family culture. The provision for testing in the native language also applies to individuals who rely on alternative or augmentative communication systems (such as deaf, blind, physically handicapped).

In addition to these requirements, Public Law 94-142 provides specific rights relating to due process for families of individuals with disabilities. Due process rights include the following:

Educational records:
1. Right to review and obtain free copies of educational records
2. Right to be informed of the location of all records

3. Right to an objective explanation of information in records
4. Right to have inaccurate records removed or amended
5. Right to a hearing when appropriateness of records is disputed

Confidentiality:
1. Right to be informed prior to releasing records
2. Right to refuse records disclosure to other agencies or people

Notice:
1. Right to notice before a child's educational program is altered. Notice must be in advance of the change in identification, placement, service, and so on. Notice must also be in the family's native language or the principal mode of communication.
2. Right to be informed of proposed action, rationale for the action, description of alternative procedures or placements, and justification for not adopting alternatives
3. Right to be notified of each evaluation procedure including tests and formal reports that will be used as a foundation for actions

Consent:
1. Right to provide consent for evaluation, classification, placement, or change in the educational program
2. Right to revoke consent at any time

Evaluation:
1. Right to obtain from the school district a comprehensive case study evaluation that includes multiple measures and criteria. The evaluation must address all areas associated with the suspected disability, be conducted by a multidisciplinary team, and be completed within 60 days of referral for special services.
2. Right to reevaluation whenever warranted by changes in the student's condition, whenever requested by family members or professionals, and at least every three years

Independent review of evaluation:
1. Right to obtain an independent evaluation when questions arise about the quality or appropriateness of the district's evaluation
2. Right to be reimbursed for the cost of an independent evaluation if it is determined through a due process hearing that the district's evaluation is inappropriate
3. Right to consider the independent evaluation when making classification, placement, and programming decisions

Least restrictive environment:
1. Right for the family member to be educated to the maximum extent possible with age matched nonhandicapped peers
2. Right to frequent and systematic attempts (as through technological aids, consultative and itinerant services, special instructional methods, and so on)

to accommodate the student in regular education settings prior to removal to segregated placements

3. Right to participate with nonhandicapped peers during nonacademic activities (such as lunch, athletics, school organizations, and other activities)

Mediation and resolution of differences:

1. Right to request an impartial due process hearing if family members and the school district fail to agree to questions of identification, evaluation, placement, or the provision of a free and appropriate public education
2. Right to be informed of procedures for filing a due process action including the availability of no or low cost legal and/or advocacy services
3. Right to have the hearing administered by an independent officer not employed or inappropriately influenced by the school district and disclosure of the qualifications of the hearing officer
4. Right to a public hearing attended by all family members and counsel for the family. The cost of counsel is provided by the school district if the family prevails in the judgement.
5. Right to present evidence and cross examine school district witnesses
6. Right to be informed of evidence that will be disclosed by the district five days in advance of the hearing
7. Right to obtain a written transcript of the hearing as well as findings of facts and the decision of the hearing officer
8. Right to appeal to the state court system
9. Right to retain the student in the current placement with all provisions of the current IEP in effect during the due process proceedings

Education of the Handicapped Act Amendments of 1986

The Education for All Handicapped Children Act was amended by Public Law 99-457. The most important effect of the amendments was that rights and protections accorded under Public Law 94-142 are provided for students ages three to five. Prior to the amendments, state educational agencies were required to provide educational services to 3, 4, and 5-year olds only if they were provided for individuals who are not handicapped. Otherwise provisions of Public Law 94-142 were restricted to individuals ages 5–21.

Rather than requiring the development of individualized education programs, the amendments require the use of an individualized family service plan. This plan provides a broader and more comprehensive service delivery approach: levels of performance; goals and objectives; criteria, procedures, and time tables for evaluating progress; specific services and service providers are directed not only at the individual needs of the child, but the general needs of the family. In addition to these elements, the family service plan must include the designation of a case manager responsible for coordinating efforts delivered on behalf of the child and family.

Education of the Handicapped Act Amendments of 1990

The amendments of P. L. 94-142 included a change in title to the "Education of Individuals with Disabilities Education Act." It further changed all references from "handicapped children" to "children with disabilities."

The Education of Individuals with Disabilities Act extends the provisions of P.L. 94-142 to children and youths with autism and traumatic brain injury. Further, the law requires schools to provide transition services to learners with disabilities. Transition services are described as coordinated activities leading to movement from school to post-school outcomes. They may include "post-secondary education, vocational training, integrated employment, continuing and adult education, adult services, independent living, or community participation." (Sec. 602(a)(19). Consistent with this provision, IEPs must contain a description of required transition services. These services should be developed no later than the 16th birthday and should continue annually.

The Education of Individuals with Disabilities Act further defines rehabilitation counseling and social work as related services. The law requests public comment on the definition of "attention deficit disorder." Finally, it stipulates that states may be sued in federal court for violations of the law.

The Americans with Disabilities Act of 1990

The *American with Disabilities Act of 1990,* Public Law 101-336, addresses the needs of adult Americans with disabilities. While direct implications for school-aged individuals residing with their families and not employed are limited, the act offers optimism for full integration upon completion of school. Its overriding goal is to reduce segregation and discrimination of individuals with disabilities in society. Specifically, Congress argued that "the Nation's proper goals regarding individuals with disabilities are to assure equality of opportunity, full participation, independent living, and economic self-sufficiency for such individuals."

Requirements of the act extend to private and public facilities and services. These may include employment, housing, recreation, transportation, and telecommunication services and facilities. In general, the law requires that all reasonable accommodations allowing persons with disabilities be provided so that these individuals can participate in services and activities. Many of the rights and services identified in Tables 2-1 and 2-2 are included within the act.

One of the stronger provisions is that businesses with over 14 employees may not discriminate against individuals with disabilities during application, hiring, advancement, discharge and in the terms, conditions, and privileges of employment. Employers must make reasonable accommodations for individuals with disabilities. These may include: scheduling, adapting materials and equipment, providing augmentative or alternative communication methods, and so on.

SUMMARY

Early in this chapter we described the chronological progression of societal views toward individuals with disabilities. We noted that early civilization's treatment of individuals with disabilities was shaped by the increased *threat to survival* imposed by the responsibility of caring for the individual. Euthanasia was practiced in response to the diminished capacity for the family unit to survive. It was considered more moral to abandon or kill individuals with disabilities than expose the larger family unit to the hardship of extraordinary care. Subsequent cultures were substantially influenced by *superstitious beliefs* in the care and treatment of individuals with disabilities. Human exceptionality was explained through parapsychological phenomena such as the presence of demons, witches, or other evil spirits. Treatment was generally conducted by spiritual leaders empowered with ritualistic methods. As civilization progressed, so did the rational treatment of individuals with disabilities. The next era focused on the provision of *services* to exceptional people. Scholars and religious and political leaders advocated the benevolent care of individuals with disabilities. This period heralded the advent of specialized facilities and treatment methods for individuals with disabilities. Along with attention to serving individuals with disabilities came special attention to the *science* of treatment. Physicians and scholars have increasingly come to understand the epidemiology and control of physical, psychological, and social disorders.

It is important to reemphasize that current practice emphasizes service and science. However, remnants of the less functional survival and superstition eras continue to exist. We encourage advocacy efforts to ensure that each and every individual with disabilities is served in a matter befitting of human dignity. This includes integration into the mainstream of society, freedom from pejorative labels and restrictions, and appropriate shelter and care that provides for basic human needs. Further, we encourage advocacy efforts dedicated to expanding the general study of disability. Broad-based research focusing on the cause and treatment of disabilities must continue. Equally important, advocacy efforts must be directed to providing full access to effective treatments for all individuals with disabilities.

To these ends we identified three forms of advocacy ranging from more laissez-faire to directive approaches. The first, *social support advocacy,* is the most general and least directive. It involves broad political action on behalf of individuals with disabilities. Voting for school board members and legislators with special sensitivities to individuals with disabilities is one social support approach. Another is lobbying for increased appropriations and protective legislation for social services. As we highlighted, the general goal of social support advocacy is to reduce the need for more intrusive methods. Ultimately, however, not all advocacy needs are addressed through broader social and political action. Therefore, the next more intrusive method, *interpersonal advocacy,* is often required. Interpersonal advocacy includes ongoing informal or specialized formal interactions between the advocate and service provider. Meetings to develop individualized education programs, transition plans, or family service plans are discrete opportunities for interpersonal advocacy. Interpersonal advocacy may also fall short in assuring rights and services for individuals with disabilities. Therefore, more focused and binding advocacy methods are required. We describe these as *legal advocacy.* Legal advocacy by its very nature is adversarial. It invokes the due process provisions of law and often results in hearings before an impartial hearing officer. Because of likely negative side effects associated with legal advocacy, we suggest employing it only as a last resort.

A major element of this chapter includes specific rights and services to which individuals with disabilities are entitled. Tables 2-1 and 2-2 summarize each of these rights and services. These rights and services are accorded through the Fourteenth Amendment to the United States Constitution. They are further defined by litigation and legislation.

Final sections of this chapter summarize the most influential court cases and laws affecting rights and services for individuals with disabilities. The most comprehensive and authoritative of these is Public Law 94-142 and its subsequent amendments. The law stipulates that a free and appropriate public education must be provided to all students (ages 3–21). It also establishes standards for the manner in which educational services are to be planned and implemented. Finally, it includes due process provisions that ensure students and their family members specific rights.

This chapter highlights the implications of social evolution and legal issues for families of individuals with disabilities. As noted in the preceding chapter, this emphasis is warranted because family members are most intimately aware of and concerned for the needs of the individual. Equally important, they are often in the most tenable position to influence the nature and extent of efforts on behalf of their children and youth.

The next chapter will provide a more direct focus on families of students with disabilities. We provide an overview of the influence of individuals with disabilities on other family members. Equally important, we discuss approaches used by family members to uphold the rights and obtain necessary services for their children.

History of Services and Rights

1. Four major determinants of the conditions under which persons with disabilities have lived are described by Hewett and Forness (1977).

2. The *threat to survival* influence was influenced by the harsh physical environment faced by all individuals. As a result of these influences, children and youths with disabilities were abandoned or killed so nondisabled family members would have a better chance to survive.

3. The *superstition* period was influenced by family members and community leaders attributing disabilities to activities of mythical beings. Pseudoreligious rituals were used in an attempt to change norm-violating behaviors.

4. The *service* influence included thoughtful attention and support for the needs of persons with disabilities. The work of Dorothea Dix, Louis Braille, Jean-Marc-Gaspard Itard, Edouard Seguin, Sigmund Freud, B. F. Skinner, Alfred Binet, and Ivan Pavlov exemplified this influence.

5. The *science* period included both pseudoscientific efforts, such as trephining and bloodletting, and empirical science. The latter, characterized by the objective study of disabilities

and their treatment, exerts a major influence on our current practices.

Contemporary Parent and Professional Advocacy

6. Advocacy strategies can be characterized under the headings of *social support, interpersonal,* and *legal.*

7. *Social support* includes general actions that enhance the quality of life for all members of society regardless of disability. Social support advocacy is often unobtrusive and informal. As such, social support advocacy may reduce the need for more direct and intrusive procedures. Unfortunately, social support advocacy may not be sufficient to address the needs of some individuals with disabilities. Donations to benevolent organizations, lobbying for disability rights legislation, and so on exemplify social support advocacy.

8. *Interpersonal advocacy* involves direct interactions by the learner, family, or others in an effort to improve services and rights. Unlike social support advocacy, interpersonal advocacy is directed at specific needs of an individual. It also follows a formal action plan. Participation in IEP meetings and other formal planning sessions exemplify interpersonal advocacy.

9. *Legal advocacy* involves applying due process provisions under the law to ensure appropriate treatment for a specific individual with disabilities. Legal advocacy is the most formal and adversarial of the three advocacy approaches.

10. Family members advocating on behalf of their disabled child or youth should generally strive to use the least intrusive method of advocacy prior to adopting a more formal and adversarial advocacy method.

Advocacy Outcomes

11. The United States Constitution, judicial action, and legislation accord specific rights to individuals with disabilities. These rights are enumerated in Table 2-1.

12. Four conditions may operate to deny individual rights. These include: absence of legal precedents, limited representation of individuals who are unable to self-advocate due to cognitive or expressive language limitations, limited knowledge of service providers, lack of good faith efforts on the part of professionals.

13. Existing legislation mandates rights that must be accorded to persons with disabilities. These rights are enumerated in Table 2-1.

14. Modern service delivery approaches emphasize placement in the least restrictive and most normal setting, support for individuals with more severe disabilities, individualization of instruction, cultural fair testing, and attention to the needs of individuals throughout the age range.

15. Existing legislation mandates services that must be provided to persons with disabilities. These services are enumerated in Table 2-2.

16. Court cases further clarify the rights and services that should be provided persons with disabilities. Summaries of the findings of the more influential cases are provided in this Chapter.

17. Influential legislation that addresses the rights and services that should be provided for persons with disabilities is included.

REFERENCES

Armstrong v. Kline 476 F. *Supp.* 583 (1979).

Barton, L. E., Johnson, H. A., & Brulle, A. R. (1986). "An evaluation of the effectiveness of an extended year program." *Journal of the Association for Persons with Severe Handicaps, 11,* 136–138.

Board of Education of the Hendrick Hudson Central School District v. Amy Rowley, 458 U.S. 176 (1982).

The Americans with Disabilities Act of 1990.

Board of Education of the Hendrick Hudson Central School District v. Amy Rowley, 102 S.Ct. 3034 (1982).

Brown v. The Board of Education of Topeka, Kansas, 347 U.S. 483 (1954).

Cartwright, G. P., Cartwright, C. A., & Ward, M. E. (1989). *Educating special learners* (3rd ed.). Belmont, CA: Wadsworth Publishing Co.

Cleland, C. C. & Swartz, J. D. (1982). *Exceptionalities through the lifespan.* New York: Macmillan.

Coleman, J. C. (1972). *Abnormal psychology and modern life.* Glenview, IL: Scott Foresman.

Crosson, A. (1977). *Advocacy and the developmentally disabled.* Eugene, Oregon: Rehabilitation Research and Training Center in Mental Retardation, University of Oregon.

Cruzan v. Webster and the State of Missouri

Diana v. (California) State Board of Education, C-70 37 PFR (1970).

The Education of All Handicapped Children Act of 1975, 20 U.S.C. Sections 1400–1461.

Education of the Handicapped Act Amendments of 1986, 20 U.S.C. 1471 *et seq.* and 1419 *et seq.*

Family Educational Rights and Privacy Act of 1974, 20 U.S.C. 1232(g).

Hallahan, D. P. & Kauffman, J. M. (1991). *Exceptional children: Introduction to special education* (5th ed.). Englewood Cliffs, N.J.: Prentice-Hall.

Handicapped Children's Protection Act of 1986, 20 U.S.C. Section 1415(e)(4).

Hewett, F. M., & Forness S. R. (1977). *Education of exceptional learners.* Boston: Allyn and Bacon.

Individuals with Disabilities Education Act of 1990.

Meyen, E. L. (1982). *Exceptional children and youth.* Denver, CO: Love.

Mills v. Board of Education of the District of Columbia, 348 F. *Supp.* 866 (1972).

PARC, Bowman et al. v. Commonwealth of Pennsylvania, 334 F. *Supp.* 279 (1971).

Rothstein, L. F. (1990). *Special education law.* White Plains, NY: Longman.

Rehabilitation Act of 1973 (Section 504) 29 U.S.C. Section 794.

Smith v. Robinson 468 U.S. 992 (1984).

Rehabilitation Act Amendments of 1986

Topeka, Kansas, 347 U.S. 483 (1954).

Turnbull, A. P., Strickland B. B., & Brantley J. C. (1982). *Developing and implementing individualized education programs.* Columbus, Ohio: Merrill.

Wolf, N. (1985, June). Lawscore: Handicapped kids' lawyers' fee bill introduced. *American Bar Association Journal,* p. 31.

Wyatt v. Aderholt, 334 F. *Supp.* 1341 (1971)

Zilboorg, G., & Henry, G. W. (1941). *A history of medical psychology.* New York: W. W. Norton.

3

PARENTAL RESPONSES, ROLES, AND RESPONSIBILITIES

Ming-Gon John Lian
*Department of Specialized
Educational Development,
Illinois State University*

Gregory F. Aloia
*The Graduate School and
University Research Office,
Illinois State University*

*All families, especially those with
a child who has a disability, are unique,
complex, multifaceted, active, ever changing social units.*

Chapter Objectives

After completing this chapter you will be able to:

1. Identify eight historical roles that parents of children with disabilities have assumed or been assigned by professionals
2. Describe the major roles, significant mission, and importance of family
3. Describe parents' general expectations associated with the birth of a child
4. Describe general feelings of parents and other family members to the birth of a child with a disability
5. Describe successive adaptations during six different phases in families with a child with disabilities
6. Explain the purpose of identifying parental feelings and reactions to the birth of a child with a disability

7. Identify the influence of type and degree of disabilities on parental reactions

8. Explain ethnic and cultural influences on parental reactions

9. Identify the influence of family structure, stability, and characteristics on the reaction to a child with a disability

10. Describe the extended family's reactions to the birth of a child with a disability

11. Identify internal and external resources that contribute to coping responses of parents who have a child with disabilities

12. Describe parents' experiences in the life cycle of a family with a child who has a disability

13. List the seven major functions of a family

14. Identify evolving roles and responsibilities of parents who have a child with disabilities

15. Suggest approaches for enhancing positive parent-professional relationships

Key Terms and Phrases

birth expectation
community resources
ethnic and cultural influence
extended family
external resources
family characteristics
family functions
family life cycle
family stability
family structure
friends and neighbors
governmental agencies
internal resources
parent-professional relationships

parental adaptations
parental reactions
parental responses
parental responsibilities
parental roles
parentalplegia
professional organizations
P.L. 94-142
P.L. 99-457
religious organizations
sibling attitudes
stressors
type and degree of disability

INTRODUCTION

Parents are the most important people in the life of a child with disabilities. Buscaglia (1975) states that no matter how many professionals work with a child during his or her life, none will have a more influential, lasting, and significant effect than that of his or her parents. In order to better understand parental responses, roles, and responsibilities, there should be an effort to study these topics across time and from diverse points of view. Topics addressed in this chapter include impact of disabilities on parents, resources for coping responses of parents, evolving roles and responsibilities of parents, and parent-professional relationships.

PARENTAL SUPPORT AND ADVOCACY

In the historical development of enhancing education and related services, parents of children with disabilities played an important role. These parents made efforts to share their experiences, develop team work and mutual support, advocate for legislation and litigation, obtain financial assistance, protect rights of children with disabilities, promote education and related services, and support professional personnel preparation and training (Lian, 1984). They founded and participated in organizations that had tremendous influence on education and related services for children with disabilities.

Turnbull and Turnbull (1990) present an overview of the historical roles that parents have assumed or been assigned to by professionals over the years. As parental roles are discussed in detail in Chapter 1, we will only briefly review them here. Although these roles have not occurred within an exact chronological time frame, they reflect in a general sense the type and degree of involvement by parents over time. The eight roles identified by Turnbull and Turnbull (1990) in which parents were viewed were:

1. The source of their children's problems
2. Organization members
3. Service developers
4. Recipients of professionals' decisions
5. Learners and teachers
6. Political advocates
7. Educational decision makers
8. Family members

Turnbull and Turnbull (1990) indicate that parents began being viewed as the source of the problem as a byproduct of the eugenics movement in the late nineteenth century. As is noted in Chapter 2, one of the goals of this movement was to stop the spread of degeneracy in society by preventing those thought to be "mental defectives" from reproducing. The result was that many laws were passed that discriminated against persons with mental retardation. Marriages were regulated; sterilizations and institutionalizations increased dramatically. They go on to list some specific disabling conditions for which parents were scorned, including autism, asthma, emotional disorders, or other "maladaptive personality traits" and results of "inappropriate child-rearing practices." Turnbull and Turnbull (1990) state that "it was typical in the 1940s and 1950s for professionals to describe parents of children and youth who are autistic or psychotic as rigid, perfectionistic, emotionally improvised, and depressed" (p. 3).

Faced with a less-than-supportive public, and professionals who viewed them as part of the cause, parents began to organize. Local parent groups were formed that spawned many state and national organizations. These organizations have enabled parents to have a positive impact in many areas that have benefited children with disabilities.

Turnbull and Turnbull (1990) identify the next role that parents assumed as that of service developers. During this phase, which lasted through the 1950s and 1960s, the primary emphasis of parents was getting services for their children who were excluded from public schools due to their disabilities. The specific action undertaken by the many varied organizations took several different forms. Some organizations provided direct service, others served as liaison between public and private agencies, while others assumed the role of watchdogs and advocates. This commitment to service continues to this day with parents investing much time and energy insuring that their children receive appropriate services.

From the 1950s to the 1970s, the relationship between parents and professionals was essentially unidirectional with parents being the passive and grateful recipients of professional advice and direction. Parents tended to be blamed if they did not cooperate or do what the professionals asked them to do (Taylor, 1976). As Turnbull and Turnbull (1990) state, ". . . first, professionals were expected to make educational decisions and then interpret these decisions to parents; and, second, parents were expected not to question professionals and to be appreciative recipients of services" (p. 10). One example was that parents were expected to be "counseled" through home visiting if their children with mental retardation were to be integrated into society. Sonnenschein (1981) describes the historical perspective in which parents were viewed as vulnerable clients in need of assistance; service recipients with whom professionals should not get too involved; patients in need of therapy; responsible parties for their children's condition; less intelligent persons; adversaries with whom professionals should be careful to deal; and victims of labeling (for example, "denying," "resistant," and "anxious" parents).

Although parents today are not as passive or as "humbly" grateful as they have been in the past, some professionals still hold the belief that they should be. This professional attitude is very counter-productive to effective parent-professional relationships (Turnbull, 1983).

The political and social climate of the 1960s and 1970s, supported by findings in psychology and education, encouraged parents to be more active as teachers of their children. Although this idea started with parents of economically deprived children, it was soon applied to parents of children with all disabling conditions. As perceived by professionals, parents have learned and become an influential factor contributing to their children's progress and achievement in areas such as changing behaviors (Turnbull & Turnbull, 1990).

Although parent training is not as popular today as it was in the past, there is still a need for information and training, but not in as structured a setting as formal training sessions (Turnbull & Turnbull, 1990). Also, parents prefer the terminology of "collaborating parents" or "assisting parents," rather than "training parents" or "educating parents." Every effort should be made to eliminate the image that parents are untrained, less competent, or less active people.

The next phase identified by Turnbull and Turnbull (1990) emphasized the role of parents as political advocates for their children. From the 1960s through the 1980s, court decisions and laws noted in the preceding chapter fundamentally changed the way society treated persons with disabilities. Although the impact of parental advocacy was felt in many areas (such as institutional care, community services, personnel training, and so on), it was in education that the greatest gains were achieved. The crowning accomplishment was the guarantee that children with disabilities had a right to a free, appropriate, public education (in *Pennsylvania Association for Retarded Citizens* v. *Commonwealth of Pennsylvania,* 1971 and P.L. 94-142, the Education for All Handicapped Children Act, 1975).

Enactment of P.L. 94-142 dramatically transformed the role of parents and altered their relationships with professionals. No longer are they viewed as recipients of information or passive players in the education of their children. They are now seen as active decision-makers. As noted in the previous chapter, parental informed consent must be obtained before almost any action regarding children with disabilities is undertaken. Although much still needs to be done, the law clearly empowered parents to be full participating members of the team that plans and implements education for their child.

Today, parents are viewed by professionals as members of an integrated social family unit with special needs and roles of their own. Turnbull and Turnbull (1990) state that it is necessary to identify and address all family members' needs, including the parents, in order to enhance successful family life. Any experience affecting one family member will affect all because members in a family are so interrelated.

> *For example, a mother might be so heavily involved in teaching her child and participating in educational decision-making that she neglects to spend adequate time with her husband and other children and ignores her own personal needs. Whereas the earlier focus was almost exclusively on the parents (or mother) and their involvement with their child with an exceptionality, now more attention is being given to the diverse needs of each family member and the competing demands in terms of time and responsibility placed on parents. (Turnbull & Turnbull, 1990, p.16)*

IMPACT OF DISABILITIES ON PARENTS

Although there are similarities in the ways parents react to the birth of a child with a disability, there are also many other factors that mitigate a wide range of parental responses. This section will examine those common attributes, as well as those factors that result in differential responses. The following topics will be discussed:

- Uniqueness of each family
- Generalized expectations associated with the birth of a child
- Generalized reactions to the birth of a child with disabling conditions
- Research findings and qualifiers on parental/family reactions
- Parental expectations related to the type and degree of disabilities
- Basic family structure, stability, and characteristics and the reaction to a child with a disability
- Sibling reactions
- Extended family's reactions

Uniqueness of Each Family

All families, especially those with a child who has a disability, are unique, complex, multifaceted, active, ever changing social units. Turnbull, Barber, Behr, and Kerns (1988) describe the role and importance of a family:

> *The family, the oldest and most fundamental social institution, is the major source of individual beliefs, values, and codes of behavior. The pivotal role of the family in the nurturing, socialization, education, and career development of its individual members has important implications for the field of education in general and special education in particular. (p. 82)*

Each family should be viewed individually because of its specific members, structure, social and cultural backgrounds, and life experiences. Turnbull et al. (1988) emphasize two major concepts about family: the uniqueness of the individual in a family and the specific need to individualize instruction. In addition, the cultural aspect of a family is another factor that makes each family unique. McGoldrick (1982) indicates that "ethnicity is deeply tied to the family, through which it is transmitted" (p. 3). Family and ethnicity are intertwined and inseparable, and should be studied together. Ethnicity is a major determinant of family patterns and belief systems (McGoldrick, 1982). There are no two families alike and each family has its own unique ethnic values, and special goals and objectives that the family members agree upon and work together to achieve. In the community of special education and related services, there has been increasing awareness of the importance of promoting cultural sensitivity when appreciating and working with culturally and linguistically diverse families, especially those from minority populations (Ferguson & Ferguson, 1991; Lian, 1990a; Lynch & Stein, 1987). Box 3-1 provides an example of encouraging service providers to prevent cultural and linguistical discrimination in their work with persons who have disabilities, and to recognize and respect the preferences of each family.

Every family is important and carries a significant mission. Fewell (1986a) makes the following observations:

> *Throughout history and across cultures, the family has been the primary agency for survival. Although the forms of families vary, the tasks are universal. Parents or parent surrogates across all cultures assume the responsibility for transmitting to their offspring the competencies required by the social, economic, and political forces of their society or social group. (p. 4)*

Fewell (1986a) also emphasizes the importance of each family member and his/her influence on others:

> *Family members do not operate in vacuums. Members are influenced and changed by other members, and by the circumstances in which they exist.*

BOX 3-1 • Cultural Sensitivity Resolution

WHEREAS, individuals with severe handicaps who are also culturally and linguistically diverse may be disadvantaged in educational assessment, placement, and instructional processes because of the potentially discriminatory effects of language and culturally biased testing procedures and instruments.

WHEREAS, the unique linguistic and cultural backgrounds of individuals with severe handicaps and their families are not well recognized and utilized in education and habilitation programs designed to serve individuals with severe handicaps.

WHEREAS, the recognition of unique linguistic and cultural characteristics is fundamen-

tal to good school/home cooperation and to the design of programs that promote maximum individual development and learning.

THEREFORE BE IT RESOLVED, THAT the Association for Persons with Severe Handicaps encourages all service providers to implement culturally and linguistically nondiscriminatory procedures in their work with individuals who have severe handicaps. Because of the central role familial/cultural factors play in development, planning for individual programs must take into account familial preferences and linguistic origins of the individual with severe handicaps.

Source: TASH Newsletter, July 1988, *14*(7), p. 11. Reprinted with permission of the Association for Persons with Severe Handicaps, Seattle, Wa.

> *If society's goal is to help families carry out their caregiving tasks, then it is necessary that we understand the influences that family members and their environments have on one another. (p. 4)*

This view is confirmed by Turnbull and Turnbull (1990), who point out that whatever happens to one family member will influence all other members in the family.

Powell and Olge (1985) suggest that parents recognize the uniqueness of their families. Family members, with or without a disability, tend to compare themselves to other families. They may not be aware that many other families also have a full range of problems that are hidden from public scrutiny.

Parents of a child with disabilities were once considered to be in an abnormal group. We are beginning to realize that these parents are regular family members just like the rest of the community (Turnbull & Turnbull, 1990). It has been indicated that, in schools, special education teachers should mainstream themselves before their students with disabilities are mainstreamed. So should parents. Families of children with disabilities are unique, normal families in the community, not "handicapped families." Kaplan (1986) says that working with families should start from the "health" point of view (that is, family growth and development), not from the "pathology" point of view (as indicated in traditional medical, psychological, and therapeutic models).

Generalized Expectations Associated with the Birth of a Child

In order to understand the reaction of parents, let us examine the basic expectations that parents associate with the birth of a child. Most prospective parents are faced with excitement, the task of planning for the future, learning the meaning of being parents, and, in the case of giving second or further birth of a child, preparing older brothers and sisters. Fewell (1986a) says that these parents have "long-nurtured hopes and dreams."

The birth of a child, whether disabled or nondisabled, may create both positive and negative situations in the family. Buscaglia (1975) states,

> *Birth, for most families, is a time for rejoicing, for pride, for gathering together loved ones and sharing with them in the celebration of a renewal of life . . . For other families, birth may not be as joyful an occasion. On the contrary, it may be a time for tears, despair, confusion and fear. It may demand a totally new life of all involved, full of mysterious and unique problems. (p. 25)*

It is important to note that all parents need help during and shortly after the birth of their child. Hollingsworth and Pasnau (1977) state that "parental defenses are normal. All parents need others to help them understand and accept even the healthy, nondisabled child. It is not pathological that all parents deny and/or intellectualize to ward off severe anxiety" (p. 95). As Murphy (1976) emphasizes, when counseling parents of children with disabilities, we see "identification of our commonalities as more vital than identification of our differences" (p. 11).

Waisbren (1980) finds that, during the first 18 months after a child's birth, parents of disabled and nondisabled children are strikingly similar. There are no significant differences in terms of parents' physical health, social involvement, activities with the baby, marital relationships, and plans for the future.

Later, differences between families become easily observed in personalities, resources, values, size, and harmony. These differences will likely impact how a family responds to a child with a disabling condition. Although no two families will respond identically, researchers have found common stages that almost all families pass through as they adjust to a member with a disabling condition.

Generalized Reactions to the Birth of a Child with Disabling Conditions

Although there are similarities in the ways parents react to the birth of a child with a disabling condition, there are also many other factors that mitigate a wide range of parental responses. This section will examine those common attributes, as well as those factors that result in differential responses. Murray and Cornell (1981) posit that parental reactions at the birth of a child with disabilities are based upon the belief that the grief they experience is the result of the loss of an expected "normal" child. The type and degree of parental reactions are highly related to the degree to which the child's birth deprives the parents of their dreams and fantasies relating to the child.

Farber (1975) lists the successive adaptations in families when having a child with severe mental retardation:

1. **Labeling Phase.** *The family looks at the removal of the bases for the existing role arrangements and finds that major understandings underpinning family relationships may have to be renegotiated.*
2. **Normalization Phase.** *The family makes a pretense of maintaining its normal set of roles. Family members try to be considerate of each other for role lapses in an attempt to keep family life as normal as possible. The family presents a face of normality to the outside and seeks to maintain liaisons with the world of normal families.*
3. **Mobilization Phase.** *The family members intensify the time and effort given to family demands, without, however, giving up their claim to normality as a family.*
4. **Revisionist Phase.** *The family, in isolating itself from community involvements, can no longer maintain an identity of normality, and it revises age and sex standards in its organization of family roles. This revision represents an attempt to maintain cohesiveness in an uncaring and lack-of-understanding world.*
5. **Polarization Phase.** *The family, finding itself unable to maintain its coherence in a complacent or perhaps hostile world, turns its attention inward to seek the sources of this complacence or hostility within the family.*
6. **Elimination Phase.** *The polarization eventuates in arrangements to preclude contact with the offending person himself. In this phase, the family seeks to renegotiate (with whatever resources remain) to regain those roles regarded as normal (p. 251).*

As a result, parents pass through a sequence of feelings and reactions (Murray, 1980, p. 151).

1. **Failure to Believe.** *Parents do not accept a diagnosis and continue shopping for a new diagnosis or cure. Parents also may minimize the seriousness of the disability as they develop coping mechanisms.*
2. **Self-Blame.** *An overwhelming feeling of guilt may often be initiated by the parent. Parents may experience regret about some of the things they think they should not have done.*
3. **Anger and Self-Pity.** *These two emotions often are closely aligned. Parents feel helpless and unable to change the disabling condition, and this helplessness often develops into either anger or pity. Parents will displace their anger onto the professional, the spouse, or the institution. Self-pity and/or depression can be expected from parents of children*

with disabilities and should be permitted as parents wrestle with how to cope with their problem.

4. **Giving and Sharing.** *A common type of parental reaction that usually takes place following failure to believe, self-blame, and anger and self-pity, is seen as parents volunteer to help other parents of children with disabilities, or as they begin to help teachers and other educational personnel. They may also become very involved with their child's activities.*

Some other parental reactions are identified on Featherstone's (1980) emotional response list of fear, anger, loneness, guilt and self-doubt, and marital stress. Menolascino (1974) indicates three stages of parental acceptance: rejecting the diagnosis (shock and denial), feeling guilty, and responding to the child's and their personal needs and making efforts to handle and control the situation. Roos (1985) states that parents of children with mental retardation are at-risk to be misunderstood and mistreated which may cause the following reactions: loss of self-esteem, shame, ambivalence, depression, self-sacrifice, and defensiveness. Gordon (1975) lists possible parents' concerns about the birth of a child with disabilities, including loss of confidence in their worth as procreators and individuals, feelings of inadequacy and hurt, ruin of dreams and hope, unhappiness, rejecting the child and each other, withdrawal, irrationality, uncontrollable anger, depression, not being able to communicate, fear and uncertainty, frustration, helplessness, guilt-ridden feelings, resentment, anxiety, and acceptance. He indicates that it is helpful for parents to share feelings with other parents. In his own experience, he finds it extremely helpful for enhancing group dynamics if parents and professionals are relaxed and at ease with each other.

Giving birth to a child is stressful. It causes even more stress if the child has a disability (Suelze & Keenan, 1981). In addition to a variety of feelings and reactions, parents also face a number of sources of stress. Peterson (1987) summarizes these **"stressors"** as:

> *. . . additional expenses and financial burdens; actual or perceived stigma; heightened demands on time as a result of caretaking requirements for the child; difficulties with basic caretaking tasks such as feeding, bathing, dressing; decreased time for sleep; social isolation from friends, relatives, neighbors; reduced time for leisure or personal activities; difficulties in managing the child's behavior; interference with routine domestic responsibilities; [and] general feelings of pessimism about the future (pp. 422–423).*

Sharing their experiences as parents of a child with hemophilia, Massie and Massie (1975) cite the health-worshipping tendency in our society as a major cause of sources of stress. "Every family with a handicapped or chronically ill child shares the same problems: lack of money, isolation from the health community, prejudice, misunderstanding in the schools, loneliness, boredom, [and] depression" (p. xi). Parents' potential to cope effectively with these sources of stress is related to factors such as severity of the child's disability, the family's stability, and its internal and external support (Peterson, 1987). These factors will be discussed later in this chapter.

In addition to the reactions following the birth of a child with a disability, a number of parents and families may also face the situation of having a child with a terminal illness. These parents and families may have further feelings of shock, denial, sadness, guilt, hostility, bargain, depression, and anger which need to be dealt with before acceptance can occur (Green, 1971; Lian 1990b).

It should be noted that the purpose of identifying parental feelings and reactions is not to produce an uncaring chronology of parents' movement from one stage of feelings and reactions to another. Rather, it is to provide appropriate assistance. Professionals are encouraged to determine exactly what services parents need and prefer at each specific stage.

Menolascino (1974) emphasizes the importance of an initial multidisciplinary diagnostic evaluation and interpretation interview which can be crucial to further intervention. To achieve an effective initial interpretation interview with parents, he suggests that professionals need specific skills such as utilizing knowledge of the disabling condition, being able to explain and discuss the condition at a parental level of understanding, and having an understanding of the family dynamics. In addition, professionals should learn and practice to become active listeners, community resource users, and caring helpers or facilitators. And overall, parents should be recognized as full and equal participating members on the educational and related services team. There should be positive attitudes and sharing and working together as a team. Professionals should try to accept parents, and learn to listen and encourage them. Professionals should share all relevant information, enhance clear and successful communication, and provide methodological and technical assistance for parents' selection and decision of goals and approaches. At many stages of parental reactions, professionals may find parental mentorship and peer support to be very helpful.

Safford and Arbitman (1975) reaffirm that societal attitudes toward individuals with disabling conditions affect not only the individual but also those family members and friends closest to them. Hollingsworth and Pasnau (1977) use the theory of defense mechanisms to interpret parents' and families' responses such as denial, guilt, projection, anger, shame, and over-protection. They state that the existing disabling condition of a child may be perceived as a threat. This is because parents view their child as an extension of themselves, and having a child with a disability may cause them to lose hope of having a healthy and normal child. They may concentrate more on this concern, rather than on the immediate needs of the child. This defense mechanism may have already been greatly decreased since today, society tends to show fewer negative attitudes toward individuals with disabilities and their families, and instead provides them with more understanding, support, and assistance. As Turnbull (1985) describes, ". . . over the years the sensitivities of people have far outnumbered the insensitivities" (p. 138). She indicates that the sensitivity of her extended family, friends, and neighbors to her child with a disability is positive and rewarding.

Another factor causing parents' negative responses is related to professionals' comments and prognosis statements, including those generally reported in media. Unfortunately, many of these comments and prognosis statements have been inaccurate. In Baby Jane Doe's case of the early 1980s, for example, Baby Keri-Lynn was described as follows: ". . . she wouldn't live all that long and as long as she did live, she would be profoundly retarded and in constant pain, would always be bedridden, would never be able to learn anything and would never be able to recognize anyone, even her parents. In grim sum, her quality of life would be so low—the press implied—that her departure would be a blessing to her parents and, of course, to herself" (Hentoff, 1991, p. 3). It was found that, during her first seven years of life, this child "was not in pain, that she laughs and plays with her parents and other children, and recognizes her parents with no trouble at all" (Hentoff, 1991, p. 3). Several of her pediatric surgeons said that, if the court ruled for her to receive more aggressive treatment, she would do even better in terms of mobility, education, and intelligence.

Being a parent, Gorham (1975) found a number of "ironies" about living with a child with disabilities prior to enactment of P.L. 94-142, including: (a) parent's responsibilities for monitoring the child's progress through the fragmented service system; (b) parent's efforts to seek help from a non-school medical professional, such as the physician who actually has minimal exposure to the total need of the child and the family; (c) the highly specialized diagnostician who is less concerned, and may be less willing to deal with the parent's situation and feelings; (d) recommendations made by professionals to place the child in an institution; (e) not being allowed to read confidential information about the child; (f) lack of commu- nity-based group homes, foster homes, and respite care facilities and programs; (g) lack of free and appropriate public education; and (h) being made to feel guilty by the concept of normalization. These "ironies" tend to make parents feel guilty, and feel bad or incompetent about themselves.

It is important to note that parents of a child with disabilities may have both positive and negative responses. Waisbren (1980) reports that parents tend to see themselves more negatively and express more **negative feelings** toward their young children with developmental disabilities soon after birth. They tend to contact more medical and hospital personnel and end up with more uncertainty. Their negative feelings include hopelessness, anger, and rejection, which center on the child's appearance or lack of ability. However, Waisbren (1980) also finds that parents can have **positive feelings** toward their children with developmental disabilities, too, including their feelings toward the child as good-natured and easy-going. Other positive reactions include more volunteer activity related to the child, better understanding of individual differences, and being more tolerant toward others.

A family's experience, such as feeling pain when having a member with a disability, being labeled because of symptoms, beliefs about the cause of illness, attitudes toward medical and therapeutic personnel, or desire for treatment, will be strongly influenced by the family's ethnic and cultural background (McGoldrick, 1982). For example, Turnbull et al. (1988) summarize white, Anglo-Saxon Protestants' values as "self-reliance, self-control, achievement, and self-determinism" and Mexican-Americans' values as "cooperation, interdependence, collectivism, and cohesiveness" (p. 86). Professionals in education and related services should be willing to make efforts to understand such cultural and ethnic influence when providing services. For more information about specific ethnic families, such as Italian, Hebrew, Asian, Hispanic, African-American, or Caucasian families, readers are encouraged to study the work of McGoldrick, Pearce, and Giordano (1982) and Heward and Orlansky (1992).

For parents who fail to traverse the several stages of feelings and responses successfully, the disabling condition that directly impacts the child could then produce a secondary disabling condition called parentalplegia. Murray and Cornell (1981) defined **parentalplegia** as:

> *a secondary psychophysiological (stress induced) condition that evolves among parents of handicapped children. . . . It is the inability on the part of parents to adjust to the handicap of their children. . . It is recognized by extremes in resulting parental attitudes toward their child's handicap. . . The parents adaptability and efficiency in daily living is radically affected by their inability to adjust to the condition of their child. (p. 201)*

It is important for education and related services professionals to understand parental responses and to assist parents in an efficient way so that parentalplegia can be prevented. If necessary, counseling and other services should be sought.

Parental Reactions Related to the Type and Degree of Disabilities

Parents' expectations relating to their child may be influenced by different types and degrees of disabling conditions. Mental retardation may be one of the most difficult conditions for parents to accept. Parents may be "devastated" by this diagnosis, especially when they realize that their child is going to carry a stigma that has been highly related to isolation, dependency, and institutionalization in our society (Fewell, 1986a). In addition, Turnbull et al. (1988) indicate that a family's reaction to a specific type of disability may be influenced by their great values and general lifestyle. They describe the possibility that families with high achievement goals may react positively when having a gifted child. On the contrary, families that do not place great value on achievement and education may perceive the birth of a child with giftedness as a threat.

Families of a child with hearing or visual impairments may develop stronger social ties with other families facing the same disabling condition. It is not unusual that persons with severe hearing loss and their families get together to form a "deaf community." Part of the reason is that these persons and family members may feel more comfortable in using specific non-English sign language within their group. Turnbull et al. (1988) describe different challenges for a family caused by different types of disabilities:

> *A child with a language impairment possibly could create problems for the family as it tries to establish meaningful, constructive communication; a child with health problems may require extended hospitalizations and expensive medications; and a child who is blind needs special adaptations in learning self-care and leisure skills. A family may do quite well with one exceptionality but not with another. (p. 85)*

Many disabling conditions may have associated conditions or secondary/multiple conditions, such as speech/language/communication impairments, social disabilities, and behavioral disorders. The impact of having a child with a disability may be more difficult when the child displays maladaptive behaviors as well as when there are other family conflicts (Nihira, Meyers, & Mink, 1980).

The severity of disability is another factor with specific implications for parents. Children with mild conditions, such as learning disabilities and mild mental retardation, may not be identified until school readiness screening. This might cause parents to regret not having had the opportunity for early intervention. The advantage, however, would be that these children have been treated as normal throughout their infant, toddler, and early childhood years (Fewell, 1986a).

Once of school age, another advantage for children with mild disabilities would be a greater opportunity to be mainstreamed and integrated among other children without disabilities in the least restrictive environment. By this time, parental reactions may be varied, depending on each individual family's perception and experience relating to mild disabilities.

Fewell (1986b) indicates that parents of children with moderate disabilities may face ambiguity and feel puzzled or stressed, especially if at times their child is perceived as "normal," and at other times they are not. Generally speaking, families of a child with severe disabilities tend to experience more stress than those of a child with mild disabilities (Turnbull et al., 1988). However, children with severe disabilities are generally identified at birth or shortly after. Although the early diagnosis is often a source of great sadness accompanied with loss of self-esteem, feelings of shame, ambivalence, depression, self-sacrifice, and/or defensiveness (Roos, 1985), these children tend to receive early assistance and intervention. Parents and professionals need to consider the differential impact of different types and severity of disabling conditions. Accurate information provided for parents may decrease ambiguity, help parents to set appropriate goals and expectations, and start home intervention activities as early as possible (Fewell, 1986a).

Basic Family Structure, Stability, and Characteristics and the Reaction to a Child with a Disability

Turnbull et al. (1988) describe how family structure, stability, and characteristics vary:

Families differ in how many children they have, the number of parents, the presence and number of stepparents, extensiveness of the extended family network, and preferences and extensiveness of live-in members of the family who are unrelated by blood or marriage. The parents may be married, divorced, or reestablished, or they may have some other type of arrangement. The notion of two parents living in the home, the father working, and the mother devoting full-time care and attention to two children and their collie dog is a myth of modern society. (p. 86)

Professionals in education and related services need to be aware that, in the future, there will be increasing numbers of unmarried or divorced single parents in the family as well as more working mothers. These trends in society impact on the special needs of persons with disabilities.

In addition to the form of a family, family size may also have influence. The number and birth order of children in a family lead to various situations. More children in a family seems to result in less parental-caring time, but more sibling help and support (Turnbull et al., 1988). Again, the situation may differ from one family to another.

Through family harmony and quality of parenting and child rearing practices, parents can better cope with the impact of having a child with disabling conditions at home. Nihira et al. (1980) suggest that parents provide an educationally stimulating environment, a home with cohesiveness and harmony, a culturally stimulating atmosphere, along with positive educational expectations, to enhance their children's adaptive competence and social adjustment.

Sibling Reactions

Having a brother or sister with a disability in the family provides siblings with special experiences and causes specific reactions. Crnic and Leconte (1986) indicate that

. . . being the sibling of a handicapped child evokes a range of emotional responses, from pride to enjoyment to irritation and resentment. At times, it is just plain confusing. While these emotions may seem little different from those characterizing all sibling relationships, the potential for more extreme responses exists, given the ongoing stress related to the presence of a handicapped child. (p. 76)

In a survey conducted about thirty years ago, Farber (1963) found that boys and girls, especially those who were frequent interactors with their brothers or sisters with disabilities, placed less emphasis on life goals concerned with success in personal relations, including having many close friends, focusing life around marriage and the family, and on being a respected community leader. Siblings may feel guilty about their bitter or negative feelings (Grossman, 1972). These situations may have changed today by factors such as an increase of public awareness and acceptance, legal protection of family rights, and more positive involvement of regular school and community systems. Simeonsson and Bailey (1986) maintain that advocacy and public policy efforts are the two major factors that can cause this change.

Powell and Olge (1985) report that siblings of persons with disabilities may focus on play and social interactions, friends, extra family duties and caregiving responsibilities, and loss of freedom when describing their personal experience. This is especially true when there are few positive parental attitudes and when, in lower-income families, there are extra caregiving responsibilities for siblings to manage (Fewell, 1986a). Nevertheless, these siblings felt advantaged. In fact, many siblings make career decisions and become human service professionals because of their brothers or sisters with disabilities (Powell & Olge, 1985). Grossman (1972) finds that siblings of a person with a disability seem to be more tolerant and more goal-oriented. Powell and Olge (1985) state:

> . . . *they are more understanding of human problems; that they accept people better; and that they are less judgmental and more easy going. Several said that they learned to teach; others said they developed practice; still others claimed to have learned to deal effectively with embarrassment . . . that their family communicates more effectively . . . their family members [were] closer, more open, and more honest with each other as a result of their experiences. (p. 176)*

Siblings' adjustment was found to be related to a number of factors, such as family size, age, gender, severity of disabilities, and definition of disabilities. Positive adjustment of siblings is associated with small families, siblings who are younger than the child with a disability, male child with a disability, same gender of sibling and the child with a disability, severe level of impairment, and undefined, ambiguous nature of impairment (Simeosson & McHale, 1981; Simeonsson & Bailey, 1986). The oldest child, most often the daughter, tends to serve as a surrogate parent in caring for a younger brother or sister with disabilities (Bossard & Boll, 1956).

Table 3-1 lists 20 strategies for parents in responding to siblings of children with a disability. These strategies are suggested by Powell and Olge (1985), based on their observations and interviews of a number of siblings. Additional information on sibling relations is provided in the following chapter.

Extended Family's Reactions

In addition to siblings, other members of the extended family are also affected in varying degrees by the birth of a child with disabilities. Their reactions to the birth and corresponding degree of support for the parents can be a source of comfort or pain for parents of a newborn child with disabilities (Ferris, 1980).

TABLE 3-1 • Suggested Strategies for Parents to Respond to Siblings

1. Be open and honest.
2. Value each child individually.
3. Limit caregiving responsibilities.
4. Use respite care and other supportive services.
5. Be fair.
6. Accept disability.
7. Put together a library of children's books on disabilities.
8. Schedule special time with each sibling.
9. Let siblings settle their own differences.
10. Welcome other children and friends into the home.
11. Praise siblings.
12. Recognize that parents are the most important, most powerful teacher of their children.
13. Recognize the uniqueness of each family.
14. Listen to siblings.
15. Involve the siblings.
16. Require the child with a disability to do as much for himself or herself as possible.
17. Recognize each child's unique qualities and family contribution.
18. Encourage the development of special sibling programs.
19. Help establish a sibling support group.
20. Recognize special stress times for siblings and plan to minimize negative effects.

Source: Powell, T. H., & Olge, P. A. (1985). *Brothers and sisters—A special part of exceptional families.* Baltimore, MD: Paul H. Brookes.

Having a child with mental or physical disabilities may cause some negative, or even disruptive, changes between the child's parents and grandparents. Parents may receive less support from the child's grandparents, especially those who are paternal, when compared to parents and grandparents of nondisabled children. Sonnek (1986) states that "maternal grandmothers were perceived as providing help to their daughters; paternal grandmothers were perceived as being unsympathetic to their daughters-in-law for the child's handicapping condition or placing excessive burden on their sons" (p. 108). However, the situation can be exactly the opposite. Vadasy and Fewell (1986) find grandparents happen to be most helpful when there is a child with dual sensory impairments in the family.

Grandparents are especially vulnerable by their unique position as parents of the mother and father. They tend to grieve at two levels; first, the "loss" of the expected grandchild and, second, at the knowledge of the increased burdens placed on their own offspring. The degree to which grandparents are impacted is also reflected by the degree to which they can be supportive and provide encouragement for the parents (Fewell, 1986a).

RESOURCES FOR COPING RESPONSES OF PARENTS

The ability of parents to respond to the stress of having a child with a disabling condition is based on two categories of resources available to them: internal resources and external resources.

Kirk and Gallagher (1989) find that some families are successful in coping with having children with disabilities, while some are not. Families that are successful "call on internal and external means of support for the strength to deal with the special needs of their children" (p. 22).

Internal Resources

There are five internal resources that are closely related to parents' coping responses. These five resources are described in the paragraphs that follow.

The Degree of Perceived Control or
Lack of Control of the Situation

Using its own internal resources, a family can find it somewhat easier to adjust to life with a child with disabilities (Gallagher, 1986). Examples of internal resources are:

1. *A mother who is satisfied with her marriage*
2. *A father who is supportive*
3. *Financial security*
4. *A commitment to a set of values (for example, strong religious beliefs)*
5. *The support of relatives, friends, and parents of other children with handicaps (Kirk & Gallagher, 1989, pp. 22–23)*

Families may perceive the situation of having a child with disabilities in different ways. As a result, some may withdraw, while others may see it as a challenge. Turnbull and Turnbull (1990) give specific examples:

> *If we interpret an event negatively, we think of it as threatening our well-being or creating needs—in other words, it is stressful to us. If, on the other hand, we interpret an event positively, we think of it as enhancing our well-being or satisfying our needs—in other words, we cope . . . When we use an internal coping strategy, we revise our interpretations about an event that was originally perceived negatively, so that all or part of it can be perceived positively or at least neutrally. (p. 362)*

Extended Family

Interactions in extended families with grandparents and other relatives such as uncles and aunts may be complex (Gabel & Kotsch, 1981). However, these extended family members may provide support and help (Caplan, 1976; Vadasy &

Fewell, 1986). Professionals have started to realize the potential of grandparents as a significant source of support (Fewell, 1986a). Sonnek (1986) suggests that programs for extended family members, such as: (a) the family, infant, and toddler project; (b) the family intervention project; and (c) the grandparents' workshop, should focus on supporting the entire family and utilizing the existing helping relationships and patterns in the extended family on a day-to-day basis for effective family functioning.

Parental Relationships, Health, Energy, Morale, and Spiritual Perspective

Friedrich (1979) reports that degree of maternal satisfaction with the marriage is the single most significant factor in the mother's ability to cope with her child with a disability. This theme is supported by Fewell, Belmonte, and Ahlersmeyer (1983) who report that mothers rate spouses out of a possible nineteen other persons as the most significant support person when it comes to coping with the birth of a child with disabilities.

Generally speaking, parents who are in better health have more physical and/or emotional strength to cope with the situation of having a child with a disability. Parents with increased energy and morale may be more able to meet the needs of the child and maintain successful family life. On the contrary, parents may have more difficulty coping with stressful situations when they do not feel well (Turnbull & Turnbull, 1990).

Turnbull and Turnbull (1990) also include parents' religious views as one major component of internal resources. They stress that some parents may cope well with spiritual support, while others may not. Caplan and Killilea (1976) stated:

> *Many of us had been struck by the importance of religious metaphors in certain mutual help groups. We thought the more we knew about religion and religious concepts and how they operate in people's lives, the better we might understand about the nature of such things as conversion process (p. 95).*

Religious viewpoints and emphasis on human physical and mental abilities may influence parental acceptance of a disabling condition and their coping responses (Wolfensberger, 1967). In addition, certain religious doctrines and practices may increase or decrease some parents' feelings of guilt and, again, influence their coping responses (Zuk, 1959).

Problem Solving Skills

Hornby (1989) suggests that professionals not only try to understand parents' needs, but also make efforts to get to know and utilize parents' strengths in order to increase their competency and participation in problem solving situations. These situations may include needing non-biased diagnosis and assessment, participating in individualized educational planning, deciding placement in specific programs, finding effective instructional or interventional strategies, dealing with challenging behaviors, and/or enhancing smooth and successful transition from school to community.

As discussed later in this text, effective communication skills, including active listening, paraphrasing, behavioral describing, perception check, and conflict management are helpful problem solving skills (Scharf, 1990). These communication skills can be successfully developed among parents through collaboration or workshop efforts.

Problem solving by parents may be enhanced by employing the following steps (Turnbull & Turnbull, 1990):

1. Defining the problem, describing its related issues, and dividing the problem into resolvable and unresolvable parts
2. Brainstorming alternatives by listing all possible "free-spirited" and "nonjudgmental" options for solutions
3. Evaluating alternatives by the criteria set with all family members' agreement
4. Selecting and implementing an appropriate alternative by family members being assigned specific responsibilities

Available Financial and Related Resources

Having a child is expensive. Having a child with a disability is even more costly, due to increased need for health and medical care, therapy, day and nursery care, transportation, adaptive equipment for mobility, and other accommodations. Parents tend to be overwhelmed by the additional financial needs. One parent often has to stay home. Such extra costs may lead to financial insecurity in the family (Singer, Irvin, Irvine, Hawkins, & Cooley, 1989). Unfortunately, our society has not developed a financial support system "to support families as primary caregivers . . . [and assist families] to carry out their responsibilities" (Fewell, 1986a, p. 26).

External Resources

A number of external resources can be helpful. These resources include friends, neighbors, professionals, and community agencies/organizations. Turnbull et al. (1988) include relatives, friends, neighbors, members in religious or community organizations, co-workers, and professionals in the "extrafamilial subsystem" of family interactions network. People in this subsystem provide various assistance, such as offering child care, helping perform household chores, and giving financial and emotional support.

Friends

Both parents and their children need friends' support to cope with a disabling condition. Turnbull and Turnbull (1990) state, "Friendships between people with and without a disability can provide social support for the person with a disability, as well as for his family" (p. 360). Friends should include not only other families of children with disabilities, but also families of children without disabilities.

Although families of children with disabilities tend to meet and become friends with families of children with the same disabilities, "the promotion of social networks with families whose children are normally developing would also appear to be an important goal" (Bailey & Winton, 1989, p. 107).

As a parent of a son with severe disabilities, Ahlgren (1985) sees no difference between her family and supporting friends—in her definition and experience, they are all family. Her friends were always there to express interest, concern, and sympathy, and to offer help and support when there were frustration, challenging behaviors, negative medical or educational diagnoses, and various parental feelings. Her friends include people in the community, such as the policeman, neighbors, the grocery clerk, professionals, and other parents of children with disabilities. Most importantly, these friends give Ahlgren's family and her son dignity. Together they "create a real and strong demonstration and affirmation of [her son] Todd's—and all the others who share his challenge—capacities to grow, to be an individual, and to survive" (p. 3).

Neighbors

A number of people and families live close to the family of a child with a disability. They are neighbors who provide "a[n] important source of support with short-term assistance such as babysitting, meals during an illness, and care of property in one's absence" (Fewell, 1986a, p. 5). In addition, neighbors can also provide emotional and moral support and, thus, increase community awareness and positive attitudes toward persons with disabling conditions. Moeller (1986) invites parents to look at themselves and review their own sensitivity and vulnerability. She asks parents to learn to differentiate a smile from a passerby as out of pity or out of friendliness and to review their own emotional guard. It is with mutual trust that a helping relationship can be established with friends and neighbors.

Professionals

Educators, rehabilitation specialists, counselors, and related human service personnel may provide professional assistance to help parents cope with the challenge of having a child with disabilities. Begab and Richardson (1975) suggest the following:

> It is essential to build trust between consumers and professionals. Opportunities for joint planning for common objectives seem to foster collaboration and trust. Openness on the part of professionals is also useful. A community-oriented program such as BDS sees no contradiction in consumers operating their own programs provided the programs are effective, well run, and do not duplicate existing services. Another reasonable way of promoting better professional and consumer understanding is through the mechanism of establishing procedures for the joint evaluation of the effectiveness of services and "normalization" experiences. The results of the studies would enable us to plan more realistically and collaboratively in the future (p. 413).

Professionals should be trained to get to know parents and families through functional and productive approaches, such as active listening and helping parents to relax. They should provide parents with valid and understandable information. Finally, they should work together with parents as a team for planning and achieving realistic goals (Hollingsworth & Pasnau, 1977; Lian, 1984).

There have been efforts by administrative and inservice professionals to help school personnel establish and maintain productive relationships with parents. For example, Brock and Shanberg (1990) provide guidelines for conflict resolution and prevention of unnecessary due process hearings. Scharf (1990) describes parent workshops for enhancing communication skills, problem solving and conflict managing strategies in order to achieve more positive and productive parent-school relationships.

Community Agencies/Organizations

Walker (1989) lists a number of community resources for family support services. Many of these resources assist families in (a) keeping children with disabilities at home; (b) strengthening their caregiving capacities; and (c) increasing the quality of life of persons with disabilities and their families. In addition to governmental agencies and projects, Fewell and Vadasy (1986) include other resources for parents and families, such as national disability, special education and rehabilitation organizations, written resources (directories and guides), specific resources (according to types of services or disabling conditions), sport organizations, and religious groups.

Lian (1990b) suggests the following community resources for parents of children with disabilities:

1. **Governmental agencies** such as offices for supplemental social income, the American Printing House for the Blind, Head Start agencies, the department of mental health and developmental disabilities, the department of child and family services, the department of public aids, the department of rehabilitation services, the state office of human rights and advocacy, the state planning council on developmental disabilities, state and local libraries, and local park and recreation agencies
2. **Professional organizations** such as the Council for Exceptional Children (CEC), The Association for Persons with Severe Handicaps (TASH), organizations for children with learning disabilities, American Association on Mental Retardation (AAMR), and the American Alliance of Health, Physical Education, Recreation and Dance (AAHPERD)
3. **Service organizations** such as the Easter Seal Rehabilitation Center, the United Cerebral Palsy Association, YMCA, YWCA, the March of Dimes Birth Defects Foundation, the Epilepsy Foundation, the Cystic Fribrosis Foundation, and the National Lekotek Center
4. **Parent support groups** such as the Association for Retarded Citizens (ARC),the National Society for Autistic Children and Adults, the Spina Bifida

Association of America, The Muscular Dystrophy Association of America, and the National Society for Children with Down Syndrome; and

5. **Charity groups** such as the Lion's Club, Rotary Club, Salvation Army, United Way, and the International Shriners.

In addition to the above community resources, there are also educational organizations (Espinosa & Shearer 1986) and community health-care systems (Mallory, 1986). **Educational organizations,** such as school districts, regional special education cooperatives, and educational learning resource centers, provide parents with systematic education and related services, including assessment, prereferral intervention, individualized educational planning, implementation, and progress evaluation, school health and school nurse, counseling, physical, occupational, and speech/language therapy, and transportation. **Community health-care systems** offer diagnosis, referral, treatment, and financial assistance (for example, constant care allowance, health maintenance organizations, or HMOs, and alternative payment mechanisms) (Mallory, 1986).

Religious organizations in the community can be another source of support for parents and families of a person with disabilities. Fewell (1986b) lists four major kinds of religious groups' support. **Instrumental support** includes material goods and services such as food, medical supply, and transportation for medical treatment, money and gift certificates, and other forms of goods and services for those in need, whether church members or not. **Emotional and social support** can be provided through a pastor's active listening, consultation, and prayer; church members' fellowship, music, social, and recreational activities; and the church congregation's sharing and support. Joining a religious organization, parents of a child with disabilities may look for two different kinds of **educational support.** The first is the opportunity for their child to participate in church activities and to be involved in religious programs. The second is to help parents to carry out their responsibilities of raising a child with disabilities. Religious organizations provide their members with **structural support** through the major developmental milestones in church life, including baptism, membership, marriage, death, rituals, and corporate worship such as "the Catholic Mass, the prayer meeting, the church or temple service" as well as "a religious organization's stated principles or beliefs that are central to the organization in the forms of written scriptures, creeds, and doctrines" (Fewell, 1986b, p. 308). Through these different kinds of support, parents and families of children with disabilities may develop a feeling of belonging to a church or community family. Parents may no longer feel alone when coping with the situation of having a child with disabilities.

However, it is not uncommon that parents of children with disabilities do not turn to religious organizations for help and support. Possible reasons include: (a) different theological explanations on disabilities; (b) church groups and personnel who are not trained or prepared for counseling parents and families of children with a disability; and (c) parents, as well as the society, tend to see disabilities as a medical, instead of a religious, problem (Drew, Logan, & Hardman, 1984).

As society becomes more and more complex, many of the duties that used to be performed by families are transferred to agencies and organizations outside the family. For example, education may be shifted from the home to the school (Winch, 1971). It is recommended that parents and families have the opportunity to be away from the child with a disability at regular intervals (Hollingsworth & Pasnau, 1977). This can be achieved through friends, neighbors, baby-sitters, day care services, foster family care, or the formal respite program of some social agencies and organizations (Adams, 1975). Kirk and Gallagher (1989) pinpoint the significance of **respite care** provided by community agencies:

> *One of the primary stressors of life with a severely handicapped child is day-to-day care—feeding, dressing, toileting. A dependent child must have someone's help to survive. Often the emotional and physical demands of that care leave the caregiver (usually the mother) with no strengths for other relationships or activities. Community agencies now offer respite care to families with handicapped children. A trained individual comes into the home for a certain number of hours a week or for a weekend a month, to relieve the primary caregiver (p. 24).*

Singer et al. (1989) find that, besides general support of respite care and case management, intensive intervention can significantly decrease parents' depression and anxiety. Such services may include stress management, parenting skill training, support groups, and community-based respite care. When assisting parents to cope with the situation of having a child with disabilities, Spiegel (1982) suggests that the following be kept in mind:

> *(a) the value patterns characteristic of the family's culture of origin; (b) where the family is in the acculturation process—that is, what values have been or are being changed at the time of intervention; (c) the family's understanding or misunderstanding of mainstream American values; [and] in the case of cross-cultural marriages, . . . (d) what conflicts have occurred between two native value patterns. (pp. 45–46)*

Collaborative assistance should be provided to enable parents and families to utilize internal and external resources. These resources can be located and arranged to be helpful for each individual family's specific needs and goals.

EVOLVING ROLES AND RESPONSIBILITIES OF PARENTS

After exploring the historical and contemporary view of parental rights and responses in this chapter, we now come to roles parents play and responsibilities they take in the life of their child with disabilities. The following topics will be addressed:

- Parents' experiences in the life cycle of a family
- Transitional stages
- Major functions of a family
- Evolving roles of parents

Parents' Experiences in the Life Cycle of a Family

The type and degree of the disabling condition, along with other factors, may influence a family's involvement throughout the life span of the individual with a disability. It is also important to note that such influencing factors do not occur only during certain stages in the life span. As Turnbull et al. (1988) state, "Families grow and change over the life cycle" (p. 102). The evolving roles of parents should be examined through the major life cycle of the family as well as the major functions that a family provides the child. Turnbull and Turnbull (1990) identify the following stages in a life cycle: the couple, childbearing and preschool years of the child, school age, adolescence, and adulthood.

The Couple

Two persons are joined together and form a new family. Before they have children and become parents, there are only two individuals in the family, the husband and wife, unless there were children from previous marriages. Each family member assumes certain roles, including earning family income and making and maintaining a home. More importantly, this couple provides company and partnership for each other. They provide psychological and emotional support for each other. They try to establish new priorities and traditions which are the results of "a blending of the values, goals, and expectations of the two families of origin" (Turnbull et al., 1988, p. 103). A strong nuclear family depends on the teamwork of the couple, before and after a child is born. When the wife becomes pregnant, the couple "psychologically prepare for the changes in family structure and new responsibilities (financial, temporal, and psychological) that the infant will bring" (Peterson, 1987, p. 410). At the birth of a child, the couple shares expectations and feelings, and helps each other to adjust, plan, and work out a possible way to accomplish the increasingly complicated tasks in the family.

Childbearing and Preschool Years

During the period from birth to infancy, parents take care of "the child's many physical demands, his/her very real pain, his/her physical discomfort, his/her needs for special diets, his/her frequent doctor's appointments and special medications" (Buscaglia, 1975). Parents at this stage may be under pressure and face challenging and stressful situations. Parents work so hard that sometimes they even forget or ignore their own physical and emotional needs and demands. By creating a positive social environment, the task of parenting leads to a two-way interaction and establishes a reciprocal relationship between the child and the family (Peterson, 1987).

As the child starts to grow and become independent, parents must guard against overprotection. They must avoid setting limits on the child's opportunities to explore the outside world. We all understand and agree that parents are the very first teacher of the child. Parents are always there to help, encourage, praise, and to respond to the child for his or her continuous growth and development (Heward & Orlansky, 1992). Children learn many things from parents, such as daily living skills, values, and self-esteem and self-confidence. At the same time, parents at this stage have increased their awareness of available community resources relating to the child's early intervention and start to search for, and participate in, appropriate school programs.

School Age

At this stage, parents pay increased attention to educational and socialization aspects of the child (Turnbull et al., 1988). School-related issues relating to the development of friendships emerge. With the trend for decentralized special education service delivery and increased regular education initiative (REI), more children with disabilities are integrated into their neighborhood public school settings. Parents care about their children being accepted by their teachers and nondisabled peers. There have been suggestions that parents actively participate in integration teams and programs to enhance acceptance and socialization. Examples of opportunities for such participation are the teacher assistant team (TAT) in the prereferral support system and the integrated IEP approach (Hayek, 1987; York & Vandercook, 1991).

Adolescence

During adolescence, parents observe their children with disabilities transfer from primary school to intermediate, junior high, and senior high school education. Rapid physical and psychological changes occur during this stage. Turnbull and Turnbull (1990) describe the issue of puberty:

> *Puberty, the beginning of sexual maturity, usually marks the start of ado-lescence, which is accompanied by a host of developmental tasks including: (a) development of self identity; (b) development of a positive body image; (c) adjustment to sexual maturation; (d) emotional independence from parents; and (e) development of mature relationships with peers of both sexes. (p. 121)*

Parents at this stage can be helpful in meeting the child's increasing physical-care or self-care needs as well as his or her needs to cope with stress. However, children at this stage may reject parents' opinions and authority. Facing the fact that their children are growing into adulthood, parents need to review their own roles and accept and encourage their children's self-initiatives.

Wilcox and Bellamy (1982) identify differences between roles of parents with children in early intervention or elementary programs and those with secondary-age students with disabilities. Parents more often find longitudinal skill sequences to follow in preschool and elementary curriculum based on children's normal development. For secondary students, parents and educators may need to switch to non-sequential curricular options, such as vocational preparation, domestic skill training, community living, and leisure/recreational development. As a result, "the values of parents are more important and more apparent in educational programming for secondary students because there are no established skill sequences per se" (Wilcox & Bellamy, 1982, p. 21).

Adulthood

The child with disabilities completes his or her formal education and enters the post-secondary stage in the family life cycle. Adults with disabilities enter the community for independent living, employment, marriage and child rearing, recreation, and related daily life. Brotherson, Turnbull, Bronicki, Houghton, Roeder-Gordon, Summers, & Turnbull (1988) indicate three major causes of stress during this stage:

1. Transition to adulthood can be one of the most stressful situations in a life cycle for families in general.
2. Families are moving from a familiar system (the school) into an unfamiliar system (the community adult service agencies).
3. Families of adults with disabilities may have little experience in change of teachers, classrooms, and activities in high schools, and may accept the adult services as they are.

After interviewing 48 parents of young adults with mental or physical disabilities, Brotherson et al. (1988) found three of the largest needs to be residential arrangements, socialization, and employment. These needs for support and assistance become obvious because federal laws do not mandate post-secondary rehabilitation services (Hill, Seyfarth, Banks, Wehman, & Orelove, 1987). Parents at this stage need to accept the fact of possible separation of parents and children and actively participate in team efforts to utilize all available community resources and accomplish the transition from school to community.

Transition Stages

The family life cycle is not only a number of separate stages, or milestones, it also includes the **developmental transition** from one stage to another in an ongoing manner (Turnbull et al., 1988). This type of transition period may be as critical as during each specific stage for which parents and families need to adjust. As a result, different stresses may occur during a transition period. Turnbull and Turnbull (1990) identify two factors that may reduce stress: (a) the special events to lead a family into a new developmental stage, such as "a wedding, bar mitzvah, graduation, or funeral" (p. 136) which may have already been modeled by other families in a specific culture and are not entirely unknown to the family; and (b) the timing of transition to provide the family with plenty of time to prepare.

There are other kinds of transition periods, or **nondevelopmental transitions** (Turnbull et al., 1988), that exist when a regular stage in the life cycle is interrupted or terminated, such as premarital or extramarital pregnancy, separation, divorce, school dropout, and death of a family member. The interruption or termination of the traditional family life cycle may cause situations such as single parents, decrease of financial support, and shrinking of the extrafamilial support network (Turnbull et al., 1988). Sometimes, a regular family life cycle may be reestablished through remarriage, family counseling, or family rehabilitation services.

Weiss and Weiss (1976) find that people in transition are often faced with:

1. *obsessive review,*
2. *anger, guilt, and related emotions,*
3. *uncertainty regarding the self,*
4. *tendency to false starts, and*
5. *self-doubt and loss of self-confidence. (pp. 217–218)*

Parents and families with the above situations may need special resources for support and counseling services.

Major Functions of a Family

Turnbull, Summers, and Brotherson (1984; 1986) list seven specific areas in which families are responsible for each of their members (see Table 3-2). Kirk and Gallagher (1989) summarize these responsibilities parents and families need to fulfill; they also emphasize increased responsibility when there is a member with disabilities in the family:

> *To function, a family must generate income, protect and maintain its members and home, nurture and love one another, and see to it that children are socialized and educated. When a child is handicapped, these responsibilities grow larger. There is the expense, the time, the energy needed to care for the child; the extra concern for the child's safety; the difficulty of helping the child develop a good self-image and social skills; and the problems of seeing to it that the child receives an appropriate education. Every ordinary task becomes more difficult, and more stressful. (p. 21)*

For a child with disabilities to receive appropriate education and related services, parents face extra responsibilities "including teaching and counseling the child, managing behavior, dealing with their other nonhandicapped children and other significant people, maintaining the parent-to-parent relationship, and relating to the school and community" (Heward & Orlansky, 1992, p. 486). Parents and professionals need to be efficient in two major tasks in order to fulfill family functions. They must be able to utilize available internal and external resources. Equally important, they must be able to make effective arrangements for family

TABLE 3-2 • Major Responsibilities of a Family

1. The economic responsibility to generate income and provide financial support for living costs and related payments

2. The domestic and health care responsiblity to meet the daily needs of food, clothes, health and medical care, and safety

3. The recreational responsibility to provide leisure environment and activities

4. The responsibility for self-identity to increase each family member's sense of belonging

5. The affectionate responsibility to show and share love, care, emotional feelings, and companionship

6. The responsibility for socialization to develop social skills and enhance interpersonal relationships

7. The educational and vocational responsibility to assist and support schooling and career selection and preparation

Source: Turnbull, A. P., Summers, J. A., & Brotherson, M. J. (1984). *Working with families with disabled members: A family systems approach.* Lawrence, KS: University of Kansas.

dynamics and successful teamwork. These tasks can be achieved by efforts such as parent collaboration services, workshops, and ongoing support.

Evolving Roles of Parents

Parents may play more than one role in the life of their children with disabilities. Kirk and Gallagher (1989) identify parents as (a) team members to be observers of the child, valuable sources of information for professionals, teachers, and trainers of the child, and reinforcers of the child's learning and application of skills at home; (b) helpers for the child to adapt to his or her disability; and (c) advocates to stimulate legislation and public awareness and community support. Gorham (1975) indicates that parents are "the primary helper, monitor, coordinator, observer, record-keeper, and decision-maker" (p. 524) for their child.

Peterson (1987) lists alternative roles through which parents can participate in the child's program: observers, audience, providers of services and information, decision makers and team members, liaisons or representatives, advocates, disseminators, and fund raisers, counselors, friends, and supporters, learners or trainees, teachers or tutors of their children, volunteers, aides, or assistants, and just people.

Bernal and North (1978) suggest involving parents as "change agents" for their children, especially when there is personpower shortage, revised service delivery approaches, or use of nonprofessionals and paraprofessionals in the child's program. Thurman and Widerstrom (1990) indicate that many programs for young children with disabilities rely almost entirely on parents as primary change agents in their children's learning environments. Readers of this chapter should also be reminded that there are a great number of parents who teach their own children through home schooling arrangements (see Box 3-2).

BOX 3-2 • Importance: Home Schooling Children with Disabilities

In addition to the issues and concerns that have been discussed regarding parents of children with disabilities, there is a population of parents that are dealing with the education of their children with disabling conditions by teaching them at home.

Over the past few years, there has been a dramatic rise in the number of children being home schooled in this country (Wendel, Konnert, & Foreman, 1986). Although the exact number is not known, it is estimated that there were approximately 10,000 home educators. This figure has jumped to 260,000 (Lines, 1987) with estimates of a million children (Zakariya, 1988) and the numbers growing each year.

The home education movement has grown in both its complexity and diversity. Home schoolers reflect almost every point on the social, political, economic, religious, and philosophical spectra in our society. The movement's multifaceted nature is seen in many ways, but especially in: (a) the composition of the families involved; (b) the curricula and teaching methods employed; and (c) the characteristics of the children taught at home.

Home schooling has also generated much controversy. The mere mention of home schooling can elicit strong reactions from people. Whether it be about its basic legality, the issue of state's rights versus parental rights, the socialization of the children or the concern that "teaching children at home is like practicing medicine without a license" (Wilson, 1988), home schooling can be a very charged issue.

The legal and legislative ramifications stimulated by home schooling have been felt in recent years in almost every school district, state legislative body, and judicial system throughout the country. However, cases relating to some aspect of home schooling have been before the courts for almost 100 years

(from *Commonwealth* v. *Roberts*, 1893; *Meyer* v. State of Nebraska, 1923; *Pierce* v. *Society of Sisters*, 1925; *State* v. *Massa*, 1967; *Wisconsin* v. *Yoder*, 1972; *Perchemlides* v. *Frizzle*, (1978); *Deleconte* v. *State of North Carolina*, 1985; *Dept. of Social Services* v. *Emmanuel Baptist Preschool*, 1987; and *Blackwelder* v. *Safnauer*, 1988.

The number of home-schooled children with disabilities may be extrapolated from data included in the 10th Annual Report to Congress on the implementation of the Education for All Handicapped Children Act (EHA), as well as the estimate of all home schoolers provided by Lines (1987) of 260,000 and Zakariya (1988) of one million children. According to the 10th Annual Report, the number of individuals with disabilities between the ages of 6 and 17 is 3.7 million or 8.9% of the resident population (Gerber & Levine-Donnerstein, 1989). Therefore, taking 8.9 as the percentage of students with disabilities between the ages of 6–17 and applying it to the range of estimates of all home schoolers, the number of children with disabilities home-schooled would range from about 25,000 to 89,000.

What is not known is if there are other factors within the home-schooled population that would increase or decrease the actual numbers than would be predicted by the 8.9% figure found in the 10th Annual Report.

Although some scholarly research efforts about home-schooling have been reported in the literature, they have been too specific, incomplete and/or insufficient in size or scope to provide clear insights as to what is happening with home-schooled children who have a disability. Almost nothing is known about the parents of home-schooled children with disabilities. In light of the topics discussed in the chapter, much is still to be learned about this topic.

Through the years, there have been evolutionary changes in the role of parents. Parents' roles have changed from "volunteer-fund-raiser, paraprofessional, observer-student, and decision-maker" to "advocate, planner-organizer, case manager-coordinator, and collaborator" (Espinosa & Shearer, 1986, p. 271). Through these new roles parents no longer should be treated as passive second-class agents in the education and related services of their children. Instead, they should be treated as equal partners and positive and active managers.

PARENT-PROFESSIONAL RELATIONSHIPS

Conflicts have traditionally existed between parents and professionals. This is especially true when parents had negative experiences with professionals. As a result, parents might lose confidence in professionals and become hesitant to utilize professionals as a resource. However, as Cain (1976) indicates, as parent groups became more actively involved in their children's life and got into further enhancement of education and related services, "the need for professional assistance overcame their objections" (p. 39). He points out that professionals can provide parents with skills relating to "fund-raising, public relations, medicine, social work, psychology, and teaching" (p. 39) and, as a result, parents increase their positive attitudes toward the professionals.

Another factor that leads to the improvement of parent-professional relationships is the increased willingness and efforts of professionals to accept parents and their children with disabilities and to utilize more appropriate and productive approaches when working with them. This section will discuss the key changes in parent-professional relations and related topics to enhance these relationships—changes in parental relationships with key professionals; and guidelines for enhancing productive parent-professional relationships.

Changes in Parental Relationships with Key Professionals

During the past 15 years, tremendous changes have occurred in the roles and relationship of parents with professionals who work with their children (see example in Box 3-3). The key professionals may include medical personnel (for example, the physician) educational personnel (the teacher), and other related service providers (the psychologist, therapist, social worker, and counselor).

Physicians
The physician usually is the first person to inform parents that they have a child with genetic defects, mental retardation, or other moderate to severe disabilities.

BOX 3-3 • One Family, Two Generations: Parents' and Professionals' Reactions to the Birth of Children with Disabilities

The attitudes of professionals and parents toward the birth of a child with disabilities have changed dramatically in many ways over the past several years. These changes, in part, have been influenced by many factors, legal decisions, legislative enactments, increased education, exposure and general shifts in societal values.

First Generation: The year was 1950; the place was a public hospital somewhere in America and the event was the birth of a child with spina bifida. As a common practice at that time, the mother was alone and heavily drugged in the delivery room while in a side room the father was anxiously awaiting news about the birth of his child. The well intended but misguided physician and nurses immediately recommended several standard options, "Forget you have a son. Don't go near him; he will be a vegetable. He will be dead in the next two years. Put him in an institution. You rest now and we will take care of everything."

The mother was confused, greatly saddened and alone as she was wheeled into the recovery room and tried to sort through the traumatic events of the past few hours. Her initial attempts to see her son were met with simplistic condoning remarks such as, "Now, now, just rest. You don't want to see it. It will be too painful. It'll take time, but you'll get over this."

The father was allowed to see his wife. He too was subjected to the same "onslaught" of professional opinions and attitudes. The medical staff in their attempts to "help him" accept, adjust and accomodate this reality only ladened him with guilt, confusion and increased pain. All during this time, their son was placed in a crib without any care or attention or medical treatment. Everyone was waiting for the child to die.

The mother's repeated requests to see her son were rebuffed but, with the aid of the father, they demanded to see and hold their son. This resulted in much discussion and verbal disagreement with the nurses. Finally more

than ten hours after his birth, the physician reluctantly and begrudgingly brought the newborn son to the mother's bed for the parents to hold.

Epilogue: The mother and father did not institutionalize their son, but instead gave him a loving and caring home for the seven years in which he lived.

Second Generation: Twenty-seven years later, another older son of the same parents was anxiously awaiting the birth of his second child. His wife was in her seventh month of pregnancy and went into premature labor. Arriving at the hospital, they were met by the emergency room staff and led quickly to the delivery room. The labor was closely monitored and support was provided in every possible way. A son was born with many problems —respiratory, cardiovascular, and several other evident physical deformities. A team of physicians from the intensive care—pediatrics ward was waiting to begin the best possible medical treatment with their son immediately.

As this mother was being wheeled into the recovery room, the father was introduced to a social worker who specialized in support for families who meet with an unexpected crisis. The social worker briefly explained that she was there to help in any possible way and offered her support.

The father followed his son into the intensive care treatment room where the nurses were very supportive of the father's presence and encouraged him to remain as long as he desired with his son while treatment was being administered. The father was able to stay with his son and visit the mother to monitor the treatments they were receiving.

The mother was moved to a room immediately down the hall for close proximity to her son as well as her husband. The mother was asked if she wanted to see her son and then encouraged to visit the child in the intensive care ward making accommodations for any needs the parents might also have.

BOX 3-3 • *Continued*

Epilogue: Despite everything medically possible being done, their son died of complications after three days.

These two examples dramatically reflect the changes that have occurred in one generation in society's attitude toward handicapped children. Although as a society we have come a long way from the mentality expressed by the medical community of the 1950s, there was one additional irony in the experiences of the sec-

ond generation. At one end of the hospital, their son was being treated with the finest medical technology available to try to save his life despite his handicaps, but, at the other end of the hospital, children with similar defects were being aborted. We have come a long way in society's attitudes toward the handicapped, but we still have a long way to go to resolve the inherent contradictions.

Source: The above document was written by the sibling of the original parents. He gave permission to reprint the story.

However, the way physicians inform parents and the information they give to parents has been widely criticized (Drew, Logan, & Hardman, 1984). Three major factors causing the criticism are: (a) general negative attitudes toward persons with a disability; (b) lack of awareness of contemporary trends of deinstitutionalization and community-based integration; and (c) lack of up-to-date information relating to education and related services available in the community. In view of this, Hardman, Drew, and Egan (1987) recommended that: (a) physicians receive more training relating to medical, psychological, and educational aspects of persons with special needs; (b) community physicians be willing to treat common illness of persons with disabilities; (c) physicians be willing to refer patients to specialists with expertise in a specific disability area; and (d) physicians be able to refer persons with disabilities and their parents to available community resources.

Teachers

Teachers in traditional schools might expect all students to demonstrate high-standards of academic performance and socially appropriate behavioral patterns. Children deviating from the norm group were encouraged to leave the group so that the group learning activities and progress would not be interrupted. Parents might be blamed for the child's low school performance and "abnormal" behavior and were asked either to "shape up" the child before bringing him/her back to school, or to place the child in a special school, or a self-contained special classroom for remediation.

This situation has been changed with the passage of P.L. 94-142. Parents are involved in the child's free, public, appropriate education in the least restrictive environment. Parents have rights to be an equal partner and a contributing member on a team for the child's assessment, placement, and individualized educational planning. P.L. 99-457 emphasizes family-centered early childhood services. Recently, parents started to serve in prereferral intervention groups, such as the teacher assistance team (TAT) to prevent segregation, as well as to participate in integration projects, such as Project CHOICES ("Children Have Opportunities in Integrated Community Environments"), to bring students with disabilities back to their neighborhood schools (Hayek, 1987; Hohulin, 1990). Parents are active in-charge persons who take initiatives in their children's education and related services. The teacher's role has thus changed to become a facilitator and work closely with parents as a team.

Related Service Providers

Because of the multiple disabling conditions and needs of a child with disabilities, team work is essential in providing education and related services (Jeffe, Lian, Martin, May, Reiner, & Surfus, 1988). The coordination of multidisciplinary efforts has evolved during the past two or three decades and team members have become increasingly productive. This evolution went through three major stages: multidisciplinary, interdisciplinary, and transdisciplinary approaches (Lian, 1986). In the *multidisciplinary team approach,* every team member worked independently with the child, solving part of the child's problem. The child and his/her parents might need to face the burden of transportation between service providers who preferred not to get together to discuss the child's case or have the child's records released. In the *interdisciplinary team approach,* team members still worked independently with the child and, then, scheduled to get together in staffing. Each team member reported evaluation results and the child's progress to the team. The child might be discussed as a whole in staffing, but still treated and served separately after staffing. In the *transdisciplinary team approach,* team members work closely together whenever needed before, during, and after the child's staffing. Each team member is willing to introduce and share his/her own expertise with others and there are numerous follow-up interactions, coordination, and cooperation among team members in the education and related services for the child. As the team approach moves toward more sharing and interaction, the importance of the parents' role is increasingly identified and parents tend to find more openness among educationally related service personnel. Parents and these service providers work together on a regular and continuous basis. Again, parents become active consumers and participants in requesting and maintaining high quality related services.

Guidelines for Enhancing Productive Parent-Professional Relationships

Heward and Orlansky (1992) point out that productive parent-professional relationships are valuable for the parent, the professional, and, most importantly, the child.

They suggest a series of Do's and Don'ts for professionals to interact more appropriately with parents:

1. *Don't assume that you know more about the child, his needs, and the ways in which those needs should be met than do the parents.*
2. *Speak in plain, everyday language.*
3. *Don't let generalizations about parents of handicapped children guide your efforts.*
4. *Don't be defensive toward or intimidated by parents.*
5. *Maintain primary concern for the child.*
6. *Help parents strive for realistic optimism.*
7. *Start with something parents can be successful with.*
8. *Don't be afraid to say, "I don't know." (p. 512)*

When working for students with mental retardation, Roos (1985) suggests the following parent-professional relationships:

1. *Parents should be accepted as full-fledged members of the multidisciplinary team. They should be considered as colleagues, and their contributions should be treated with respect.*
2. *Parents and professionals should recognize that they may have preconceived notions about each other that may interfere with working together. Destructive stereotypes and negative expectations should be openly discussed whenever possible.*
3. *Professionals should try to accept parents where they are (in their attitude toward mental retardation) and develop a listening skill that encourages full disclosure.*
4. *Professionals should be particularly attuned to the existential anxiety experienced by parents of retarded children, and they must be willing to listen to expression of these anxieties.*
5. *Professionals should share with parents all relevant information that is the basis for planning and decision making.*
6. *Clear two-way communication is essential to productive parent-professional interaction.*
7. *Professionals should have the prime responsibilities for selecting the methods and techniques to be used, and parents—or, when appropriate, the clients themselves—should be ultimately responsible for selecting goals and objectives.*
8. *Parents as well as professionals need support and encouragement as they try to cope with the problems and frustrations of helping a retarded individual. Natural reinforcement, praise, encouragement can be very useful.*
9. *Parents and professionals should guard against competing against each other. They need to be constantly aware of the possibility of competitive rivalries and of the temptation to use each other as scape-*

goats or to undermine each other's efforts with the retarded client (pp. 254–255).

Box 3-4 illustrates efforts in a preschool program to enhance parent-professional team partnership. Kugelmass (1982) suggests that efforts should be made to enhance parents' feelings of belonging to the school and their active participation in the school program. Such feeling and participation can be achieved by the openness of the school for parents to be formally and informally involved. This would eventually help reinforce positive parental responses and attitudes and many other factors essential to positive achievement in school programs for students with disabilities.

BOX 3-4 • Team Partnership/Family Participation Rights

As participants in the S.P.I.C.E. Program, you are partners on the team. Partnership entails certain rights and responsibilities. Here are some questions that you, as family members and team partners may find useful as you define your roles.

- Am I honest with team partners about child's abilities and skill levels?
- Do I share information about my child and family that will help determine the services we need?
- Am I committed to the plan we made up as a team? Can I and will I take responsibility for some of the strategies and activities?
- Am I contributing to the plan in any way (equipment, ideas, time, decision)?
- When I disagree or am disappointed, do I talk to the rest of the team about it?
- Do I ask for clarification, more information or help in making choices?

- Do I communicate the importance of my family's priorities and values effectively— can I negotiate some compromises without demanding?
- Do I consider the knowledge, skill and experience of other team members, and also their time, schedules and priorities?
- Are most (if not all) of the outcomes my own ideas?
- Are the services in my plan a reflection of the needs and strengths that I have identified for my child and family?
- Is there open-ended and two-way sharing of information? Am I invited to meetings, given a chance to talk? Am I listened to and taken seriously?
- Are outcomes, plans, home programs, etc., stated in language I understand? Are they clear about what each team member's role is in the plan?
- Is the assessment process shaped by my priorities and concerns as well as by my child's characteristics and abilities?

Note: Part of these questions are from *Into our lives. A guidebook to the individualized family service plan (IFSP) process* (pp. 38–39) of the Family Child Learning Center, 90 West Overdale, Tallmadge, Ohio.

Source: Parents involvement handbook (1990). Reprinted with permission of Services for Parent Infant Child Education (S.P.I.C.E.) Program, MARC Center, Normal-Bloomington, Il.

SUMMARY

Knoblock (1982) emphasizes the importance of educating and intervening on behalf of children with a disability in the context of a social system. The family is a major unit in the social system that should not be neglected. Parents are most important people for their children's successful growth, development, and learning. Throughout the history relating to education and related services for students with disabilities, parental rights, reactions, resources for coping responses, roles and responsibilities, and relationships with professionals have undergone tremendous change. Parents and other family members, including siblings, grandparents, and others in the extended family, are faced with a variety of feelings, reactions, and responses when having a child with a disability. These feelings, reactions, and responses may change as life goes on, especially when there are available supporting internal resources (the degree of perceived control of the situation, parental relationships, health, energy, morale, and spiritual perspectives, problem solving skills, and available financial and related resources) and external resources (friends, neighbors, professionals, and community agencies and organizations).

Parents' roles and responsibilities also change in the family life cycle at each critical transition stage, including the couple, child bearing and preschool years, school age, adolescence, and adulthood. Through the changing roles and responsibilities of parents and other family members, family functions are fulfilled and the goals achieved. The relationships between parents and professionals have changed, too, including those between parents and medical personnel, educational personnel, and related supporting service personnel.

All the changes in parental rights, reactions, resources for coping responses, roles and responsibilities, and relationships with professionals have been in the same direction from passiveness and isolation toward activeness and integration. This chapter emphasizes the uniqueness of each family. As we are moving into the next decade, evolutionary changes will continue for more inclusiveness and, we expect, more positive outcomes for students with disabilities.

A special part of family relations discussed only briefly here is the roles and reactions of siblings. The next chapter will explore in greater detail the influence of a child with disabilities on his or her brothers and sisters.

Parental Support and Advocacy

1. Parents of children with disabilities have been cast into eight specific historical roles.

2. Enactment of P.L. 94-142 dramatically transformed the role of parents and altered their relations with professionals.

3. Parents today are not as passive or as "humbly" grateful as they have been in the past.

Impact of Disabilities on Parents

4. There are similarities in the ways parents react to the birth of a child with a disability.

5. All families, especially those with a child who has a disability, are unique, complex, multifaceted, active, ever changing social units.

6. Every family is important and carries a significant mission.

7. Family members are influenced and changed by other members, and by the circumstances in which they exist; family members, with or without a disability, tend to compare themselves to other families.

8. Most prospective parents are faced with excitement, the task of planning for the future, learning the meaning of being parents and, in the case of giving second or further birth of a child, preparing older brothers and sisters.

9. The birth of a child, whether disabled or nondisabled, may create both positive and negative situations in the family.

10. All parents need help during and shortly after the birth of their child.

11. Parental reactions at the birth of a child with disabilities are based upon the belief that the grief they experience is the result of the loss of an expected "normal" child.

12. The successive adaptations in families when having a child with severe mental retardation are: labeling phase, normalization phase, mobilization phase, revisionist phase, polarization phase, and elimination phase.

13. The purpose of identifying parental feelings and reactions is to provide appropriate assistance.

14. Societal attitudes toward individuals with disabling conditions affect not only the individual but also those family members and friends closest to them.

15. Parents of a child with disabilities may have both positive and negative responses.

16. Parents' negative feelings may include hopelessness, anger, and rejection, which center on the child's appearance or lack of ability.

17. Parents have positive feelings about their children with disabilities, too, including their feelings toward the child as good-natured and easy-going.

18. For parents who fail to traverse the several stages of feelings and responses successfully, the disabling conditions that directly impact the child may then produce a secondary disabling condition called parentalplegia.

19. Parents' expectations relating to their child may be influenced by different types and degrees of disabling conditions.

20. Mental retardation may be one of the most difficult disabilities for parents to accept.

21. Families of a child with hearing or visual impairments may develop stronger social ties with other families facing the same disabling conditions.

22. Parental reactions to a child with mild disabilities may be varied; some take the mild disability seriously, some not so, depending on each individual family's perception and experience relating to mild disabilities.

23. Families differ in how many children they have, the number of parents living in the home, the presence and number of stepparents, extensiveness of the extended family network, and preferences and extensiveness of live-in members of the family who are unrelated by blood or marriage.

24. There will be an increasing number of unmarried or divorced single parents in the family, as well as more working mothers.

25. The number and birth order of children in a family lead to various situations; more children in a family seems to result in less parental-caring time but more sibling help and support.

26. Through family harmony and quality of parenting and child rearing practices, parents can better cope with the impact of having a child with disabling conditions at home.

27. Having a brother or sister with a disability in the family provides siblings with special experiences and causes specific reactions.

28. Siblings used to place less emphasis on life goals concerned with success in personal relations, including having many close friends, focusing life around marriage and the family, and on being a respected community leader.

29. Siblings may feel guilty about their bitter or negative feelings.

30. Sibling reactions to a child with disabilities may be changed by factors such as an increase of public awareness and acceptance, legal protection of family rights, and more positive involvement of regular school and community systems.

31. Siblings' adjustment was found to be related to a number of factors, such as family size, age, gender, severity of disabilities, and definition of disabilities.

32. Extended family's reactions to the birth and corresponding degree of support for the parents can be a source of comfort or pain for parents of a newborn child with disabilities.

33. Grandparents are especially vulnerable by their unique position as parents of the mother and father.

Resources for Coping Responses of Parents

34. The ability of parents to respond to the stress of having a child with a disabling condition is based on internal and external resources.

35. There are five internal resources closely related to parents' coping responses: perceived control of the situation; extended family; parental relationships, health, energy, morale, and spiritual perspective; problem-solving skills; and available financial and related resources.

36. A number of external resources can be helpful for parents' coping responses, including friends, neighbors, professionals, and community agencies/organizations.

Evolving Roles and Responsibilities of Parents

37. Parental roles and responsibilities are closely related to parents' experiences in the life cycle of a family, transition stages, and major functions of a family.

38. The type and degree of the disabling condition may influence a family's involvement throughout the life span of the individual with a disability.

39. The family life cycle is not only a number of separate stages, or milestones, but also includes the developmental transition from one stage to another in an ongoing manner.

40. There are seven specific areas in which families are responsible for each other: economic, domestic and health care, recreation, self-identity and sense of belonging, affection, socialization, and educational and vocational training.

41. Parents may play more than one role in the life of their children with disabilities.

42. Parents' roles have changed from volunteer fund-raiser, paraprofessional, observer-student, and decision-maker to advocate, planner-

organizer, case manager-coordinator, and collaborator.

Parent-Professional Relationships

43. Conflicts have traditionally existed between parents and professionals.

44. Professionals can provide parents with skills relating to fund-raising, public relations, medicine, social work, psychology, and teaching and, as a result, parents increase their positive attitudes toward professionals.

45. Tremendous changes have occurred in the roles and relationships between parents and professionals.

46. The key professionals may include medical personnel, educational personnel, and other related service providers.

47. Productive parent-professional relationships are valuable for the parent, the professional, and, most importantly, the child.

48. There are several do's and don'ts for professionals to interact more appropriately with parents, such as speak in plain, everyday language; don't be defensive; help parents strive for realistic optimism; and don't be afraid to say, "I don't know."

REFERENCES

Adams, M. (1975). "Foster family care for the intellectually disadvantaged child: The current state of practice and some research perspectives" in M. J. Begab & Richardson, S. A. (Eds.), *The mentally retarded and society: A social science perspective* Baltimore, MD: University Park Press (pp. 267–285).

Ahlgren, C. (1985). "Families and friends." *TASH Newsletter, 11*(7), 3.

Bailey, D. B., & Winton, P. J. (1989). Friendship and acquaintance among families in a mainstreamed day care center. *Education and Training in Mental Retardation, 24*(2), 107–113.

Begab, M. J., & Richardson, S. A. (1975). *The mentally retarded and society: A social science perspective*. Baltimore, MD: University Park Press.

Bernal, M. E., & North, J. A. (1978). A survey of parent training manuals. *Journal of Applied Behavior Analysts, 11*, 533–544.

Bossard, J. H., & Boll, M. (1956). *The large family system*. Philadelphia: University of Pennsylvania Press.

Brock, K. A., & Shanberg, R. (1990). "Avoiding unnecessary due process hearings." *Journal of Reading, Writing, and Learning Disabilities International, 6*(1), 33–39.

Brotherson, M. J., Turnbull, A. P., Bronicki, G. J., Houghton, J., Roeder-Gordon, C., Summers, J. A., & Turnbull, H. R. (1988). "Transition into adulthood: Parental planning for sons and daughters with disabilities." *Education and Training in Mental Retardation, 23*(3), 165–174.

Buscaglia, L. (1975). *The disabled and their parents: A counseling challenge.* Thorofare, NJ: Charles B. Slack.

Cain, L. F. (1976). "Parent groups: Their role in a better life for the handicapped," in J. B. Jordan (Ed.), *Exceptional child education at the bicentennial: A parade of progress.* Reston, VA: CEC (pp. 37–42).

Caplan, G. (1976). "The family as a support system," in G. Kaplan & M. Killilea (Eds.), *Support systems and mutual help: Multidisciplinary explorations.* New York: Grune & Stratton (pp. 19–36).

Caplan, G., & Killilea, M. (Eds.), (1976). *Support systems and mutual help: Multidisciplinary explorations.* New York: Grune & Stratton.

Crnic, K. A., & Leconte, J. M. (1986). "Understanding sibling needs and influences," in R. R. Fewell & Vadasy, P. F. (Eds.), *Families of handicapped children: Needs and supports across the life span.* Austin, TX: Pro-Ed (pp. 75–98).

Drew, C. J., Logan, D. R., & Hardman, M. L. (1984). *Mental retardation: A life cycle approach.* Columbus, OH: Merrill Publishing Co.

Espinosa, L., & Shearer, M. (1986). "Family support in public school programs," in R. R. Fewell & P. F. Vadsy (Eds.), *Families of handicapped children: Needs and supports across the life span.* Austin, TX: Pro-Ed (pp. 253–277).

Farber, B. (1963, February). "Interaction with retarded siblings and life goals of children." *Marriage and Family Living, 25,* 96–98.

Farber B. (1975). "Family adaptations to severely mentally retarded children," in M. J. Begab & Richardson, S. A. (Eds.), *The mentally retarded and society: A social science perspective.* Baltimore, MD: University Park Press (pp. 247–266).

Featherstone, H. (1980). *A difference in the family: Life with a disabled child.* New York: Basic Books.

Ferguson, P. M., & Ferguson, D. L. (1991). "Parent and professional perspectives: Sexuality and culture in the lives of people with severe disabilities." *TASH Newsletter, 16*(3), 9–10.

Ferris, C. (1980). *A hug just isn't enough.* Washington, DC: Gallaudet College Press.

Fewell, R. R. (1986a). "The handicapped child in the family," in R. R. Fewell & P. F. Vadasy (Eds.), *Families of Handicapped Children: Needs and supports across the life span.* Austin, Texas: Pro-Ed (pp. 3–34).

Fewell, R. R. (1986b). "Support from religious organizations and personal beliefs," in R. R. Fewell & P. F. Vadasy (Eds.), *Families of handicapped children: Needs and supports across the life span.* Austin, TX: Pro-Ed (pp. 297–316).

Fewell, R. R., Belmonte, J., & Ahlersmeyer, D. (1983). *Questionnaire on family support systems.* Unpublished manuscript, Experimental Education Unit, University of Washington, Seattle, WA.

Fewell, R. R., & Vadasy, P. F. (Eds.), (1986). *Families of handicapped children: Needs and supports across the life span.* Austin, TX: Pro-Ed.

Friedrich, W. N. (1979). "Predictors of the coping behavior of mothers of handicapped children." *Journal of Consulting and Clinical Psychology, 47,* 1140–1141.

Gabel, H., & Kotsch, L. S. (1981). "Extended families and young handicapped children." *Topics in Early Childhood Special Education, 1,* 29–35.

Gallagher, J. J. (1986). "The family with a child who is handicapped," in J. J. Gallagher & B. Weiner (Eds.), *Alternative futures in special education.* Reston, VA: CEC (pp. 13–14).

Gerber, M., & Levine-Donnerstein, D. (1989) "Educating all children: Ten years later." *Exceptional Children, 56*(1) 17–27.

Gordon, S. (1975). *Living fully: A guide for young people with a handicap, their parents, their teachers and professionals.* New York: John Day.

Gorham, K. (1975). "A lost generation of parents." *Exceptional Children, 41,* 521–525.

Green, B. R. (1971). "Discussions on death and on death education," in B. R. Green & D. P. Irish (Eds.), *Death education: Preparing for living.* Cambridge, MA: Schenkman (pp. 69–124).

Grossman, F. K. (1972). *Brothers and sisters of retarded children: An exploratory study.* Syracuse, NY: Syracuse University Press.

Hardman, M. L., Drew, C. J., & Egan, M. W. (1987). *Human exceptionality: Society, school, and family* (2nd. ed.). Newton, MA: Allyn & Bacon.

Hayek, R. A. (1987). "The teacher assistant team: A pre-referral support system." *Focus on Exceptional Children, 20*(1), 1–7.

Hentoff, N. (1991). "Whatever happened to Baby Jane Doe?" *TASH Newsletter, 16*(2), 3. (Reprinted from *Washington Post,* December 11, 1990).

Heward, W. L., & Orlansky, M. D. (1992). *Exceptional children* (4th. ed.). Columbus, OH: Merrill Publishing Co.

Hill, J. W., Seyfarth, J., Banks, P. D., Wehman, P., & Orelove, F. (1987). "Parent attitudes about working conditions of their adult mentally retarded sons and daughters." *Exceptional Children, 54*(1), 9–23.

Hohulin, J. (1990). "A case for integration." *IL-TASH Newsletter, 5*(2), 5, 9.

Hollingsworth, C. E., & Pasnau, R. O. (1977). "Mourning following the birth of a handicapped child," in C. E. Hollingsworth & R. O. Pasnau (Eds.), *The family in mourning: A guide for health professionals.* New York: Grune & Stratton (pp. 95–99).

Hornby, G. (1989). "A model for parent participation." *British Journal of Special Education, 16*(4), 161–162.

Jeffe, D., Lian, M-G. J., Martin, T. J., May, M. L., Reiner, L., & Surfus, J. (1988). *A special education service delivery guide for students with physical disabilities and/or health impairments.* Chicago: Illinois Spina Bifida Association.

Kaplan, L. (1986). *Working with multiproblem families.* Lexington, MA: Lexington Books.

Kirk, S. A., & Gallagher, J. J. (1989). *Educating exceptional children* (6th ed.). Boston: Houghton Mifflin.

Knoblock, P. (1982). "Introduction to teaching autistic children," in P. Knoblock (Ed.), *Teaching and mainstreaming autistic children.* Denver, CO: Love Publishing Co. (pp. 1–14).

Kugelmass, J. (1982). "Parent-school partnership: The essential component," in P. Knoblock (Ed.), *Teaching and mainstreaming autistic children.* Denver, CO: Love Publishing Co. (pp. 195–216).

Lian, M-G. J. (1984). "Counseling parents of exceptional children." *Special Education Quarterly, 11,* 18–22.

Lian, M-G. J. (1986). "More successful team work for the education of students with severe handicaps." *IL-TASH Newsletter, 1*(5), 2, 8, 10.

Lian, M-G. J. (1990a). "Enhancing ethnic/racial minority involvement." *TASH Newsletter, 16*(5), 1–2.

Lian, M-G. J. (1990b). *Getting to know individuals with physical disabilities and/or health impairments.* Normal, IL: Illinois State University.

Lines, P. M. (1987) "An overview of home instruction." *Phi Delta Kappan, 68*(7), 510–517.

Lynch, E. W., & Stein, R. C. (1987). "Parent participation by ethnicity: A comparison of Hispanic, black, and Anglo families." *Exceptional Children, 54*(2), 105–111.

Mallory, B. L. (1986). "Interactions between community agencies and families over the life cycle," in R. R. Fewell & P. F. Vadasy (Eds.), *Families of handicapped children: Needs and supports across the life span.* Austin, TX: Pro-Ed (pp. 317–356).

Massie, R. & Massie, S. (1975). *Journey.* New York: Knopf.

McGoldrick, M. (1982). "Ethnicity and family therapy: An overview," in M. McGoldrick, J. K. Pearce, & J. Giordano (Eds.), *Ethnicity and family therapy.* New York: Guilford Press (pp. 3–30).

McGoldrick, M., Pearce, J. K., & Giordano, J. (Eds.), (1982). *Ethnicity and family therapy.* New York: Guilford Press.

Menolascino, F. J. (1974). "Understanding parents of the retarded—A crisis model for helping them cope more effectively," in F. J. Menolascino & P. H. Pearson (Eds.), *Beyond the limits: Innovations in services for the severely and profoundly retarded.* Seattle, WA: Special Child Publications (pp. 172–209).

Moeller, A. T. (1986). "The effect of professionals on the family of a handicapped child," in R. R. Fewell & P. F. Vadasy (Eds.), *Families of handicapped children: Needs and supports across the life span.* Austin, TX: Pro-Ed (pp. 149–166).

Murphy, A. T. (1976). "Parent counseling and exceptionality: From creative insecurity toward increased humaness," in E. J. Webster & A. J. Weston (Eds.), *Professional approaches with parents of handicapped children.* Springfield, IL: Charles C. Thomas (pp. 3–26).

Murray, J. N. (1980). *Developing assessment programs for the multi-handicapped child.* Springfield, IL: Charles. C. Thomas.

Murray, J. N., & Cornell, C. J. (1981). "Parentalplegia." *Psychology in the Schools, 18,* 201–207.

Nihira, K., Meyers, C. E., & Mink, I. (1980). "Home environment, family adjustment, and the development of mentally retarded children." *Applied Research in Mental Retardation, 1,* 5–24.

Peterson, N. L. (1987). "Parenting the young handicapped and at-risk child," in N. L. Peterson (Ed.), *Early intervention for handicapped and at risk children: An introduction to early childhood special education.* Denver, CO: Love Publishing.

Powell, T. H., & Olge, P. A. (1985). *Brothers and sisters-A special part of exceptional families.* Baltimore, MD: Paul H. Brookes.

Roos, P. (1985). "Parents of mentally retarded children: Misunderstood and mistreated," in H. R. Turnbull & A. P. Turnbull (Eds.), *Parents speak out: Then and now.* Columbus, OH: Merrill Publishing Co. (pp. 245–257).

Sacken, D.M. (1988). "Regulating nonpublic education: A search for a just law and policy." *American Journal of Education, 96,* (3) 394–420.

Safford, P. L., & Arbitman, D.C (1975) *Developmental intervention with young physically handicapped children,* Springfield, IL: Charles C. Thomas.

Scharf, M. K. (1990). *The effects of communication training on parent participation in school programs for children with disabilities.* Unpublished doctoral dissertation, Illinois State University, Normal, IL.

Services for Parent Infant Child Education Program (1990). *Parent involvement handbook.* Normal-Bloomington, IL: S.P.I.C.E., MARC Center.

Simeonsson, R. J., & Bailey, D. B. (1986). "Siblings of handicapped children," in J. J. Gallagher & P. M. Vietze (Eds.), *Families of handicapped persons.* Baltimore, MD: Paul H. Brookes (pp. 67–77).

Simeonsson, R. J., & McHale, S. M. (1981). "Review: Research on handicapped children: Sibling relationships." *Child: Care, Health, and Development, 7,* 153–171.

Singer, G. H. S., Irvin, L. K., Irvine, B., Hawkins, N., & Cooley, E. (1989). "Evaluation of community-based support services for families of persons with developmental disabilities." *Journal of the Association for Persons with Severe Handicaps, 14*(4), 312–323.

Sonnek, I. M. (1986). "Grandparents and the extended family of handicapped children," in R. R. Fewell & P. F. Vadasy (Eds.), *Families and handicapped children.* Austin, TX: Pro-Ed (pp. 99–120).

Sonnenschein, P. (1981). "Parents and professionals: An uneasy relationship." *Teaching Exceptional Children, 14*(2), 62–65.

Spiegel, J. (1982). "An ecological model of ethnic families," in M. McGoldrick, J. K. Pearce, & J. Giordano (Eds.), *Ethnicity and family therapy.* New York: Guilford Press (pp. 31–51).

Suelzle, M., & Keenan, V. (1981). "Changes in family support networks over the life cycle of mentally retarded persons." *American Journal of Mental Deficiency, 86*(3), 267–274.

Taylor, F. C. (1976). Project COPE. in E. J. Webster (Ed.), *Professional approaches with parents of handicapped children.* Springfield, IL: Charles C. Thomas (pp. 146–190).

Thurman, S. K., & Widerstrom, A. H. (1990). *Infants and young children with special needs: A developmental and ecological approach* (2nd ed.). Baltimore, MD: Paul H. Brookes.

Turnbull, A. P.(1983). "Parental participation in the IEP process," in J. A. Mulick & S. M. Pueschel (Eds.), *Parent-professional participation in developmental disabilities services: Foundations and prospectics.* Cambridge, MA: The Ware Press (pp.107–123).

Turnbull, A. P. (1985). "The dual role of parent and professional," in H. R. Turnbull & A. P. Turnbull (Eds.), *Parents speak out: Then and now*. Columbus, OH: Merrill Publishing Co. (pp. 137–141).

Turnbull, A. P., Barber, P., Behr, S. K., & Kerns, G. M. (1988). "The family of children and youth with exceptionalities," in E. L. Meyen & T. M. Skrtic (Eds.), *Exceptional children and youth*. Denver, CO: Love Publishing (pp. 81–107).

Turnbull, A. P., Summers, J. A., & Brotherson, M. J. (1984). *Working with families with disabled members: A family systems approach*. Lawrence, KS: University of Kansas.

Turnbull, A. P., Summers, J. A., & Brotherson, M. J. (1986). "Family life cycle: Theoretical and empirical implications and future directions for families with mentally retarded members," in J. J. Gallagher & P. Vietze (Eds.), *Families of handicapped persons*. Baltimore, MD: Paul H. Brookes (pp. 45–66).

Turnbull, A. P. & Turnbull, H. R. (1990). *Families, professionals, and exceptionality: A special partnership* (2nd. ed.). Columbus, OH: Merrill Publishing Co.

Vadasy, P. F., & Fewell, R. R. (1986). "Mothers of deaf-blind children," in R. R. Fewell & P. F. Vadasy (Eds.), *Families and handicapped children*. Austin, TX: Pro-Ed (pp. 121–148).

Waisbren, S. E. (1980). "Parents' reactions after the birth of a developmentally disabled child." *American Journal of Mental Deficiency, 84*, 345–351.

Walker, P. (1989). "Resource review: Family support services." *TASH Newsletter, 15*(4), 2–3.

Wendel, J., Konnert, W., & Foreman, C. (1986). "Home schooling and compulsory attendance law." *School Law Bulletin, 17*, 1–8.

Weiss, H. G., & Weiss, M. S. (1976). *Home is a learning place: A parent's guide to learning disabilities*. Boston: Little, Brown.

Wilcox, B., & Bellamy, G. T. (1982). *Design of high school programs for severely handicapped students*. Baltimore, MD: Paul H. Brookes.

Wilson, S. (1988). "Can we clear the air about home schooling?" *Instructor, 97*(5), 11.

Winch, R. F. (1971). *The modern family*, (3rd ed.). New York: Holt, Rhinehart & Winston.

Wolfensberger, W. (1967). "Counseling the parents of the retarded," in A. A. Baumeister (Ed.), *Mental retardation: Appraisal, education and rehabilitation*. Chicago: Aldine (pp. 329–400).

York, J., & Vandercook, T. (1991). "Designing an integrated program for learners with severe disabilities." *Teaching Exceptional Children, 23*(2), 22–28. Chicago: Aldine.

Zakariya, S. (1988). "Home schooling litigation tests state compulsory education laws." *American School Board Journal, 175*(5), 45–46.

Zuk, G. H. (1959). "The religious factor and the role of guilt in parental acceptance of the retarded child." *American Journal on Mental Deficiency, 64*, 139–147.

4

SIBLINGS OF CHILDREN WITH DISABILITIES

James A. McLoughlin
School of Education,
University of Louisville

Catherine Senn
Learning Disabilities Association
of Kentucky

Chapter Objectives

After completing this chapter you will be able to:

1. Describe three positive and three negative aspects of living with a brother or sister who has a disability

2. Describe one positive and one negative way siblings can affect their brothers or sisters who have disabilities

3. Identify three factors that determine the impact of having a brother or sister with a disability and explain the implications for siblings

4. Explain the different feelings and issues siblings must deal with as their brother or sister with a disability moves through his or her preschool, school, and adult years

5. Explain the significance for a sibling of having a family that does not function well, have open communication, or provide mutual support

6. Explain the relevance of the age of the siblings and the socioeconomic status of the family

7. Describe the social stigma with which siblings must deal in school and in social situations

8. Explain some of the issues that worry siblings as they get older

9. Explain why it may be difficult for the child who has a disability to watch the developmental experiences of their siblings

10. Describe two positive and two negative ways siblings may cope or adapt to living with a brother or sister who has a disability

11. Identify five special needs of siblings and one way to meet each of them

12. Identify two organizations that serve as support groups for siblings

13. Explain why siblings and their needs should be included in family assessment and individualized family service plans

14. Describe three ways siblings can be a resource to the family

15. Explain the role of siblings as advocates for themselves and for their brothers and sisters who have a disability

Key Terms and Phrases

adaptive responses
adaptive strategies
advocacy
age of majority
at-risk preschool children
autism
behavior management
caretaking responsibilities
cerebral palsy
communication board
coping responses
emotional overlays
family assessment
family stressors
family styles
family system
guardianship
hearing impaired
individualized family
  service plan
invisible exceptionality

learned helplessness
legal liability
mediating factors
mental retardation
mobility
National Information Center
  for Children and Youth
  with Handicaps
overachievers
overidentify
PL 99-457
scapegoats
semi-independent care
severely multiply handicapped
sibling rivalries
sign language
social stigma
socioeconomic status
stages of adjustment
support groups
surrogate parent role

INTRODUCTION

It is important to consider the siblings of children with disabilities in addressing issues of advocacy. Integral members of the family support system, they are frequently afterthoughts in studies of family dynamics and needs. The focus most typically is placed upon the parents and child with the disability. Questions about siblings are few in family needs surveys, and parental responses indicate a relatively lower priority among their concerns (Bailey & Simeonsson, 1988).

Siblings and their needs can only be considered in the context of the whole family system. As noted in the previous chapter, the significance of their role lies in their interactions with parents and the child with the disability. The siblings are likely to demonstrate a range of adaptive responses to having a brother or sister with a disability. How they adapt to the situation depends upon familial, psychological, and personality influences (Crnic & Leconte, 1986). For this reason, there is a lack of uniformity in the formal research about the relationships of siblings and their brothers and sisters with disabilities and the mutual effects they have on one another. This reciprocal relationship between the children complicates the effort to present a clear profile of who is affecting whom and in what way. Suffice it to say that any discussion of siblings and their needs will contain some factors peculiar to any developing person and others to living with a child who has a disability.

IMPACT OF DISABILITIES ON SIBLINGS

Even in the most functional and healthy family, there are emotional overlays for siblings. However, siblings of children with disabilities tend to react in unique ways related to the special dynamics created in the family around the child's disability. The range of emotional feelings is similar to that reported for parents (McLoughlin, 1993), but is different because of the reasons and sources of the feelings. Also, siblings are very dependent upon the parents to determine how the feelings and reactions will be dealt with and resolved.

Positive Reactions

There have been many reports of positive and negative outcomes to being raised with a child who has a disability. Grossman's (1972) interviews and more recent ones (Vine, 1982) provide testimony that siblings develop greater empathy and understanding for people with disabilities. They become more tolerant and patient with others and learn how to be helpful to others. Siblings become more mature and responsible as well as develop pride in their brother's or sister's accomplishments (Powell & Ogle, 1985). That pride has to be related to the obvious contribution they make to the cognitive and social development of the child who has a disability through their play, caretaking, reinforcement, and general communication and interaction. As a younger sister of a person with cerebral palsy said:

*I have a different outlook on life than many other people my age. I under-
stand that you can't take anything for granted. And you have to be able to
look at the positives, where the balance falls. With Jennifer, there are
negatives, but there's so much more that's good.*

*I'm very involved now with activities for persons with mental retarda-
tion. Sometimes I get upset at some of the nonhandicapped people who work
with me and seem to be involved as some kind of an ego trip . . . like, 'Look
at me and what a nice person I am for helping out these poor helpless
people.' I feel like I understand so much more about persons with handicaps
and how they feel trying to overcome so many frustrations. We're proud of
what Jennifer can do. (PACER Center, 1987, p. 19)*

Negative Reactions

Without well informed parents and a functional family, siblings run the risk of
dealing with their natural feelings in an unhealthy fashion. As a result they may
develop inappropriate behaviors and long-lasting emotional problems related to the
experience. Some siblings have reported the need for counseling in later life to deal
with issues related to having a brother or sister who has a disability (Cleveland &
Miller, 1977; Vine, 1982).

Siblings may feel a myriad of feelings including resentment, jealousy, guilt,
grief, fear, shame, embarrassment, and rejection. None of these feelings are bad but
they may arise from a misunderstanding of the situation and a misinterpretation of
parental behavior. However, all too often, parents do not assist siblings in dealing
with these feelings nor help resolve them satisfactorily.

The resentment and jealousy stems from the extra attention parents and others
give the child who has a disability. This translates into less quality time with their
parents, a reality faced by this parent:

*It was difficult or impossible at the time to see the situations in which the
siblings were being slighted. The slights were not intentional and there was
no lack of love. When Marianne and her older sister, Patricia, were four
and five years old, respectively, I enrolled them in dance class. This was one
of the first realizations I had as a parent that they were not getting as much
time, energy, and effort as their little sister with a disability. After that, I can
recall making a conscious effort to change things. I remember how important it became that their costumes for the dance recitals were all that they
should be. I remember sitting the children down and saying, 'Jane takes
more of Mommy's time and energy. It isn't that I love her more; it is just that
she needs more. You see, she needs more car rides for her doctor visits and
evaluations, and more time for her programs. So it ends up that she gets
more of my time. (Horne et al., 1988, p. 9)*

Also, siblings may resent the special concessions made to the child who has a
disability in terms of rules and regulations. It may become difficult for the sibling

to accept that family schedules and other aspects of family life are structured around the needs of the child who has a disability such as scheduling therapy or tutoring. They may not be able to have certain clothes, music, vacations, and other possessions because family resources are devoted to the child with a disability.

Most of all, siblings are often expected to help out with their brother or sister and that demand may become burdensome, especially if they have not been taught how to communicate, play, and assist the child with a disability. Their self-concept may be damaged if they are regularly thrust into situations in which they do not feel successful. There is a possibility that they could harm the child with a disability if they do not feed, move, or otherwise care for him or her properly. Without adequate training in behavior management, they may reinforce "learned helplessness," that is, the sibling does everything for the child who has a disability and reinforces the belief that they cannot do anything for themselves.

As a result of being treated this way, siblings may feel rejected and develop a low self-esteem unless they have a strong support system. This feeling can be intensified by a lack of knowledge about their brother's or sister's condition and how they are expected to behave. Friends may ask questions that they cannot answer accurately or comfortably. They may also become fearful of developing the condition, catch it, or pass it on to their own children some day. As this sister of a child who has mental retardation said:

> *When I was young I used to get pretty good grades, but I went through a very painful period wondering when my grades would change and I would "grow retarded" like my sister. I never talked with anyone about those fears. Initially, I was afraid to talk about this because I dreaded the answer. Later, when I understood what retardation was, I felt guilty that I had such thoughts. (Horne et al., 1988, p. 7)*

There can be losses associated with having a sister or brother with a disability. Parents may expect siblings to take care of the child with a disability a great deal and to assume surrogate parent roles for which they are ill-equipped. Siblings may lose elements of their childhood. They may also lose their playmates who do not want to be around the child with a disability. At school and in the community they may have to confront people who are being abusive to the child with a disability.

Without suitable guidance and support, siblings may react negatively to these demands and pressures. They may start acting out to get attention or withdraw as a form of protection. Drugs, alcohol, sex, and other diversions are possible outlets for their frustration. They may overidentify with the child who has a disability and assume a parental role long before they have the knowledge or skills.

Impact of a Sibling on the Child Who Has a Disability

It is important to realize that while the child who has a disability is affecting the sibling, the reverse is also happening for better or worse. Siblings can model appropriate language, motor, social, and other skills for the child with a disability. They are wonderful playmates and can provide for many enjoyable experiences. They are invaluable assistants in performing the daily chores of life under the unique restrictions associated with the exceptional condition such as wheelchairs, hearing aids, and so forth.

On the other hand, if siblings do not choose to interact with their brother or sister who has a disability, the child's self-concept may be adversely affected. Without the stimulation and encouragement offered by siblings, the child with a disability may not develop as well or as quickly. If siblings are difficult children themselves, parents may have less time to devote to meeting the needs of the child with a disability.

EVOLVING IMPACT ON SIBLINGS THROUGH THE LIFESPAN

Siblings will react differently to their brother or sister who has a disability as that child progresses through his or her lifespan from preschool years, through the years of school, and into adulthood. There are a number of factors that determine or mediate the nature of their response and the intensity of the experience. They include: the nature of the disability; family functionality and lifestyle; family culture and resources; the age, gender, and experience of the siblings; the broader support system available; and other stressors in the family.

Mediating Factors

The Nature and Severity of the Disability

The nature and severity of the disability may or may not be an influential factor. If the child with a disability has an "invisible" exceptionality like a specific learning disability, the sibling may have less need to explain the child's problem to other children than if the child has an obvious behavioral condition like autism. A child with severe disabilities may require more caretaking by family members than a child who is hearing impaired. A sibling may find a brother's or sister's behavioral or emotional disorder more disruptive to live with than a visual impairment, as this 21-year-old brother of an older autistic person did:

> *At times, when we were younger, I really hated our family situation. I used to think my sister was anywhere but here and I'd think, sometimes, that maybe she should be put in an institution. Now that I am older and have learned more about institutions, I don't think that anymore.*
>
> *. . . But family outings in public were rare. Stacy was too volatile and unpredictable to allow many good times together. The family has a lake*

cabin, but our times there have been private, avoiding possible explosions in public.

I've felt much sorrow, both for Stacy and myself. I'd never want children of my own to experience what I have or what Stacy goes through.

Someday, if I do marry and have children, I really hope that no person will have needs that have to be so much more important than everyone else's. (PACER Center, p. 22, 23)

Skrtic, Summers, Brotherson, and Turnbull (1983) caution against assuming that the impact increases with the severity of the exceptionality. Siblings with brothers or sisters with mild disabilities may more often be in social situations where they must face problems of embarrassment, the need to protect them from teasing, and the need to explain their disabilities. More severe disabilities may place less demands on siblings because the child with a disability is being cared for by others and less likely to accompany them to school and social situations.

Family Functionality and Lifestyle

As noted in the previous chapter, how well a family functions as a healthy social system has a great deal to do with sibling coping ability. The presence and involvement of the parents are especially critical since they model for the siblings appropriate attitudes and coping behaviors. Open communication is a key for sibling adjustment to a brother or sister who has a disability. It provides for a clarification of roles and an outlet for emotional reactions. A family's functionality and willingness to address issues openly decides what siblings are asked to do and how reasonable and healthy it is.

The impact is largely due to the parents' attitudes and reactions to the child who has a disability, especially the father (Garguilo, 1985). Sometimes the parents do not share similar perceptions of the situation and siblings are left confused. In one survey of parents of at-risk preschool children, mothers felt a greater need than fathers for assistance in discussing problems and reaching solutions and in learning how to support each other during difficult times (Bailey & Simeonsson, 1988). In these families the siblings are not as likely to get the support they need.

When the child who has a disability has an emotional or behavioral disorder, there may be a greater challenge to the family to cope well. In one survey of mothers and fathers of children with attention deficit disorder with hyperactivity, the mothers perceived their family as less supportive and more stressful than parents of children without disabilities (Brown & Pacini, 1989). The result can be deficits in parenting and family management with the siblings deprived of positive parental role models.

The family's lifestyle and child-rearing practices also determine how the parents and siblings respond. Mink, Nihara, and Meyers (1983) found five family styles among the families of children labeled trainable mentally retarded they studied: cohesive, harmonious; control-oriented and somewhat unharmonious; below average in openness and unharmonious; child oriented and expressive; little stimulation and stressful. Needless to say, a family that responds to stress by exercising more control and closing communication does not provide a conducive environment for siblings who need to work out their feelings and learn about what is going on.

This is particularly critical since parents themselves have a variety of reactions to the birth and raising of a child with a disability. Siblings who observe these fluctuations in feelings may become very confused and scared. Parents have to be careful not to impose their own anxieties and stifle healthy communications (Diamond, 1981). As parents go through their stages of adjustment to the child's disability, it is not unreasonable to expect that the siblings must also. Siblings must appropriately grieve the loss of the "real" brother or sister they expected and accept the one they have as parents must (DeLuca & Solerna, 1984).

Family Culture and Resources

As was discussed in Chapter 2, the culture of the family influences the family's response to the child with a disability. Some cultural groups deny the disability, ignore the person, or kill them; others care for them and protect them from harm. Another culture makes a place for them in the society and sees to their needs; they may even revere them for their differences. Still another culture may strive to arrange the environment to include the person with a disability as much as possible and enhance their self-confidence.

Socioeconomic status directly affects the sibling's experience. The availability of family resources to buy services frees family members from direct responsibilities and indirectly from deprivation of their own needs. Research indicates that siblings within lower-class families tend to assume more caretaking responsibilities, while middle-class children are not as affected by issues related to stigma and acceptance (Crnic & Leconte, 1986). Also, the responses of mothers of preschool at-risk children indicated that adequacy of resources directly determined their sense of emotional and physical health and commitment to carry through with needed services (Dunst, Leet, & Trivette, 1988).

This does not mean poor families necessarily take care of their children with disabilities less well by intent and that siblings in these families suffer more. Rather, the research suggests that the nature of poor families is to have more stress due to the lack of basics and that they have to draw on other resources to meet the challenge, such as their culture, religion, extended family, and so forth.

Sibling Age, Gender, and Experience

The age of the sibling dictates what they may notice and understand about the situation and what they are expected to do. Crnic and Leconte's (1986) review of the literature indicates that first born and older siblings seem generally less affected by the presence of a sibling who has a disability, while younger male siblings may have more adjustment problems. Some studies indicate that females, particularly if the oldest, are more involved with the child who has a disability and later in life may require counseling to resolve related issues (Cleveland & Miller, 1977).

It is important to recognize the effect of experience on how siblings may react. Siblings who have more positive interactions with their brother and sister are more likely to adapt well. More knowledge about the condition and training in adaptive forms of communication may also help. Most of all, working with their parents and professionals in successfully helping the child who has a disability grow can be a major determinant of a positive experience.

Support Systems

The availability of a healthy, involved extended family and support system can guarantee a more positive impact over time. Peers with whom siblings can talk out their frustrations and feelings are helpful; peers who are accepting and understanding of the child who has a disability also are a support. Professionals who serve the child with a disability can assist the sibling when they take them into account in planning services. They may offer special support groups for siblings or at least counsel them informally.

Of course, siblings need the appropriate kinds of services for their brother or sister who has a disability to be available. As this sister of a younger person with a disability who requires community services and housing explains:

> When people ask me what my needs are as a sibling of a person with severe disabilities, I tell them that I need the commitment from society that every person has a right to a basic quality of life. I believe that my sister has a right to live and work in her community, and a right to lead a life of her own, with some assistance. For me to be powerful in my collaboration with Karen in meeting these goals, I need resources to make this commitment become a reality. (Horne et al., 1988, p. 7)

Other Family Stressors

Families struggling with alcoholism, drug addiction, and other stressful issues tend to find it more difficult to cope with a child who has a disability. Accidents, severe family illnesses, and other events may detract from the kind of support siblings might get in the family.

Preschool Child Who Has a Disability

When the child who has a disability is an infant or of preschool age, the sibling may experience fewer demands. Sibling relationships seem to be less stressful when both the sibling and child with a disability are younger (Crnic & Leconte, 1986). They are expected to be playmates and sources of entertainment. Certainly siblings are expected to take care of the child who has a disability and let them tag along.

If the sibling is young, they may not understand everything that is going on around the child who has a disability and, consequently, alternate between feeling afraid, anxious, and angry. They wonder what is wrong with them if parents spend so much time with the child who has a disability. It is hard for them to understand the reasons why they are getting less attention: parents may be overwhelmed with responsibilities, driven by guilt to give all their energy to the child with a disability, escaping from the family, feeling unfit as parents, or are truly incompetent in the situation (Chinn, Winn, & Walters, 1978).

For a while, the sibling may mimic the child with the disability or regress in his or her own development. Siblings may engage in other attention getting strategies.

School-Age Child Who Has a Disability

At this age, siblings are apt to have more questions about the condition of the child who has a disability and what is expected of them. Peers and others are querying them more about it and they need answers. Professionals may be calling upon them to provide information and to become involved in the program for the child with a disability. They may have to attend support groups, learn new information, and develop skills in sign language, behavior modification, and so forth.

This is the period during which the social stigma of having a brother or sister who has a disability becomes really intense, as described by this sister of a deaf child who is transferring from a special school to a public one:

> *A lot of people make fun of him, and it hurts me so much, too. He knows he's different, but he really hasn't felt he is. It's hard to hear him ask Mom why a kid will act mean to him.*
>
> *One time I got so angry at some kids, I went out and asked them how they'd feel if they were John. They said they weren't deaf so they didn't have to worry. I didn't accomplish much, but telling them how I felt helped me.*
>
> *A good friend and I have talked over how worried I am about what will happen to John in high school next year. My friend said he and my other good friends will help me talk to the other kids—maybe if the freshmen know that my friends and I are ready to pounce, it will be a deterrent. (PACER Center, 1987, pp. 12–13)*

Siblings may feel embarrassed by the behavior or looks of the child who has a disability and dread having friends over to the house, especially to participate in family events like meals. Parents may rely on siblings to accompany the child who has a disability to school and convey messages, carry medications, and otherwise act as a surrogate during the school day.

This is also the period when caretaking activities may increase. It is a consistent finding in the research that siblings become caretakers and parent surrogates, especially if they are the older females in the family (Crnic & Leconte, 1986). When both parents have jobs and money is in short supply for sitters and daycare, the role of siblings increases in this area.

Siblings begin to experience restrictions on what they want and want to do. The drain on family resources may prevent some purchases. Parental time and attention to help out with homework and recreation may deter them from developing closer relationships with their parents. Siblings may become frustrated with the lack of flexibility in family structure and activities due to the needs of the child who has a disability.

The gaps between their own development and the child with a disability now become more apparent. For the younger sibling, this is particularly confusing. They see how much more they can do in academic, social, and other areas. For this reason they may feel guilty about their achievements and try to hide them. Since they are children themselves, there is apt to be a gap between what they know is going on and how they react to living with a sibling who has a disability, as this sibling explains:

> *But I feel bad when John sees me go off with my friends and wonders why he doesn't have many. He'll be at home when I'm out having fun, and it makes my Mom feel bad. I feel guilty and I don't know how to handle it.*
>
> *But he doesn't want to talk about the social problems of being deaf and he doesn't want us to be hurt on his behalf. When he was going through the real bad period before he went to the special program in another school, one night I heard Mom crying. I knew exactly how she felt, and we talked for a long time. (PACER Center, 1987, pp. 13–14)*

Some siblings handle the adjustment well. Others resort to various devices. If they are overachievers and stars, they may try to make up for their sibling by striving to be the best in everything. If they are scapegoats, they may react to the stress and lack of attention by rebelling and engaging in inappropriate behavior.

Adult Sibling Who Has a Disability

As the brother and sister who has a disability gets older, siblings may worry about their responsibility to support and take care of the person when their parents are deceased. If parents have not been explicit about future plans, siblings are left to figure it out for themselves. They may also be concerned about the prospects for jobs, marriage, and living arrangements outside the home for the person. Issues of guardianship need to be settled.

They may develop a dread of family functions, not knowing how the adult who has a disability will behave or whether he or she will draw attention to themselves. They may hesitate to bring friends home and lie about the existence of the person. They may hesitate to tell the person about their own activities to avoid having to involve their brother or sister.

In cases of emotional and behavioral disorders, siblings may worry about the harm their brother or sister may cause to another person. When their brother or sister has a cognitive disability, the family's legal liability may be a concern. In some cases siblings have to deal with decisions about residential or semi-independent care.

Impact on the Child Who Has a Disability as the Sibling Develops

Conversely, we can expect the child who has a disability to be affected by their siblings as they move through their developmental periods. When their siblings are *preschoolers,* the child with a disability may enjoy having them as playmates if they are similar in age or somewhat younger. Since they are both developing skills, the gaps between themselves may not be as obvious. However, as the sibling gets older, the developmental differences may become more apparent to the child who has a disability and it is apt to affect his or her self-esteem.

The child with a disability may be frustrated in trying to keep up with the siblings. If older, the child may have a hard time competing with even younger siblings. They may choose to associate with younger children outside the home so they can feel more comfortable. In order to guarantee more pleasant experiences together, children with disabilities and their sibling need to be taught how to play together and interact. Use of sign language or a communication board, choice of toys and games, and other adaptive strategies are essential.

When the siblings enter *school,* children with disabilities may find it helpful and enjoyable to share that experience if they have been taught how to do so. There is a danger that the child with a disability may feel jealous of their sibling's accomplishments in academic and social areas. Parents must ensure that praise is given to both, although for different kinds and levels of work.

The child who has a disability may also become angry because of how much more protective parents are with them than siblings and the lesser amount of independence they are allowed. Parents should be encouraging their child with a disability to be independent. However, when appropriate boundaries need to be set, parents must explain that all the children have restrictions, but some are different.

This is the period when siblings are developing more interests and relationships outside the home that may not include the child who has a disability. The child may feel abandoned as their siblings draw away and feel saddened over the loss of their attention. In some cases, siblings may be avoiding the child who has a disability out of embarrassment felt in new school and community situations. Parents need to clarify for both the child and siblings how to maintain their relationship while developing new separate interests. It helps if the child with a disability is finding new interests and friends outside the home, too.

As siblings become *adults,* the child who has a disability can benefit from the experience of siblings who are learning about careers, employment, dating, and other activities. They can accompany their siblings and learn a great deal in a comfortable fashion.

However, the person with a disability may feel abandoned when their sibling goes off to college, the military service, or gets married, as illustrated by this brother of a person with a seizure disorder and learning disability:

Before I used to feel uncomfortable giving him advice and talking about what I'd learned about something like dating when Tom hadn't had a chance to have any experience in that respect yet. Now that he's able to lead a more independent life and have more social experiences of his own, it's easier to talk together.

There's still some envy and bitterness on Tom's part when I come home and we're together again. Especially when he sees me going out to be with my friends, he can get mad and resentful. (PACER Center, 1987, p. 27)

Parents and the sibling need to discuss what is happening and explain that the relationship will not cease but be different. The child who has a disability may also be sad that they do not have a job, special belongings, a family, freedom, money, and the like. Parents must work hard to help the person have some close friends and prevent the child who has a disability from becoming too dependent on them.

COPING RESPONSES

In a healthy, functioning family environment, siblings and other family members have a variety of coping strategies to deal with the stresses and challenges associated with living with a child who has a disability. Siblings should be able to go to their parents and professionals involved with their brother or sister and vent their feelings and frustrations. They should be taught to ask questions and know how to use books, films, and other resources to learn more about the exceptionality and its implications. Siblings can learn to use artwork and journals to deal with their feelings and communicate with others. Many siblings use humor as a healthy coping mechanism.

It is essential that siblings have their own hobbies and areas of interests independent of the child who has a disability that they can turn to for their own identity. The same is true about having a group of friends they can associate with without their brother or sister always being involved.

However, there are many less healthy ways that siblings may use to cope with their reactions to exceptional brothers or sisters. Siblings may become troublesome at home or school in order to get parental attention. They may withdraw into a fantasy world. They may ignore their brother or sister, turn to friends exclusively, and deny the existence of the exceptional condition.

Drugs, sex, alcohol, and food are only a few things that can be misused to compensate for what a sibling is missing in their home life with a person who has a disability. They may even become workaholics and overachieve in academics, sports, and other areas to relieve unfounded feelings of guilt and accomplish unreasonable goals of making things better at home. Some siblings get too involved in the life and affairs of the child with a disability and almost become a surrogate parent. While commendable, the sibling may harm their own development. Parents and professionals must intervene and relieve siblings of such self-imposed burdens.

SPECIAL NEEDS OF SIBLINGS

Siblings need a variety of things to ensure a positive experience with a brother or sister who has a disability. The most prominent ones are: mature, informed parents; information, skills, and support groups; an opportunity to grow and develop as an individual; positive involvement in the program for the child with a disability; planning for the future of the child with a disability and clarification of the sibling's role; and a close, meaningful relationship with the child who has a disability.

Mature, Informed Parents

Siblings need parents who can be positive role models and who can make them feel loved and cared for. They need to feel they have their own place in the family and are not an afterthought. Parents need to make a conscious effort to include them when planning family events and take the sibling's needs into account. Siblings need to know that they are not responsible for their brother or sister who has a disability and should feel free to decline to care for them or to be involved if they wish (Turnbull & Turnbull, 1990).

Parents who take care of their own needs model a valuable lesson to siblings. Also they need to explain stresses and tensions in the family so that siblings know the sources of them and how to deal with them. Siblings may be confused by parents' changing reactions to the child with a disability as they try to adjust to different issues. Sibling needs can be met as demonstrated by 90 siblings of adults who are mentally retarded, most of whom reported that their adult life was not adversely affected by their sibling because of a positive adaptation to the sibling, supportive parents, and coping strategies (Cleveland & Miller, 1977).

What is especially difficult for siblings is how they fit into the family in relationship to the child who has a disability. Parents may treat that child differently and make certain allowances for him or her. Siblings notice this and may wonder about how fair that is. Parents need to explain special rules and arrangements for the child with a disability and help the sibling put them into perspective so they do not feel cheated or overlooked. See Box 4-1 for questions siblings may need to have answered about parenting of children who have disabilities and issues of equity. As a sister of an older person with mental retardation explains:

> One person's disability can change almost everything about a family. I think families have to talk about it and acknowledge what's occurring.
>
> Also, I think parents will have to create communication opportunities between themselves and their children. Parents will probably have to ask some leading questions, too, because kids won't initiate telling their folks about some of the bad things they feel. Their feelings can include a lot of guilt and shame—not the kind of things that children feel very proud of themselves for feeling. But I think it's important that the emotions be brought into the open and discussed. (PACER Center, 1987, pp. 30–31)

BOX 4-1 • Questions Siblings Have for Parents

Will you help me understand more about the exceptionality? What does it really mean?

Will you share with me your feelings/strategies regarding my brother or sister?

Will I have the same problems as my brother or sister?

How do I explain the exceptionality to my friends?

Why is so much time given to my sibling?

Why do you have different expectations for me? Is it fair?

What is my responsibility? Why? Is it fair?

What is the best way to communicate with my sibling?

How do I deal with unacceptable behavior?

How do I deal with my roller coaster emotions—showing love and understanding at times and shame, fear, hatred, jealousy, etc. at other times?

Will I be punished for these feelings?

Why do I feel guilty when I am successful in school?

What will happen in the future?

Information, Skills, and Support Groups

Siblings who lack information and experience have a hard time putting things into the proper perspective (Featherstone, 1980). Parents need to provide information about the exceptional child's condition, its etiology, and what can be done about it, as indicated by this sibling:

> *My Mom and Dad had told us right away when they realized something was wrong with John's hearing. They helped us to understand that there was nothing that could be done to make his deafness go away and that we would need to help him and be especially kind.*
>
> *They explained right away what they would need to do to help John. I think it's really important to include other kids in the family right away. One of my friends didn't know for a long time what was wrong with her sister, and it was really confusing for her. If kids are in on it from the beginning, they can start adjusting along with their parents and learn how to live with it. Even if you don't know exactly what's wrong for awhile, it's still better that everyone understand there may be something wrong than to go through a long period of seeing that one kid is different but never talking about why. (PACER Center, 1987, p. 14)*

Siblings need to know what it means for them. Will they get the condition? Will their children? Is it contagious? However, siblings need only so much information at one time so parents and professionals must regard this need as an ongoing one. Meyer, Vadasy, and Fewell (1985) have composed an excellent book for siblings with this need in mind.

Siblings also need some guidance on how to deal with predictable situations. Other children and adults may ask them what is wrong with their brother or sister. They need to be taught what to say and how to say it in their own words; also they should learn to be comfortable saying "I don't know" or "Ask my mother."

Siblings need basic skills in communications and behavior management so they can relate with their brother or sister. They need to know sign language, how the hearing aid works, how to use the wheelchair, proper lifting and feeding techniques, remedial reading approaches, and others depending upon the nature of the exceptionality. It is appropriate to prepare them for emergency situations when the safety and life of the child with a disability might depend on swift, effective action. Such background supports the development of a meaningful sibling relationship.

PL 99-457's initiative means greater involvement of siblings in the services for the child who has a disability. Siblings need to know about the assessment and planning process and something about the services given their brother or sister. If they are given a role in the program, their tasks should be clearly laid out and expectations well defined. Schools and therapists can hold special training for siblings in these areas. Siblings have been successfully taught to use behavior management techniques with their exceptional brothers and sisters and, in the process, begin making more positive statements about them (Schreibman, O'Neill, & Koegel, 1983).

Siblings definitely need support groups of their own to provide a forum to learn new information and to share their experiences with one another. Parent organization, clinics, and therapists often organize groups of siblings to discuss their feelings and deal with mutual issues. Siblings can work out their negative feelings in a supportive environment and without the fear of offending parents and the brother and sister who has a disability. The sharing of experiences and resources can do much for the sibling's self-confidence. See the suggestions in Box 4-2 for organizing such a support group.

See Box 4-3 for a list of publications about or for siblings and of organizations specifically designed around the needs of siblings.

Self-Identity

Siblings need special understanding, attention, support, and recognition for their unique contributions to the family system (Powell & Ogle, 1985). With the proper instruction and support, there is every likelihood that siblings will benefit immeasurably from living with the child who has a disability. Without it, the opposite can occur. It is critical that the sibling's self-identity not be confused with that of the child who has a disability. Also it must be nurtured in spite of the attention needed by the exceptional child.

Siblings need to be recognized and affirmed for themselves, independent of achievements and deeds. Their accomplishments should be recognized and applauded, and not overlooked because of the attention the child with a disability receives. They should be encouraged to have their own friends, games and

BOX 4-2 • How to Start a Sibling Support Group

I. Select a time and location for the first meeting.

    A. Evenings or weekends are preferred.

    B. Meeting place must be easy to find.

    C. Provide clear directions for locating the meeting place within the facility.

    D. Location should be easily accessible to public transportation.

    E. A quiet, comfortable setting is important.

II. Publicize the first meeting widely using different media.

    A. Include the name and telephone number of a person willing to be contacted for further information.

    B. Provide information to organizations representing the target population.

    C. Contact school counselors and the special education department of the local schools.

    D. Contact psychologists, psychiatrists, physicians, and community health facilities.

    E. Provide the newspaper with articles, ads, and press releases.

    F. Provide radio stations with public service announcements.

    G. Request appearances on radio/television talk shows.

    H. Prepare posters and/or brochures.

III. Decide who will lead the first meeting. Remember, the goal is that the group become self-sufficient.

IV. Have a backup plan in the event:

    A. Only one person attends.

    B. One hundred people attend.

    C. It is difficult to begin discussion.

    D. Someone monopolizes the discussion.

V. Establish basic ground rules at the beginning of the meeting:

    A. One person speaks at a time.

    B. No person will be allowed to monopolize discussion.

VI. Suggested peer support group framework:

    A. Establish a limited amount of time for informal conversation.

    B. Each member should be given a specific amount of time to speak. It is critical that the leaders encourage participants to express themselves fully and state present realities. Others should listen quietly and respectfully. The leaders should make every attempt to assure others are paying attention rather than considering their own feelings and difficulties.

    C. When each member has been given allotted time, any issues agreed on by the group can be returned to for further discussion.

    D. Each person should have an opportunity to say something they like about the group meeting and one thing they will do to meet their goals during the coming week.

    E. Provide information regarding the next meeting prior to closing the meeting.

VII. The support group should determine the following:

    A. When and how often to meet.

    B. What to do beyond sharing experiences.

    C. Issues to be discussed.

hobbies, and time to themselves. While it is reasonable to expect siblings to play with and otherwise take care of the child with a disability sometimes, it should not be a fulltime occupation. As one sibling recommends:

> *In my experience, and from discussions with other siblings of people with disabilities, I have learned that the best way to foster a positive relationship*

BOX 4-3 • Sibling Bibliography and Organizations

BIBLIOGRAPHY

General Interest:

Attitude toward disability: A bibliography of children's books. Santa Monica: Pediatric Projects. (Available from Pediatric Projects, Inc., P.O. Box 2175, Santa Monica, CA 90406.)

Family life: Jerry got lost in the shuffle: Problems of a sibling. (1982). *The Exceptional Parent. 12*(4), 45–51. (Available from Psy-Ed Corporation, 1170 Commonwealth Ave., Boston, MA 02140.)

Lobato, D. (1983). Siblings of handicapped children: A review. *Journal of Autism and Developmental Disorders, 13*(4), 347–364.

Meyer, D. J., Vadasy, P. F., & Fewell, R. R. (1982). *Sibshops: A handbook for implementing workshops for siblings of children with special needs.* Seattle: University of Washington Press. (Available from University of Washington Press, P.O. Box 50096, Seattle, WA 98145-5096.)

Quicke, J. (1986). *Disability in modern children's fiction.* Cambridge: Brookline Books. (Available from Brookline Books, P.O. Box 1046, Cambridge, MA 02238.)

Ross, B. M. (1981). *Our special child: A guide to successful parenting of handicapped children.* New York: Walker Publishing. (Available from Walker Publishing Company, Inc., 720 Fifth Ave., New York, NY 10019.)

Shulman, S. (1988). The family of the severely handicapped child: The sibling perspective. *Journal of Family Therapy, 10*(2), 125–134.

Siblings: A bibliography of children's books. Santa Monica: Pediatric Projects. (Available from Pediatric Projects, Inc., P.O. Box 2175, Santa Monica, CA 90406.)

Smith, P. M. (1984). *You are not alone: For parents when they learn that their child has a handicap.* Washington, DC: National Information Center for Children and Youth with Handicaps. (Available from NICHCY, P.O. Box 1492, Washington, D.C. 20013.)

Stewart, D. A., Benson, G. T., & Lindsey, J. D. (1987). A unit plan for siblings of handicapped children. *Teaching Exceptional Children, 19*(3), 24–28. (Available from The Council for Exceptional Children, 1920 Association Dr., Reston, VA 22091)

Therrien, V. L. (1985). *For the love of siblings who cope with special brothers and sisters.* Salem, NH: Salem Association for Retarded Citizens. (Available from Salem Association for Retarded Citizens, 8 Centerville Dr., Salem, NH 03079.)

Walkowski, T. R., & Baurhenn, S. W. (Eds.). *"Am I the only one?": Written by and for brothers and sisters of physically and multiply handicapped children.* Buffalo: United Cerebral Palsy Association. (Available from United Cerebral Palsy Association of Western New York, Inc., Children's Center, 4365 Union Rd., Buffalo, NY 14225.)

Magazines and Newsletters:

The Brown University Child Behavior and Development Letter (Formerly *Raising Kids*). A newsletter published monthly that focuses on the many aspects of normal development in young children, and often includes articles on disabilities and health issues. (Available from The Brown University Child Behavior and Development Letter, P.O. Box 3352, Providence, RI 02906.)

The Exceptional Parent. A magazine for parents of children with disabilities published eight times a year. (Write: Psy-Ed Corporation, 1170 Commonwealth Ave., Boston, MA 02134.)

For Sibs Only (ages 4–9 years) and *Sibling Forum* (ages 10 & up). Each newsletter is published four times a year by Family Resource Associates. (Write: Family Resource Associates, Inc., 35 Haddon Ave., Shrewsbury, NJ 07701.)

BOX 4-3 • *Continued*

Sibling Information Network Newsletter. A newsletter for siblings, published quarterly. (Write: Sibling Information Network. Connecticut's University Affiliated Program on Developmental Disabilities, 991 Main St., East Hartford, CT 06108.)

Special Parent/Special Child. A newsletter published bi-monthly to promote effective family functioning between parents and special children. (Available from: Special Parent/Special Child, Lindell Press, Inc., P.O. Box 462, South Salem, NY 10590.)

Videotape:

Like an Ordinary Brother: The Cares of Siblings. A 20-minute color video featuring five brothers and sisters of individuals with handicaps who talk about their common experiences and feelings. Available in 1/2" for rental or purchase. (Write: Media Services, Child Development and Mental Retardation Center, WJ-10, University of Washington, Seattle, WA 98105.)

Organizations:

The Sibling Information Network. Connecticut's University Affiliated Program on Developmental Disabilities, 991 Main St., East Hartford, CT 06108. Telephone (203) 282-7050.

Siblings for Significant Change. 105 East 22nd St., New York, NY 10010. Telephone (212) 420-0430.

Parent Advocacy Coalition for Educational Rights (PACER) Center. PACER is a Center of "parents helping parents." PACER's programs help parents and children become informed and participating members in the life of a child with disabilities. In addition to a resource listing of publications and a newsletter, PACER offers many workshops. Write: PACER Center, Inc., 4826 Chicago Ave. South, Minneapolis, MN 55417. Telephone (612) 827-2966.

Siblings of Disabled Children. A program of Parents Helping Parents, offers two groups, one for ages 8–12, and one for ages 13–17. The objective is to give siblings special attention relating to their needs around being a member of an exceptional family. Their newsletter is called, *Sibling Squabble.* Write: Parents Helping Parents, Inc., 535 Race St., Suite 220, San Jose, CA 95126. Telephone (408) 288-5010.

Sibs Publishing Company. The Sibs Publishing Company was established as a network for sibling support. Publications encourage siblings to share their experiences and ideas. Inquiries and information exchange are welcomed. Write: Sibs Publishing Company, 15 Barnes Circle, Salem, MA 01970. Telephone (508) 745-2719.

Source: From National Information Center for Children and Youth with Handicaps, *News Digest,* 1988, volume 11, pp. 11–12. Adapted with permission of the National Information Center for Children and Youth with Handicaps.

among family members and a strong commitment to each other is to let them choose the levels and intensity of involvement with each other. I have noted that for me, these levels have fluctuated over time and during various circumstances. My relationship with Karen was strengthened when I came to view my involvement with her as a collaboration. Collaboration can be encouraged, but never coerced. (Horne et al., 1988, p. 7)

Planned Involvement

Siblings need to be included in the family assessment mandated by PL 94-457 (Bailey & Simeonsson, 1988). Questions about siblings should be inserted regularly into family needs assessment instruments. Siblings should be interviewed themselves about their needs and feelings and observed in their interactions with the child with the disability. See Box 4-4 for interview questions that might be addressed to siblings or, if they are too young, to parents. They can be observed while they play, tutor or assist, or interact socially with their brother or sister: see Box 4-5 for some factors to be mindful of. It is important to take into account normal sibling rivalries and interactions and not assume everything that occurs is related to the exceptionality.

When the individualized family service plan is being developed, it may be appropriate to include siblings in the discussion if for no other reason than that they know what is going on. Their needs should be incorporated into the IFSP and appropriate services provided, perhaps in the areas mentioned before. Parents should also periodically assess the family environment to see how the needs of family members are being met and what adjustments are needed.

It is important to include siblings in interventions to increase their knowledge and give them a chance to discuss their own needs (Turnbull & Turnbull, 1990). There are many ways for siblings to encourage their brothers or sisters to move, speak, or behave correctly. Since siblings associate with the child who has a disability in a variety of settings, they can encourage the use of skills learned in one type of setting in another one.

BOX 4-4 • Interview Questions for Siblings

Do you understand your brother/sister? Have reasons for his/her behavior been explained to you?

How do you feel about your brother/sister?

Do you resent the amount of time/resources that your parents spend on your brother/sister?

Do you have an opportunity to express/discuss these feelings with your family?

Do you have the opportunity to help make decisions about your sister/brother?

Do you belong to a group for siblings? If not, would you like to join a group to share your feelings?

How do your friends react to your brother/sister?

What responsibilities do you have for your brother/sister? Do you think it is fair?

Do you think about your brother/sister's future?

If you had a chance to talk with parents who have children with and without disabilities, what would you tell them about the sibling experience?

BOX 4-5 • Observation of Siblings and His/Her Brother/Sister

Does the sibling show respect and understanding?

Does the sibling model appropriate behavior?

Does the sibling allow his/her sister/brother appropriate amount of freedom?

Does the sibling offer stimulation and encouragement?

Does sibling show pride in accomplishments of his/her sister/brother?

Is there appropriate sharing?

Does the sibling consider the safety of his/her sister/brother?

Does the sibling reinforce "learned helplessness"? Does the sibling have the idea that his/her brother/sister can't do anything themselves?

Does the sibling demonstrate any negative feelings such as resentment, jealousy, etc.

Future Plans

For their own peace of mind, siblings need to know about future plans for the child with a disability, as explained by this sibling:

> *I know it is easier to say that siblings should be involved in planning for the future care of the brother and sister with disabilities than it is to involve them. I also know that the emotional ramifications of this are sometimes subtle and not always easily recognized. With respect to financial planning, Moms and Dads don't usually sit down with their kids and say, 'OK, folks, I want to let you know the details of our finances now and our financial prospects for the future.' This topic is difficult for parents and children alike. But you must attend to this in some way if the family members are going to be prepared to take over the care of, or responsibility for, a person with disabilities. I remember all too well the day I finally got the courage to ask my Mom about her insurance provisions for my sister. Her answers were anticlimactic compared to the effort and energy I had spent getting the courage to ask the question (Horne et al., 1988, p. 7).*

It is inaccurate to assume that siblings perceive things as their parents do. When parents and their sons and daughters without disabilities were asked about the children's future involvement, only 41 percent of the parents thought their children would assume partial care for the child with a disability, while over two-thirds of the children anticipated having such a role (McCullough, 1981). It is considerably less stressful for siblings to have the details worked out in advance (Skrtic et al., 1984).

When planning for the future of a child who has a disability, parents and siblings should consider such things as mobility, social and communication skills, education, and the individual's own ideas about where to live and work. Here is information the National Information Center for Children and Youth with Handicaps (Horne et al., 1988) suggests be developed and stored in a place accessible to siblings:

1. Develop financial plans for future care. It is important to consult an attorney with experience in devising wills for those who have an heir with a disability. The exceptional person may become ineligible for certain social services if he or she receives an inheritance.
2. Know your state's laws regarding guardianship and independence. Parents cannot assume they will remain the child's guardian after he or she reaches the age of majority. They need to determine how much supervision the exceptional person will need and put in writing the first and second choice guardians.
3. Siblings should know where all educational, vocational, and medical records are kept.
4. Document where the person who has a disability can receive medical care and the financial resources and arrangements made for this care.
5. Parents and siblings need to investigate the eligibility requirements for governmental programs like Supplemental Security Income, vocational rehabilitation, independent living centers, employment services, parent and disability groups.
6. Parents and siblings need to find out about the range of available community services.
7. Since the needs of the person who has a disability change over time, parents and siblings should regularly address questions such as those in Box 4-6.

Close and Meaningful Relationships

The greatest need that siblings have and the outcome of all the other needs is to have a close, intimate relationship with their brother or sister. Like all relationships,

---

BOX 4-6 • Questions for Future Planning

What are the needs of the sibling with a disability?

How will these needs change?

What can be expected from local support groups in the community?

What is and will be my level of involvement?

Is the involvement financially, emotionally and psychologically realistic for me?

How will the responsibility be shared with other family members?

Are my career plans compatible with my responsibilities for my brother or sister with a disability?

Will my future spouse accept my brother or sister?

Source: From National Information Center for Children and Youth with Handicaps, *News Digest,* 1988, volume 11, p. 11. Adapted with permission of the National Information Center for Children and Youth with Handicaps.

it has to be established on the basis of mutual trust and understanding. That requires a lot of work on the part of the sibling and the devotion of much time with their brother or sister. Parents and professionals have to provide guidance along the way and encourage the relationship. Barriers to sound, sight, movement, speech, and other natural functions make the attainment of the goal all the more difficult. However there are many siblings who can testify to the rewards to both themselves and the person who has a disability, as indicated in Lisa's letter to her autistic sister in Box 4-7.

SIBLINGS AS A RESOURCE FOR THE FAMILY

There are many potential contributions that siblings can make at different points in the life cycle based on these family functions: economic, physical care, rest and recuperation, socialization, self-definition, affection, guidance, education, and vocational functions (Skrtic et al., 1984). Not all siblings should be asked to assume these responsibilities.

The most important contribution is to the family system that sustains all the members. A sibling who has love and respect for the child who has a disability and interacts positively with him or her has a central role to play in the family. A special and unique bond between siblings and their brother or sister can foster and encourage the positive growth of the entire family.

Siblings can serve as valuable role models in speech, mobility, socialization, and academics. They provide stimulation and opportunities to practice learned skills in a way that parents and professionals cannot emulate. Siblings can assist with home training programs in behavior management (Schreibman, O'Neill, & Koegel, 1983). They also have been shown to be able to teach brothers or sisters self help skills like snack preparation, bedmaking, and teeth brushing (Swenson-Pierce, Kohl, & Egel, 1987).

Siblings can also engage in their own form of advocacy for themselves and for their brother or sister. They advocate for themselves by seeking their own needs, expressing them openly, and getting them met in a healthy way. They can become informed about the exceptional child's condition, available resources, the implications for them, and appropriate roles to play. They need to determine their true feelings about their brother and sister and find healthy, appropriate vehicles of expression. They adamantly resist the role of primary caretaker and strive to be a supportive sibling. They fight the temptation to become the "perfect one" in the family.

Siblings can be very effective in educating and sensitizing other children and adults to the needs of children who have disabilities. They can learn to do so informally during play or casual conversation. They can form "Kid Power" groups as the Turnbull's daughter did to acquaint others with her brother (Turnbull & Turnbull, 1990).

BOX 4-7 • **Letter from Sibling to her Exceptional Sister**

March 27, 1992

Dear Tina:

I suppose a good place to start would be the earliest memories of something being different. It wasn't really explained to me at that age, but I remember hushed discussions between mom and dad about your problems. Maybe I would have been confused if they had tried to explain it to me, maybe not.

You couldn't do many of the things I could and at first, I tried to tell myself that it was because you were younger. I perfected denial. I didn't want to think that there was a "real" problem. I wanted to live in a fantasy world where you were what was considered normal (I have since determined that there is no "normal"). I wanted to live in a world where there was no frustration, no fear, no sadness and especially no guilt.

Something I want you to realize about this letter is that it is full of "me and I." You see, I won't ever be able to understand what you have had to live with and through. I do know that you are a stronger person than I could ever be because of it. You are a survivor and I pray that you will always be a survivor.

I also know how I felt each time you had a seizure, each time I saw the kids teasing you, each time I was allowed to go somewhere or do something that I knew you couldn't and wouldn't be able to do.

I wish then that I had had some understanding of what you were experiencing. I could have, should have and hopefully would have been a better sister and friend than I ever was. If only I had persevered when you had pushed away. If I could have always been there, maybe you would never have withdrawn from the hugs, kisses and smiles that used to play more a part in our lives than they do now. It's the same as the flower that is planted in the shade and repressed, eventually, it doesn't grow.

Our world is an imperfect place. We are all aware of it. However, for such an imperfect world, we lack acceptance of people whom we consider less than perfect. We are supposedly more intelligent than animals, however, unlike many animals we do not protect our weaker, or less perfect, but are like the animals that must crush and destroy any weaker of the species. People are afraid of what is different and I must admit that I am too. Hopefully not as much as most people but unfortunately more than many.

Someday I hope to be able to express to you how much you do mean to me. Your innocence, your acceptance, your pleasure at simple things, the uncomplicated way you accept people and give love. I think you look at things the way God intended. You still trust and have faith that all is good. It would be so wonderful if good is all you ever received from people.

This is only a beginning of what I should have said to you years ago. Don't give up on me. I love you dearly and maybe I will someday be capable of letting you see just how much I do love you. You have a wonderful gift of sweetness and trust. Maybe someday I'll grow up to be just like you, until then, don't give up on me.

I love you.

Lisa

SUMMARY

The needs and role of siblings of persons with exceptionalities must not be overlooked. Siblings should be considered in the context of the whole family system and of the normal sibling relationship to avoid attaching special meaning to issues that are part of being a family member and a sibling. On the positive side, they are reported to develop greater empathy, understanding and tolerance of individual differences. On the negative side, they may be put under great emotional strain, be called upon too much as a caretaker, and adopt inappropriate coping strategies.

The impact of having a brother or sister who has a disability is determined by a variety of mediating factors. The challenge may be related to the nature and severity of the disability. How well a family functions as a healthy, communicating, and mutually affirming unit determines much of the impact; the role of parents as models cannot be overstated. The cultural values and expectations help to set the role for siblings, and the family's economic condition decides how much of the caretaking falls to siblings.

The reactions of siblings is somewhat determined by their age, gender, and amount of experience in coping with the challenges of having a brother or sister with disabilities. Siblings meet the challenges better with a strong family, peer and community support system. Other family issues like alcoholism also determine the impact of having a family member with a disability.

The impact on the sibling extends the full lifespan of the person who has a disability. There seems to be less stress associated with the preschool years of the exceptional child particularly if the sibling is also young. However, the schooling period may mean an increase in demands for the sibling to be a caretaker. Also the sibling must deal with the social stigma of the disability and find appropriate ways to interpret the brother or sister to their friends and other peers at school and in the community. When the person who has a disability is an adult, siblings must decide upon future plans for them along with their parents.

For their part, the person who has a disability has his or her own struggles as they watch the younger or older sibling progress through life. Developmental differences become more apparent over time and the exceptional person has a difficult time competing even with younger siblings. They may feel jealous about their school achievements and resent their independence and network of friends. They may feel abandoned as siblings go off to college, the military service, and marriage.

Siblings of persons with disabilities use different coping strategies. Those with a well functioning family rely heavily upon parents and other family members to address their feelings, provide information, teach them how to communicate and interact, and enjoy an independent life. Less healthy responses include acting out or withdrawal behaviors, denial of the child with a disability, misuse of drugs or alcohol, and assuming unrealistic responsibilities for the child who has a disability.

Siblings need many things to insure a meaningful relationship with their brother or sister who has a disability. Parents need to be available for guidance, nurturing, support, and assurance. They must maintain an open communication system and model appropriate coping strategies themselves. Information should be shared freely, and the siblings should be encouraged to ask questions. They may need to be taught how to behave around their brother or sister who has a disability in terms of adaptive communication approaches and behavior management. Special support groups for siblings should be provided. Sibling self-identity should be nurtured in the family and their place as independent family members affirmed.

Sibling involvement in the family should be planned by careful assessment of their needs and their incorporation into the individualized family service plan. Siblings need to know the expectations for them in the service plan for the person with a disability. Planning for the future care of the person with a disability should involve siblings so they are assured of their responsibilities and have an opportunity to accept them. Most of all, siblings need a meaningful relationship with their brother or sister.

Siblings serve as a resource for their families. Siblings who have love and respect for the child with a disability encourage the positive well-being of the whole family. They serve as valuable role models in speech, mobility, socialization, and academics. Siblings can be helpful in teaching and reinforcing skills in a variety of areas. They can be strong advocates for their own needs and those of their brother or sister who has a disability.

In conclusion, it is important to consider siblings in any effort to meet the needs of families with persons who have disabilities. Siblings' own well-being depends upon how well equipped they are to form a meaningful and positive relationship with their brother or sister with a disability. They can be a significant resource in assisting the person who has a disability if properly taught and supported. Parents must recognize the unique role they have in modeling a positive attitude toward the person with a disability. Siblings can be a positive force and advocate.

Introduction

1. It is important to consider the siblings of children with disabilities in addressing issues of advocacy.

2. Siblings and their needs can only be considered in the context of the whole family system.

3. Siblings are apt to demonstrate a range of adaptive responses.

4. There is a lack of uniformity in the formal research about the relationships of siblings and their brothers and sisters with disabilities.

Impact of Disabilities on Siblings

5. Siblings tend to react in unique ways related to the special dynamics created in the family around the child's disability.

6. Siblings develop greater empathy and understanding for people with disabilities.

7. Siblings become more mature and responsible as well as develop pride in their brother's or sister's accomplishments.

8. Siblings may develop inappropriate behaviors and longlasting emotional problems.

9. Siblings may feel resentment, jealousy, guilt, grief, fear, shame, embarrassment, and rejection.

10. Due to parental expectation that they take care of their brother or sister with the disability, siblings may lose elements of their childhood and, perhaps, even playmates.

11. Without suitable guidance and support, siblings may start acting out or withdraw as a form of protection.

12. Siblings can model appropriate developmental behaviors and be wonderful playmates and valuable assistants.

13. If siblings do not choose to encourage their brother or sister, they may deter their development or provide poor models and distract needed attention from parents.

Evolving Impact on Siblings Through the Lifespan

14. Siblings will react differently to their brother or sister with a disability as that child progresses from early childhood through adulthood, depending on certain mediating factors.

15. The nature and severity of the disability may or may not be an influential factor.

16. How well a family functions as a healthy social system has a great deal to do with sibling coping ability. Open communication among family members, positive parental attitudes and reactions to the child with a disability, and supporting family lifestyles and child-rearing practices are critical factors.

17. The culture of the family influences whether it denies and ignores or accepts and nurtures the child with a disability. Socioeconomic status is a critical factor.

18. Reviews of research indicate that first born and older siblings seem less affected by the presence of a sibling with a disability, while younger male siblings and the oldest female siblings have more adjustment problems.

19. The availability of a healthy extended family and support system, including childhood peers and professionals, can guarantee a more positive impact over time.

20. Sibling relationships seem to be less stressful when both the sibling and child with a disability are younger.

21. When the person with the disability enters school, there may be an increase in demands to take care of their brother or sister and to explain the disability to schoolmates.

22. As they realize the gaps between their development and achievement and that of their brother or sister, siblings have many mixed feelings.

23. When persons with a disability become adult, siblings may worry about their responsibility to support and take care of them when their parents are deceased.

24. Siblings may find family functions uncomfortable due to the unpredictability of their brother's or sister's behavior or worry about the potential harm their brother or sister may cause themselves or others.

25. Developmental differences become more apparent over time and the person with the disability may resent the achievements and social life of their brother or sister.

26. They may feel abandoned as siblings go off to college, the military service, and marriage.

Coping Responses

27. Siblings with a well functioning family rely heavily upon parents and other family members to address their feelings, provide information, teach them how to communicate and interact with their brother or sister, and enjoy an independent life.

28. Less healthy responses include acting out or withdrawal behaviors, denial of the child with a disability, misuse of drugs or alcohol, and assuming unrealistic responsibilities for the child with a disability.

Special Needs of Siblings

29. Siblings need a variety of things to ensure a positive experience with their brother or sister with a disability.

30. Siblings need parents to be available for guidance, nurturing, support, and assurance.

31. Siblings need parents to maintain an open communication system and model appropriate coping strategies themselves.

32. Siblings need to know the nature of their brother's or sister's disability, its etiology, and what it means for them.

33. Siblings need basic skills in adaptive communications and behavior management so they can relate to their brother or sister and prepare for being involved in planning and delivering services for their brother or sister.

34. Siblings need support groups of their own to provide a forum to learn new information and to share their experiences with one another.

35. Siblings need special understanding, attention, support, and recognition for their unique contributions to the family.

36. Siblings need to be recognized and affirmed for themselves, independent of achievements and deeds.

37. Sibling involvement should be planned through careful assessment of their needs and their incorporation into the individualized family service plan.

38. Siblings need to know about future plans for the person with the disability and parental expectations for their involvement.

39. Siblings and parents should develop systematic future plans and review them regularly.

40. The greatest thing that siblings have and the outcome of all the other needs is to have a close, intimate relationship with their brother or sister.

Siblings as a Resource for the Family

41. Siblings who have love and respect for the child with a disability encourage the positive well-being of the whole family.

42. They serve as valuable role models of developmental skills.

43. They can sensitize and educate others concerning the needs of persons with a disability.

REFERENCES

Bailey, D. B., & Simeonsson, R. J. (1988) "Assessing needs of families with handicapped infants." *Journal of Special Education, 22*(1), 117–127.

Bailey, D. B., & Simeonsson, R. J. (1988) *Family assessment in early intervention.* Columbus, OH: Merrill Publishing Company.

Brown, R. T., & Pacini, J. N. (1989). "Perceived family functioning, marital status, and depression in parents of boys with attention deficit disorder." *Journal of Learning Disabilities, 22,* no. 9, 581–587.

Chinn, P., Winn, J., & Walters, R. (1978). *Two-way talking with parents of special children.* St. Louis: C. V. Mosby.

Cleveland, D. W., & Miller, N. (1977). "Attitudes and life commitments of older siblings of mentally retarded adults: An exploratory study." *Mental retardation, 15,* 38–41.

Crnic, K. A., & Leconte, J. M. (1986). "Understanding sibling needs and influences," in R. R. Fewell and P. F. Vadasy (Eds.), *Families of handicapped children.* Austin, TX: Pro-Ed (pp. 75–98).

DeLuca, K. D., & Solerno, S. C. (1984). *Helping professionals connect with families with handicapped children.* Springfield, IL: Thomas Press.

Diamond, S. (1981). "Growing up with parents of a handicapped child: A handicapped person's perspective," in J. Paul (Ed.), *Understanding and working with parents of children with special needs.* New York: Holt, Rinehart, and Winston (pp. 23–50).

Dunst, C. J., Leet, H. E., & Trivette, C. M. (1988). "Family resources, personal well-being, and early intervention." *Journal of Special Education, 22*(1), 108–116.

Featherstone, H. (1980). *A difference in the family: Life with a disabled child.* New York: Basic Books, Inc.

Garguilo, R. (1985). *Working with parents of exceptional children.* Boston: Houghton Mifflin Company.

Grossman, F. K. (1972). *Brothers and sisters of retarded children.* Syracuse, NY: Syracuse University Press.

Horne, R., Schmieg, P., Place, P., McGill Smith, P., Prickett, J., & Valdivieso, C. (1988). "Children with disabilities: Understanding sibling issues." *News Digest,* (11), 1–12.

McCullough, M. E. (1981). "Parent and sibling definition of situation regarding transgenerational shift in care of a handicapped child." (Doctoral dissertation, University of Minnesota). *Dissertation Abstracts International, 42,* 161B.

McLoughlin, J. A. (1993). "Working with families of exceptional children," in W. H. Berdine & A. E. Blackhurst (Eds.), *An introduction to special education* (3rd edition). Riverside, NJ: Macmillan Publishing.

Meyer, D. J., Vadasy, P. F., & Fewell, R. R. (1985). *Living with a brother or sister with special needs: A book for sibs.* Seattle: University of Washington Press.

Mink, I. T., Nihara, K., & Meyers, C. E. (1983). "Taxonomy of family life styles." *American Journal of Mental Deficiency, 87*(5), 484–497.

PACER Center. (1987). *Brothers and sisters talk with PACER.* Minneapolis, MN: Parent Advocacy Coalition for Educational Rights, 4826 Chicago Avenue South, 55417, (612) 827-2966.

Powell, T. H., & Ogle, P. A. (1985). *Brothers and sisters: A special part of exceptional families.* Baltimore: Paul H. Brookes Publishing.

Schreibman, L., O'Neill, R. E., & Koegel, R. L. (1983). "Behavioral training for siblings of autistic children." *Journal of Applied Behavior Analysis, 16,* 129–138.

Skrtic, T. M., Summers, J. A., Brotherson, M. J., & Turnbull, A. P. (1984). "Severely handicapped children and their brothers and sisters," in J. Blacher (Ed.), *Severely handicapped young children and their families: Research in review.* New York: Academic Press (pp. 215–246).

Swenson-Pierce, A., Kohl, F. L., & Egel, A. L. (1987). "Siblings as home trainers: A strategy for teaching domestic skills to children." *Journal of the Association for Persons with Severe Handicaps, 12*(1), 53–60.

Turnbull, A. P., & Turnbull, H. R. (1990). *Families, professionals, and exceptionality* (2nd ed). Columbus: Merrill Publishing Company.

Vine, P. (1982). *Families in pain.* New York: Pantheon Books.

5

NONTRADITIONAL FAMILIES OF CHILDREN WITH DISABILITIES

Sandra Alper
Department of Special Education,
University of Missouri-Columbia

Paul Retish
Department of Special Education,
University of Iowa

Chapter Objectives

After completing this chapter you will be able to:

1. Describe recent economic and social changes and their impact on U.S. families
2. Describe the various family constellations that are termed nontraditional families
3. Discuss single parent families of children with disabilities
4. Define seven different residential options that fall under the label of foster care for persons with disabilities
5. Describe characteristics of children with disabilities who are placed for adoption
6. Describe the unique needs and challenges to families of children with disabilities who face poverty
7. Discuss the problems faced by children with disabilities who are victims of chemical and/or physical abuse
8. Describe misconceptions held about parents who experience disabilities

Key Terms and Phrases

child abuse
emergency shelter
family foster home
fetal alcohol syndrome
foster care
group home
independent living
noncustodial biological parents

nontraditional families
prenatal drug exposure
Public Law 96-272, the Adoption
    Assistance and Child Welfare Act
secure facility
single parent families
support groups
traditional families

NONTRADITIONAL FAMILIES

Changing Demographics of the U.S. Family

Recent social and economic changes in modern society have had profound influences on the U.S. family. The availability of birth control, increased numbers of women entering the work force, a divorce rate of nearly 50 percent, an increased number of teen pregnancies, the growing number of single parent families, increased numbers of dual career families, and alternative living styles, such as living together before marriage, have all changed the profile of the "typical" U.S. family. In fact, according to 1990 census data, only about 26 percent of households in the United States were occupied by the "traditional family" of two married adults with children.

The U.S. family is affected by politics and public controversy. Issues surrounding discrimination in the workplace, welfare support for dependent children, and availability of child care facilities shape the family. We live in a time when the family is being reshaped by public, political, and private decisions (Collins, 1986).

These rapidly occurring changes in society have affected the amount of resources, time, and energy available to care for and nurture children. For example, as the number of working mothers, single parents, and other nontraditional family constellations increase, the need for adequate and affordable child care has become acute. As the number of dual career couples with children rises, the time and energy available to give to children has, in many cases, decreased. The phenomenon of the "latchkey child" is common today.

Two additional factors add to the complexities and difficulties posed by a rapidly changing society. First, an ever more sophisticated medical technology allows more premature, at risk, and infants with severe disabilities to survive. Infants who even five years ago could not have survived due to their fragile condition now may be saved.

Second, there has been a dramatic and tragic increase in the number of infants who are exposed to drugs prior to birth. In 1989, urban hospitals in California and Massachusetts reported that the percent of births linked to prenatal exposure to drugs ranged from 10 to 25 percent (Halfon, 1989, reported by Kanagawa, 1991). These infants often have multiple disabilities.

Divorce is another factor that has affected the traditional family. Over the last two decades, the proportion of divorced persons doubled. Divorce rates are consistently highest for persons under the age of 30. The divorce rates for blacks quadrupled between 1960 and 1987 and increased almost as much for whites (Levitan, Belous, & Gallo, 1988).

The outcomes of divorce, especially for women and their children, can be devastating. Regardless of the magnitude of their needs, there is little support actually given to this type of family by service organizations. Only 54 percent of all women who are divorced, but who have not remarried, actually receive child support. Less than 37 percent of all divorced, separated, never married, and remarried women receive child support (Collins, 1986).

Data on divorce reveal only part of the picture. The number of single-parent families has increased significantly since 1970. However, the most dramatic change in the structure of the traditional family has been the increased number of nonfamily households (Levitan, Belous, & Gallo, 1988). Persons living alone represent the overwhelming majority of nonfamily households. High divorce rates and the large proportion of persons living outside the family indicate major changes in family structure. These changes pose problems for the individuals involved, as well as for the larger society.

The changing family has altered the role of the members of the family. Daycare has become one of the prime concerns of families. In many families, men have assumed more responsibility for childcare. Some large corporations (for example, Rockwell, IBM, Kodak), concerned with the quality of care for employees' children, have become involved in providing daycare services. Other industries have begun efforts to establish schools on the work site. Data from these efforts are few, but there is some indication that absentee rates are reduced and that job satisfaction has increased.

The economy has also affected the family. With skyrocketing costs of medical services and support systems, more and more families are concerned about how to continue to provide the necessary and quality care that many people with disabilities need. It is frequently difficult to obtain medical insurance for individuals with a disability. The cost of innovations such as computer assisted reading and communication devices is prohibitive to many families. Medications that are used by only a limited number of people are not produced in quantities that make them affordable for the average family.

Economics, changing family characteristics, cutbacks in services, stress from work or family, social pressures, and a variety of other stressors can result in less than quality care for an individual with a disability. Though these problems exist to some extent for all members of society, they are particularly difficult for the family of a person with a disability. Service delivery options are often limited and expensive. We are in need of policies that make it a priority to provide basic medical care to all citizens, regardless of their ability to pay.

In the next sections, we consider some of the coping strategies used by traditional and nontraditional families of persons with disabilities. Then, we consider children with disabilities within several different nontraditional family groupings.

Coping with Disability

Each of us copes differently with our life situations. Some individuals are able to ask for and accept assistance. Others may wish to handle the problems themselves. Woven throughout these individual and cultural differences is the issue of the rights of the individual with a disability. No matter how we cope, we also need to be sure that we are not depriving the person with a disability of the right to function as normally as he or she possibly can.

One often overlooked resource that families may have to assist in getting through the daily routine is humor. As Pearlman and Scott (1981, p. 13) stated:

> *Finally, there is an element of coping that cannot be omitted. In every life there are times to be humorous, joyous, and even silly. Special parents have more right to enjoy such times than most. Do not deny yourself pleasure and fun. You well deserve it.*

Other information on coping is found in the business management literature on stress reduction. West (1990) indicated that effective managers prioritize goals and set timelines. The successful executives let go of what they cannot control and concentrate instead on what can be accomplished. The parent or sibling of a person with a disability needs the same type of organizational skills; the development of strategies that can lead to accomplishing necessary tasks.

Coping should not be done at the expense of ambition or lowering one's aspirations. Some children with a disability and their parents have been discouraged in attempts to reach goals that professionals have deemed unattainable. Self-empowerment, problem solving, and learning to make prudent choices are all important aspects in development that, unfortunately, many professionals and parents have failed to teach to individuals with disabilities.

Hitchings, Hitchings, and Retish (1987) found that many parents, when discussing their aspirations for their loved one with disabilities, were primarily concerned about care and safety. These parents did not place a high priority on work skills or independence. Instead, they wanted services that would ensure that their child would be cared for once the parents were no longer alive.

Another resource for those with disabilities and their families has been the emergence of support groups. National associations representing many disability areas have formed parent support groups, as well as groups composed entirely of individuals with disabilities. One encouraging outcome has been groups made up of those who represent themselves such as *People First,* a self-help and advocacy group for persons with mental retardation.

Due to the efforts of support groups, we are beginning to see the availability of auto, medical, and life insurance for individuals with disabilities. Using generic community facilities, having access to transportation, and developing innovative systems to enable small numbers of people to live in the community are other goals of groups such as these.

Two Case Studies

Frances and Albert visited their 23 year-old daughter who had been living in an institution for 17 years. They found their daughter quite upset and looking disheveled. Angry, they asked the staff what was going on and found that there was a lack of trained personnel to work with their daughter. As a result, she had far fewer opportunities to leave the institution than she wanted. As they were returning home, they discussed bringing their daughter home but realized they could not handle her alone. They also realized they no longer wanted to leave her at the institution. While attending the local ARC (Association for Retarded Citizens) meeting, they talked about their frustration. Other parents suggested that they contact a local agency that provided surrogate family care through group homes. After about one year, Frances and Albert were able to arrange for their daughter to move into a group home where she now lives with three other women. What they like best is that their daughter enjoys the group home, is learning new skills, and the family can frequently visit each other.

LaVerne is a 34 year-old who has not lived with her natural parents since she was eight years old. When she was 19 she was moved from an institution to a local group home that was designed for individuals with disabilities. She lived in this home for three years, then asked to live in an apartment by herself. The organization placed her in an apartment with two others under close supervision. This arrangement lasted 18 months with LaVerne continually asking for her own privacy and living quarters. In staffings, she demanded to be placed in another apartment, but the organization said she was not ready because she did not have a job. LaVerne said she would find a job on her own. She proceeded to find a job in the housekeeping department of a large hospital and, on her own, moved to a different apartment. The staff tried to convince her to return to the supervised apartment, but she refused. Finally, she was allowed to live without supervision. For the last three years, LaVerne has lived in her own apartment with no significant difficulties.

One can conclude from these vignettes that persons with disabilities are finally having the opportunity to experience life in the community, with all of its' joys and frustrations. One important function of the family and the support system is to enable the individual with a disability to take advantage of opportunities and make appropriate choices. Too often, persons with disabilities are taught to be almost totally dependent on others.

We have reviewed some of the social and economic factors that have changed the structure of the family. These changes have resulted in an increase in the number of nontraditional families. Several different constellations of nontraditional families are described in the next section, along with their unique characteristics and needs.

Single-Parent Families of Children with Disabilities

There were 3.2 million single-parent households with children in 1970. That number rose to 6.7 million by 1984 (Norton & Glick, 1986). Bristol, Reichle, and Thomas (1987), in their review of the literature, noted the lack of any comprehensive national data set describing single-parent families of children with disabilities.

Bristol et al. (1987) found some data that indicate the divorce rate may be higher in families with children with disabilities. For example, Price-Bonham and Addison (1978) concluded that the divorce rate in families with children with disabilities is three times the national average. But, when level of income and education are held constant, there is no difference in the divorce rates between parents with disabled and nondisabled children. Whether or not having a child with disabilities increases the likelihood of divorce is unknown at the present time.

The results of some studies have indicated that single mothers of children with disabilities may experience a high degree of stress. Parents of children with disabilities may be in particular need of respite care (Wikler, 1979). There is disagreement in the literature as to whether or not single parents of children with disabilities provide more or less enriching home environments (Bristol et al., 1987).

Bristol et al. (1987) pointed out that our knowledge of single-parent families with children with disabilities is limited by methodological differences in the design of experimental studies. Their review of literature revealed that some studies of single parents included only young, unmarried mothers of children with disabilities, while others included older mothers who were divorced. Still other investigations included both groups.

Another problem that makes it difficult to interpret the results of research in this area is that the effects of different levels of education and economic status of the parent may have just as much effect on a child as the parents' marital status. In addition, studies focused on single parents have typically included single mothers and their children. Much less is known about single fathers and their children. (Bristol et al., 1987).

Inhinger-Tallman (1986) discussed several factors related to successful adaptation and functioning after divorce of parents who have children. These factors included parental personality factors, adequate income, good parent-child communication, consistent routines in the home, frequent noncustodial parent contact with the child, lack of continuing conflict between the parents, and availability of affordable and quality daycare.

Bristol et al. (1987) cautioned against making generalizations about what services are needed by single-parent families. Single-parent families are not all alike. For example, vocational training and child care skills may be needed by an adolescent, unmarried mother. But the needs of an older, well-educated, divorced parent might be very different.

Many questions remain to be answered about single parents of children with disabilities. What services are needed by the parent and what services are needed by the child in these families? How do the needs of the young, undereducated, poor, unmarried parent differ from those of the parent who is older, divorced, educated, and successfully employed? What role do single fathers of children with disabilities play and what are their needs? Finally, what are the significant differences between single and dual parent families of children with disabilities?

Foster Care

Foster care is increasingly exercised as a placement option for children and adults with disabilities. Hill, Lakin, Novak, and White (1987) described foster care as including any one of a number of out-of-home placements that provide 24-hour substitute care. These out-of-home placements become necessary when the natural family cannot or will not provide adequate food, shelter, and emotional nurturance to children. The term foster care includes the following options (Hill et al., 1987, p. 81):

- **Family foster home:** Residential care around the clock in a permanent or temporary family setting, including potential but unfinalized adoptive families and licensed or reimbursed relatives.
- **Group home:** 24-hour residential facility serving 20 or fewer clients. May or may not offer an educational program.
- **Group home 21+:** Residential care facility for 21 or more persons with disabilities. May or may not offer educational or therapeutic services.
- **Emergency shelter:** Facilities used only for short-term placement during crisis or emergency situations, pending arrangements for long-term care.
- **Secure facility:** 24-hour residential care facility of any size in which all exits and entrances are under the exclusive control of staff.
- **Independent living:** A residence in which an individual is allowed to live without a paid caretaker.
- **Parents or relatives:** Return of a child to the parents' or relatives' home, with ongoing assistance and support or supervision provided.

Beginning in the late 1960s and continuing today, concepts such as normalization, least restrictive environment, and full community participation for persons with disabilities have been stressed (such as Wolfensberger, 1977). These philosophical positions hold that persons with disabilities should have the opportunity to live in normal, stable, and familylike environments in the community. Foster care placements can be consistent with these goals.

The Adoption Assistance and Child Welfare Act of 1980, Public Law 96-272, established as a national policy permanency planning for children. Supporters of this law were concerned about the harmful effects of multiple out-of-home place-ments on children and youth. Primary goals of PL 96-272 were to reduce the number of children in foster care, reduce the duration of foster care, and promote more stability in the lives of foster children through case management and family-based support services (Hill et al., 1987, p. 1).

The Administration on Developmental Disabilities funded a national study of foster care placements for persons with disabilities (Hill et al., 1987). These authors analyzed data available on foster care placements on a state-by-state basis. While the report focused on persons with mental retardation or developmental disabili-ties, many of the results undoubtedly have implications for persons with other disabilities. The major findings of this report relative to number of children in foster care, disabilities experienced by these children, operation of foster programs, and longitudinal trends are summarized below.

Number of Children in Foster Care Placements

At the time of the Hill et al. (1987) report, there were approximately 261,000 children living outside their own homes in foster care. Children living with relatives other than the parent were included in this figure only if the relatives were licensed and/or reimbursed by the state. Fifty-four thousand children in foster care place-ment had some type of disability, including 14,000 children who experienced mental retardation (Hill et al., 1987).

Approximately 77 percent of children in substitute care were in family foster homes, while 10 percent lived in group homes with 20 or fewer residents. Thirteen percent of the children in foster care resided in large residential facilities.

Children with Disabilities in Foster Care

Data were available from 32 states on the number of children with disabilities in foster care. While 75 percent of children without disabilities in foster care were placed in family foster care, only 64 percent of children with disabilities were in family foster care homes. Hill et al. (1987) noted that these children were more often placed in group residences with 20 or more residents than were foster children without disabilities (24 percent versus 14 percent).

Data on type of handicapping condition are incomplete because of two difficulties. First, not all states report the number of children in foster care by specific type of disability. A number of states report only the presence of children in foster care who have special needs or learning difficulties with no reference to specific disabilities. Second, as Hill et al. (1987) pointed out, there is a wide degree of variation among states in the eligibility criteria employed in classifying children by disability. Of the 25,000 children and youth with disabilities in states reporting type of disability of children in foster care, approximately one-third were labeled mentally retarded, while 38 percent were reported to be emotionally disturbed. These figures should be considered only as rough estimates because of incomplete data sets mentioned above.

Operation of Foster Care Programs

Hill et al. (1987) obtained information on three specific aspects of operating foster care programs in their study: (a) training requirements of foster care operators, (b) case management, and (c) interagency cooperation. Thirty-three states reported information on training requirements. Sixteen states required some type of formal training for foster care providers, ranging from 4 to 20 hours. In five states training requirements were determined by individual county agencies. Three states reported no formal requirements for in-service or pre-service training of foster care providers.

Hill et al. (1987) defined case management as monitoring the progress and providing needed resources to persons in foster care on an individual case-by-case basis. This function is most typically provided by county or regional social service agencies. There were differences noted in monitoring and evaluation between foster homes serving children with and without disabilities (Hill et al., 1987). Foster care for children and youth with disabilities was, in general, more highly regulated, with more safety and training regulations. Case managers for children with disabilities tended to have greater responsibilities and be more directly involved in program development and planning. Foster care providers serving children with disabilities tended to be better funded and have more support services and consultation available than providers for children without disabilities (Hill et al., 1987, p. 40).

Hill et al. (1987) asked respondents in their study if there were any formal written interagency agreements regarding coordination of services between agencies providing foster care to children with and without disabilities. Eleven states had such agreements, while 21 did not. In states with written interagency agreements, these statements specify responsibilities of each agency relative to referral, coordination of services, licensing, and economic accountability. One state reported that due to lack of funding, generic county agencies were often left with the responsibility of providing foster care services to children with multiple disabilities.

State respondents were asked if there were any significant differences in selection criteria of foster families of children with and without disabilities. Seventeen states reported there were such differences and 11 states reported no differences in requirements. The 17 states that reported differences described foster parents of children with disabilities as expected to have more "competence, skills, and experience with the specific kinds of problems experienced by the child" (p. 43).

Interestingly, seven state respondents argued that generic foster homes serving both children with and without disabilities were advantageous. These respondents cited factors such as opportunities to interact with nondisabled peers, the chance to be in a family type setting, and opportunities to observe and model normal behaviors. Three respondents argued that there is more emphasis on "permanence planning and referral for adoption from generic foster homes" than in foster homes serving only children with disabilities. These respondents considered foster care serving only children with disabilities as regimented and stigmatizing (Hill et al., 1987, p. 44).

Longitudinal Trends in Foster Care

Respondents in the Hill et al. (1987) study were asked if there were any recent trends regarding foster care for children with disabilities. Nineteen states replied yes. Philosophically, these respondents favored generic foster care that resembled "normal" family settings whenever children could not be raised by natural or adoptive parents. Hill et al. (1987) noted that both state and federal governments are beginning to provide more flexibility in supporting such placements. States are establishing supplemental economic aid to support children and youth with disabilities in generic foster homes. "Respite care, increased case management, and training for foster parents of children with disabilities are also increasing" (p. 46).

Finally, Hill et al. (1987) reported a higher than expected prevalence rate of disabilities in children placed in foster care. If the population of children in foster care were representative of a typical demographic group, approximately 10 percent of these children could be expected to have a disability. Hill et al. (1987) found that over 20 percent of children in foster care had disabilities. Whether the presence of a disability contributes to foster care placement remains unknown. A number of respondents indicated a need for more emphasis on prevention, support services delivered to children in their own homes, short-term placements during crises, and long-term services directed at maintaining family relationships.

Adoptive Parents

The field of adoption has begun to focus on the needs of the child rather than of parents since passage of P.L. 96-272 (Deiner, Wilson, & Unger, 1988, p. 15; Hardy, 1984). Adoption of "perfect" newborns is occurring less frequently than in the past because fewer and fewer healthy infants are available for adoption (Hyde, 1982). At the same time, there has been an increase in the number of older children with disabilities in need of permanent homes. The majority of these children are moved through a succession of foster homes (Hardy, 1984).

Costin and Rapp (1984) estimated that nearly half of all children in foster care could benefit from permanent adoption. Most of these children are considered to have special needs, are older, and/or members of minority groups. Nearly 40 percent of these children are black (Hardy, 1984).

Increasing our knowledge of who adopts children with disabilities should be helpful for professionals working with adoptive families. Hardy (1984) reported that adoptive parents are a diverse group. Many are people who were once overlooked as adoptive parents, including single men and women, older parents whose biological children are grown, and middle to lower income families who desire to provide a permanent, nurturing home.

Glidden (1986) identified two distinct groups of adoptive parents. The first group included less goal-oriented families. The second group of adoptive parents described by Glidden was made up of highly educated, families motivated to help a child from less fortunate circumstances.

Deiner, Wilson, and Unger (1988) studied 105 families who had adopted special needs children in Delaware between 1979 and 1987. They conducted extensive interviews with these families, using the Family Adaptability and Cohesion Evaluation Scales (FACES III), developed by Olson, Portner, and Lavee (1985).

The participants in the Deiner et al. (1988) study were predominantly white, had a median income of $19,000, and were active in church. The mean age of the mothers was 42 years, while the mean age of the fathers was 45 years at the time of adoption. Seventy percent of these families had served as foster parents to the child they adopted. Seventy-three percent of these parents had adopted one child, while 27 percent had adopted two or more children. The most frequently reported reason for adopting was to provide "security and stability for the child."

The average age of the adopted children was eight years, nine months at the time of adoption. Half of these children were in foster care by the age of two years. The average length of time they spent in foster care before final adoption was seven years. Family dynamics were measured with FACES III. Deiner et al. (1988) described these families as "adaptable, flexible, and with family members who were very close to one another." (p. 15)

Based on their own data, as well as statistics reported by other researchers, Deiner et al. (1988) made the following recommendations regarding adoption of children with special needs:

1. Children need to be made eligible for adoption at a young age.
2. Children should be placed in foster care settings that are likely to lead to adoption.
3. Adoption agency personnel need to give increased attention to older, single-parent, lower income, and other nontraditional families. These families often adopt children with special needs.

FAMILIES WITH UNIQUE CHALLENGES

Families who live in poverty, families in which substance abuse and/or physical abuse and neglect occur, families who live in sparsely populated rural areas and those in the center of large urban areas, and parents who themselves have a disability all present unique needs and challenges (see Turnbull & Turnbull, 1990).

Poverty

According to 1989 Census Bureau statistics, a family of three was judged poor if its annual income was under $9,885. Families who have difficulty in obtaining and maintaining adequate housing, food, and medical care may find it particularly difficult to participate in their children's schooling. The logistical and economic difficulties of arranging transportation, time off from work, and child care for other children in the home may make a visit to their child's school an unlikely event (Turnbull & Turnbull, 1990).

Homelessness is a growing problem linked to poverty. Single-parent families may make up as many as one-third of the population of homeless persons (Turnbull & Turnbull, 1990). The Children's Defense Fund estimated from 1989 Census Bureau Data that the youngest Americans have the highest chance of being poor, with 20.1 percent of children under six years of age living in poverty.

Families in Urban Areas

Repetto (1990), in a report on vocational education, noted the many challenges faced by educators and families living in urban areas. Decreases in population, employment, services, and financial revenues have occurred simultaneously with increases in unskilled immigrant groups, teen parents, drug abuse, and homelessness (Hill, Wise, & Shapiro, 1989, cited in Repetto, 1990).

Families in central urban areas are faced with problems that can jeopardize the welfare of their children. The National League of Cities (Born, 1989, cited in Repetto, 1990) identified the following obstacles: (a) 20 percent of the children living in urban America live in poverty; (b) housing costs have increased three times faster than per capita income; (c) young people in the United States abuse drugs more than youth in other industrialized countries; and (d) 75 percent of this country's mothers find it difficult to obtain adequate child care (p. 1).

The National Center for Education Statistics reported that dropout rates for youth in inner cities were significantly higher than for youth attending nonurban schools (Kaufman & Frase, 1990, cited in Repetto, 1990). In some urban areas the rate of failure to graduate from high school approaches one half.

Urban schools face a multitude of special needs. Repetto (1990) noted that the majority of these districts had found it necessary to initiate a variety of special programs for pregnant and parenting students, students who abused drugs, and those who were at risk for dropping out.

Repetto's (1990) review of best practices literature indicated that successful urban education programs are characterized by high standards for all students, curricula that stress the relationship between school and real-life demands of living in the city, and cooperative efforts between schools, employers, social service providers, and families. After reviewing data on a number of successful urban school programs around the nation, Repetto (1990) concluded that collaborative relationships between schools and other agencies in the larger community are necessary to resolve the many problems faced by educators in urban areas.

Families in Rural Areas

Rural areas are defined here as geographic areas with less than 150 people per square mile. Helge (1988) reported that disproportionate numbers of poverty stricken families and minorities often reside in rural areas.

Families of children with disabilities in these areas may feel isolated and lonely. They are often faced with unique day-to-day burdens such as driving long distances to take their child to needed services and having little contact with other parents and support systems (Turnbull & Turnbull, 1990).

Shortages and difficulties have been noted in providing many needed services to persons with disabilities residing in rural areas. These include: audiology and speech-language pathology (London, 1986), vocational education (Mori, 1983), and school psychology (Fagan, 1988). Personnel in rural settings also find it difficult to provide adequate transportation and recreational services for students with severe disabilities (Hamre-Nietupski, 1982).

Personnel shortages impact the delivery of education services. School districts in rural settings tend to be more isolated in the overall state services delivery system. These school districts must contend with a disproportionate concentration of services in urban settings. School districts must also cope with significantly higher attrition rates among their personnel than their urban counterparts. Finally, school districts must integrate information and knowledge from a variety of disciplines without the help or support of ancillary personnel. These are critical needs if persons with disabilities in rural settings are to receive educational, vocational, domestic, and recreational opportunities in natural, integrated environments.

Substance Abuse

Children born of substance abusing parents are threatened by multiple physical, emotional, nutritional, and medical risk factors. In the alarming number of cases where the infant is exposed to drugs or alcohol before birth, the interaction of the resulting disabilities with a potentially unhealthy and unsafe home environment poses even greater risks (Kanagawa, 1991).

Two specific groups of infants prenatally exposed to drugs and born with disabilities are receiving increased attention today. The first group includes infants born with fetal alcohol syndrome (FAS). Pregnant women who abuse alcohol are at risk for giving birth to a child with intellectual, emotional, and/or physical disabilities. Children with FAS may be mentally retarded, smaller in physical size than normal, irritable or hyperactive, and have irregular features of the nose, chin, or eyes. FAS is considered to be a leading cause of mental retardation in the United States.

The second group of infants born with disabilities due to prenatal exposure to drugs are the cocaine or "crack babies." These infants also show a wide range of problems including hyperirritability, poor feeding patterns, irregular sleeping patterns, low birth weight, premature birth, and respiratory problems. In addition, approximately 75 percent of instances of AIDS in newborns are linked to maternal abuse of drugs during pregnancy (Kanagawa, 1991).

In her review of literature, Kanagawa (1991) noted that children born to parents who abuse drugs and alcohol often face a home environment poorly suited to meet the needs of a young child. Some of these babies are left in the hospitals and abandoned. These infants may be cared for by relatives on a voluntary basis without any supports or financial aids, or they may be placed in some type of substitute care setting. Halfon (1989, cited by Kanagawa, 1991) reported that drug-related foster placements in Los Angeles increased by 1,100 percent between 1981 and 1987.

How the field of special education will meet the challenges presented by these children born to substance abusing parents remains to be seen. Kanagawa (1991) recommended the following:

1. Individualized services should be focused on the unique needs and problems of both the child and the primary caregiver.
2. Services to these children are best delivered within a family setting. This might include family, foster, or adoptive home settings, as long as they are stable environments with at least one permanent caretaker.
3. Caregivers must be viewed as equal partners in service and development delivery.
4. Comprehensive services should be coordinated across agencies.
5. Services should be delivered without discrimination or value judgments relative to cultural diversity and alternative lifestyles.

Physical Abuse

Child abuse is a significant problem in contemporary U.S. society. The United States has the highest rate of reported child abuse and neglect of any industrialized country in the world. Parents in all socioeconomic and cultural groups emotionally and physically abuse their own children (Meier and Sloan, 1984). Estimates of the number of abused children who have physical, intellectual, or emotional disabilities vary widely and range from 8 to 55 percent (Blacher & Meyers, 1983; Daly & Wilson, 1981; Frodi, 1981).

In some cases, child abuse may cause disabilities. In other situations, the abuse may result from the presence of some preexisting disability (Turnbull & Turnbull, 1990). Some children with disabilities may be difficult to manage, hard to comfort, or unresponsive to their parents (Blacher & Meyers, 1983). Parents who were abused in childhood and are prone to aggression as a result may respond to such children with abusive behaviors (Turnbull & Turnbull, 1990). Repeated instances of physical and emotional abuse over a long period of time may increase the severity of disability (Meier & Sloan, 1984).

While the presence of a disability may place the child at risk for abuse, Turnbull and Turnbull (1990) pointed out that it would be incorrect to assume that the majority of children with disabilities are abused. The largest number of children with disabilities are not abused or neglected.

Schools and other agencies are developing educational programs in an attempt to teach children to discriminate between appropriate and inappropriate touching, and between appropriate punishment and physical abuse (Turnbull & Turnbull, 1990). Children are encouraged to report sexual or physical abuse to a trusted adult. These programs are critical because abuse of a child is often denied in a family. In sexual abuse, the child may be intimidated by the abusing adult into keeping the abuse a secret. The child may be too afraid or embarrassed to report the abusive behaviors of an adult on whom he or she is dependent.

Professionals are mandated by law to report instances of suspected child abuse. Professionals are not in agreement as to whether the family should be informed as to who filed the report. While many states guarantee confidentiality, it may still be possible to determine the identity of the informant (Turnbull & Turnbull, 1990).

Another point of disagreement among professionals is how to end child abuse. Removing the child may cause grief and marital discord for the parents (Meier & Sloan, 1984) and result in confusion, emotional trauma, and loss of a permanent family setting for the child. Some legal professionals have demanded the abusing parent be removed from the home and ordered to undergo therapy or counseling. This approach attempts to avoid punishing the child with the trauma of being removed from the home and placed in foster care. Both approaches result in disruption of the family unit. While it was once widely held by social service and legal professionals that it is always in the child's best interest to remain with the natural parents, this view is now frequently debated in professional circles and courts of law.

Meier and Sloan (1984) pointed out that child abuse is one of the most frustrating and difficult problems encountered by professionals. Working with children whose parents purposely and repeatedly injure them can be very painful. It is also frustrating to realize that we have not yet developed any interventions that are effective on a long-term basis. Sadly, many abused children grow up to become adults who repeat the pattern of abuse and neglect with their own children.

Parents Who Experience Disabilities

One result of the recent emphasis on protecting the legal and human rights of persons with disabilities is that more of these individuals are allowed to experience heterosexual relationships such as friendships, dating, and marriage. Some of these persons will become parents.

Turnbull and Turnbull (1990) identified two sensitive issues that arise when persons with intellectual or psychological disabilities become parents. First, there are social and legal prohibitions against persons who are mentally retarded or mentally ill having children. In some states, these individuals can be legally barred from marriage or reproduction. In other cases, parents may decide to obtain some form of birth control for their children with disabilities when they reach sexual maturity with or without the child's consent. As Turnbull and Turnbull (1990) pointed out, these same restrictions are typically not applied to persons who have different problems that might raise questions about their ability to parent, such as chronic drug abuse or a history of violence.

The second issue involving parents who have disabilities noted by Turnbull and Turnbull (1990) is the assumption of parental incompetence. While low IQ does not preclude the possibility that an individual can raise healthy children, it means that supports for both the parent and child are needed. Child care skills, homemaking skills, consumer skills, assistance with managing finances, and vocational training may be needed by the parent. We should remember, however, two important points. First, these same skills are needed by many parents without disabilities. Unfortunately, parenting skills are still learned "on-the-job" by most individuals. Second, child abuse and neglect occur across all social, economic, and educational levels.

Noncustodial Biological Parents

Over half a million children are growing up in settings other than their natural homes. Many of these children have disabilities. Some biological parents have been legally forced to relinquish custody of their children because the courts have deemed them unfit parents. Child abuse and neglect have often occurred in these cases. Other parents, however, have voluntarily made the decision to give up custody of their child. In still other instances, parents have opted to retain legal custody of their child but to place the child in a residential setting other than their own home.

What factors might compel parents to place their child outside of the home? What are the effects of such a decision on the parents, the child, siblings, and other family members? These are important questions. They are questions that are difficult to answer for several reasons. First, the factors involved in the decision to keep a child with disabilities in the home or to place that child outside of the family home are many and complex. How a particular family copes with a child with disabilities is influenced by many factors including amount of resources and information available to the family, level of income, education, family dynamics, religion, and federal, state, and local policies in effect that apply to persons with disabilities and their families. Every family is unique. Generalizations are hard to make.

Decisions made by families about where a child with disabilities will reside are also influenced by the scientific knowledge base available. For example, prior to 1975, many professionals believed that competitive employment, living in the community, and attending integrated schools were beyond the capabilities of persons with moderate to severe disabilities. Today these same goals characterize state-of-the-art programs. We now know more about the learning capabilities of these individuals and, as a result, have developed more effective teaching strategies.

Another reason that makes it difficult to answer questions regarding noncustodial biological parents is that the field of special education focuses on the child to a much greater extent than the family. We have a much richer understanding of children with disabilities than of their families. This almost exclusive emphasis on the child is evident in demographic data collected by federal and state agencies. While many statistical profiles of children who are placed outside of the home are available, very few statistics are collected on the biological families of these children.

SUMMARY

As we have seen, some nontraditional families of children with disabilities may have different cultural and ethnic backgrounds from the professionals with whom they have contact. Cultural differences in standards, values, and child rearing practices can result in conflict between professionals and the families for whom they serve as an advocate. Issues surrounding cultural differences that confront professionals and nontraditional families are discussed in the next chapter. Values and standards relative to child rearing, family structure, and the role of children outside the dominant society are discussed. Factors that can impede or facilitate communication between persons with cultural differences are addressed. Finally, strategies to minimize the inevitable conflicts that may arise are presented.

Nontraditional Families

1. The U.S. family has been significantly affected by several recent social and economic changes including divorce, large numbers of women entering the job market, teen pregnancies, and lack of high quality and affordable child care.

2. Medical technology is available that enables infants born with severe and multiple disabilities to survive.

3. There is an increased number of infants who are prenatally exposed to drugs. Many of these children are born with disabilities.

4. These social and economic changes have resulted in a growing number of nontraditional families, many of whom are responsible for the care and nurturance of children with disabilities.

5. Traditional and nontraditional families of children with disabilities may utilize a variety of coping styles, including developing expectations that are reasonable for the entire family.

6. Some families have found support groups helpful as they struggle with day to day demands.

7. One out of five families with children under the age of 18 is a single-parent household.

8. There are not enough data available on single-parent families of children with disabilities to make generalizations about this group.

9. Single mothers differ on a number of variables, including age, level of education, and economic status. The needs of these individuals and their children vary widely.

10. There are virtually no studies of single fathers of children with disabilities.

11. Foster care includes any one of a number of out-of-home placements that provide 24-hour substitute care.

12. Public Law 96-272, the Adoption Assistance and Child Welfare Act of 1980, established the concept of permanency planning for children as a national policy. Today, the emphasis is on stable, familylike foster placements likely to lead to permanent adoption of children.

13. While approximately 75 percent of children without disabilities in foster care were placed in family foster homes, only 64 percent of children with disabilities in foster care were placed in family foster care homes.

14. There is a higher than expected prevalence rate of disabilities in children placed in foster care. According to one national study, over 20 percent of children in foster care have disabilities.

15. The typical child available for adoption is approximately nine years old and often has a physical, emotional, or intellectual disability. Nearly half of these children are black.

16. Many individuals who would not have been considered as adoptive parents a few years ago are adopting children. Many are single, older parents whose children have grown, and/or middle to lower income families who have a genuine desire to provide a stable home to a child.

Special Challenges

17. Families that have a great deal of difficulty in obtaining food, shelter, and health care often find it extremely difficult to participate in their children's school program.

18. Homelessness is a growing problem in our society. Small children are now the fastest growing group of homeless persons in the United States.

19. Families in central urban areas are faced with a number of problems that can result in negative outcomes for their children. These include poverty, high rates of unemployment, widespread availability of drugs, and high costs of housing.

20. In some urban areas the rate of failure to graduate from high school is nearly one-half.

21. Studies indicate that only through a partnership of schools and other community agencies can urban education begin to solve its problems

22. Rural areas are defined as geographic areas populated by fewer than 150 people per square mile.

23. Difficulties in providing services to children with disabilities and their families in rural areas center around large distances between families and services and personnel available.

24. Two groups of children who are prenatally exposed to drugs are children who are born with fetal alcohol syndrome and those whose mothers used cocaine during pregnancy. These infants often face a multitude of problems including physical and intellectual difficulties as well as unhealthy, unsafe home environments. They are often at risk for abuse, neglect, and multiple caretakers.

25. The United States has the highest rate of reported child abuse of any industrialized country in the world.

26. Estimates of the number of abused children who have disabilities range from 8 to 55 percent. Whether or not child abuse causes disabilities or results from the presence of some preexisting disability in the child is unknown.

27. Due to increased emphasis on protecting the legal and human rights of persons with disabilities, there is an increased probability that these individuals will become parents.

28. Some people object to the idea of persons with mental retardation or mental illness becoming parents. It is extremely difficult to separate parenting difficulties due to low IQ from those due to lack of resources or bad parenting models.

29. Low IQ or emotional problems should signal to professionals that supports for both the parent and the child are likely to be needed.

30. Some parents have voluntarily given up custody of their child with a disability, or retained legal custody but placed the child in a residence other than the natural home.

31. The factors involved in decisions of whether or not to keep a child with disabilities in the home are many and complex. A family's ability to keep a child with disabilities in the home is influenced by amount of resources and information available, level of income, family dynamics, religion, other demands on the family members, and many others. It is difficult to make generalizations about these families.

REFERENCES

Adoption Assistance and Child Welfare Act of 1980, P.L. No. 96-272, 94 Stat. 500 (1980). (Codified at 42 U.S.C. 670 et seq., 1982).

Blacher, J., & Meyers, C. C. (1983). "A review of attachment formation and disorder of handicapped children." *American Journal of Mental Deficiency. 87*(4), 359–371.

Born, C. E. (1989, September). *Our future and our only hope: A survey of city halls regarding children and families.* Washington, DC: National League of Cities.

Bristol, M. M., Reichle, B. R. & Thomas, S. T. (1987). "Methodological caveats in the assessment of single-parent families of handicapped children." *Journal of the Division for Early Childhood.* Council for Exceptional Children, *11,* 134–142.

Collins, R. (1986). *Sociology of marriage and the family.* Chicago, IL: Nelson-Hall.

Costin, L. & Rapp, C. (1984). *Child welfare: Policies and practice* (3rd ed.). New York: McGraw Hill.

Daly, M. & Wilson, M. (1981). "Abuse and neglect of children in evolutionary perspective," in D. Tinkle and R. Alexander (Eds.), *Natural selection and social behavior: Recent research and new theory.* Concord, MA: Chiron Press.

Deiner, P. L., Wilson, N. J., & Unger, G. (1988). "Motivation and characteristics of families who adopt children with special needs: An empirical study." *Topics in Early Childhood Special Education, 8*(2), 15–29.

Fagan, T. K. (1988). "The historical improvement of the school psychology service ration: Implications for future employment." *School Psychology Review, 17*(3), 447–458.

Frodi, A. M. (1981). "Contribution of infant characteristics to child abuse." *American Journal of Mental Deficiency, 85,* 341–349.

Glidden, L. (1986). "Families who adopt mentally retarded children: Who, why, and what happens." In J. Gallagher & P. Vietze (Eds.), *Families of handicapped persons* (pp. 129–142). Baltimore, MD: Paul H. Brookes.

Halfon, N. (1989). "Born hooked: Confronting the impact of perinatal substance abuse." *Hearing before the Select Committee on Children, Youth, and Families, April 27, 1989,* (pp. 203–213). Washington, DC: U. S. Government Printing Office.

Hamre-Nietupski, S. (1982). "Implementing a community-based educational model for moderately/severely handicapped students: Common problems and suggested solutions." *Journal of the Associations for the Severely Handicapped, 7*(4), 38–43.

Hardy, D. (1984). "Adoption of children with special needs: A national perspective." *American Psychologist, 39*(8), 901–904.

Helge, D. (1988). "Serving at-risk populations in rural America! *Teaching Exceptional Children, 20,* 17–18.

Hill, B. K., Lakin, K. C., Novak, A. R., & White, C. C. (1987). "Foster care for children and adults with handicaps: Child welfare and adult social services (Report No. 23)." Minneapolis, MN: University of Minnesota, Department of Educational Psychology.

Hill, P. T., Wise, A. E., & Shapiro, L. (1989, January). *Educational progress: Cities mobilize to improve their schools.* Santa Monica, CA: The RAND Corporation.

Hitchings, S., Hitchings, W., & Retish, P. (1987). "Parent perspectives of vocational services for moderately retarded individuals." *Journal of Career Development, 13*(4).

Hyde, M. (1982). *Foster care and adoption.* New York: Franklin-Watts.

Ihinger-Tallman, M. (1986). "Member adjustment in single parent families: Theory building." *Family Relations, 35,* 215–221.

Kanagawa, L. O. (1991). *Infants prenatally exposed to drugs: Policies for case management and support of primary caregivers.* Manuscript submitted for publication.

Kaufman, P., & Frase, M. J. (1990). *Dropout rates in the United States: 1989.* Washington, DC: U. S. Department of Education, Office of Educational Research and Improvement.

Kubler-Ross, E. (1975). *Death, the final state of growth.* Englewood Cliff, NJ: Prentice Hall.

Levitan, S., Belous, R., & Gallo, F. (1988). *What's happening to the American Family?* Baltimore, MD: The Johns Hopkins University Press.

London, M. (1986). "Rural school system recruitment and retention of speech-language pathologists." *Rural Special Education Quarterly, 7,* 14–16.

Meier, J. H., & Sloan, M. P. (1984). "The severely handicapped and child abuse," in J. Blacher (Ed.), *Severely handicapped young children and their families: Research in review.* Orlando, FL: Academic Press (pp. 247–272).

Mori, A. A. (1983). "A survey of the perceived importance and frequency of practice of career education tasks by secondary teachers at residential schools for the blind." *Journal of Special Education, 19*(3), 29–36.

National School Boards Association. (1989). *A survey of public education in the nations' urban school districts.* Alexandria, VA: Author.

Norton, A. J., & Glick, P. E. (1986). "One parent families: A social and economic profile." *Family Relations, 35*(1), 9–17.

Olson, D., Portner, J., & Lavee, Y. (1985). *FACES III.* St. Paul: University of Minnesota, Family Social Science.

Pearlman, L., & Scott, K. (1981). *Raising the handicapped child.* Englewood Cliffs, NJ: Prentice Hall.

Price-Bonham, S., & Addison, S. (1978). "Families and mentally retarded children: Emphasis on the father." *The Family Coordinator, 27*(3), 221–230.

Repetto, J. (1990). "Issues in urban vocational education for special populations." *Technical Assistance for Special Populations Program, 2*(4), 1–4.

Sarachan-Deily, A. B. (1986). "Preparation of teachers to work with communicatively handicapped students in rural schools." *Rural Special Education Quarterly, 7*(3), 6–9.

Turnbull, A. P., & Turnbull, R. H. (1990). *Families, professionals, and exceptionality: A special partnership.* (2nd ed.). Columbus, OH: Merrill Publishing Co.

U. S. Department of Education, Office of Special Education and Rehabilitative Services (1987). *Ninth annual report to Congress on the implementation of PL 94-142. The Education for all Handicapped Children's Act of 1975.* Washington, DC.

West, J. (1990). *Executive development program.* Iowa City: The University of Iowa, College of Business.

Wikler, L. (1979). *Single parents of mentally retarded children: A neglected population.* Paper presented at meeting of the American Association of Mental Deficiencies, Miami, FL.

Wolfensburger, W. (1977). "The principle of normalization," in B. Blatt, *An alternative textbook in special education.* Denver, CO: Love Publishing Co.

6

PARTNERSHIP WITH MULTICULTURAL FAMILIES

Anjali Misra
State University of New York-Potsdam

Chapter Objectives

After completing this chapter you will be able to:

1. Identify four major cultural groups in the United States
2. Define cultural diversity and cultural pluralism
3. Explain the benefits of partnerships with culturally diverse parents for the school, teacher, parents, and students
4. List the responsibilities of teachers and other professionals in special education toward multicultural families
5. Identify one verbal and one nonverbal communication style typical of the four major cultural groups
6. Specify techniques that teachers can use for overcoming communication barriers with multicultural families
7. Describe the standards and values related to child rearing, discipline, disabilities, and schooling among the four cultural groups and identify how they differ from Anglo-American standards
8. Develop strategies for identifying conflicting standards and values
9. Specify strategies for resolving conflicts and monitoring outcomes of parent-teacher communication
10. Develop techniques to build a meaningful relationship with multicultural parents of students with disabilities

Key Terms and Phrases

African American	facilitating effective partnership
Asian-American	Hispanic American
barriers to communication	identifying existing conflict
child rearing	interpreters
communication	monitoring cultural integrity
communication patterns	Native American
cross-cultural communication	nonverbal communication
cultural beliefs	Pluralism
cultural pluralism	resolving conflict
culture	school role
discipline	stage theory
diversity	standards and values
dominant culture	verbal communication
exceptionality	

INTRODUCTION

Cultural diversity permeates all aspects of U.S. life including the school system. Teachers and other professionals must work closely with families from a variety of cultural backgrounds. The likelihood of contact between teachers and multicultural families of students with disabilities is particularly high. This is evident from statistics which reflect overrepresentation of culturally diverse children in the population of students with disabilities. Unfortunately, current teacher preparation programs do little to equip special education teachers and other professionals to recognize and foster relationships with culturally diverse families. The result is frustration and anxiety when a teacher's attempts to communicate with parents are unsuccessful. At the same time, parents of students who have disabilities feel neglected and alienated from their child's education. Teachers, parents, and, most of all, students sustain the adverse circumstances generated from a breakdown in essential communication.

Teachers must realize that the needs of the culturally different family vary from those of a typical Anglo-American family. Methods of communication that are useful with most families may be ineffective in a multicultural context. Differences between the Anglo American and other cultures, in communication styles as well as in values and belief structures, may pose barriers to collaboration and interpersonal relationships. This chapter describes the communication patterns, standards, beliefs, and values of four major cultural groups in the United States. Cultural practices related to upbringing and discipline of children with disabilities and parental perceptions regarding the school's role are discussed. Potential barriers and conflicts that result from cultural differences are identified. Finally, techniques for resolving conflicts and monitoring outcomes are suggested. We believe that the techniques suggested will provide special education teachers with skills to create an atmosphere of positive acceptance and understanding with multicultural families.

CULTURE AND DIVERSITY

Culture is the collective beliefs and knowledge that govern social behavior. Culture includes the language of the people, their standards and perceptions, the ways in which they display anger or joy, and the gestures they use during a conversation. These aspects of life are influenced by the country, neighborhood, and family in which people grow up. Simply stated, a society's culture consists of whatever it is one has to know or believe in order to operate in a manner acceptable to its members (Goodenough, 1957).

The United States, a somewhat new society, is home to people of various national origins. Multiple origins have created a society in which different cultures come together within a multicultural environment. The sizeable cultural groups, apart from the predominant Anglo American, that inhabit the U.S. include African American, Hispanic American, Asian American, and Native American. Subsumed within each major category are various smaller cultural groups that contribute to the nuances in cultural diversity within this country.

African American is the term used for all people whose ancestry is traceable to Africa. Within the Hispanic population, the primary subgroups in order of population size include those of Mexican heritage, Puerto Rican, Cuban, Central and South American, and others (Caribbean and Spanish). Asian Americans, too, originate from different countries. Prior to 1970, 65 percent were from China and Japan. Since the Vietnam war, people from Vietnam, Laos, Cambodia, Korea, and the Philippines have emigrated to the United States. Native Americans, the smallest cultural group, belong to over 500 tribes with approximately 200 languages (McDonald, 1989). The largest reservation tribe is the Navajo and the second largest is the Oglala-Sioux (Bennett, 1990).

The diversity introduced in a society by various subgroups expounding unique cultures is compounded by numerous other differences. These differences include variations in the length of time a group of people have lived in the United States, reasons for seeking immigration, ties with family members left behind, and differences in socio-economic status. Families who have resided in the United States for several generations have adapted the lifestyle of the majority through the process of acculturation. They may have little or no ties with people in their homeland, whereas, recent arrivals may be undergoing emotional hardships waiting to be reunited with the family left behind. Reasons for leaving the home country vary. For example, some Hispanic families were well off in their home countries but came to the United States for further advancement of economic lifestyle or to receive higher education. Other families represent the poor working class from Latin America whose primary goal was to obtain jobs. Many recent Central American immigrants left their country to escape civil war and severe economic crisis and are poor and uneducated (Penfield, 1989). Therefore, diversity results not only from different national origins, but also from unique events surrounding the settlement of a group of people in this country. Differences in beliefs, values, and standards will reflect distinct life circumstances and must be considered in the study of diversity.

Pluralism

Diversity has been a way of life in the United States; however, perceptions regarding acculturation and assimilation of diverse cultures have undergone dramatic shifts. The melting pot theory of national assimilation entailed blending into the mainstream culture at the cost of losing original culture and language. In the 1960s, ethnicity was viewed as un-American and discouraged. Cultural pluralism, a new philosophical orientation, respects the individuality and uniqueness of every cultural heritage. Some people fear that separatism, fragmentation, and intergroup rivalry will result from strengthening and maintaining cultural identity. This misconception is a result of lack of awareness and understanding of other cultures. The basis of current national planning, policy, and service delivery is the notion that forcing cultural change is unlawful and goes against democracy. Accordingly, school personnel must acquire competencies to bridge cultural gaps and collaborate with parents from various cultural backgrounds.

Prevalence

Researchers predict that by 1995, African, Asian, and Hispanic Americans will constitute one-third of the total U.S. population (Cornelius, 1990). The largest subgroup today is African American, encompassing 11 percent of the population. Hispanic Americans make up the second largest group; but, they are expected to be the largest group by the year 2000 (Macias, 1985). Asian Americans are next, followed by well over 1.5 million Native Americans.

These projections have implications for our schools. Teachers will be more likely to teach multicultural students and interact with their families. The student population is a good indicator of parent population. Students from multicultural backgrounds account for approximately 15 percent of the national school population (National Coalition of Advocates for Students, 1985). A breakdown by subgroups in 1986 showed that African-American students made up 16 percent of public school population, Hispanic students constituted 10 percent, Asian students were 3 percent, and Native Americans accounted for 1 percent (Ramirez, 1988). In many large city school districts multicultural students represent nearly 80 percent of the population (Ramirez). In the state of California, the multicultural student population is projected to be 52 percent of the total school population by the year 2000.

Statistics on dropout rates, school-related problems, and disabilities among multicultural students are astounding. The dropout rate among Anglo Americans is 15 percent, for African Americans it is 21 percent, and among Hispanic Americans the rate is an amazing 39 percent. In some large school districts such as Chicago and New York, the Puerto Rican dropout rate exceeds 70 percent (Santiago, 1986). Dropout rates for Native-American and Asian-American students have not been as well documented. However, given current educational status, the situation for Native-American students is similar to or worse than that of African Americans (Gay, 1989). Asian Americans appear to be the only group with a dropout rate on par with Anglo-American students (Census of Population, 1980). It is also reported that 90 percent of the students suspended from schools come from multicultural backgrounds (National Coalition of Advocates for Students, 1985).

Multicultural students are disproportionately overrepresented among school-age children and youth who are classified as disabled (Salend, Michael, & Taylor, 1984). One-third of all students who are disabled come from multicultural backgrounds (Kamp & Chinn, 1982). For example, 28 percent of students labeled mentally retarded are African American. Learning disability is the most prevalent category assigned to Hispanic students (Cummins, 1986b). These figures highlight long standing school-related problems among certain cultural groups. Students from multicultural backgrounds are more likely to be considered academically slow, placed in lower track grouping, socially isolated, and faced with the consequence of lowered teacher expectations.

Special education personnel must be alerted to these statistics because they are legally mandated to work on a frequent basis with parents of students who are disabled and/or experience school related problems. To face the challenge of working with multicultural families of students with disabilities, schools must foster cultural pluralism. Teachers who adopt the philosophy of respect and mutual understanding of all cultures will be better prepared to accommodate the needs of their students. Collaboration with families of these students may successfully prevent many failures and gradually reverse the direction of current statistics.

Responsibility to Multicultural Families

All students and their families are entitled to appropriate educational services, irrespective of social or cultural differences. It appears that students from multicultural backgrounds are more susceptible to school failure and are more likely to be labeled. To uphold student rights of receiving an appropriate education, school personnel have the responsibility of extending greater flexibility to meet the needs of culturally diverse families.

Inadequately prepared teachers may be unable to establish meaningful links with parents. They often assume parental apathy and disinterest contribute to lack of family participation (Dunn, 1987). On the contrary, parents may have high aspirations for their children and are eager to participate (WongFillmore, 1983). Cultural factors such as beliefs about the school's authority in decision making or lack of resources may be the factors resulting in their absence from school activities (Turnbull & Turnbull, 1990). Some parents simply may not know how to make a contribution and are excluded from taking an active role. Special education teachers must learn as much as possible about multicultural families and their reasons for nonparticipation. Furthermore, teachers and other school professionals must provide all necessary educational information to parents. They must open channels of parental participation through frequent and insightful communication.

Special education teachers have the responsibility of recognizing cultural differences and attributing equal status to all cultures. Numerous reports of frustration and anxiety faced by both parties during parent-teacher conferences are available (Lynch & Stein, 1982; Morgan, 1982; Turnbull & Turnbull, 1990). These feelings are magnified when teachers and parents cherish different values, standards, and beliefs and/or communicate using a different language or style. Teachers have the responsibility of encouraging parents to make their contribution despite language barriers. Parents must not be made to feel inferior or incompetent due to their lack of familiarity with a new language or a way of education. A study of cultural beliefs and communication patterns will assist special education teachers in encouraging parental participation.

Teachers have the responsibility of explaining school expectations to multicultural parents. They must share information on how students learn, what they learn, and materials used in school. In keeping with legal regulations (P.L. 94-142), special education professionals must familiarize parents with an educational process unique to this country. Teachers have the responsibility of explaining the detailed, systematic, and oftentimes bureaucratic and tedious process through which special education services are provided. Parents also need to know the unique evaluation methods used in the U.S. schools so they may participate in their children's achievements. Empowerment of multicultural families will take more effort than required for Anglo-American families.

Schools vary in their abilities to fulfill their responsibilities towards multicultural families of students with disabilities. Large school districts in urban areas where cultural groups have resided over long periods of time may be better equipped. They may have staff from diverse backgrounds or have learned from past experiences. Small, rural, and isolated communities face a greater challenge due to limited resources, lack of trained ethnic personnel, and/or poor models of delivery. Irrespective of logistical hurdles, schools must make every attempt to seek and develop resources to fulfill their responsibility. According to Ortiz (1988), successful schools acknowledge the pluralistic composition of the school society and provide ways for all families to participate actively in programs and activities.

Benefits of Multicultural Family Involvement

Legal and ethical forces are frequently emphasized as primary reasons for integration and involvement of multicultural families. These factors ensure that the innumerable advantages of involving multicultural families in the educational process are not ignored. Schools, teachers, parents, and, most of all, students can benefit from parental involvement (See Table 6-1).

Cultural diversity contributes to the richness and splendor of a society. Multicultural families can do the same for the school environment. They can contribute by introducing new styles of dress, food, and music to the school's cultural events. This creates an atmosphere parallel to current societal composition and offers

TABLE 6-1 • Benefits of Multicultural Family Involvement with Schools

Who benefits	Benefits
School	Experience unique languages, dress, food, and music
Teachers	Receive help with assessment, IEP's, instruction, communication with students, and understanding individual student needs
Parents	Gain insights about school policies and teacher expectations, acquire confidence
Students	Exhibit gains in school performance

valuable preparation to youngsters who must encounter the "real" world. Reality dictates that students be ready for a multicultural society.

Taking a narrower perspective, family involvement can help special education teachers and other school professionals educate the increasing numbers of multicultural students in today's special education classrooms. The multicultural student is a sum total of various experiences, influenced by two different cultures, beliefs, and attitudes. It is indisputable that special educators cannot attend to the unique needs of culturally diverse students with disabilities without a firm grasp of behaviors that derive from individual cultural backgrounds. Parents can provide information on how their child learns, how he or she handles accomplishments and failures, and why he or she behaves in certain ways. The individualized education plan can be tailored to include realistic goals and objectives suitable to the multicultural backgrounds of the student. Also, parents can add essential facts to the detailed assessment process that accompanies special education placement and service delivery. Their contribution could, perhaps, prevent misdiagnosis, mislabeling, and inadequate instructional programming. Parents can also assist teachers in planning everyday instruction. For example, they could translate key concepts and words that may facilitate communication between the teacher and student. Most importantly, parent involvement provides teachers with the opportunity to obtain first-hand knowledge about cultural standards and values that influence educational practice and expectations.

Parents from different cultures are often unfamiliar with the special education process. Involvement with teachers can provide opportunities to learn about school policies, teaching methods, and teacher expectations. Parents benefit by learning skills to cope with their child's disability and develop confidence in their interactions with school personnel. Other important benefits, such as consistency in reinforcement for student accomplishments, greater individualization of instruction, and increased task engagement, may result from parental participation.

When culturally diverse families are involved as partners in their children's education, parents develop a proficiency that communicates itself to children and results in academic gains (Cummins, 1986a). Research with students without disabilities from multicultural backgrounds supports the notion of gains in school performance as a result of parent teacher collaboration. Students whose limited

English-proficient parents were enrolled in tutoring showed significant gains in English language acquisition and reading achievement (Simich-Dudgeon, 1987). Similarly, significant changes in language acquisition were evident among students whose parents assisted them in Spanish language instruction (Lindholm, 1987). In another study (Tizard, Schofield, & Hewison, 1982), illiterate parents and parents with minimal English competency read to their children with positive results. Of particular interest to special educators was the finding that gains were most apparent among students who were experiencing difficulty in learning to read.

Despite testimonials and research support for parent involvement, actual participation by culturally diverse families is limited. Empirical research targeting multicultural families of students with disabilities is in its beginning phases. In a survey of Hispanic parents, Lynch and Stein (1987) found that only 45 percent felt they had contributed to the assessment process and 50 percent said they were not actively involved with IEP development. It appears that multicultural families pose a dilemma to most school professionals. Family needs are not fully understood and, therefore, not accommodated by school personnel (Correa, 1989). Special attempts must be undertaken by special education teachers and related service providers to engage multicultural families in a productive relationship.

A key to establishing such a relationship is effective verbal and nonverbal communication. Meetings with multicultural families demand additional effort, understanding, and sensitivity to communication. Reality is often just the contrary. Hillard (1980) issues a stern warning to practitioners and states that professionals who exhibit discomfort with other cultures, due to ignorance, dislike, or fear, must honestly reevaluate their role as educators. The next section provides an overview of communication patterns typical of different cultural groups. Conflicts resulting from cultural differences in communication are discussed. Finally, readers are provided with suggestions to overcome these conflicts and cultivate a meaningful dialogue with multicultural families.

COMMUNICATION

Effective communication is the key to building a positive, productive, and enduring relationship between school personnel and multicultural families. Special education teachers and other school professionals must modify their current communication techniques an/or learn novel ways of communicating with families of culturally diverse students who are disabled.

Researchers and educators have provided valuable information to assist teachers in communicating with parents (Losen & Losen, 1985; Shea & Bauer, 1985). Insights regarding seating arrangement, introductions, choice of language, feedback system, questioning, body language, and so on have been enumerated. Some authors have described parental personalities and outlined suitable responses to execute during various scenarios. For example, Losen and Losen (1985) provide teachers with tips on how to deal with sensitive or volatile parental behavior during IEP meetings. They suggest, never raise your voice in response to an angry parent, listen carefully, and write down complaints while reassuring parents that you will attempt to alleviate their realistic concerns. Little research, however, is available on how to communicate with parents from different cultures. Consequently, teachers may feel helpless when confronted with parents who sit passively during a meeting, do not make eye contact, or fail to display an emotional reaction when told shocking information. Such reactions may be typical for a cultural group and not signs of deviance. Table 6-2 outlines some verbal and nonverbal communication patterns typical for the four major cultural groups. The following section discusses

TABLE 6-2 • Communication Patterns of Different Cultural Groups

Cultural Group	Communication	Typical Characteristic
Hispanic American	Language Patterns	Spanish and dialects Omission of final sounds Pronunciation of /ch/ as /sh/, /th/ as /t/ or /d/, /y/ as /j/ No discimination in /b/ and /v/
	Discussion	Do not question authority figures
	Nonverbal	Physical contact during conversation acceptable Distance between people less than among Anglo Americans
African American	Language Patterns	English and dialects Grammar and semantics vary from standard English
	Discussion	Forthright, active participation, turn-taking considered restrictive
	Nonverbal	Aversion of eyes may signify respect
Asian American	Language Patterns	Chinese, Korean, Japanese, and others Vary with language, for example, Chinese is tonal; Korean is atonal, highly inflected, and polysyllabic
	Discussion	Passive, avoid attention to self, courteous, respect authority, and avoid confrontation
	Nonverbal	Eye contact avoided with elders Great distance during conversation Do not touch high status or opposite sex members
Native American	Language Pattern	Several languages and dialects Slow and soft with several pauses
	Discussion	Participation limited, take turns, do not interrupt, giving and receiving compliments is embarrassing
	Nonverbal	Gentle handshake Periods of silence acceptable Eye movements and gestures preferred to excessive verbal communication

these patterns in detail. Next, discrepancies between dominant and minority communication styles are investigated and suggestions are offered to overcome potential miscommunication.

Verbal Communication

Verbal communication is essential in an educational environment where people share vital information, offer valuable opinions, and make consequential decisions about educational programming. Many multicultural families do not speak the language of the dominant group. Even when verbal communication is possible, through the mediation of an interpreter, cultural differences impact on language usage and communication. Teachers must be aware of cultural differences in the use of grammar, semantics, phonology (pitch, rhythm, and tempo), and discussion modes (ways in which to engage in discussion) to prevent potential sources of misunderstanding. Culture-specific verbal communication styles are described below. The information is based on the limited literature published on this topic. We warn readers to avoid generalizations because past experiences, training, and level of education create innumerable variations in communication patterns. Readers must not assume that all members of a group necessarily share the characteristics typical of the group. For example, a Mexican-American parent may speak English with natural proficiency and not speak Spanish, speak both English and Spanish, or be proficient only in Spanish.

Hispanic

The official language of Hispanic people is Spanish. There are several variations in dialect depending on geographic area of origin. Some linguistic patterns include omission of certain final sounds; pronunciation of /ch/ as /sh/, /th/ as /t/ or /d/, /y/ as /j/; lack of discrimination between /b/ and /v/; and an absence of short i sounds. Frequently endings that denote plural or past tense are omitted. The American English intonation pattern is unnatural to Spanish speakers and their voice may not go up at the end of a question or down at the end of a declarative sentence. All syllables receive equal stress in Spanish (Loridas, 1988). Hispanic parents may hesitate to participate in a meeting, restricted not only by language barriers, but due to communication modes that discourage questioning of authority figures in the school setting.

African American

African Americans demonstrate dialect differences in verbal communication, especially grammar and semantics. Standard American English may pose a problem for them as their language usage may to standard English speakers. Differences may also be evident in discussion modes (Longstreet, 1978). Typically, African Americans are forthright in stating their opinions. They confront issues without attempting to restrict their emotions (Turner, 1987). Their culture emphasizes active participation during a discussion. Taking turns is considered too restrictive (Ratleff, 1989).

Asian American

Asian-American language varies relative to the culture of origin. For example, spoken Chinese is tonal and any change in tone denotes a different meaning for the same character or phonogram. Korean language is highly inflected, polysyllabic, and atonal (Loridas, 1988). Intonation and tonal patterns influence spoken English. Asian traditions of courtesy, formality, deference to authority, extreme modesty when speaking of one's own family, and belief in maintenance of harmony during social interactions have strong influence on verbal communication (Loridas, 1988). Addressing others, especially elders, by first name may be uncomfortable or even unacceptable to some. For this reason Koreans consider it proper to ask someone's age so they may establish their position and communicate accordingly (Armstrong, 1986). Asians will rarely engage actively in group discussions and tend to minimize attention to themselves (Kitano, 1973). Receiving compliments may be a cause for embarrassment. Asian parents often do not respond with "thank you," but appear humble and deny the action. Too many compliments may seem insincere. Asking or answering questions, voluntarily expressing opinions, or discussing personal matters is customarily circumvented (Brower, 1983). Open criticism, disagreements, sarcasm, and abruptness are avoided in favor of maintaining harmony. They may be willing to tolerate personal injustice rather than engage in adversarial situations to exert rights. For example, if a Japanese parent is pushed to express an opinion about a disputable action, the response would probably be "it's difficult to say" instead of a direct "no". This is done to spare the listener the unpleasantness of such a reply (Armstrong, 1986).

Native American

Native Americans have several languages and dialects. The speech patterns of the majority tends to be leisurely and full of pauses in comparison to Anglo-American speech. They speak softer and communication takes place at a slower rate (Loridas, 1988). Native Americans may not participate in a conversation unless they believe their contribution is exceptionally worthwhile. Interrupting another person while he or she is speaking is considered impolite. Taking turns and mutual respect influence communication patterns. This trend may originate from the formal historical procedure, the native circle, wherein everything (food, water, conversation) moved in a clockwise fashion (Loridas, 1988). Native Americans may find non-native speech too loud and fast and a hindrance to comprehension. Questioning is viewed as a sign of incompetence and failure to acquire information independently. Cooperation, rather than individualism, is stressed in Native American culture. Therefore, attention to the individual, through praise, may cause embarrassment.

Nonverbal Communication

Nonverbal communication is an essential component through which individuals express themselves during a conversation. Frequently, what remains unspoken may convey more meaning than what is expressed orally. It is estimated that over 65 percent of what transpires during a typical conversation is through nonverbal forms of communication (Knapp, 1972). Nonverbal communication includes gestures, expressions, body movements, distance between individuals, and the frequency, quality, and location of touch (Longstreet, 1978). People are not always consciously aware of nonverbal messages they transmit during a conversation. However, because a large part of interaction is governed by nonverbal cues, awareness of cultural differences is critical to monitor and prevent miscues. Typical nonverbal communication patterns among different cultural groups are discussed below. Again, readers must be cautious about making faulty overgeneralizations.

Hispanic American

Hispanic Americans customarily touch and make physical contact to the extent considered insulting among Anglo Americans (Curt, 1984). Hugging as a form of greeting is common among friends and family. Women of the same age and social status will kiss on the cheek and men shake hands firmly and beat each other on the back. Required distance between people is not maintained or expected. Touching is used spontaneously during a conversation to emphasize a point or share an emotion (Dodd, Nelson, & Peralez, 1988).

African American

Similar to their verbal communication patterns, African Americans are direct and unreserved in nonverbal communication styles. They are forthright and may use physical gestures to enhance the content of verbal communication. They participate actively and may react with nonverbal responses to the comments of others. Eye contact, however, is sometimes avoided out of respect.

Asian American

Like verbal communication, nonverbal actions among Asian Americans are governed by customs of deference, respect, and formality. Eye contact, especially with older people, is avoided during conversations. In some Asian cultures, people tend to stand further apart during a conversation, especially with those whose status demands respect. A smile may signify a range of emotions such as happiness or sorrow, agreement or disagreement, or understanding or lack of understanding (Morrow, 1987). Asians do not like to be touched by unfamiliar people. Display of physical familiarity with older or high status individuals is particularly offensive. Pointing at someone is considered rude; instead a gesture with the palm of the hand facing down is used to recognize someone (Loridas, 1988). Traditionally, heterosexual display of affection is forbidden (Bennett, 1990). It is, however, not uncommon to see males walking holding hands with each other and females with other females. This does not signify a homosexual relationship.

Native American

Native Americans prefer a gentle handshake to an overly firm one. Because of slow speech patterns, periods of silence are acceptable. Use of a variety of eye movements, gestures, and body language for communication is preferred to excessively verbal modes.

TABLE 6-3 • Examples of Misconceptions During Communication with School Personnel

Misconceptions	Cultural Explanations
Parents are passive	May require time to consider and discuss issues
Do not respond during discussion	Verbal (Yes, um-hmm) or nonverbal (nodding) responses may not be part of culture
Lack interest or are preoccupied	May not make eye contact due to respect for authority
Do not ask questions	Sign of respect for school decision making process
Passively accept suggestions, do not disagree or give personal opinion	Hesitate to practice personal rights
Show discomfort when complimented	Avoid attention to self
Appear uncomfortable when greeted	Touching may be unacceptable

Barriers to Communication

Verbal and nonverbal communications styles which differ from those prevalent in the dominant culture may create barriers when culturally diverse people meet (See Table 6-3). Ignorance, lack of acceptance, or lack of sensitivity about different forms of communication are common reasons for barriers. Ignorant teachers assume all communication is governed by the same verbal and nonverbal patterns and standards. This may result in covert or overt oppressive attitudes when dealing with culturally diverse families of students with disabilities. The outcome is misunderstanding that damages and/or impedes the development of positive relationships. Barriers may result from differences in language, styles of communication, and variations in the symbolism of nonverbal communication.

Interpreters are used to bridging the language barrier. Despite this, several educational concepts such as learning disabilities, teaching strategies, and evaluation techniques challenge accurate translation and explanation (Marion, 1980). These problems are magnified during interactions with newly arrived Americans who may be illiterate and unable to comprehend the standard form of language used by the interpreter. Schools may also be confronted by languages that have no written form (Rueda & Prieto, 1979).

Other communication barriers are an outcome of differences in communication styles. For example, Anglo-American culture encourages expression of personal views and concerns during a discussion. Asian parents, who may be used to careful reflection and analysis, may feel frustrated by the lack of opportunity to present their opinion during a spontaneous, fast-paced meeting. Presenting views by interrupting others may be considered impolite; consequently, some parents may prefer to remain silent. Another barrier results from the Anglo-American need for feedback during conversation in the form of "Ok, alright, I understand." Absence of signals which convey receptivity or acknowledgement make most speakers uncomfortable. Their immediate reaction is to fill the silence by talking more quickly or with fewer pauses. Accelerated speech limits the gaps that many parents require for silent consideration and interjection. Anglo-American teachers may not recognize that feedback takes a different form in some cultures. For example, Japanese parents may make frequent sounds such as "mm mmm" accompanied by head nodding to show they are listening. This may be interpreted as a signal to hurry up and finish. Such obstacles to active participation may discourage attempts at discourse and create a breakdown in communication.

Differences in cultural nonverbal communication patterns, described previously, provide several sources of possible barriers because they are often contradictory to popular nonverbal language usage. A clear example is the use of eye contact during a conversation. Anglo Americans expect and encourage eye contact during a conversation. They feel uncomfortable if the conversational partner does not look them in the face while talking. Poor eye contact may be interpreted as lack of interest, flighty attention, or preoccupation on the part of the listener. A breakdown in communication may occur as a result of this common misconception. Cultural implications of such behavior must be recognized and respected.

Overcoming Communication Barriers

Special education teachers and other professionals must recognize the cultural value of diversity in communication and refrain from instantaneous judgments regarding the merit of a particular communication style. To establish meaningful communication, teachers must initially come to terms with their personal biases. They must go beyond the tendency to attribute a superior or inferior status to particular ways of communication. Guidelines, including tips for overcoming verbal and nonverbal communication impediments and suggestions for effective use of an interpreter, are described below.

Tips for Overcoming Verbal and Nonverbal Barriers
The following suggestions may help teachers in creating an environment of openness and mutual respect.

1. Take care to address parents as "Mr." or "Mrs." This may be more familiar and acceptable than use of "Ms." or an informal use of first name. Formality and respect are essential especially, with older members of the family.
2. Make an attempt to learn and use words and phrases in the family's native language. This conveys interest, preparation, and acceptance on your part and may serve as an ice breaker. For example, in Spanish buenos dias means good day and adios is good-bye. Such attempts must not exceed boundaries of genuine interest. Smith (1981) warns against going too far, stating that African Americans often resent Anglo professionals who try to use black slang or mannerisms.
3. Never use condescending statements deriving from generalizations such as, "I have a good friend who is an Indian," "Do you Japanese believe in God?" or "Where did you learn to speak such good English?"

4. Do not automatically slow down or simplify speech when you hear an unfamiliar accent. Lack of familiarity with the dominant language or imperfect fluency does not imply inferiority or limited comprehension and awareness (Kumabe, Nishida, and Hepworth, 1985). Remember that the most eloquent English speakers of a multicultural origin are those who are fluent in their own language.

5. Allow longer time between comments and provide frequent encouragement for questions and reactions. Do not expect an immediate response to a question. If one is not forthcoming, the common assumption is that the person has no answer, does not care, or is upset. Avoid filling silent time with more language even though silence may be uncomfortable to you. Remember that second language speakers may require more time to comprehend and generate meaningful answers.

6. Culturally diverse parents require careful explanation of the purpose and need of evaluative and educational procedures related to their child who has a disability. Categorical labels, placement options, curricular objectives, and numerous other concepts must be meaningfully communicated. Communication replete with jargon and confusion delivered in a patronizing manner is extremely counterproductive. Find out exactly what was unclear and offer clarification and/or elaboration using different words. It does not help to repeat information louder or faster.

7. Be aware that some Asian or Hispanic parents will not willingly express feelings to someone outside their family. Initial meetings may be extremely formal and reserved, and this pattern may persist over a period of time. Provide as much encouragement to develop parental trust in your intentions regarding the well being of their child. Relatedly, do not take lightly any comments, questions, or suggestions made by parents because they may be the outcome of considerable thought and reflection.

8. Special attention must be given to nonverbal behavior. A parent who maintains shorter distance than "acceptable" is not conveying a negative message. Similarly, someone who does not maintain eye contact may actually be attending very carefully to everything you say. It is important to consciously watch your reactions. Remember nonverbal behaviors may be linked to cultural communication patterns and are not meant to offend you.

Effective Use of an Interpreter

Legal mandates require that conferences be conducted in the native language of parents. Selection of a translator may be critical to ensure parental participation. Besides being fluent in both languages the interpreter must be one who is familiar with curricular and educational issues. Unskilled translators may convey inaccurate information, especially because several terms and concepts in special education are extremely technical and difficult to translate. The translator must be knowledgeable about differences in values between the school and home (Blakely, 1984). Parents must feel relaxed and comfortable while discussing confidential matters through the translator. It is conceivable that interpreters may threaten unknowing parents into accepting something without complete explanations.

School personnel, therefore, must trust the translator to carry out his or her responsibilities in an ethical manner. Meeting with the interpreter prior to meeting parents may be extremely useful in explaining the purpose of the conference and in clarifying his/her role in communicating with the family. Translators must be told their role is to facilitate communication to the best of their ability, be sensitive to the needs of both parents and school, and refrain from convincing unsuspecting parents about any issue (Blakely, 1984). Recruiting and training individuals such as social workers, college students, family members, and local community members to be mediators may help schools provide parents the support they need (Correa, 1989).

Teachers must be cognizant of family situations wherein the husbands work and are familiar with the English language; however, their wives remain home and have limited exposure to the dominant culture. Although communication with the father may be easier, often mothers are the primary caretakers of children and must be involved to the maximum extent possible. Teachers must allow the father time to translate for the mother and solicit her opinion as much as possible. Failure to do so may minimize the role of maternal participation in the child's education. Often, teachers rely on their language proficient students to be mediators for facilitating communication with parents. Teachers must be warned that although parents may receive the information, they may not entirely trust their child to convey accurate content.

Some additional areas require consideration when services of an interpreter are employed. Teachers must realize that translations will necessitate a longer meeting time than may be necessary for a regular meeting. They must schedule time accordingly. Conversation that must be translated back and forth is often frustrating and a strain to a smooth flow of ideas. School personnel must not lose patience or display frustration during trying moments. Parents are probably experiencing similar frustrations. Professionals must guard against the natural inclination to sidestep and abbreviate important issues in an attempt to minimize repetition and explanation. Marion (1980) states that professionals may withhold information because of the belief that culturally diverse families are unable to grasp the complexities of the special education process. He affirms that school personnel often consider meetings with culturally diverse families a strain and actively avoid participation. Such an atmosphere discourages two-way communication and further detaches parents who may be inclined not to question authority, request clarifications, or disagree publicly. Planning and implementing cross-cultural communication is time-consuming and tedious, however, the long-term benefits are priceless (Langdon, 1988).

Sensitivity to different communication styles will help bridge the gap of cultural differences. However, there are other considerations in developing an effective partnership with multicultural families. These include a study of standards and values of different cultural groups and how they impact the education of students with disabilities. Cultural belief systems governing fundamental areas such as the family structure, child rearing and discipline, family reactions to exceptionality, and perceptions of the school's role that influence a child's schooling are described next. Conflicts between families and schools resulting from differences in standards and values on issues deriving from these areas are discussed. Strategies to resolve such conflicts are provided.

STANDARDS AND VALUES IN CULTURES

Cultures vary in the standards of acceptable behavior and values they hold sacred. Values are defined as "the ideals, the aims and ends, the ethical and aesthetic standards, and the criteria of knowledge and wisdom embodied within it, taught to and modified by each human generalization" (Valentine, 1968, p. 7). Standards and values are mirrored in the way people belonging to different cultures live their lives and conduct important traditions with the aim of maintaining common goals. Standards and values are used as measures to guide the actions, attitudes, evaluations, and justifications of people and those around them. Although people may readily adopt material and technological changes from the dominant society, value and belief systems are deeply ingrained and unlikely to change. Knowledge of diversity regarding standards and values is essential for working with multicultural families. No matter how well versed teachers may be in verbal and nonverbal communication, liaison can collapse if standards and values and their impact on beliefs and behaviors are not considered.

Recognition of values that guide the family structure, beliefs about child rearing, expectations related to male and female roles, reactions to exceptionality, and philosophy about the school's role in education is essential for working with culturally diverse families. The following section describes standards and values in relation to several aspects of family life and schooling within the four major subcultures in the United States.

Family Structure

The family has different meanings for people from different cultures. The family unit, its physical make-up, and the expectations and lifestyles of its members vary according to cultural values. Awareness of the family structure aids teachers in understanding parental concerns, attitudes, actions, and behaviors related to their child's education. Although cultural beliefs related to family structure remain intact when families immigrate to the United States, family members may be physically separated. A majority of immigrants have families in more than one country. They may feel bereft of ongoing contact and close participation with the extended family. In cases where members are waiting to be reunited with the rest of the family the experience can be very emotional and stressful. Other families may have resided in the United States for a long duration and have no ties with their country of origin. It is important to consider all these factors when we study traditional patterns of family structure within different cultures.

Hispanic

Hispanic people live in large, extended families; it is common to find several generations sharing the same household. Cooperation and solidarity are strong virtues that support this family structure. Individual needs are superseded by the needs of the larger unit and problems are solved within the confines of a closeknit unit. The Hispanic family in the United States is under economic pressures and occupies a low social status. Poverty, illiteracy, poor health, unemployment, and high birth rates are grim problems facing Hispanic families (Dieppa & Montiel, 1978).

African American

Contrary to views that the majority of African Americans live in matriarchal, low-income families, many grow up in a middle-class background. Forty percent of African-American families are headed by a single female; of these 54.6 percent live below the poverty level (Jacobs, 1986). Employment rates are lower among African Americans than among Anglo Americans (Gollnick & Chinn, 1986). Many African-American families include extended relatives who may reside together or maintain intimate contact with each other. Families have strong kinship bonds and members are a source of support and solidarity to each other (Utley & Marion, 1984).

Asian American

Like the Hispanics, Asian Americans place utmost value on the family unit and live together as a joint family. Strong regard of mutual respect, obedience to elders, and denunciation of personal fulfillment binds family members. Problems are dealt with privately by the family rather than shared with outsiders. Unlike Hispanic and African families, a majority of Asian-American families are not plagued by problems related to poverty and broken households.

Native Americans

Native-American families include all relatives. Families commonly live together or in close proximity to each other (Loridas, 1988). Cooperation, mutual respect, and positive interpersonal relationships are considered necessary for group survival. Clan members are frequently considered to be as close as relatives and participate in daily family activities.

Child Rearing and Discipline

Child rearing practices differ across cultures and strongly influence values and behaviors of children during their early formative years. These practices reflect the strongest values of a culture and are least likely to be modified (Penfield, 1988). School personnel must be aware of diversity in the upbringing of students to prevent inaccurate judgments regarding student behavior and to ensure positive interactions with families.

Hispanic American

Many families from the Hispanic culture have a relaxed attitude toward attainment of developmental milestones, self-reliance, and independence (Falicov, 1982). Parents are generally overprotective and do not encourage early development of individualism and autonomy. Child rearing differs for males and females. The son has more freedom and is expected to take care of his sisters, even if they are older. The loyal extended family including grandparents, aunts, uncles, and older siblings provide support for the child (Falicor, 1982). The male is the authority figure and the father's role is one of the provider. He is rarely involved in child rearing. The father may, however, be responsible for defining discipline guidelines for children. Respect and obedience towards authority figures is expected. Children are expected to listen quietly and look away when they are being scolded. Values of cooperation are encouraged and competitive endeavors are often punished because they convey a threat to the integrity of the unit.

African American

According to Peters (1981), child rearing priorities among African Americans have been influenced by the exigencies of the unique economic, cultural, and racial circumstances which surround them. Parents socialize their children to become self-sufficient and competent adults. Children are taught to take responsibility early and expected to be a source of help to the family. According to Smith (1981), African-American parents expect adherence to predetermined standards of behavior in the home. Violation of rules may often lead to physical punishment.

Asian American

The Asian child grows up with a strong sense of dependence (Azuma, 1986) because child rearing fosters a particularly supportive and responsive relationship with the mother. Parents expend inordinate time and sacrifice personal needs to foster the interests of their children and family at large. Consequently, parents demand unquestioning obedience from their children. Children learn moral obligation and loyalty to the family at an early age. Exceptional courtesy and deference must be shown to the elderly (Loridas, 1988). The male child is valued more than the female. Fathers are usually the authority figures and do not engage in intimate conversations with their children—a responsibility delegated to the mother. Children are expected to listen when parents speak without questioning their views. Public display of affection among parents or between parents and children is embarrassing and discouraged. According to interviews conducted by Kobayashi-Winata (1989), Japanese parents used verbal commands, reprimands, shaming or guilt induction, and explanations as primary disciplinary techniques with the children. These methods are preferred because they explain to the child why compliance is important for the group (Chan, 1986). External means of control emphasize consequences of individual actions and do not serve everyone. In addition to parents, older extended family members have the right to discipline the child.

Native American

Natural parents are usually not the sole caretakers of the child. The grandmother may be largely responsible for the upbringing of the child. Among some groups an informal adoption process results in children being raised by those not related by blood (Medicine, 1980). A clansperson may play a role of greater significance in a child's life than the biological father. Caretakers do not believe in reprimanding or scolding a child to gain compliance. Instead, a quiet and private explanation of the misbehavior and its consequences on others is sufficient to ensure a change. The goal of discipline is not simple obedience but eventual self-discipline. Not unlike Asian children, Native-American children are taught to respect cooperation and rights of others around them. They are expected to learn by observation and listening rather than asking and questioning. Individuals are judged on their actions rather than words. Children have a short childhood and assume adult responsibilities at an early age (Loridas, 1988). It is not uncommon to see them accompany parents to several places of entertainment or work. They are trained to make personal choices and decisions and to become self-reliant.

Reaction to Exceptionality

Cultural values and beliefs regarding disabilities strongly influence how a family will cope with a child who is disabled. Parental aspirations for children are culturally governed to some extent and have a bearing on their reactions to exceptionality. In some cultures, children with disabilities are considered a burden whereas in others, they are perceived as God's gift to the family and given special care and love. These attitudes determine the upbringing, education, and life goals families have for their children with disabilities. As emphasized before, generalizations based on common practices must not be attributed to all members of a particular group.

Hispanic American

Children with disabilities are rarely institutionalized because the extended family assumes the responsibility of child care. Some families may keep the child hidden at home rather than risk loss of family pride by letting others know of the child's disability. It is common to attribute the child's disability to "God's will" and seek direction from religious sources (Loridas, 1988). Values related to sex and status of the child also influence family reactions and ability to cope with disabilities. Traditional emphasis on the role of the eldest male child makes it particularly difficult for the family to deal with their first born male's disability (Gelb, 1982). The family might experience less stress if a younger female child were disabled.

African American

The practice of reliance on the family eases the demands of daily care of a child with a disability among African-American families. Another vital source of support is the church which provides families with comfort and advice during their ordeal.

These factors may account for why some African-American families react with less distress than families from other cultures.

Asian American

Views of disability are strongly influenced by cultural characteristics of "shame and pride" and notions regarding causes of exceptionality (Chan, 1986). A disability may bring overwhelming shame to the family. The family status is compromised because the child with a disability is viewed incapable of propagating the family name through economic and/or academic achievements (Morrow, 1987). Physical problems are more easily accepted than behavioral or emotional problems which are often associated with strong stigma. The cause of disability is attributed to fate or factors out of personal control. Some parents may consider the birth of a child with a disability a punishment for past sins. Whatever the cause, maintenance of emotional strength without complaints is considered an expression of dignity (Chan, 1986). Asian Americans may be reluctant to seek help for their child with a disability, preferring to manage the problems within the larger family as much as possible. Families, however, are generous while caring for children with disabilities (Gelb, 1982).

Native American

Native-American families are more inclined than any other group to integrate the child with a disability into the family without seeking external assistance (Heward & Orlansky, 1988). They may resist attempts by special education professionals to remove children to be educated in remote settings. Stewart (1977) indicates that children with disabilities are mostly accepted and taught to assume useful roles, suitable with their abilities, in the community. They are not segregated into special classrooms for students with disabilities. In most instances, the birth of a child with a disability is viewed as resulting from "prenatal choice" by the infant and the event may not solicit negative or tragic reactions (Stewart, 1977).

Perception of School's Role

Expectations regarding the role of schools in education vary. Often, perceptions are governed by the educational philosophy of the country of origin and the educational system in which parents received their schooling. Similarly, notions about interactions with school personnel are governed by past experiences and unique cultural values and beliefs.

Hispanic American

Hispanic parents are accustomed to entrusting their children to teachers who are expected to extend the role parents play at home (Penfield, 1988). Parents do not consider it appropriate to interfere with educational issues considered to be in the realm of school professionals (Grossman, 1984). Some parents may have never attended school themselves and feel inadequate when faced with school related issues. Questioning teachers or discussing their child's participation in certain activities is considered disrespectful to the teacher who is viewed as an authority in the school context. Parents have full confidence in the course of action taken on behalf of their children. Results of interviews conducted by Lynch and Stein (1987) indicated that Hispanic parents felt that teachers know what is best for their child and 97 percent rated professionals working with their children as effective.

African American

Although experiences and values vary within the African-American community, they have generally had the common experience of living "in a unique but mundane extreme environment of subtle-to-overt racism" (Peters, 1981, p. 220). These experiences play a role in parental perception of the school's role in education. Parents who have children with disabilities may be particularly frustrated with schools that have promoted overrepresentation of African-American children in classes for the mentally retarded. They may express anger and confusion over labeling based on behaviors that are culturally different and not a reflection of particular disabilities (Marion, 1980).

Asian American

Asian-American families hold views similar to those of Hispanic parents and attribute educational decision making to the schools. School personnel are treated with respect and their advice is followed. This regard is evident from the fact that Asian parents rarely address teachers in an informal manner. They always use the proper title, often referring to them as "Teacher". Children are raised to hold educators in high esteem and develop unquestioning respect for their authority. Education is considered immensely valuable and essential for upward mobility and success (Loridas, 1988). Children are encouraged to strive hard and excel in school. Schools are expected to provide activities primarily geared towards teaching academic skills. Early education which emphasizes play and learning through creative experiences may be considered frivolous compared to the wealth of information that must be acquired from books (Loridas, 1988). Parents may expect teachers to give regular homework to their children.

Native American

Native-American parents also maintain respectful silence during a meeting, allowing educators to make important decisions (Bryde, 1971). Questioning is not a form of verbal interaction in communication patterns of Native Americans. Schooling is considered essential for the acquisition of knowledge; however, excelling for personal fame is considered disgraceful.

Culturally governed belief systems will influence how children are raised and the expectations parents have for the future. These values will influence all communications and interactions that parents have with school personnel. Conflicts may arise when standards and values clash. Teachers and other professionals must be aware of cultural differences in values and beliefs to best serve their multicultural students. The following section provides methods of anticipating and identifying conflicts in standards and values. Several suggestions for overcoming and resolving conflicts are also presented.

CONFLICTS WITH THE DOMINANT CULTURE

Cultural diversity in standards and values that influence family life, child rearing practices, and perceptions of school's functions may create conflict when expectations governed by dominant cultural values guide multicultural contacts. Conflicts may arise between the expectations special education teachers and other school professionals have for students and their families and in the role parents are willing to assume in their child's education.

Conflicts may be manifested in overt and/or covert ways. Parents may openly oppose suggestions offered by the special education teacher and argue about the relevance of particular programs and services for their child. Conversely, parents may express their discomfort by terminating communication with the school and boycotting meetings. Or, parents may attend meetings but maintain a passive role. Such situations are frustrating and anxiety provoking for both teachers and parents. Teachers get discouraged when their persistent attempts at including parents are rejected. At the same time, parents feel schools are unresponsive to the unique needs of nonmainstreamed cultures and do not respect their ethnic identities (Berger, 1987). Comer (1986) states that many schools are simply reluctant to involve parents representing minority cultures. Conflicts resulting from lack of awareness of differences in values and standards must be resolved to amend existing conditions and pave the way for positive exchange between school and home.

Information about cultural standards and values provides teachers a resource for anticipating conflict when working with multicultural families. Areas of potential conflict must be investigated to confirm and identify the nature of the conflict. Accurate identification of disparate values is essential prior to planning strategies for preventing and/or resolving conflicts in an amicable manner. Finally, the relationship between teachers and parents must be constantly monitored to ensure continued success in working with multicultural families of children with disabilities.

Anticipating Conflict

Awareness and anticipation of conflict can be extremely significant in understanding, restructuring, and positively manipulating the sequence of events during communication with parents. A comparative study of Anglo-American standards and values and values of other cultural groups can provide special education teachers valuable insights regarding potential sources of conflict. A review of culture specific values and beliefs outlined above reveal substantial deviation from mainstreamed views in almost all areas of educational importance.

Generally, most cultural groups tend to emphasize an extended family structure that is different from the dominant society's nuclear family. Among Anglo Americans, individual rights supersede the need of the group and relationships with relatives are not as important as the needs of immediate family members. Among Asian and Hispanics, extended family members play the primary role in dealing with personal problems and parents may not be willing to discuss their child's problem with school personnel. Relatedly, parents may have responsibilities (as towards other family members) that take away from the time they can devote to their child's problem. It is also possible that, due to clearly defined authority roles, the mother may not feel comfortable voicing her opinion or discussing personal issues without having consulted her husband and older members of the family.

Conflicts may also surface during discussions related to student behavior in the classroom. Special education teachers may expect their students to actively participate in the classroom by asking questions, engaging in inquiry and debate, demonstrating creativity and problem solving, taking part in competitive games, and displaying independence in daily work. Parents, when confronted by teachers who believe that failure to meet these expectations is a shortcoming, may feel frustrated or oppose what they perceive as unfavorable qualities. Similarly, parents who are unfamiliar with disciplinary techniques commonly used in schools may not be willing to implement them at home. Schools must anticipate these conflicts and be prepared to deal with them on an individual basis.

Schools can also expect conflicts resulting from differences in beliefs about the role school personnel play in education of children. Anglo-American teachers expect parents to display interest in their child's progress by actively receiving and giving feedback and assuming responsibility for their child's educational program. The special education system grants parents the right to question and, if required, contest in court, decisions made by school authorities. This is in conflict with the view that teachers are authority figures who must determine and tell parents. This conflict makes it difficult for many multicultural parents to participate in a special education program that requires decision making and parental consent at almost every stage of the process.

Special education personnel face other challenges with regard to conflicting values. Conflict may result from the training provided to special education teachers who are typically presented with a stage theory (including shock, denial, anger, sadness, resignation, and acceptance) to understand the psychological impact of raising a child with a disability. This model, derived exclusively from research with white middle class families, cannot be applied universally to culturally different families (Gelb, 1982). Another conflict arises when multicultural parents have to comprehend a highly legalized and structured special education system. Special education personnel are puzzled by resistance to what they discern as a beneficial, revolutionary, and hard-fought system of providing for the rights of the child with a disability. It is not uncommon to hear of resistant parents who refuse to accept the child's disability and prefer to absorb the problem within the family network. They do not want to face the shame of publicly acknowledging a humiliating label for their child. Also, many new immigrant families fear the unknown consequences of legal processes and bureaucratic scrutiny in a strange land. Working within the dictates of cultural diversity in providing education for students with disabilities will impact the success of parental involvement.

Identifying Existing Conflict

Special education teachers and other school professionals must systematically investigate conflicts that interfere during communication with culturally diverse families. Understanding the backgrounds different families bring with them to the school setting is essential to achieving maximal educational outcomes for students with disabilities. Schools are encouraged to develop procedures that permit all personnel working with culturally diverse families to acquire information about beliefs and preferences of individual families.

Schools can gather information about cultural beliefs, values, habits, and customs through questionnaires, interviews, and/or telephone surveys. Questionnaires may be sent home with students or distributed during a school meeting. Commercially developed and validated assessment instruments specific to multicultural families are rare. One device that may be useful is the family needs survey (Bailey & Simeonsson, 1988). This instrument assesses a family's need for information, support in communicating their child's problems to others, community services, and sources of financial assistance.

Parent interviews are particularly useful because the interviewer can modify questions based on parent responses and/or nonverbal cues. Interviews may be conducted by teachers, teacher aides, volunteers, social workers, and school-community liaisons. Interviewers must have expertise in conducting interviews or be trained in effective communication with culturally diverse families. For example, when faced with differences in values, beliefs, and priorities it is imperative that interviewers remain nonjudgmental and do not display adverse emotions either verbally or nonverbally. Also, they must be able to convey openness and a genuine interest in helping the family (Hanson & Lynch, 1989). Language barriers must be considered and school personnel must be aware that interpreters may be needed. Telephone surveys are an alternative to interviews but are less desirable than the latter due to lack of personal contact. However, many schools may have to depend on telephone communication due to economic and personnel constraints. The purpose and intent of any survey must be clearly explained to parents to optimize response rate and quality. The content of survey instruments can be derived from areas of anticipated conflicts and must cover all domains essential to furnish details to teachers and other personnel. Examples of questions that may be used to identify conflict are provided in Box 6-1.

We encourage teachers to modify, and/or delete questions from the list provided in Box 6-1 to suit their needs. When developing new questions, teachers must keep the format and nature of questions as nonthreatening as possible. All questions must be carefully analyzed with respect to applicability. Inclusion of questions that yield responses of no practical utility to either effective classroom practice or communication with the parents must be avoided. Appropriateness of the content may be determined by requesting other teachers to review the questions or by seeking assistance from community experts and parents who may serve on the school advisory board.

BOX 6-1 • Questions to Help School Professionals Identify Cultural Practices that May Create Conflict in Parent-Teacher Communication

1. How long has the family lived in this country?
2. Does the family maintain regular contact with the homeland?
3. How many family members reside together?
4. What is their relationship with one another?
5. What is the primary language spoken at home?
6. What language is spoken between children and adults?
7. What language do children use with each other?
8. How much time do parents and other family members spend with the student?
9. What is the nature and substance of this contact?
10. What are some social and leisure time activities in which the family participates?
11. Would the parents like to bring certain family members to school meetings?
12. What are the most important family rules?
13. What are the primary methods of discipline?
14. How does the student react to disciplinary techniques?
15. Is the student praised often? How? By whom?
16. How is the student corrected or criticized? By whom?
17. How is the student expected to behave toward older family members?
18. How is the student expected to behave toward teachers?
19. What emotions are expressed openly?
20. What emotions are never displayed?
21. What messages are communicated to children nonverbally?
22. What are the student's responsibilities at home?
23. In what specific areas does the student experience difficulty at home?
24. What are parent's educational expectations for their child?
25. How do different family members react toward the student's disability?
26. What are some future goals parents have for their child?
27. Are there external agencies or people who help the family in times of need?
28. What are the areas in which you need help from school personnel?
29. What expectations do you have from the classroom teacher?

Strategies for Resolving Conflict

Conflicting standards and values create barriers when teachers view multicultural families as inferior or poorly informed. Teachers have the obligation to empower culturally diverse families by providing them with skills and resources to deal with the school system. At the same time teachers must engage in introspection to assess personal attitudes and beliefs related to cultural differences. Probing subjective misconceptions may encourage teachers to overcome and/or conceal their reactions during encounters with culturally diverse families. Suggestions for resolving conflict are provided below.

One area of conflict is related to parental participation. To encourage parental involvement, it may be necessary to invite the extended family and other significant people to school meetings. In addition, teachers may have to alter the typical practice of interacting only with the mother because of the primary role of the father in decision making. Mothers must be allowed time to discuss important issues with their spouses and other family members.

School meetings may sometimes be the forum of parental anger, skepticism, suspicion, or distrust. Past discrimination and substandard treatment may be the cause of such reactions (Turnbull & Turnbull, 1990). This may be especially true of African-American and Hispanic families whose children have traditionally been placed in a lower track or special education classes (Reschly, 1988). Realization of historical practices must guide professionals in building a relationship of sincere trust and commitment to education. Special education teachers must assure that each student was treated fairly and assessment was conducted in a nonbiased fashion. Being an advocate for the family by conveying realistic and factual information will go a long way in establishing credence for the role of educator.

Parents may also need detailed explanations about the services recommended for their child. The necessity of sports, creative activities, and membership in clubs must be explained in the context of the total development of the child. Once parents realize the worth of various school activities they may not object to what they previously perceived as nonacademic and nonfunctional engagements. Exposing multicultural families to the special education process by arranging classroom visits and opportunities to see first hand the beneficial services provided to students with disabilities is recommended. Teachers may find that including other parents from similar cultural backgrounds or securing help from local community cultural groups and leaders may increase the comfort and confidence with which parents interact.

Conflicts regarding expectations from students must be interpreted within a cultural context. Parental unresponsiveness to particular learning and behavioral techniques must not be viewed as resistance or rejection of the special education system. Teachers must clarify their expectations regarding student performance in the classroom. Patient explanations accompanied by realistic accommodations to cultural standards are likely to result in parental acceptance. We realize that prompt and efficient action may have to be delayed in lieu of parental agreement. However, establishment of common grounds is extremely important to minimize the confusion often experienced by students who may be confronted by different expectations at home and school. Parents often experience similar dilemmas and struggle to resolve personal conflict about what values to model for their child when they realize their standards are often in conflict with the Anglo culture. They need reassurance from teachers who can empathize with their emotional discord, are willing to listen and incorporate their beliefs, and do not reflect their ways as inferior and unacceptable.

The process of encouraging parental participation must be well planned and organized. Throughout the process, the importance of parental input in the school's ability to assist the student must be emphasized. Parents must be made to feel comfortable when they express their opinion. They may require extra reinforcement to corroborate the worth of their participation. They must be convinced that teachers listen and act on their suggestion. Once this is done they will be diligent in the assistance they offer the school. At the same time, initial hesitation must be honored and not brushed off as a sign of disinterest. Extreme sensitivity to feelings of family pride, especially among Asian Americans, must be practiced. Teachers must proceed slowly by investing initial time in building rapport and trust and then cautiously explore personal matters. Direct probes regarding the student's problem may result in a dead end. Furthermore, keeping in mind the strong family support existing in several cultural groups, it may be futile to offer services such as counseling for emotional support. In fact, many families may view this as an encroachment and an insult to their psychological unity. Families may require other important information such as where to obtain necessary resources and equipment for their child, how to obtain a physician, how to protect their rights, and so on. Educators have a powerful position because of the respect attributed to their role by multicultural families. They can take advantage of this worth by empowering parents to actively participate in decision making.

Monitoring to Ensure Cultural Integrity

Follow-up procedures are necessary to assess the outcome of any endeavor. Monitoring is an essential component in the development and implementation of innovative techniques related to parental involvement. Parents and other family members must be asked to elaborate their experiences resulting from contacts with school personnel. Parental feedback can offer valuable insights regarding special efforts made by the school toward resolving conflicts.

Monitoring the outcome of parent-teacher interaction can be done through written or verbal feedback from parents. Schools can utilize different strategies to obtain written feedback. Evaluation sheets may be given to parents at the termination of every formal contact to obtain feedback on key areas. Or, a questionnaire may be mailed at the end of a term or semester.

Due to language and emotional barriers, written feedback may not be the best mode for monitoring school success in overcoming cultural impediments. As an alternative, trained people could meet with individual families or invite a small number of families to hold discussion groups. For this purpose, services of the school social worker, counselor, volunteers, or interpreters may be employed. Another alternative may be monthly meetings with all multicultural families for the specific purpose of monitoring school-home relationships. In particularly sensitive situations, home visits are recommended. Box 6-2 provides a list of questions that may be included on feedback questionnaires and used during group or personal interviews.

Finally, teachers can evaluate their performance after a meeting to ensure they practiced effective communication techniques. Box 6-3 provides a list of questions teachers can ask themselves. Self-assessment may provide valuable insights for self-modification and improvement.

Regular and ongoing evaluation is essential to ensure that special education teachers and other school personnel are following correct practices and that families are being served in accordance with their needs. Continuous monitoring also provides immediate warning of any breakdown in communication. Prompt action to resolve infractions can prevent long-lasting and irreversible damage due to ignorance of problems.

We have seen how differences in standards and values can create conflict between school personnel and families. Awareness and remediation of these differences can smooth conflicts and engage every student and his/her family in a positive educational experience. Information about family standards and values must be gathered systematically and regular evaluation must be conducted to monitor relationships with families. These data assist teachers in developing, implementing, and modifying strategies for resolving conflicts suitable to the needs of specific families. However, several general guidelines for promoting interaction

---

BOX 6-2 • Questions to Obtain Parental Feedback on School-Home Communication

1. Which method of communication do you prefer? School visits, home visits, telephone contacts, or written contact.
2. What information provided by school personnel was most beneficial to you?
3. What information did you consider irrelevant or a waste of time?
4. Would you like more in-depth information in any area(s)?
5. Was information presented in a clear and unambiguous manner?
6. Can you identify specific areas that were unclear?
7. Can you pinpoint reasons for lack of clarity?
8. Do you have any suggestions to help us communicate the information clearly?
9. Do you think school personnel were receptive to your comments?
10. Were you able to voice all questions, concerns, and suggestions that you wanted to? If not, what was the reason?
11. Were you satisfied by the overall communication? Why or why not?
12. Do you have any suggestions for improving existing communication?

BOX 6-3 • Questions for Teachers to Self-Evaluate Their Communication Skills with Culturally Diverse Parents

1. Did I address the parents appropriately?
2. Did I take the time to explain necessary information clearly?
3. Did I try to skip over or avoid discussing issues that required extensive explanations?
4. Was I sensitive to cultural differences in communication style?
5. Did I accommodate parents who appeared to require extra time during a conversation?
6. Did I repeat information when necessary?
7. Was I condescending in any way?
8. Did I stress the importance of parental suggestions in their child's education?
9. Did I convey interest in parental contributions?
10. Did the parents appear to be comfortable and communicative? If not, can I identify specific reasons for nonparticipation?
11. Overall, did I communicate satisfactorily?
12. What are some areas in which I need improvement?

---

with multicultural families can be very useful to teachers. These guidelines are described in the next section. Teachers who initiate the activities described below will be taking a positive first step in cultivating good relationships with families of their multicultural students.

FACILITATING AN EFFECTIVE PARTNERSHIP

The need for specific and systematic attempts for multicultural involvement must be impressed upon teachers so that all parents feel included in their children's education. Several suggestions for teachers are listed below. We believe these tips will provide teachers with a foundation that will assist them in accommodating and cultivating cultural diversity.

Suggestions for Teachers

1. Write down personal prejudices and negative attitudes related to multicultural practices. Make sure you do not convey attitudes that reflect judgments based on personal values. Enter every interaction with a positive attitude and a realization that you can learn from all people you meet.
2. Convey your interest in different cultures by displaying artifacts symbolizing various aspects of their life. Remember to project realistic and true elements while minimizing stereotypes.
3. Communicate your openness and willingness to work with all parents by hanging pictures and posters of students from different countries. A simple

welcome sign in different languages can convey a lot. Hallways and libraries decorated with works by famous people from different cultures transmit respect and knowledge of cultures by the school community (Gelb, 1982).

4. Be an advocate for the multicultural family. Listen carefully to their problems and investigate ways to overcome their frustrations by creating access to services (Turnbull & Turnbull, 1990).

5. Involve community cultural groups and leaders. Invite them to the school and classrooms for presentations and elicit their suggestions in working with multicultural families. Enlist the help of retired teachers, church members, and other volunteers who may informally communicate information to families.

6. Take an active interest in community activities directed towards building cultural awareness and understanding. Cultural enlightenment will enable you to respond with greater sensitivity to all families.

7. Empower parents with information about traditional school values and practices so they may alleviate both their own and their children's anxieties when they enter school.

8. Organize an informal meeting with parents from different cultural backgrounds. This may provide an excellent channel for acquiring and distributing information which is ordinarily not part of a formal agenda. Parents will get an opportunity to exchange personal experiences and receive tips from each other. A model program that does this is Project TOT (Training of Trainers) described by Ruiz, 1988. In this project, parents who are knowledgeable about special education services participate in small group seminars to educate other families.

9. Invite parents to a cultural day and ask them to share a cultural activity with students and other parents. Cultural dress and food may be required to promote interest and learning.

Teachers who project sensitivity to cultural differences will be able to create the atmosphere of mutual trust and respect. However, the task of building a partnership with multicultural families goes beyond teacher conducted activities. The educational system, the legal system, and the school system of this country must be mobilized to enhance inclusion of multicultural families. Recommendations that provide directions towards these goals are discussed below.

RECOMMENDATIONS FOR THE FUTURE

The entire educational system of the United States must start taking steps to ensure preparation among personnel who will work directly and indirectly with multicultural families. Educational laws must reflect the needs of a growing multicultural population, colleges must build their resources to provide adequate training, and schools must implement programs that reflect cultural awareness and enlightenment.

The U.S. Department of Education must increase its efforts to support research and training efforts that focus on developing effective multicultural educational programs at the school and college level. Similarly, monetary incentives must be provided to model programs that provide training in cross-cultural interactions to educators.

Collaboration across national special education agencies and agencies supporting multicultural affairs can provide an effective link between the two disciplines. Special education resource centers governed by the state and local districts must be equipped with materials and information to assist teachers in working with culturally diverse families. Resource centers must also make available a listing of community experts who may be recruited to assist teachers and families.

Preservice and inservice training on multiculturalism must be provided in schools and universities. This is of immediate importance in areas populated by large numbers of multicultural families. Future administrators, educators, and other school personnel well versed in multicultural issues must be prepared by universities. Current teacher training programs must include sensitivity to the needs of the culturally diverse student who is disabled and his/her family (Fradd, Weismantel, Correa, and Algozzine, 1988).

Schools can develop committees who are charged with the task of planning strategies to remove barriers created by cultural differences. Families of students with disabilities and community leaders must be invited to join these teams. Schools can organize and plan activities to change attitudes and create acceptance of differences. Public occasions that include multicultural students with disabilities can be arranged in collaboration with community leaders. Such activities will make students and their families visible and provide everyone an opportunity to learn from one another. It will offer an informal avenue to observe and gather aspects of another culture which may be difficult to comprehend without the opportunity to intermingle with diverse people.

Systematic efforts must be directed at recruitment and retention of culturally diverse special education professionals in our schools. The need for culturally diverse personnel to bridge the cultural gap within the school system has been stressed by researchers (Preston et al., 1984). The current declining trend in the percentage of minority teachers projects to only 5 percent minority teachers at the turn of the century. This is much less than the 12.5 percent minority teachers in 1990 (Gay, 1989).

Schools must develop parent training programs that provide information about the special education system and parental rights. Grant applications may be developed to support such programs. Parents may be recruited to serve as advisory members and support providers for other multicultural families. Furthermore, training packages including information about special education services must be developed for culturally diverse parents. Dissemination may be conducted through local agencies or through cultural groups and organizations which have direct contact with parents (Lynch & Stein, 1987).

Schools must conduct an ongoing and systematic study of needs of culturally diverse parents of students with disabilities. These data can assist in strategic planning for increasing parental involvement (Lynch & Stein, 1987).

SUMMARY

Introduction

1. The overrepresentation of culturally diverse children in the population of students with disabilities makes contact between teachers and multicultural families particularly high.

2. Differences between the Anglo-American and other cultures, in communication styles as well as in values and belief structures, may pose barriers to collaboration and interpersonal relationships.

Culture and Diversity

3. A society's culture consists of whatever it is one has to know or believe in order to operate in a manner acceptable to its members.

4. Differences in beliefs, values, and standards will reflect distinct life circumstances and must be considered in the study of pluralism.

5. Cultural pluralism respects the individuality and uniqueness of every cultural heritage.

6. School personnel must acquire competencies to bridge cultural gaps and collaborate with parents from various cultural backgrounds.

7. Researchers predict that by 1995, African, Asian, and Hispanic Americans will constitute one-third of the total U.S. population.

8. Drop-out rates, school-related problems, and disabilities are disproportionately high among multicultural students.

9. Collaboration with families of these students may successfully prevent many failures and gradually reverse the direction of current statistics.

10. Teachers have the responsibility of establishing meaningful links with parents, recognizing cultural differences, attributing equal status to all cultures, and explaining school expectations to multicultural parents.

11. Family involvement can help special education teachers and other school professionals educate the increasing number of multicultural students in special education classrooms.

12. A key to establishing good relationships with multicultural parents is effective verbal and nonverbal communication.

Communication

13. Special education teachers and other school professionals must modify their current communication techniques and/or learn novel ways of communicating with families of culturally diverse students who are disabled.

14. Teachers must be aware of cultural differences in the use of grammar, semantics, phonology, and discussion modes to prevent potential sources of misunderstanding.

15. Nonverbal communication is an essential component through which individuals express themselves during a conversation, and may convey more meaning than is expressed verbally.

16. Barriers may result from differences in language, styles of communication, and variations in the symbolism of nonverbal communication.

17. Several educational concepts such as learning disabilities, teaching strategies, and evaluation techniques challenge accurate translation and explanation.

18. To help overcome barriers, teachers should:

   a. Address parents as "Mr." or "Mrs."

   b. Refrain from using condescending statements derived from generalizations.

   c. Refrain from slowing down or simplifying speech when an unfamiliar accent is heard.

   d. Allow longer time between comments, and provide frequent encouragement for questions and reactions.

   e. Carefully explain the purpose and need of evaluative and educational procedures.

   f. Be aware that some parents will not willingly express feelings to someone outside the family.

   g. Give special attention to nonverbal behaviors.

Standards and Values in Cultures

19. Recognition of values that guide the family structure, beliefs about child rearing, expectations related to male and female roles, reactions to exceptionality, and philosophy about the school's role in education is essential for working with culturally diverse families.

20. Awareness of the family structure aids teachers in understanding parental concerns, attitudes, actions, and behaviors related to their child's education.

21. School personnel must be aware of diversity in the upbringing of students to prevent inaccurate judgments regarding student behavior and to ensure positive interactions with families.

22. Cultural values and beliefs regarding disabilities strongly influence how a family will cope with a child who is disabled.

23. Notions about interactions with school personnel are governed by past experiences and unique cultural values and beliefs.

Conflicts with the Dominant Culture

24. Conflicts resulting from lack of awareness of differences in values and standards must be resolved to amend existing conditions and pave the way for positive exchange between school and home.

25. Most cultural groups tend to emphasize an extended family structure that is different from the dominant society's nuclear family.

26. Parents and teachers may not be in agreement on what constitutes appropriate classroom behavior, the role of parents in education, and the role of school personnel in education.

27. Understanding the backgrounds different families bring with them to the school setting is essential to achieving maximum education outcomes for students with disabilities.

28. To resolve conflict related to parental participation, it may be necessary to invite the extended family and other significant people to school meetings. Teachers should consider the primary role of the father in decision-making, and allow the mother time to discuss important issues with her spouse and other family members.

29. Educators have a powerful position because of the respect attributed to their role by multicultural families. They can take advantage of this worth by empowering parents to actively participate in decision making.

30. Monitoring is an essential component in the development and implementation of innovative techniques related to parental involvement.

31. Alternative strategies to written feedback include discussion groups, monthly meetings with all multicultural families, and home visits.

Facilitating an Effective Partnership

32. Educators should enter every interaction with a positive attitude and a realization that one can learn from all people.

Recommendations for the Future

33. The educational system, the legal system, and the school system of this country must be mobilized to enhance inclusion of multicultural families.

34. Schools should recruit and retain culturally diverse special education professionals, develop parent training programs, plan strategies to remove barriers created by cultural differences, and conduct ongoing and systematic studies of needs of culturally diverse parents of students with disabilities.

REFERENCES

Armstrong, M. (1986). *Expressions of social conventions and language features in Arabic, German, Japanese, and Korean and their importance in proficiency oriented classroom.* Dallas, TX: Paper presented at the Annual Meeting of the American Council on Teaching of Foreign Language. (ERIC Document Reproduction Service No. ED 278 270).

Azuma, H. (1986). "Why study child development in Japan?," in H. Stevenson, H. Azuma, & K. Hakuta (Eds.), *Child development and education in Japan.* New York: W. E. Freeman.

Bailey, D. B., & Simeonsson, R. J. (1988). "Home-based early intervention," in S. L. Odom & M. B. Karnes (Eds.), *Early intervention for infants and children with handicaps: An empirical base*. Baltimore: Brookes.

Bennett, C. I. (1990). *Comprehensive multicultural education: Theory and practice*. Boston, MA: Allyn and Bacon.

Berger, E. H. (1987). *Parents as partners in education: The school and home working together*. Columbus, OH: Merrill.

Blakely, M. (1984). *Americans talking. . . . Listen! How some Hmong, Kher, Lao and Vietnamese view American schools*. Eugene, OR: Lane Community College. (ERIC Document Reproduction Service No. ED 241 652).

Brower, I. C. (1983). "Counseling Vietnamese," in D. R. Atkinson, G. Morten, & D. W. Sue, *Counseling American minorities*. Dubuque, IA: William C. Brown.

Bryde, J. F. (1971). *Indian students and guidance*. Boston, MA: Houghton Mifflin.

Chan, S. (1986). "Parents of exceptional Asian children," in M. D. Kitano, & P. C. Chinn (Eds.), *Exceptional Asian and youth*. Washington, DC: ERIC Exceptional Child Education Report.

Comer, J. P. (1986). "Parent participation in the schools." *Phi Delta Kappan, 67*(6), 442–226.

Cornelius, G. (1990). "A border issue in teacher training: Respecting the diversity of children." *The Journal of Educational Issues of Language Minority Students, 7*, 111–117.

Correa, V. I. (1989). "Involving culturally diverse families in the educational process," in S. H. Fradd, & M. J. Weismantel (Eds.), *Meeting the needs of culturally and linguistically different students: A handbook for educators*. Boston, MA: College Hill Press.

Cummins, J. (1986a). "Empowering minority students: A framework for intervention." *Harvard Educational Research, 56*, 18–36.

Cummins, J. (1986b). "Psychological assessment of minority students: Out of context, out of focus, out of control?," in A. C. Willig & H. D. Greenberg (Eds.), *Bilingualism and learning disabilities: Policy and practice for teachers and administrators*. New York: American Library.

Curt, C. J. N. (1984). *Nonverbal communication in Puerto Rico*. Cambridge, MA: Lesley College, Evaluation, Dissemination, and Assessment Center.

Dieppa, I., & Montiel, M. (1978). "Hispanic families: An exploration," in M. Montiel (Ed.), *Hispanic families: Critical issues for policy and programs in human services*. Washington, DC: COSSMHO.

Dodd, J. M., Nelson, J. R., & Peralez, E. (1988). "Understanding the Hispanic students." *The Rural Educator, 10*(2), 8–13.

Dunn, L. (1987). *Bilingual Hispanic children on the U.S. mainland. A review of research on their cognitive, linguistic, and scholastic development*. Circle Pines, MN: American Guidance Service.

Falivoc, C. J. (1982). "Mexican families," in M. McGoldrick, J. K. Pearch, & J. Geordano (Eds.), *Ethnicity in family therapy*. New York: The Guilford Press.

Fradd, S. H., Weismantel, M. J., Correa, V. I., & Algozzine, B. (1988). "Developing a personnel training model for meeting the needs of handicapped and at risk language minority students." *Teacher Education and Special Education, 11*, 30–38.

Gay, G. (1989). "Ethnic minorities and educational equality," in J. A. Banks, & C. A. M. Banks (Eds.), *Multicultural education: Issues and perspectives*. Boston, MA: Allyn and Bacon.

Gelb, S. (1982). *A guide to working with minority language students in special education*. Washington, D. C.: Office of the State Superintendent of Public Instruction, Olympia Division of Instructional and Professional Service. (ERIC Document Reproduction Services No. ED 302 880).

Gollnick, D. M., & Chinn, D. C. (1986). *Multicultural education in a pluralistic society*. Columbus, OH: Merrill.

Goodenough, W. H. (1957). "Cultural anthropology and linguistics." *Georgetown University Monograph Series on Language and Linguistics, 9*, 167.

Grossman, H. (1984). *Educating Hispanic students: Cultural implications for instruction, classroom management, counseling and assessment*. Springfield, IL: Charles C. Thomas.

Hanson, M. J. & Lynch, E. E. (1989). *Early intervention: Implementing child and family services for infants and toddlers who are at-risk or disabled.* Austin, TX: Pro-Ed.

Heward, W. L., & Orlansky, M. D. (1988). *Exceptional Children.* Columbus, OH: Merrill Publishing Co.

Hillard, A. (1980). "Cultural diversity and special education." *Exceptional Children, 46,* 584–588.

Jacobs, J. E. (1986). "An overview of black America in 1985," in J. D. Williams (Ed.), *The state of black America 1984,* Washington, DC: National Urban League, Inc.

Kamp, S. H., & Chinn, P. C. (1982). *A multiethnic curriculum for special education students.* Reston, VA: Council for Exceptional Children.

Kitano, H. (1973). "Highlights of institute on language and culture: Asian component," in L. A. Bransford, L. M. Baca, & K. Lane (Eds.), *Cultural diversity and the exceptional child.* Reston, VA: Council for Exceptional Children.

Knapp, L. (1972). *Nonverbal communication in human interaction:* New York: Holt, Rinehart, & Winston, Inc.

Kobayashi-Winata, H. (1989). "Child rearing and compliance: Japanese and American families in Houston." *Journal of Cross-Cultural Psychology, 20*(4), 333–356.

Kumabe, K. T., Nishida, C., & Hepworth, D. H. (1985). *Bridging ethnocultural diversity in social work and health.* Honolulu: University of Hawaii.

Langdon, H. W. (1988). *Interpreter/translator in the school setting module.* California State Department of Education/Special Education Resource Network Cross-Cultural Unit. Sacramento, CA: California State Department of Education.

Lindholm, K. J. (1987). *Mount Miguel Spanish program report on 1985–1986 data collection.* Unpublished manuscript, Center for Language Education and Research, University of California, LA.

Longstreet, W. (1978). *Aspects of ethnicity: Understanding differences in pluralistic classrooms.* New York: Teachers College Press.

Loridas, L. (1988). *Culture in the classroom: A cultural enlightenment manual for educators.* Detroit, MI: Michigan State Department of Education, Wayne County Intermediate School District. (ERIC Document Reproduction Service No. ED 303 841).

Losen, S. M., & Losen, J. G. (1985). *The Special Education Team.* Newton, MA: Allyn & Bacon.

Lynch, E. W., & Stein, R. C. (1982). "Perspectives on parent participation in special education." *Exceptional Education Quarterly, 3,* 56–63.

Lynch, E. W., & Stein, R. C. (1987). "Parent participation by ethnicity: A comparison of Hispanic, Black, and Anglo families." *Exceptional Children, 54*(2), 105–111.

Macias, R. F. (1985). "National language profile of the Mexican origin population in the United States," in W. Conner (Ed.), *Mexican Americans in comparative perspective.* Washington, DC: Urban Institute Press.

Marion, R. L. (1980). "Communicating with parents of culturally diverse exceptional children." *Exceptional Children, 46,* 616–623.

McDonald, D. (1989). "A special report on the education of native Americans: Stuck in the horizon." *Education Week, 7*(4), 1–16.

Medicine, B. (1980). "American Indian family: Cultural change and adaptive strategies." *Journal of Ethnic Studies, 8*(4), 13–23.

Morgan, D. P. (1982). "Parental participation in the IEP process: Does it enhance appropriate education?" *Exceptional Education Quarterly, 3,* 33–40.

Morrow, R. D. (1987). "Cultural differences: Be aware." *Academic Therapy, 23*(2), 143–149.

National Coalition of Advocates for Students (1985). *Barriers to excellence: Our children at risk.* Boston, MA: Author.

1980 Census of Population, Vol. 1, Characteristics of the Population. Chapter C. Social and Economic Characteristics, Part 1, U.S. Summary. Report No. PC-80-1-C1 (Washington, DC: Bureau of the Census, U.S. Department of Commerce, December, 1983).

Oritz, A. A. (1988). "Evaluating educational contexts in which language minority students are served." *Bilingual Special Education Newsletter,* 1–3.

Penfield, J. (1989). *The Hispanic student: Questions and Answers.* Highland Park, NJ: Penfield Associates. (ERIC Document Reproduction Service No. ED 315 497).

Peters, M. F. (1981). "Parenting in black families with young children: A historical perspective," in H. P. McAdoo (Ed.), *Black families*. Beverly Hills, CA: Sage.

Preston, D., Greenwood, C. R., Hughes, V., Yuen, P., Thibadeau, S., Critchlow, W., & Harris, J. (1984). "Minority issues in special education: A principal-mediated inservice program for teachers." *Exceptional Children, 51*, 112–121.

Ramirez, B. A. (1988). "Culturally and linguistically diverse children." *Teaching Exceptional Children, 20*(4), 445–446.

Ratleff, J. E. (1989). *Instructional strategies for crosscultural students with special education needs*. Sacramento, CA: Resources in Special Education.

Reschly, D. J. (1988). "Minority MMR overrepresentation and special education reform." *Exceptional Children, 54*, 316–323.

Rueda, R., & Prieto, A. G. (1979). "Cultural pluralism-implications for teacher education." *Teacher Education and Special Education 2*, 27–32.

Ruiz, N. T. (1988). "The Optimal Learning Environment (OLE) Curriculum Guide: A resource for teachers of Spanish-speaking children in learning handicapped programs." Unpublished manuscript, University of California at Davis, Division of Education.

Salend, S. J., Michael, R. J., & Taylor, M. (1984). "Competencies necessary for instructing migrant handicapped students." *Exceptional Children, 51*, 50–55.

Santiago, I. S. (1986). "The education of Hispanics in the United States: Inadequacies of the Melting Pot Theory," in Dietmar Rothermund and John Simon (Eds.), *Education and the integration of ethnic minorities,* New York: St. Martin's Press.

Shea, T. M., & Bauer, A. M. (1985). *Parents and teacher of exceptional students: A handbook for involvement*. Boston, MA: Allyn and Bacon.

Simich-Dudgeon, C. (1987). "Involving limited-English proficient parents as tutors in their children's education." *ERIC/CLL News Bulletin, 10*, 3–4.

Smith, E. J. (1981). "Cultural and historical perspectives in counseling blacks," in D. W. Sue, (Ed.), *Counseling the culturally different: Theory and practice*. New York: John Wiley.

Stewart, J. L. (1977). "Unique problems of handicapped Native Americans," in *The White House conference on handicapped individuals*. Washington, DC: U.S. Government Printing Office.

Tizard, J., Schofield, W. N., & Hewison, J. (1982). "Collaboration between teachers and parents in assisting children's reading." *British Journal of Educational Psychology, 52*, 1–15.

Turnbull, A. P., & Turnbull, H. R. (1990). *Families, professionals, and exceptionality: A special partnership*. Columbus, OH: Merrill Publishing Co.

Turner, A. (1987). *Multicultural considerations: Working with families of developmentally disabled and high-risk children: The Black perspective*. Los Angeles, CA: Paper presented at the conference of the National Center for Clonical Infant Programs. (ERIC Document Reproduction Service No. ED 285 360).

Utley, C. A., & Marion P. (1984). *Working with black families having mentally retarded members*. Paper presented at the annual meeting of the American Association on Mental Deficiency, Minneapolis, MN.

Valentine, C. A. (1968). *Culture and poverty: Critique and counter-proposals*. Chicago, IL: University of Chicago Press.

WongFillmore, L. (1983). "The language learner as an individual: Implications of research on individual differences for the ESL teacher," in M. A. Clarrie & J. Handscombe (Eds.), *On TESOL 1982: Pacific perspectives on language learning and teaching*. Washington, DC: TESOL.

7

GROUP APPROACHES TO CONSULTATION AND ADVOCACY

Jeanne T. Amlund
The Pennsylvania State University-McKeesport

CarolAnne M. Kardash
University of Missouri-Columbia

Chapter Objectives

After completing this chapter you will be able to:

1. List the common features and distinguishing characteristics of three models for program planning and evaluation team interaction
2. Describe the potential impact of team context variables on program planning and evaluation team effectiveness
3. Discuss the advantages and disadvantages of the consensus model for team decision-making
4. Describe the two conceptual perspectives upon which models of team development are based
5. Describe and discuss the potential value of team maintenance activities
6. List the essential context and functional differences between program planning and evaluation teams and training and support groups
7. List facilitative techniques that may contribute to the effectiveness of training and support groups
8. List the distinguishing characteristics and the common features of three model group empowerment and advocacy training programs

Key Terms and Phrases

active listening
consensus decision-making
equilibrium model of team
  development
expectation state
group cohesion
intentional positioning
interdisciplinary model
multidisciplinary model
norms
participation structures
phase model of team
  development

procedures
program planning and
  evaluation team
quasi-member status
role definition
role release
sociopetal seating arrangement
status differentiation
supportive communication
  environment
training and support group
transdisciplinary model

INTRODUCTION

This chapter is about being effective in groups and facilitating the participation and effectiveness of group members. The perspective taken here is that special educators need to be able to function effectively both as group members and as facilitators of appropriate parent participation. The key role that parents may have in ensuring continuity of program services has already been established in previous chapters. The need for collaborative rather than adversarial parent-professional relationships is clear when costs, in terms of time and energy, as well as money, far outweigh any benefits for students with disabilities, the parents, or the school (see Box 7-1).

Facilitating productive parent participation requires that professionals discard unfounded notions that blame parents for the problems of their children who are disabled. Keep in mind that limited participation by parents does not necessarily reflect lack of concern for their child's welfare. Conversely, active participation by parents should not be interpreted automatically as troublemaking. An all too common parent perspective is best expressed in the following excerpt from a letter written by the parents of a disabled student to a university professor with whom they had consulted:

> *We try to discuss our concerns and share what we know about our son in our meetings with the school people but we cannot communicate with them. We think we've tried to make Jason's teacher's work a lot easier in some ways, but she sees only that we complain a lot. We would be more sympathetic if his teacher hadn't been on the attack from almost the first moment—aggressively determined to show that whatever problems Jason had were beyond her control and needed to be dealt with by us doing something*

BOX 7-1 • Local School Loses Round in Rift With Mom

Parent wins meeting on autistic son's schooling.

The mother of a local school student has won a round in her two year legal battle over her autistic son's educational program.

The Office of Special Education last week ordered the local school to hold a meeting with the mother to discuss the school's behavior management plan for her fourth grade son. But the ruling might not bring any changes in how the boy is educated.

State officials ruled that the school system denied the mother her right to be fully involved in the determination of her son's behavior management plan.

The superintendent of the district said the district will appeal. Federal law requires that school districts work with parents to write an Individualized Education Program for every special education student.

Under his current IEP, this child, age 10, spends part of every school day in a class for Educable Mentally Handicapped children.

With the backing of the local Center for Autism, the mother contends that her son is not retarded and does not belong with retarded children.

Autism does not affect intelligence said the director of the Autism Center. "This boy can pick up Fortune Magazine and read it phonetically, but he could not tell you what it means because he is not interested" the director said. "With TV Guide he'll be able to tell you more than you want to know."

The mother has contested the district's plan through a hearing process with the State Department of Elementary and Secondary Education for each of the last three years. The first hearing examiner ruled in her favor, but the district won on appeal and has won every other hearing on the IEP since then. The state education department is slated to rule on the larger case by December 14.

Federal law includes a stay-put provision, which means that the IEP cannot change while it is being appealed. At the beginning of the school year, the mother asked for a meeting to review her son's behavior management plan.

"My son is prone to spontaneously recite the television schedule in the middle of class," his mother said. The current behavior management plan calls for sending him to the back of the classroom, then to the hall and then to the principal's office if the behavior continues.

The mother said her son is prone to wander off, because autistic children have no sense of danger.

The Elementary School principal replied that meeting to review the student's behavior management provision was not possible under the stay-put provision.

But last week, the coordinator of special education ruled in favor of the mother's request, and ordered the school to hold the meeting within 30 days.

The mother has been contesting her son's Individualized Educational Program for more than two years.

The school estimated that the legal battle has cost the financially strapped district more than $15,000 for each of the past two years. The district is spending money from its reserves this year and anticipates laying off five teachers at the end of the school year.

The mother said the district could save the money and hassle of a legal fight if it would just do what she considers right. The superintendent said the district has won all the major battles, and the responsibility for the legal expenses lies with the child's mother.

Note: From *Columbia Daily Tribune,* November 28, 1990. Adapted with permission. Names of actual participants and other identifying particulars have been altered so as to maintain confidentiality.

to Jason at home. We hope you are able to help your students understand that parents don't have to be the enemy (personal communication, March 15, 1991).

The focus throughout this chapter is on groups and the interaction of individuals as group members, rather than on individual behavior, or the larger organizational context within which groups function. The chapter begins with an exploration of the variables that influence the effectiveness of *program planning and evaluation teams,* followed by discussion of the variables that influence the effectiveness of *training and support groups.* Program planning and evaluation *teams* are groups that have a specific task to accomplish or decision to make as a primary goal. These teams may be responsible for determining eligibility for service, determining effectiveness of existing programming, or evaluating potential program alternatives. In contrast, training and support *groups* are groups that have learning, growth, or development of group members as a primary goal. These groups may be focused on establishing supportive networks, providing and sharing information, or training specific skills.

Please note that we use the word *team* throughout this chapter to refer to a formal group composed of parents and professionals. Teams meet in school settings and are invested with official authority to make decisions, evaluate programs, or change educational plans for students with disabilities. On the other hand, we use the word *group* to refer to an informal group composed of parents, people with disabilities, and professionals. The goals of such groups are support, training, and advocacy. These latter groups have no formal status within the school setting, nor are they empowered with any official authority. There are important differences in the contexts within which these two types of groups function, in the roles and interaction patterns among members, and in the procedures established to achieve group goals.

PROGRAM PLANNING AND EVALUATION TEAMS

Since the passage of Public Law 94-142 in 1975, parents have been included as members of the team that is required to evaluate assessment information and to formulate placement decisions for students with disabilities. As highlighted in a previous chapter, parents, along with professionals from those disciplines appropriate to the specific student's disability, serve as members of the multidisciplinary team required by P.L. 94-142. The 1986 Amendment to P.L. 94-142 (P.L. 99-457) provides for parent participation in planning transitional services for secondary students with disabilities, and requires parent participation in team planning and management for infant and early intervention programs.

Models for Team Interaction

McGonigel and Garland (1988) in their examination of current practices identified three general models for structuring team interaction: (a) the multidisciplinary model; (b) the interdisciplinary model; and (c) the transdisciplinary model.

Multidisciplinary Model

The multidisciplinary model structures team interaction around the individual contribution of each team member, with the focus on each member's own special expertise. In theory, this perspective includes the expertise of the parent and accords equal importance to the contribution of each team member in the formulation of a cooperative program plan. In practice, focus on members as spokespersons for their areas of expertise rather than as collaborative team members often results in minimal parent involvement in the program planning process. Recommended interventions and responsibility for implementation and follow-up may have a disciplinary focus, resulting in independent pursuit of specific goals rather than collaborative effort and mutual commitment (see Figure 7-1).

Interdisciplinary Model

The interdisciplinary model, like the multidisciplinary model, structures team interaction around the individual contribution of each team member, but team members focus on communicating their data and integrating the data contributed by other team members. This perspective uses formal participatory structures to specifically solicit contributions from all team members including parents, and accords time as well as equal importance to the contribution of each team member. One team member is designated as responsible for overall implementation of the team plan and for maintenance of communication with other team members as needed (see Figure 7-2).

Transdisciplinary Model

The transdisciplinary model, like the two previous models, structures team interaction around individual contributions of team members. Team members in the

Multidisciplinary Model

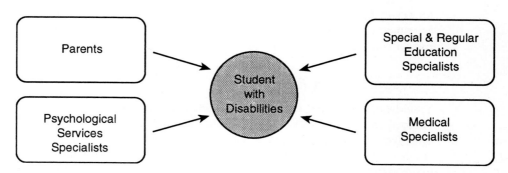

FIGURE 7-1 • Structure of Team Member Interaction from the Perspective of the Multidisciplinary Model

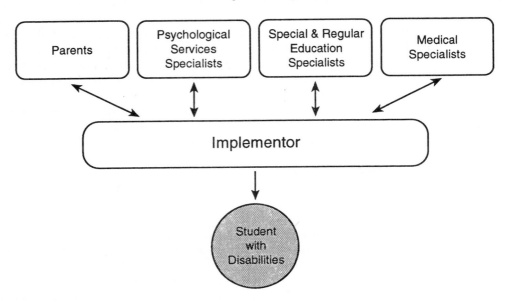

FIGURE 7-2 • **Structure of Team Member Interaction from the Perspective of the Interdisciplinary Model**

transdisciplinary model, however, are responsible for teaching other team members the essentials of their disciplines and for learning the essential terminology and basic interventions of other disciplines represented on the team. This adds a participant development component to the team function. An additional component in the transdisciplinary model is the use of what has been termed *role release,* which refers to the sharing of roles and responsibilities among team members. Direct responsibility for implementation of an intervention is assigned to a facilitator selected by the team (see Figure 7-3). The transdisciplinary model has evolved specifically in conjunction with infant intervention programs where parent participation is a central concern (Landerholm, 1990).

Assessing Team Functioning

Ysseldyke, Algozzine, and Mitchell (1982) conducted an observational analysis of videotapes of 34 special education team meetings to determine the extent to which effective team practices were used. On the basis of their analysis they concluded: "Important procedures simply do not occur, and there is little effort to encourage all team members to participate" (Ysseldyke et al., 1982, p. 312). The four factors identified by Ysseldyke et al. (p. 312) as important for facilitating team effectiveness were: (a) *consensus decision-making* (that is, ensuring that all team members

Transdisciplinary Model

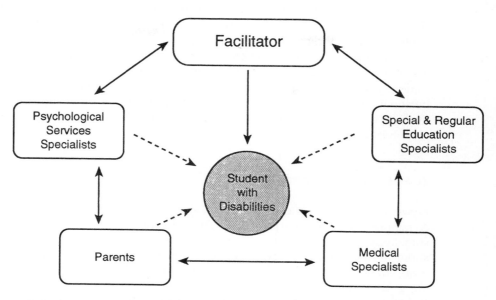

FIGURE 7-3 • **Structure of Team Member Interaction from the Perspective of the Transdisciplinary Model**

understand the decision to be made and contribute to the decision-making process); (b) *clarity of goals* (that is, ensuring that the goals to be attained and the procedures for measuring progress toward goal attainment are understood by all team members); (c) *structured separation of activities* (that is, ensuring that the decision-making process proceeds in a systematic and orderly fashion); and (d) *nonspecialized participation* by team members (that is, ensuring that all team members engage in the decision-making process without regard to role or specialty).

The factors identified by Ysseldyke et al. are similar to those measured by Glaser and Glaser's (1985) *Team Effectiveness Profile* (TEP). The purpose of the TEP is to enable teams to improve their task performance and work satisfaction by identifying obstacles that can hinder team effectiveness. The five TEP factors are: (a) *team mission, planning, and goalsetting* that includes clear statements of purpose; (b) *organization* that specifies team members' roles, relationships, and responsibilities; (c) *operating processes* that include procedures for guiding problem solving, decision-making, conflict management, and meeting format and quality; (d) *interpersonal relationships* that include procedures for facilitating trust and interaction among all team members; and (e) *intergroup relations* that focus on identification of factors that facilitate cooperation with other teams.

More recently, Huszczo (1990) identified seven components of successful teams. Five of these components are markedly similar to those identified by Glaser and Glaser (1985). The two additional components added by Huszczo were: (a) *talent* (Do team members possess the skills necessary to accomplish team objectives, and are they willing to lend their skills to team goals?); and (b) *reinforcement* (Do team members openly acknowledge and appreciate each others' efforts and contributions to the team?).

It is clear that considerable consensus exists among researchers and practitioners interested in team and organizational behavior in business and nonbusiness settings regarding the importance of goals, structure, procedures, roles, and interpersonal patterns of interaction. Identifying problems in team functioning is relatively easy given this consensus. However, methods for promoting more efficient team functioning remain more elusive.

Team Context Variables

Team and Individual Goals

A feature common to the many definitions of a team is that members share something that defines the existence of the team. The most familiar definition stipulates the sharing of a common goal or motivation (Fisher & Ellis, 1990). Setting clear, immediate goals and restating long-range team goals at each team meeting are goal clarifying behaviors associated with effective team functioning.

In many cases, teams fail to set clear goals at the beginning of their meetings, despite the importance of this activity to effective team functioning. For example, Ysseldyke et al. (1982) reported that explicit statements of the purpose of the meeting occurred in only 35 percent of the 34 special education placement team meetings they observed. Moreover, statements regarding the decisions to be made occurred in only 12 percent of the meetings they observed.

Ideally, team goals mutually agreed upon by parent and professional team members should take precedence over individual goals. When incompatibility between individual and team goals exists, a competitive orientation may arise that diminishes effort and cooperation among team members. To deal with goal conflicts, Gouran (1988) recommends "Trying to establish an acceptable degree of congruency between individual and group goals . . . [and] when there are grounds for agreement . . . exploit[ing] the opportunity to create a more cooperative . . . environment" (p. 204).

The newspaper story in Box 7-1 illustrates what can happen when there is an unresolved conflict between individual and team goals. We might speculate that both the child's mother and the professionals on the IEP team shared a mutual goal—the welfare of the child and a desire to see him succeed in school. On the other hand, individuals on the team appeared to disagree concerning how the behavior management plan specified in the IEP should be implemented. Specifically, the story suggests that the major point of contention centered on the provision that the child be sent into the hall if his inappropriate behavior continued. The mother appears to have questioned the appropriateness of this proposed action given the possibility that the child might wander off if left in the hall unsupervised. An inability to resolve these competing individual goals likely contributed heavily to the subsequent court action.

In our view, the court case may well have been averted had the team focused on finding a common ground, rather than emphasizing points of disagreement. Emphasizing disagreements often leads to a deadlock where no one is satisfied with the team decision. Based on our own past experiences as special education teachers, we believe that, in many cases, both parents and professionals come to IEP meetings with fixed ideas concerning not only the problems to be addressed, but with their own favored solutions for solving those problems. When this occurs, the team meeting can easily disintegrate into a competitive situation where team members are primarily concerned with advocating for their own solutions rather than evaluating alternatives. Focusing on commonalities and mutual goals becomes exceedingly difficult, *but not impossible,* in such situations.

Role Definitions, Norms, and Procedures

Role definitions are specifications for the unique and collective contribution that each member is to make to the accomplishment of team goals. Role definitions specify the position of each parent and professional relative to other team members. *Norms* establish the range of behaviors that are acceptable within the team context. *Procedures* define for team members how and in what order the tasks for which the team is responsible will be accomplished. As teams develop, informal roles, norms, and procedures evolve, and expectations regarding how parent and professional team members interact will solidify (Fisher & Ellis, 1990). Clear delineation of roles, norms, and procedures is associated with effective team functioning.

The importance of role definition is underscored in a study of personnel in the Bureau of Education conducted by Fenton, Yoshida, and Kaufman (cited in Ysseldyke, 1982). Fenton et al. reported that in over half of the placement team meetings they surveyed, the majority of team members failed to recognize that they had responsibility for making a decision. Moreover, school professionals involved in these meetings expressed considerable ambiguity regarding their own as well as other team members' roles.

Team Members

Status Systems and Expectation States. Expectations of team members are influenced by formal role and norm systems and expectation states that are external to the team. Certain team members may be viewed as more important to the team than others based on the perceived status of the groups these members represent. Status differentiation is of particular importance in the functioning of collaborative teams where consensus, rather than deference, in decision-making is needed. Team members who perceive their status as low devalue their own judgments and defer to and even endorse the judgments of higher status members, even when the judgments being endorsed are poorly conceived or in error (Gouran, 1988).

Parents or professionals on the team who perceive their status as low may fail to participate in the decision-making process at all. Nonparticipation, in turn, can lead to dissatisfaction with the team decision-making process. For example, Yoshida, Fenton, Maxwell, and Kaufman, in their 1977 study of BEH personnel, reported that "regular education teachers who are pivotal persons in operationalizing and implementing the PT (placement team) decisions are low in participation and are generally not satisfied with the PT process" (cited in Ysseldyke, 1982). Ysseldyke et al. (1982) similarly reported that in the 34 placement team meetings they observed, there "never was a statement made encouraging participation" (p. 311). Even more dismaying was Ysseldyke et al.'s finding that in none of the 34 meetings they observed were parents asked about either their understanding of the purpose of the meeting or their expectations for the meeting. Consequently, it is not surprising that Ysseldyke et al. found that the decisions made in these meetings were not challenged, that alternatives were not evaluated, and that opinions of noncontributing team members were not sought.

Given the findings above, it is clear that counteracting undue influence of specific team members is necessary for effective, collaborative team functioning. Specification of the contributing role of each parent and professional on the team must be accompanied by procedures that provide formal structure for each team member to participate. This can be done by according equal time and consideration to the ideas and suggestions of each team member. Moreover, the contribution of each parent and professional on the team should be evaluated in terms of its benefit to the learner, rather than with reference to the status, gender, or ethnicity of the contributor. Remember that participation in the decision-making process is directly related to satisfaction with the decision. Consequently, participation of parents and regular class teachers must be actively encouraged and solicited, especially in light of the fact that these are the people who will live most closely with and have the heaviest investment in carrying out the decisions that are made.

Gender and Ethnicity. As stressed in the preceding chapter, role expectations can be influenced by the gender and ethnicity of team members. Gender and ethnicity are components of a status that is external to the team. Women and minority team members, for example, may be viewed as less important to the team than other team members. As noted in the preceding section, this could lead to these team members devaluing their own judgments. Establishing team norms that preclude sexist and racist behavior is necessary, but insufficient, for ensuring that gender and ethnicity do not play a significant role in team member interaction. Studies of team interaction have repeatedly found that women and minority participants are more often ignored or interrupted during team discussions (see Miller, 1988; Smith-Lovin & Brody, 1989). Discounting the contribution of any team member is unacceptable in a collaborative team structure.

Verbal Communication Style and Content. The perceived value of what is said is determined, at least in part, by the manner in which it is said (Fisher & Ellis, 1990). Although being fluent, articulate, and dynamic are important characteristics of effective communication, skill in adapting to the demands of a specific situation is of equal importance. A critical adaptation in special education team situations is the adjustment required in the use of what Fisher and Ellis call "special language" or jargon. "Jargon is the specialized language of a particular group of people who have training or experience in common" (p. 190). Although jargon may facilitate communication among specialists in a particular field, the use of jargon in teams that include non-specialists interferes with interdependent, interactive communication, an important characteristic of collaborative teams (Ross & Ross, 1989).

Communication environments can be classified as defensive or supportive (Fisher & Ellis, 1990). Defensive environments are created when communication is perceived to be person-focused, judgmental, reflective of a sense of superiority, or manipulative and insincere. Supportive environments are created when communication is perceived to be issue-focused, nonjudgmental, direct, and sincere. Supportive environments are characterized by mutual respect and trust that facilitate interactive communication and ongoing clarification of the issues. Effective communicators are effective listeners and clarifiers.

Nonverbal Communication. The meaning attached to what individuals have to say is influenced by nonverbal aspects of communication such as eye contact, facial expression, gestures and body movement, and intonation. Nonverbal communication is a potent variable in determining the message listeners will receive. If nonverbal aspects of communication contradict verbal statements, the nonverbal message is more likely to be believed (Anderson, 1988). If the facial expression, gestures, body movement, or intonation of a speaker contradicts what is said, what is said is not believed. What is believed depends on each listener's individual perception of the meaning of the nonverbal communication.

In our dominant culture, eye contact between speaker and listener is generally interpreted as indicating interest and inviting interaction. Although returning speaker eye contact may indicate a readiness to respond, failure to return eye contact does not necessarily indicate a desire to avoid responding. Reciprocal eye contact among team members may facilitate interaction. Team communication can be facilitated when team members are seated so they can make eye contact with each other. Eye contact among team members can communicate respect, group inclusion, and confirmation of the value of individual team member contributions (Fisher & Ellis, 1990).

Facial expressions, gestures, and body movement are particularly effective for nonverbal communication. Basic facial expressions are universal and appear to convey similar meanings across cultures (Anderson, 1988). Interest may be expressed with intentional eye focus, enjoyment with wide eyes and smiles, and surprise with upward eyebrow movement. Gestures that accompany speech can provide emphasis and help listeners to follow the flow of what is being said. Speakers often lean back as a signal that they are finished talking. Listeners who want to speak will often lean forward toward the current speaker.

Intonation (tone of voice) is an indicator of the emotional context of what a speaker is saying. Loudness can indicate anger and softness can indicate feelings of sympathy or powerlessness. Vocal qualities of speech can also provide clarification and add emphasis to what a speaker is saying, for example, a low-pitched voice can provide emphasis to a particular point.

Interaction among parents and professionals on the team can be facilitated by attending to nonverbal cues that signal confusion or surprise, the need for clarification, or the desire to respond or contribute. Effective team members are attentive and responsive to both the verbal and nonverbal communication of other team members.

Environmental Factors

Organizational Constraints. Planning and evaluation teams (IEP teams) do not operate in isolation, but in the larger organizational context of the school system. Federal government mandates, state regulations, and the demands of special interest groups all have an impact on the school system and, in turn, on teams within the school system. The interaction of components of the larger organizational system, of which teams and schools are just a part, will be the subject of the next chapter. Organizational constraints, including policies, standard practice, rules, or laws limit the "openness" of teams within the larger system.

Resources. In the broadest sense, the resources available to planning and evaluation teams are a function of organizational priorities and constraints. These priorities and constraints are beyond the direct control of the team. In the narrowest sense, each team member represents a resource deemed necessary to plan, implement, and evaluate appropriate programming for a specific student. For teams to be productive in their planning and implementation functions, the resources of each team member must be utilized effectively.

Physical Facilities. The physical environment, particularly seating arrangements, can affect communication and interaction patterns among team members. Although research findings regarding the impact of seating position on role, leadership, and team status are contradictory, Paulus and Nagar (1989) have concluded that some general assumptions regarding the effects of seating arrangements appear to be justified.

> *Sociopetal seating arrangements (small interpersonal distance, maximization of eye contact) seem to increase the degree of interaction, communica-*

tion, and friendship formation. Positions that are central (head of the table or the center of a V-shaped arrangement) are associated with the perception of leadership, tend to be selected by those who are of high status or have leadership inclinations, and may be associated with leadership behavior (p. 126).

Research appears to support the contention that it is easier for individuals seated opposite one another to interact than for those seated next to one another. Individuals seated in central positions at a table contribute more than those positioned at the corners. Although this is not surprising considering the finding that central positions tend to be selected by high status individuals, Fisher and Ellis (1990) suggest that one way to increase the participation of a particular team member might be to place that person in a central seating position.

Attention to physical arrangements for team meetings can contribute to the establishment of an environment that is conducive to productive interaction among team members. For example, use of a round or oval table provides seating that permits maximum eye contact. In addition, intentional positioning of specific team members can enhance participation.

Decision-Making

Team decisions may be made in a variety of ways. Wood (1988), in her discussion of consensus, negotiation, and voting, notes that ". . . consensus has been proclaimed the ideal (often the only acceptable) method of making decisions in a democratic society" (p. 185). Consensus is a team decision-making format whereby a decision with which most participants can agree is reached through a process of gathering information and views, discussion, and persuasion (Shivers, 1983). Laboratory research confirms the appropriateness of the consensus method when high quality decisions with maximum levels of commitment to implementation are required (Erffmeyer & Lane, 1984). Special educators advocate consensus decision making in program planning and evaluation (Landerholm, 1990; McGonigel & Garland, 1988; Ysseldyke, Algozzine, & Mitchell, 1982).

Consensus decisions, ideally, represent the collective efforts of all parents and professionals on the team who share equitably in shaping the decision and who have a high level of commitment to implementation. Consensus procedures require a supportive communication environment and promote team unity and cohesion. Issues related to the quality of consensus decisions are best summarized by Wood (1988):

Because consensus pursues agreement, decisions tend to be moderate, a practical imperative if all members are to go along. At its best, moderation offers a welcome safeguard against potential biases, extremism, and the incomplete knowledge of each individual; at its worst, moderation becomes a euphemism for watered-down decisions that mark the least common denominator among members. (p. 186)

Effective implementation of consensus decision-making procedures requires: (a) clear definition of the decision to be made; (b) clear presentation and review of necessary background information; and (c) active participation of all team members in generation and consideration of alternatives and in making the final decision.

Participation

Teams that depend on active participation of members to be effective must have role definitions, norms, and procedures that establish a supportive communication environment, provide formal procedures for participation, and reward productive interaction among team members. Physical facilities provided for the team must promote interaction. Parents and professionals on the team must have a commitment to the team process and to facilitating active participation of all team members. Individual team members should avoid monopolizing the discussion. Conversely, team members who do not volunteer opinions should be specifically asked to contribute their views (Shivers, 1983).

Active listening encourages active participation. Active listeners listen for total meaning of the message, including the emotional context as well as the verbal message, by making note of the nonverbal aspects of communication. Active listeners communicate interest, respect, empathy, and acceptance through their nonverbal behavior and their verbal responses (Gibson & Hodgetts, 1988). Responding to other team members is important in enhancing interaction and promoting understanding. Responses should: (a) be specific; (b) provide or request information; and (c) focus on issues, not individuals (Fisher & Ellis, 1990).

Consensus

Adequate consideration of alternatives, productive disagreement among team members, and the quality of the decision eventually may all depend on the degree of agreement among team members as to where the power resides in terms of decision making (Bacharach & Mitchell, 1987). Although formal authority and the consensus model dictate that decision-making power rests with the team as a whole, the influence of individual team members and the perceived power of the groups they represent can suppress productive disagreement and result in the illusion of consensus. True consensus can only be achieved when alternatives are presented and conflicting opinions are openly discussed. Open discussion of conflicts promotes consideration of substantive issues and contributes to the quality of the decisions made. Asking team members, particularly those who do not volunteer their opinion, whether they agree with specific components of the decision under consideration is essential to promoting true consensus.

Earlier in the chapter, we stressed the importance of establishing team norms that not only allow, but actively encourage, the participation of all team members in the decision-making process. In order to ensure this, we advocate that at each decision point during the meeting, the team facilitator ask each parent and professional on the team whether or not they agree with the proposed action.

As an illustration, consider again the news story in Box 7-1. The behavior management plan for the child involved three steps: (a) sending him first to the back of the classroom; (b) then sending him to the hall; and (c) finally sending him to the principal if his inappropriate behavior continued. Remember that we speculated earlier, when discussing individual and team goals, that the major point of contention between the child's mother and the other team members involved the second step of the behavior management plan. If consensus decision-making had been used at the time this plan was proposed, each team member's opinion about the plan would have been solicited. At this point, if our speculation is correct, the child's mother would have indicated that although she generally agreed with the overall goal of the plan, she had serious reservations concerning the second step of the plan. Having focused the point of disagreement on this one step, the team could then have discussed whether to drop the second step or to try and identify an alternative second step.

On the other hand, if consensus checking had revealed that the child's mother disagreed with the entire behavior management plan, the team facilitator would then have asked her whether her objections were so strong that she was unwilling for the team to proceed with the proposed plan. Were this the case, the team facilitator might have then suggested that the decision be postponed until: (a) more information was obtained; (b) team members had an opportunity to calm down and rethink their positions; or (c) a compromise was worked out (Shivers, 1983).

Models of Team Development

Models of team development are based on one of two general conceptual perspectives. Team development may be viewed as movement through an orderly and sequential series of phases or as an ongoing state of fluctuating equilibrium between the task and social dimensions of team functioning. Current research provides support for models based on both perspectives. Cissna (1984), in his review of evidence *not* supporting the existence of phases in the development of teams, found insufficient evidence to warrant discounting the phase perspective. He concluded that "Groups do change and develop in common similar ways; some things about some groups, perhaps all groups, do not change; and all groups are also unique in changing and in staying the same" (p. 25).

Phase Models

Phase models focus on sequential changes in team activity and member interaction over time. Examples of this perspective typically distinguish the task activity of the team as clearly separate from the emotional components of member interaction. Implicit in phase models is the overall increase in team capacity to complete meaningful tasks in each successive phase.

Fisher and Ellis (1990) considered the three-phase Bales model (orientation, evaluation, control), the four-phase Dunphy model (dependency, fight-flight, pairing, work), the four-phase Bennis and Shepard model (dependency, resolution-catharsis, interdependence, consensual validation), and the four-phase Tuckman model (forming, norming, storming, performing) in identifying common features of phase models of team development (all cited in Fisher & Ellis, 1990). Phase models have in common a first-phase orienting period, a middle-phase period of conflict among members, and a final-phase period of consensus and validation of decisions (Fisher & Ellis, 1990).

Equilibrium Models

Equilibrium models of team development focus on an ever changing balance between the social dimension of member interaction and the task dimension of work accomplishment. Examples of this perspective typically view the task dimension of team activity as interdependent and inseparable from the social dimension of member interaction. Implicit in equilibrium models is the continual fluctuation of team effectiveness in one dimension when team attention is directed to the other dimension. According to this perspective, a team focus on task accomplishment results in a deterioration in team social structure, whereas a focus on developing team social structure results in a deterioration in task accomplishment (Fisher & Ellis, 1990).

Special education placement and planning teams are unique in that team development often occurs over a period of years. The team is first constituted at the time of the student's potential identification as disabled and subsequently reconstituted at least twice yearly until the student no longer requires special education or graduates from school. In order to adequately address the changing needs of students as they progress through the grades, professionals representing different programs or areas of expertise join the team as additional members or replacements for professionals whose expertise is no longer relevant.

Both the phase and equilibrium models have implications for assessing and facilitating the development of special education teams. More overall time is required for initial placement and planning meetings, and, during initial meetings, more of the time available will be devoted to the orienting components of the phase model. Subsequent meetings will require less time overall, with increasingly more of the available time being devoted to the conflict and consensus/validation components of the phase model. Changes in the team participants will temporarily increase the proportion of time that will need to be devoted to the orienting phase.

For the special education team to function effectively, there must be a productive balance between the attention paid to member interaction and to the task dimensions of the equilibrium model. Clearly defining team member roles, establishing appropriate norms, and providing formal structures for participation in initial meetings (as discussed previously) will contribute to maintaining the necessary balance over the life of the team. The special education team exists in order to make important decisions about students with disabilities. Team effectiveness in making these important decisions must not be diminished, which the equilibrium perspective predicts would be the case if the team is focused on interaction issues.

On the other hand, the personal and emotional aspects of the decisions that must be made and the interaction among team members cannot be ignored.

Team Maintenance

The relationship of the parent to the program planning and evaluation team is of particular interest in terms of team development and maintenance. Moreland and Levine (1989) have proposed a five-phase model of team socialization that "both describes and explains . . . the temporal changes that occur in the relationships between a group and each of its members" (p. 143). The five phases of team membership (investigation, socialization, maintenance, resocialization, and remembrance) provide a framework for understanding changing membership status (prospective member, new member, full member, marginal member, and ex-member).

Professional members of the program planning and evaluation team frequently have served together before on other teams and often work together on a daily basis. As a result, professional team members are more likely to be familiar with how teams operate and with each other. In this sense then, the parent, unfamiliar with how teams operate and with professional team members, may be viewed as a newcomer to the team. Newcomers are assimilated as full team members during the socialization phase of the Moreland and Levine model (1989). During the socialization phase, "The individual is a quasi-member who belongs to the group but is not fully integrated into it. This situation is inherently unstable and therefore must be resolved" (Moreland & Levine, 1989, p. 145). As we noted earlier in the section on status systems and expectation states, special efforts are required to ensure that parents do not remain in this quasi-member status.

Clarification of Goals and Roles

Role negotiation is a key element of the maintenance phase of the Moreland and Levine model. Becoming a full team member depends on the team defining a specialized role for the quasi-member that contributes to the achievement of the team's goals. Clear specification of team goals and the roles of team members, particularly the role of parents, although perhaps repetitious for experienced professional team members, is essential for parents as newcomers to the team.

Enhancing Interpersonal Processes

Interpersonal effectiveness is associated with how often individuals communicate (Fisher & Ellis, 1990). Professional team members often interact on a regular basis in conjunction with their work and have a history of shared experiences. Maintaining communication with parents between formal team meetings and providing opportunities for parent/professional interaction in training and support group activities can enhance interpersonal communication among team members.

TRAINING AND SUPPORT GROUPS

As noted in the introduction, training and support groups are groups that have learning, growth, or development of group members as a primary goal. One distinguishing characteristic of training and support groups is that membership is typically voluntary. These groups may be focused on establishing supportive networks, providing and sharing information, or training of specific skills. Specific examples of these groups that will be discussed later in this chapter include empowerment training groups, advocacy skills training groups, and parent training groups.

> *In each of these cases participants need not reach agreement, nor take joint action, nor prepare a unified public presentation. The groups exist instead as arenas that encourage individuals to meet their own unique needs and goals. The purpose of such gatherings is not to submerge individual differences into a group gestalt, but to use the group's resources to enhance awareness of members' personhood and to encourage expressions of members' unique selves (Friedman, 1988, p. 20).*

Models for Group Interaction

Training and support groups vary widely in the extent to which they are: (a) leader-centered versus member-centered; (b) information-oriented versus insight-oriented; (c) structured versus unstructured; and (d) continuing (long-term) versus temporary (short-term) in nature (Rudestam, 1988). The general focus of a particular group and the immediate task or theme of the group activity will determine the characteristics of the group in terms of each of these variables.

Group Context Variables

Group and Individual Goals

Training and support group members may share a common motivation, experience, or need that draws them to the group. Group members typically choose groups having goals compatible with their own goals. Group goals must enable group members to achieve their individual goals.

Role Definitions and Norms

Roles in training and support groups are characterized by their flexibility. Roles emerge as a group progresses in response to member perceptions of specific group needs at a particular time. Rudestam (1988) observes that "There is a long list of stereotypic roles used to describe interpersonal behavior in . . . groups. Many carry colorful names . . ." (p. 108). Stereotypic role definitions may reflect personality types, character traits, and/or emotional states. There are, however, two categories of functional behavior that are necessary: (a) task functions that focus on goal attainment; and (b) maintenance functions that deal with the social and emotional climate of the group. A balance between task and maintenance behaviors is needed for groups to function effectively. Rudestam (1988) concludes that "The more flexible members can be in their roles, the more successful the group will be in reaching its ultimate goal" (p. 11).

Norms defining acceptable group behavior must be consistent with group goals but may change over the life of a group as the focus of the group or its members change. For example, sharing (in terms of information and common experience) may be an appropriate norm for group activities with a training focus (Robinson, 1988), whereas self-disclosure (in terms of feelings) may be an appropriate norm for group activities with a support focus.

Participants

Membership in training and support groups is typically voluntary and based on each individuals' perceptions of the extent to which a specific group might be able to help them accomplish their individual goals. Members expect to make progress toward their individual goals through participation in a specific group. The commitment of individual members to the group is a function of how satisfied they are with the progress they have made toward their individual goals as a result of their participation.

The nature of the relationship between training and support groups and professionals varies from group to group. Many groups are begun in cooperation with professionals. Some groups, particularly training and empowerment groups, function in continued cooperation with or even under the direction of professionals. Other groups may function more independently in efforts to ". . . handle aspects of their members' problems which the professions cannot or choose not to deal with" (Robinson, 1988, p. 127).

Group Formation and Maintenance

Facilitative Techniques

Eliciting active participation.   Establishing a supportive communication environment and providing physical facilities that promote member interaction are necessary prerequisites to active member participation. Promoting use of active listening through training or modeling activities and reinforcing the norm of reciprocity that "functions by a member's tendency to reciprocate similar behaviors in response to the behaviors of others" (Fisher & Ellis, 1990, p. 220) are useful in establishing productive patterns of interaction in training and support groups.

Promoting group cohesion.   The development of group cohesion is dependent upon group effectiveness. One way to promote group cohesion is to support group efforts to accomplish group goals. "Basically, the more effective a group is in meeting needs that attract people, the more cohesive it will be . . . When a group is cohesive, there is an atmosphere of acceptance, support, and a sense of belonging" (Rudestam, 1988, p. 115).

Group Empowerment and Advocacy Training

It should be clear that effective training and support groups are situation, goal, and member specific. In fact, the effectiveness of these groups is determined by the degree to which they are able to address the situation specific goals of their members. The following descriptions of three model empowerment and advocacy training programs serve to highlight the variety of approaches that may be effective.

Empowerment Training. The Partners in Policymaking program is a three-year, federally funded model empowerment program based in St. Paul, Minnesota. The program provides training for people who need to access services in the area of developmental disabilities. The program is designed to: (a) build participants' skills in obtaining appropriate services; (b) familiarize participants with the people and the processes involved in policymaking at local, state, and federal levels; and (c) develop skills needed to influence public policymaking. The year-long training program includes three components: (a) eight two-day, topic-focused training sessions; (b) participant completion of assigned activities (i.e., readings, making presentations, contacting policymakers); and (c) participant completion of a major project (Zirpoli, Hancox, Wieck, & Skarnulis, 1989).

Six months after completing the program, 89 percent of the 35 first-year program participants (30 parents of children with disabilities and 5 adults with disabilities) reported that the training they had received enabled them to obtain more appropriate services for themselves or their children. Many of the first-year participants reported being involved in advocacy activities including contacts with officials, serving on commissions, and making presentations during the six-month period following their completion of the program. An additional benefit attributed by participants to the program was the strong support network that the program provided, particularly the supportive relationships that developed among the program participants (Zirpoli et al., 1989).

Advocacy Skills Training. Spiegel-McGill, Reed, Konig, and McGowan (1990) describe an education program designed for parents of children with disabilities entering special education preschool programs from home-based infant special education programs. The transition program provides parents with guidance, training, and information to reduce stress and prepare them to serve as long-term advocates for their children. Group training activities are followed by individualized transition assistance sessions conducted in the homes of the participants. Topics covered in the six workshops include: (a) the effects of transition on our lives (emotional implications of change); (b) knowing your child (understanding functional skill levels); (c) program options and services (placement and service options, roles and responsibilities of various professionals); (d) effective communication (describing child skills and needs, effective responding, assertive communication); (e) educational rights (legal rights with regard to assessment, placement and program planning); and (f) putting the puzzle together (preparing for team meetings, getting help from community resources, parent organizations).

Spiegel-McGill et al. (1990) report that the first seven parents to participate in the program felt that they were well prepared to advocate for their children. Participating parents made specific mention of the value of the opportunity provided to interact with other parents of children with disabilities in the workshop sessions. Parents also emphasized the importance of the individualized follow-up sessions in helping them to personalize and apply the information provided in the workshops.

Parents Training Parents. The Chicago Public Schools offer a training program for the parents of children with disabilities who are interested in providing support to other parents of children who have disabilities. The focus of the program is on parents helping parents to access the special education services available in the Chicago Public Schools. The program provides a total of six all-day training sessions, with the first three sessions devoted to information gathering and the development of training skills and the last three sessions devoted to practice in the use of the information and skills developed during the first three sessions. In addition to providing information about special education and the role of parents in the schools, the program includes training in communication skills, use of resources, making decisions, taking action, managing stress, and working with other parents. Training materials include simulations, role-playing activities, and discussion guides (Cadavid, Carroll, Mayo, Stephens, & Wolf, 1989).

SUMMARY

In this chapter we have emphasized the interaction of individuals as they function in program planning and evaluation teams. These teams are formed to accomplish a specific task or make a decision. Increasingly, special educators are called upon to function effectively as group members and as facilitators of parent participation. Models of team interaction, team context variables, and effective practices were described.

Program Planning and Evaluation Teams

1. There are three general models representing present approaches to structuring team interaction: (a) the multidisciplinary model; (b) the interdisciplinary model; and (c) the transdisciplinary model.

2. All three models structure team interaction around the individual contributions of team members but differ in the extent to which member roles and responsibilities are shared.

3. Effective teams set clear short-term and long-term goals that are congruent with member goals.

4. Teams that counteract the effects of status differentiation by providing formal structures for participation and clear specification of the contributing role of each member foster collaboration.

5. Productive interaction among team members is enhanced when teams use sociopetal seating arrangements (see Table 7-1).

6. Effective communicators are fluent, articulate, avoid the use of "specialized language" (jargon), and are attentive to nonverbal aspects of communication.

TABLE 7-1 • Team Context Variables and Effective Practices

Variables	Effective Practices
Goals	• Set clear goals • Establish congruency between team and individual goals
Roles	• Establish clear contributing role definitions
Norms	• Establish clear norms • Define sexist and racist behavior as inappropriate
Procedures	• Establish formal structures for member participation • Establish clear procedures for accomplishing goals
Communication	• Establish a supportive communication environment • Discourage use of specialized language (jargon) • Encourage attention to nonverbal aspects of communication
Resources	• Use member resources effectively • Encourage active listening to enhance participation
Physical facilities	• Provide seating that permits maximum eye contact among members • Use intentional positioning to enhance participation

7. Team members whose communication is issue-focused, non-judgmental, direct, and sincere contribute to the establishment of a supportive communication environment.

8. Team members who are active listeners as well as effective communicators can facilitate interaction among their fellow team members (see Table 7-1).

9. Consensus decisions represent the collective efforts of team members who share in shaping the decision.

10. Effective consensus decision-making requires: (a) clear definition of the decision to be made; (b) clear presentation and review of necessary background information; and (c) active participation of all team members in generation and consideration of alternatives.

11. True consensus decisions can only be achieved when alternatives are considered and conflicting opinions are openly discussed.

12. Attention to substantive issues contributes to the quality of decisions made.

13. Team development may be viewed as an orderly and sequential series of *phases* or as an ongoing state of fluctuating *equilibrium*.

14. Current research provides support for both phase and equilibrium models.

15. The Moreland and Levine (1989) five-phase model of group socialization is particularly useful in understanding the relationship of the parent to the planning and evaluation team.

16. According to this model, the parent may be viewed as a newcomer or quasi-member of the team.

17. Special efforts are required to ensure that parents do not remain in this quasi-member status.

Training and Support Groups

18. Training and support groups, in contrast to program planning and evaluation teams, are characterized by their diversity.

19. Whether leader-centered or member-centered in their structure, the focus of training and support groups is on using group resources and setting group goals that will enable members to meet their individual goals.

20. Roles in training and support groups are characterized by their flexibility.

21. Norms are typically consistent with group goals and may change over the life of a training and support group as the goals of the group or its members change.

22. Membership in training and support groups is typically voluntary.

23. Some training and support groups function in cooperation with or under the direc-

tion of professionals and others operate independently.

24. The effectiveness of training and support groups is determined by the degree to which they are able to address the situation specific goals of their members.

REFERENCES

Anderson, P. A. (1988). "Nonverbal communication in the small group," in R. S. Cathcart, & Samovar, L. A. (Eds.), *Small group communication* (5th ed.) Dubuque, IA: Wm. C. Brown Publishers, pp. 333–365.

Bacharach, S. B., & Mitchell, S. M. (1987). "The generation of practical theory: Schools as political organizations," in J. W. Lorsch (Ed.), *Handbook of organizational behavior* Englewood Cliffs, NJ: Prentice-Hall, pp. 405–418.

Cadavid, V., Carroll, F. G., Mayo, C. L., Stephens, T. M., & Wolf, J. S. (1989, April). *Friends of Special Education: Training Manual* (Document based on presentation at the 67th Annual Convention of the Council for Exceptional Children, San Francisco, CA). Chicago, IL: Chicago Public Schools. (ERIC Document Reproduction Service No. ED 313 834)

Cissna, K. N. (1984). "Phases in group development: The negative evidence." *Small Group Behavior, 15*(1), 3–31.

Erffmeyer, R. C., & Lane, I. M. (1984). "Quality and acceptance of an evaluative task: The effects of four group decision-making formats," *Group and Organization Studies, 9*(4), 509–529.

Fisher, B. A., & Ellis, D. G. (1990). *Small group decision making: Communication and the group process,* 3rd ed. New York: McGraw Hill.

Friedman, P. G. (1988). "Group processes for individual development," in R. S. Cathcart, & Samovar, L. A. (Eds.), *Small group communication,* 5th ed. Dubuque, IA: Wm. C. Brown Publishers, pp. 20–32.

Gibson, J. W., & Hodgetts, R. M. (1988). The listening environment. In R. S. Cathcart, & Samovar, L. A. (Eds.), *Small group communication,* 5th ed. Dubuque, IA: Wm. C. Brown Publishers, pp. 367–371.

Glaser, R., & Glaser, C. (1985). *Group facilitators intervention guidebook, a quick reference to team development interventions,* 2nd ed. Bryn Mawr, PA: Organization Design and Development.

Gouran, D. S. (1988). "Principles of counteractive influence in decision-making and problem-solving groups," in R. S. Cathcart, & Samovar, L. A. (Eds.), *Small group communication,* 5th ed. Dubuque, IA: Wm. C. Brown Publishers, pp. 192–208.

Huszczo, G. E. (1990). "Training for team building." *Training and Development Journal, 44*(2), 37–43.

Landerholm, E. (1990). "The transdisciplinary team approach in infant intervention programs." *Teaching Exceptional Children, 22*(2), 66–70.

McGonigel, M. J., & Garland, C. W. (1988). "The individualized family service plan and the early intervention team: Team and family issues and recommended practices." *Infants and Young Children, 1*(1), 10–21.

Miller, F. A. (1988). "Moving a team to multiculturalism," in W. B. Reddy, & Jamison, K., Eds. Team building: Blueprints for productivity and satisfaction. Alexandria, VA: NTL Institute for Applied Behavioral Science. San Diego, CA: University Associates, Inc. (Co-publishers), pp. 192–197.

Moreland, R. L., & Levine, J. M. (1989). "Newcomers and oldtimers in small groups," in P. B. Paulus, Ed., *Psychology of group influence* (2nd ed.) Hillsdale, NJ: Lawrence Erlbaum Associates, pp. 143–186.

Paulus, P. B., & Nagar, D. (1989). "Environmental influences on groups," in P. B. Paulus (Ed.), *Psychology of group influence,* 2nd ed. Hillsdale, NJ: Lawrence Erlbaum Associates, pp. 111–140.

Robinson, D. (1988). Self-help groups. In R. S. Cathcart, & Samovar, L. A. (eds.), *Small group communication,* 5th ed. Dubuque, IA: Wm. C. Brown Publishers, pp. 117–129.

Ross, R. A., & Ross, J. R. (1989). *Small groups in organizational settings* Englewood Cliffs, NJ: Prentice-Hall.

Rudestam, K. E. (1988). "The experiential group," in R. S. Cathcart, & Samovar, L. A., Eds., *Small group communication,* 5th ed. Dubuque, IA: Wm. C. Brown Publishers, pp. 102–116.

Shivers, L. (1983). "Leadership, meeting facilitation, and conflict resolution," in H. H. Blumberg, Hare, A. P., Kent, V., & Davies, M., Eds., *Small groups and social interactions,* Vol. 2 New York, NY: John Wiley & Sons Ltd., pp. 345–355.

Smith-Lovin, L., & Brody, C. (1989). "Interruptions in group discussions: The effects of gender and group composition." *American Sociological Review, 54,* 424–435.

Spiegel-McGill, P., Reed, D. J., Konig, C. S., & McGowan, P. A. (1990). "Parent education: Easing the transition to preschool." *Topics in Early Childhood Special Education, 9*(4), 66–77.

Wood, J. T. (1988). "Alternative methods of group decision making," in R. S. Cathcart, & Samovar, L. A., Eds., *Small group communication,* 5th ed. Dubuque, IA: Wm. C. Brown Publishers, pp. 185–191.

Ysseldyke, J. E., Algozzine, B., & Mitchell, J. (1982). "Special education team decision making: An analysis of current practice." *Personnel and Guidance Journal, 60*(5), 308–313.

Zirpoli, T. J., Hancox, D., Wieck, C., & Skarnulis, E. R. (1989). "Partners in policymaking: Empowering people." *Journal of the Association for Persons with Severe Handicaps, 14*(2), 163–167.

8

INTERPERSONAL EFFECTIVENESS IN CONSULTATION AND ADVOCACY

Lech Wisniewski
Eastern Michigan University

Chapter Objectives

After completing this chapter, you will be able to:

1. Define consultation and the consultation process
2. Specify potential roles and contributions of the consultant and consultee
3. State those interpersonal skills essential to maintain positive and effective consultative and advocacy relationships
4. Define the essential components for effective interpersonal communication
5. Specify those communication techniques that elicit behavior change
6. State and identify barriers to effective communication
7. Specify those procedures available to gather data and information during the consultation process
8. Identify and specify the guidelines for developing and implementing the consultation plan
9. Define and differentiate the various consultation models available to school and community based consultants
10. Specify and illustrate the appropriateness of a specific consultation model to resolve the concerns of consultee/consultant
11. Generate a plan to resolve resistance and conflict that may occur during the consultation process
12. Specify a plan to evaluate the effectiveness of consultation

Key Terms and Phrases

advocacy consultation
attending skills
attribution
behavioral consultation
"calling the game"
clinical consultation
cognitive dissonance
confrontation
confrontational messages
critical incident technique
didactic confrontation
empathy

experimental confrontation
facilitative messages
influencing messages
interpretation
mental health consultation
process/organizational
   consultation
program consultation
regular education initiative (REI)
skills of reception
skills of sending

School and community-based professionals who provide direct and indirect services for special needs students are changing essential aspects of their professional responsibilities (Givens-Ogle, Christ, & Idol, 1991). These professionals are placing students in a variety of community-based settings, making arrangements for normalizing experiences, and requesting services that bring the school in contact with family and community. These new responsibilities are in addition to their traditional teaching and service roles. Various consultation models (for example, behavioral intervention, programmatic, and advocacy) have been employed in these interactions. These interactions between regular and special educators, family, and community have led to specific instructional and classroom management interventions (see Brann, Loughlin, & Kimball, 1991; Friend, 1984; Paolucci-Whitcomb & Nevin, 1985), the inclusion of preschool students with disabilities (Mowder, Willis, & Wilderstrom, 1986), and development of several models of school consultation (see Gallessich, 1982; Parsons & Meyers, 1984).

Special education consultation is an established aspect of the teaching responsibilities that special educators provide (Polsgrove & McNeil, 1989). However, a number of issues related to definitions, barriers, and training (Johnson, Pugach, & Hammitte, 1988) presently limit its application. One essential aspect neglected in these efforts is the interpersonal relationship that occurs during a process that involves parents and other family members, other school and service professionals, and community members.

This chapter will focus on the processes, methods, and procedural sequence involved in providing consultation services (see Figure 8-1). Consultation should not be viewed as an intervention or a technique, but rather as a problem-solving process within which intervention strategies are generated (Davis & Sandoval, 1991). Strategies for working with family members, as well as small groups and community-based agencies, will be discussed. Special emphasis will be on the interpersonal skills and problem-solving process in the consultation and advocacy relationship.

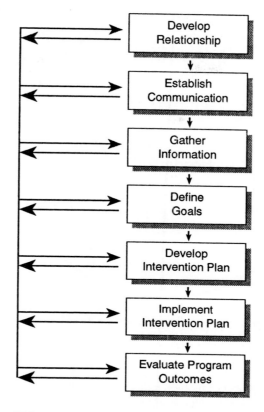

**FIGURE 8-1 • Procedural Sequence
Involved in the
Consultation Process**

CONSULTATION AND THE CONSULTATIVE PROCESS

A variety of school and community-based professionals provide services for special needs students. Often these services involve joint efforts between regular and special educators, parents and other family members, and other community-based service providers. Much of the success of an interdisciplinary process depends upon collaborative efforts with individuals who have varying backgrounds and experiences. In addition, special education and related services continue to change in response to our current data base on the most promising practices. Consultation has become a technology for change and a method to improve the special education service delivery system.

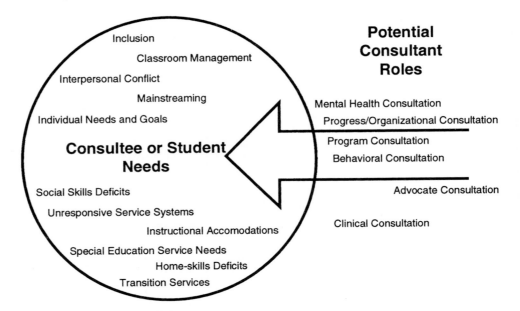

FIGURE 8-2 • Consultant Roles to Resolve Consultee or Student Needs

Consultation involves relationships with individuals or organizations employing specialized knowledge and training to resolve issues that are of concern or mutual interest (Friend, 1984). Schools and community-based service providers have employed various consultant models (Conoley & Conoley, 1982; Gallessich, 1982): to extend the knowledge of teachers and parents with the goal of preventing mental health problems, *mental health consultation* (Caplan, 1970; Bindman, 1959); to provide clinical diagnosis and recommendations for children or organizational units (for example, families and classrooms), *medical model consultation* (Schein, 1969); to implement new and innovative educational programs, *program consultation* (Sarason, 1971); to modify client's behavior using principles of applied behavioral analysis, *behavioral consultation* (Bergan, 1977; Tharp & Wetzel, 1969); to improve organizational communication and group interactions, *process/organizational consultation* (Fullan, 1982; Hall, 1979, Havelock, 1973); and to resolve conflicts associated with advocating educational or community-based services for "underpowered" children, *advocate consultation* (Chester & Arnstein, 1970; Chester & Lohman, 1971). These models provide professionals with a set of strategies to effect individual and environmental change (See Figure 8-2).

Change is a collaborative process. Existing special education consultation models emphasize collaborative relationships. Collaborative relationships are reciprocal arrangements among individuals with diverse expertise to define problems and develop solutions (Pugach & Johnson, 1988). Consultation is an indirect service delivery approach (McKellar, 1991). Consultation is also an interpersonal process in which participants have *equal* status and power. Collaborative consultation involves the contributions of all participants in this process. The role of special needs service providers is to facilitate the problem-solving process.

Collaborative consultation is also a relationship between consultant (a school or community-based specialist) and consultee (a mediator [for example, parent or guardian] or provider [for example, other teachers, school administrator, or professional] of special services). The purpose is to facilitate the welfare of the client—a student or group of students.

A variety of school and community-based specialists have knowledge and training that can be used to impact the delivery of services for special needs students. They are the consultants. The consultees are parents and other family members, classroom teachers, or other individuals who provide or mediate these services. The child's parents may not have the formal training and expertise of the service providers, but are an extremely valuable source of information about their child. Parents' ability to describe behavior in natural settings, provide developmental and medical history, and identify reinforcers is critical to the collaborative process (Skinner, 1991). The focus of these interactions between consultant and consultee is to improve the quality of services and further the growth and development of special needs students in educational settings.

In developing these interpersonal relationships, the consultant also works toward furthering the consultee's skills. The goal is to increase the consultee's ability to participate in the delivery of educational services, become more self-sufficient, and become less dependent upon the special education service delivery system (Skinner, 1991). The consultee acquires a variety of skills useful in prevention, identification, and treatment, in his or her interactions among service providers and community, and in the implementation and coordination of services.

In working with and providing services for consultee and client, consultants find that no single model of consultation adequately addresses their needs. School and community-based professionals who work with special needs students have diverse roles and responsibilities. While there exists some disagreement on the precise role that consultants should assume in providing services (see Kratochwill, 1991; Kurpius, 1991), the consultation role will reflect the consultant's training, his/her service roles, and professional responsibilities. The consultant's role will exist along a continuum, from providing direct services to student and family, to working indirectly with others to effect positive changes in systems of students (Polsgrove & McNeil, 1989). For example, parents who come to the realization that their child has a disability may experience a range of reactions: shock, denial, grief, blame and guilt (Hall & Richman, 1985). When these emotions interfere with the provision of special education services or the child's development, the professional may need to employ aspects of mental health consultation to provide support and counseling to parents during the adjustment process. In the behavioral consultation model, the consultant may design and help parents or teachers to implement behavioral interventions at school or home. When issues related to providing services are of concern, advocacy consultation may be employed to empower parents. These models of consultation provide specific guidelines to design, develop, and evaluate change strategies.

CONSULTATIVE AND ADVOCACY RELATIONSHIPS

Consultative and advocacy relationships are, first and foremost, helping relationships. In these relationships, consultants aid consultees to acquire, develop, and utilize a variety of skills necessary to further the development of special needs students (Dinkmeyer & McKay, 1973). This relationship is also a learning process that focuses upon the stimulation and growth of parenting or teaching skills and the attitudes necessary for the resolution of problems that will lead to optimal human growth and development.

As the consultant enters the process from referral to the implementation of special education services, consultee-consultant relationships are not necessarily self-motivated and voluntary. Harris and Cancelli (1991) report a continuum under which parents, teachers, and other school professionals enter the consultation process. They report several circumstances under which consultee or consultant initiate or are mandated by others to enter the process. For example, parents, initially, may be asked for permission, information, and advice. As these special education services are initiated and continue throughout their child's schooling, parents continue to face challenges that bring them repeatedly into problem-solving relationships with consultants. Occasionally, parents enter the process under circumstances of crises that require immediate attention. Under these circumstances, the school's ability to respond with the desired immediacy that parents may expect may be taxed. Teachers may be mandated to enter the process as a result of current educational mandates (for example, regular education initiative, post-secondary transition services, and so on). It is the circumstances of these relationships with parents, school, and community-based professionals that will shape educational services for the special needs students and will ultimately determine the students' independence during adult life.

As the consultant enters the process, establishes relationships, and begins an analysis of issues that concern the consultee, the consultant must assess the circumstances under which entry occurred. This is an on-going process, not a one time event. The consultation process begins whenever the consultant is contacted by an individual who believes that a situation calls for consultation services. Consultation services may be initiated by consultant, consultee, or by some third party.

Consultative and advocacy relationships involve interpersonal skills. These skills mediate the nature and productivity that leads to the development of the consultation plan. The best plans are likely to fail if the consultee fails to confide or trust the consultant, or does not participate in the plan or its management.

Several interpersonal variables have been identified that can facilitate positive consultation relationships. These variables provide consultants with general guidelines in developing productive relationships. First, consultants must convey acceptance and respect for the consultee. This establishes a sense of trust among participants. Rogers (1961) proposed the concept of unconditional self-worth as a basis for this trusting relationship. Accordingly, the consultant must convey to the consultee a respect for her as a separate person. The consultee and client have value no matter what the child's disability. The consultant can convey this by posture, gestures, and words (Margolis & Brannigan, 1986; Rocha, 1983).

Second, the consultant must develop a sense of empathy for the consultee's concerns. This perspective focuses on an understanding of the other person—how he or she thinks, feels, and sees the environment. Empathy is not agreeing or disagreeing, but rather understanding what it is like to be the consultee. Consultants must rid themselves of their internal frame of reference, personal biases, and any preconceptions (Carberry et al., 1981).

A final general guideline for consultants to consider is the importance of establishing rapport. Rapport (Rogers, 1969) is a comfortable and unconditional relationship between consultant and consultee. This relationship is established by the consultant's ability to convey a genuine interest in the consultee or client. This authenticity of interest in the welfare of the client is established through communication (see Rubin & Morrison, 1985; Westby, 1990).

COMMUNICATION

If consultation is first and foremost a helping relationship, then communication among participants is an essential aspect of that relationship. Communication skills are necessary to gather information, define goals, and develop a plan of action (Schubert, Landers, Curtin, Anderson, & Curtis, 1984).

Communication is a process where consultant and consultee both receive and send messages that influence, facilitate, and define the purpose for consultation services (Friend, 1984; Idol-Maestas & Ritter, 1985). Two essential features are required. First, consultation requires open communication. The consultant-consultee need to feel free to exchange concerns and reactions. Second, communication also needs to be effective. Effective communication is a condition whereby the message perceived and responded to by the receiver corresponds to the message intended by the sender. Research (see Conoley & Conoley, 1982; Fine, Grantham, & Wright, 1979; Polsgrove & McNeil, 1989) has provided evidence that this correspondence, between the intended and perceived message, is influenced by a number of personal, interpersonal, and environmental factors. Consultants can use this information to guide the selection of personal variables that support the nonverbal dimensions of communication. Consultants must also be cognizant of the communication process and those factors that support effective communication (see Benes, Gutkin, & Kramer, 1991). An understanding of these concepts is essential for individual or systems change (Wisniewski & Alper, 1991). These concepts are discussed in the following section.

Essential Components of Communication

In the process of understanding the consultee's concerns, both consultant and consultee create and deliver messages that are intended to lead to mutual understanding of the issues at hand. The process of communicating suggests goals and leads to the development and implementation of an intervention plan. The process also leads to the development of an evaluation plan. In the process, the consultant and consultee exchange information and each identifies the intended message of the other. Each can scan and elicit relevant information from the other. As the process moves from general to more specific issues, the basis for consultation emerges. Both consultant and consultee need to create messages that expand upon this initial basis. Finally, both need to receive messages from the other and interpret them accurately.

During the communication process, various sources of noise may interfere with consultant and consultee identifying, sending, and receiving messages. Either may reach premature closure on the issues of concern. Either may be selective of the information that is heard. Moreover, information may also be incomplete. Preconceived views also limit one's options.

Limited understanding of professional jargon will also restrict the communication process, especially for parents. Many parents feel intimidated by jargon and the feeling of being surrounded by professionals (Skinner, 1991). However, Hyatt, Tingstrom, and Edwards (1991) report that classroom teachers responded positively to the use of behavioral jargon, in that it facilitates their acceptance of a proposed intervention. Ultimately, successful consultation is a function of the communication process—a responsibility of the consultant (Witt, Erchul, McKee, Pardue, & Wickstrom, 1991). This process first includes the ability to determine and direct the topic of discussion. This in turn directly influences the consultee's willingness to collect data, to carry out treatment plans, and to determine the efficacy of that plan. In addition, the process also includes the consultant's ability to monitor communication patterns—its direction, content, and form. Breakdowns will inhibit the full utilization of the system's problem-solving skills and resources.

In the following section, specific suggestions (Benes, Gutkin, & Kramer, 1991; Parsons & Meyers, 1984) are provided to facilitate effective communication between consultant and consultee.

Skills of Reception

In receiving information, the consultant must first accurately receive and then interpret the consultee's description of the problem and its history. The consultant can employ several strategies that ensure maximum reception of the message. First, the consultant must arrange the physical environment ensuring that noise and other sources of distraction are kept to a minimum.

Second, the consultant can employ attending skills that communicate respect for and interest in what the consultee is saying. Effective attending skills require that the consultant is in front of the consultee in a physically relaxed posture, that nonverbal movements are natural, that good eye-contact is maintained, that a neutral voice is used, and that the focus of discussion is on what the other is saying.

Skills of Sending

In order to remain psychologically active in a conversation with the consultee, the consultant can send messages that communicate active involvement. Several sending skills are discussed.

Facilitative Messages

The consultant can use relatively brief questions to initiate the exchange of information. Open-ended questions (such as How? When? What? Why?) followed by facilitative messages (for example, "O.K . . .", "And . . ."; "Then . . .") create a communication pattern that positively validates the conversation and provides the consultee evidence of understanding while facilitating further information.

Influencing Messages

The consultation process has been initiated to solve a problem, resolve an issue of concern, or assist in securing special education services. All are intended to meet some consultee or client need. The consultee has perceptions, attitudes, and biases that relate to the consultation process and influence the consultant's behavior. The consultant also has skills that influence the consultee. One technique to influence the consultee's behavior is to paraphrase the message being heard. Paraphrasing provides the consultee with an essence of the message being heard. It conveys to the consultee that the consultant is actively engaged and really trying to understand what is being said.

A second influencing technique is summarization. Summarization is an attempt to reiterate critical dimensions of an issue during communication. Martens, Deery, and Gherardi (1991) report that the consultant's use of summarization encouraged the consultee to provide more detail and depth concerning the issue at hand. They also report that summarization may signal closure on a particular issue and movement to another topic.

Confrontational Messages

During the communication process, the consultant attends to and facilitates expression of the consultee's concerns. When both consultant and consultee have a clear understanding of the problem, they then need to identify strategies that are intended to resolve concerns. Sometimes the consultee is the source of resistance or conflict. Consultants may need to use additional communication skills that are more influential. Several communication techniques that lead to resolution are discussed.

Confrontation

Growth-producing experiences occur when the consultant's behavior acts as a stimulus that leads the consultee to consider the challenge. Consultants need to recognize the constructive nature that confrontation may have upon human behavior. These challenges occur when the consultee reflects upon questions, reconsiders issues of concern, or modifies some aspect of his or her behavior, attitudes, or feelings (Berenson & Mitchell, 1974). Confrontation, however, can elicit defensive reactions. For example, the consultee may counterattack, ignore, or distort the intended message.

Didactic Confrontation occurs when the consultant provides information or corrective feedback to the consultee on some aspect of his behavior. To be effective, the technique requires that the consultant provides information that: (a) is new; (b) is viewed to be important by the consultee; and (c) is descriptive. For example, parents' expectations for school achievement may be unrealistic given the nature of their child's impairment. The parents may not understand the limitations that the impairment places upon their child's ability to learn. The consultant might make specific suggestions to the parents on how their child could derive greater benefit from her educational experience.

Experimental Confrontation occurs when the consultant notes a discrepancy between verbal behavior and action. To be effective, the technique requires that the consultant point out this discrepancy—between what one says and what one does.

Calling the game is when the consultant faces the consultee's "game." Berne (1964) examined interpersonal relationships in which a hidden agenda distorted true intentions in the relationship. In a social context, games reflect different roles that are played in different situations. The "games that people play" serve as defense mechanisms. Berne provides several suggestions that consultants may find helpful. For example, the consultant may remove the reinforcement for the game being played by providing an "asocial response." In this technique, the consultant calls the consultee game and an attempt is made to move from a hidden agenda to a conscious and a deliberate discussion of the issues.

Interpretation

A second communication technique to elicit behavioral change is interpretation. Interpretation is a technique in which the consultant redefines the reality at hand. It is the presentation of an alternative frame of reference in which the consultant considers the consultee's expressed or implied feelings, attitudes, or behaviors. The consultant provides more than simple summary, feedback, and reflection. Interpretation focuses upon connections and conclusions of the consultee's attitudes with the intent of forming a hypothesis about the underlying nature of the message.

Direction

Finally, direction is a technique that gives the consultee behavioral guidance. The consultee may view the consultant as an expert. In this position, the consultant will be asked to provide direction and guidance—what to do and try. When providing advice or direction to the consultee, the consultee is called to act. Parson and Meyers (1984) suggest the following: (a) provide directions that are concise statements on new behaviors, using discreet and jargon-free language; (b) ensure that directions match the consultee's ability for action based upon a current perspective of the problem; (c) to be maximally effective, directions are presented as suggested guidelines to follow and are also presented in a tentative matter for the consultee's consideration and action; and finally, (d) directions are delivered in congruence with the consultee's understanding and readiness for action.

INFORMATION GATHERING

There are many methods and procedures for gathering information. Many aspects of school and family life, a child's relationships with his or her peers, or the child's community can provide relevant information and help determine important goals. Initial contact with the consultee will focus upon a tentative analysis. Consultee and consultant will gather descriptive information or data on issues of concern. The consultant surveys perceived needs and interests, discrepancies between current or future performance levels, or discrepancies in service needs.

If the consultant is skillful in establishing rapport, interviews are a flexible method of gathering data. Interviews can probe and shift to new areas of concern as information obtained may suggest. The consultant should regard the interview process as a joint responsibility of consultant and consultee. This shared role minimizes inappropriate diagnosis, reduces consultee resistance, and promotes shared responsibility for the intervention plan. This role may also promote growth in the consultant-consultee relationship and lead to an improved repertoire of problem-solving skills. However, interviews may not always produce the right answers. The consultee may resist change. The teacher's or parent's perceptions may signal the need for a change in classroom routines or parenting skills.

A second method for gathering information involves the use of formal or informal assessment tools to collect relevant data. Data-based approaches to consultation provide important measures of baseline levels (see Meyer & Janney, 1989). Data-based approaches also provide data necessary for formative and summative evaluation of educational programs.

IDENTIFYING AND DEFINING GOALS

The basis for consultation services are the issues that concern parents and teachers. When the goals are unknown, consultants and consultees will need to identify relevant goals. Flanagan (1954) suggests that consultants employ the *critical incident technique* to identify relevant goals (cited in DiSalvo, Nikkel, & Monroe, 1989). Using this technique, the consultee is asked to describe in detail the last time the problem arose. As the consultee narrates the issue of concern, the consultant facilitates discussions by asking explicit questions that are aimed at gathering as much information as possible. The critical incident technique can provide important information for both consultant and consultee (Parsons & Meyers, 1984). For the consultant, a data base of relevant information is generated, goals are specified, and the basis for further activities is determined. For the consultee, the technique provides a basis for establishing the collaborative relationship. The consultee's role is legitimized. He or she becomes an important and contributory member of a problem-solving team.

Depending upon the scope and sequence of consultation services to be provided, it may be helpful to write and prioritize consultation goals. This procedure provides the consultee with an opportunity to consider the magnitude of services, as well as the desired programmatic or behavioral outcomes. For the consultant, the procedure structures the resources needed and the responsibilities of participants.

DESIGNING AN INTERVENTION PLAN

Regardless of who initiates the consultation process, explicit and discriminating choices to resolve issues of concern are often rare (Davis & Sandoval, 1991). Problem-solving approaches that employ collaborative relationships to identify issues of concern, specify goals, and develop an intervention plan define the consultation process. School and community-based professionals have a variety of consultation models to guide this problem-solving process. These models identify the roles and responsibilities of consultee and consultant. Selection of any specific model will depend upon the critical variables identified earlier in the consultation process. The needs of the family and student are diverse and complex. Consultants need to have specific knowledge and expertise in a variety of intervention strategies.

Models of Consultation

Consultation is a technology for change. The focus of this change is to improve the current and future welfare of the client or consultee—the individual, small group, or organization. The consultant is the agent for that change. The target of change may be new information, the acquisition of new skills, or systems change. A number of school and community-based professionals have employed models of consultation that are intended to bring about changes intended to improve the service delivery system for special needs students.

Mental Health Consultation
A number of school and community-based professionals play an active role in promoting positive mental health in today's schools and communities. Counselors,

psychologists, social workers, and school nurses provide consultation services that focus upon prevention and remediation of a wide range of problems experienced by individuals or groups. Mental health consultation is a problem-solving process between the consultant and consultee that is intended to maximize the consultee's social-emotional development and welfare. The focus is upon increasing the consultee's understanding and coping skills, to manage both current and future mental health problems in a skillful and sensitive manner, thereby improving the mental health of the child or special needs student (Meyers, 1981).

Caplan (1970) reported several essential features of mental health consultation. First, mental health consultation is a nonhierarchical, coordinate relationship between two individuals of equal status. Second, mental health consultation emphasizes communication among participants. Consultation emphasizes a variety of indirect communication techniques to confront the consultee and lead to positive behavioral change.

Mental health consultation may be most appropriate when the consultee needs emotional and cognitive support for behavioral change (Meyers, 1981). This form of consultation may be appropriate when the consultee lacks knowledge central for an understanding of the mental health problem. For example, the consultee may attribute inaccurate conclusions about the child's behavior because of an insufficient knowledge base. In this case, consultant goals focus upon providing the consultee with this knowledge. This form of consultation may also be appropriate when the consultee lacks the professional skills to correct the mental health problem. The consultee possesses basic knowledge but lacks the skills to implement that knowledge. The consultant analyzes home, school, and community environments that lead to problem-solving interventions. The consultant teaches the consultee how to implement that knowledge. Mental health consultation may also be appropriate when the consultee lacks the parenting or professional confidence that influences the mental health of the student or child (for example, Hannah & Midlarsky, 1987). The consultee may lack confidence associated with beginning a new career or teaching assignment. Parents may lack the confidence associated with raising a child with a disability. The consultant provides this support and assistance (McClure & Lindsey, 1984). Finally, this model may be appropriate when the consultee has a personal or emotional commitment to a particular issue that interferes with his or her effectiveness as teacher or parent. The teacher may lack objectivity and be unable to maintain professional distance. The consultant provides the emotional and cognitive support to the consultee that leads to behavioral changes (Medway & Forman, 1980).

Clinical Consultation

Clinical consultation provides expert diagnosis and recommendations on problems that can be attributed to disease or a dysfunctional relationship (Gallessich, 1982; Schein, 1969). The focus is upon the student with a disability for whom the intervention is being considered. For example, the student may have a neurological basis for the disability. Educators will need to seek clinical consultation to obtain specific recommendations that will guide the student's instructional plan. If pharmacological interventions are to be prescribed, the teacher is in the unique position to assess its efficacy upon behavior and learning.

Clinical consultation may also involve the consultee. The consultee may be observed to influence the client's behavior, in which case the consultant may need to assess the consultee-client relationship. The consultee may be an organization, a small group (such as a classroom or family unit), or an individual. The intervention plan may focus upon the consultee in this relationship. Classroom and school discipline concerns (see Knoff, 1985) can be readily addressed by the consultant.

Clinical consultation involves diagnosis and amelioration of the problem. Consultation strategies focus upon the use of expert knowledge to formulate a diagnosis and develop the treatment plan. Collaborative relationships occur when the consultee is able to share authority and responsibility (see Warren & Goldsberry, 1982). The consultee can be recognized for his or her contribution to collect data, provide diagnostic information, and contribute to the problem-solving process that leads to the development of the intervention plan. The consultant-consultee relationship may vary, depending upon the professional status or capability of the consultee to contribute. If the consultee lacks in these skills, the consultant may need to be more directive. Kratochwill (1991) reports that this form of consultation is viewed to be particularly relevant when (a) the consultee or client calls for immediate, expert judgment; or (b) the consultant is more skilled to diagnose and prescribe the treatment than the consultee. While the clinical consultation model provides a prescriptive treatment, the consultee-client may not have the skill or motivation to execute the plan. This model of consultation also provides an opportunity to develop an initial relationship with the consultee-client before applying other strategies from other models of consultation.

Program Consultation

Program consultation can aid consultees (such as inservice delivery systems) bring about instructional changes through the design, development, and implementation of innovative programs (Sarason, 1971). P.L. 94-142 and its recent amendments guarantee infants, children, and youth with disabilities the right to a free and appropriate public education. Our concept of an appropriate education has and continues to change. This change reflects our current best instructional practices. As our scientific knowledge base has changed, so has our technology of teaching. New programs have been developed to reflect new knowledge.

Program consultation focuses upon helping agencies acquire a new repertoire of programmatic offerings (for example, regular education initiative). These programs are intended to reflect our current best practices in providing a free and appropriate public education for students with disabilities (Gallessich, 1982).

Behavioral Consultation

Behavioral consultation employs direct observation of human behavior in natural settings and applies social learning principles to modify behavior in school, home, and community (Iverson & Lee, 1991; Sheridan & Elliott, 1991). In this model, the consultant possesses specialized training and knowledge about the principles of applied behavior analysis. Behavioral consultation emphasizes joint efforts and responsibilities to design and develop behavioral interventions. The consultant's responsibility is to design the behavioral intervention. The consultee is primarily responsible for implementing and evaluating the behavioral intervention (Zwald & Gresham, 1982).

Cipani (1985) identified the steps involved in behavioral consultation. First, the consultant analyzes the environment. This involves identifying and prioritizing the behavioral needs and determining baseline performance levels. This analysis leads to specifying objectives. These objectives are intended to specify the behavior and the change desired of the consultee or child. Front-end analysis leads to the next step, designing and implementing the intervention program. Special consideration is given to designing and implementing a program. It is the consultee who is responsible for implementing and evaluating the intervention plan. Finally, quality assurance is determined. In this step, consumer satisfaction is assessed. Program modification or termination would occur based upon the consultee's experience with the intervention. Behavioral consultation is intended to be a collaborative effort to modify human behavior. While the consultant may possess the technical expertise, the consultee shares in the responsibilities (Bergan, 1977; Rosenfield, 1985; Tharp & Wetzel, 1969).

Process/Organizational Consultation

Process or organizational consultation is primarily concerned with modifying interpersonal interactions among group members. By improving these interactions, the overall capabilities of the service delivery system is improved (Seligson, 1987). This model focuses upon intervention strategies intended to improve interpersonal communication and decision-making responsibilities of group members (Kiesler, Collins, & Miller, 1969; Lange, 1980; Piersal & Guthin, 1983). The primary role of the consultant is to facilitate desired changes and provide a role model for the desired interactions. The consultant seeks participation of the consultee by symptomatic observation and feedback. In addition, the model employs team-building strategies (examples are brain-storming, force field analysis, nominal group techniques, and so on) to elicit desired changes (Fullan, 1982; Jerrell & Jerrell, 1981; Havelock, 1973; Heron & Swanson, 1991).

Advocate Consultation

Advocacy consultation is "an independent movement of consumers (for example, parents, people with disabilities, and children and their allies) to monitor and change human service agencies" (Biklen, 1976, p.310). Advocacy consultation focuses on intervention strategies that are intended to elicit humanistic responses from institutions—to further the goals of its disenfranchised members (Erin, 1988; Rhodes & Smith, 1980).

In the advocacy model, the consultant's role involves systems change. The institutional response is intended to accommodate the concerns of the consultee and clients. For example, schools may develop humanistic responses to the challenges parents face in securing special education services for their son or daughter (Skinner, 1991). Parents may request and be assigned a parent-advocate during the process of developing an *individualized educational plan* (IEP). This parent advocate could be a school counselor or a special educator from another school. The advocate's purpose might be to help the parents overcome feelings of being outnumbered or lacking understanding of the proceedings. The advocate may also explain legal rights and procedural safeguards, terminology and jargon, or elaborate on the educational options that are available. Since the potential for conflict is considerable, advocacy consultation is best conducted by a consultant with no vested interests (Chester & Arnstein, 1970; Chester & Lohman, 1971).

DEVELOPING AND IMPLEMENTING THE PLAN

The major goal of the consultation process is to develop and implement an intervention plan. This plan is intended to bring about change in human or organizational behavior. It is also intended to provide solutions to the daily challenges parents and service providers face in their interactions with special students. Various models of consultation have been outlined and provide consultants and consultees with potential solutions.

The major challenge facing consultants is developing collaborative relationships. The quality of collaborative relationships determines consultation outcomes. The bases for these relationships are the norms and roles of the consultation setting (Parsons & Meyers, 1984). Norms sanction who is to interact with whom and for what purpose. Norms decide the "what" and "how" of communication. What is the issue of concern? How can the solution correct that concern? As the plan develops, the consultant needs to communicate to the consultee the freedom to accept or to reject conclusions and recommendations. The focus is on heightening the knowledge, status, and power of the consultee. Eliciting suggestions and giving credit to the consultee helps to legitimize the consultee's contribution and to encourage responsibility to initiate and make decisions.

In any relationship, roles are defined by group dynamics. One may be provider, follower, or leader. One's roles may be free of conflict or lead to conflict. Consultants need to monitor their relationship with the consultee and the larger group setting. Consultants need to maintain a nonhierarchical relationship that deemphasizes their role in developing an intervention plan. By communicating choices, consultants neutralize competitive roles of interaction, maximize choices of selection, and maximize the consultee's responsibility for the plan's outcome.

Resistance and Conflict Resolution

Persistent and powerful barriers to educational change continue to limit consultation services in school, home, and community settings. In school settings, teacher roles continue to support current service delivery systems. Many special educators still spend considerable amounts of time in isolated settings in which personal involvement may lead them to validate their own practices, routines, and problem-solving strategies (Rosenfield, 1985). Some educators still prefer the pull-out approach for providing special education services, since classroom interventions may imply a change in a teacher's behavior or a change in classroom routines (Witt, 1986). In home and community-based settings, school administrators do not provide teachers the time or the necessary resources to effect change in these settings.

In addition to resistance, consultants sometimes enter relationships that are unproductive or lead to conflict. If unresolved, the consultation relationship may be terminated precipitously by the consultee. Sometimes this conflict is not with the consultee but with a third party who has authority over the service delivery system. Parents and classroom teachers may also be unwilling to implement the intervention plan developed during the consultation process (Reisberg & Wolf, 1986).

For every potential plan, there are risks. There may be the risk of failure, lost freedoms, or change. These risks may lead one to resist the implementation plan. A considerable body of research has addressed the theoretical bases for resistance, including cognitive dissonance, reactance, attribution, concerns, conflict, and commitment theories.

A general plan for managing resistance is suggested by Friend and Bauwens (1988). They suggest that consultants: (a) enlist the support of building and central office administrators; (b) actively involve all interested parties during all aspects of the process; (c) specify how the plan will aid the consultee; (d) gather data and provide feedback; (e) learn the values of the consultee and design a plan in accordance with those values; (f) request contributions and current responsibilities of the consultee; and (g) nurture a trusting relationship. Friend and Bauwens (1988) and others (Brehm & Brehm, 1981; Elksnin & Elksnin, 1989; Salend & Salend, 1984; Witt, 1986) suggest additional strategies to overcome common patterns of resistance.

EVALUATING THE PLAN

The final aspect of the consultation process is evaluation. The evaluation plan is developed prior to implementation, ensuring that relevant formative and summative information is gathered at each important milestone for making decisions. This information is then used to make adjustments or modifications, determine consumer satisfaction, or terminate consultation services. Qualitative as well as quantitative data will need to be considered in determining program outcomes.

Traditional measures of program outcomes for large groups have focused upon quantitative evaluation. Quantitative data rely on pre/post comparisons using group means and significance tests to evaluate the magnitude of desired changes. These indices, while contributing much to our understanding of consultation, have failed in other respects (Gresham, 1991). First, they have failed to provide comprehensible, user-friendly indices, particularly for parents and classroom teachers. Second, consultants have sometimes found these indices to be irrelevant. These indices tend to provide measures that are summative. Few formative measures are available that provide data on the processes that are occurring. Finally, since most consultations tend to be ecological, dependent measures often fail to provide practical significance. They report that *something* worked, but not *what* worked.

Several alternative indices are intended to address these shortcomings and involve qualitative assessment. Kazdin (1977) reports that social comparisons may be used in determining practical significance. Social comparisons can provide data that are relevant and are more likely to impact daily activities. Two measures are of greatest relevance. These are social validation and subjective evaluation. Social validation measure involves comparisons between individual or group behavior and the behavior of a referent individual or group. Subjective evaluations provide measures of consumer satisfaction and rate qualitative aspects of behavior that are essentially formative in nature.

Qualitative assessment of the developmental process in adopting an innovation is relevant to formative and summative evaluation. A recognition of developmental processes involved in adopting new school practices would create an additional evaluation dimension. Based upon research involving concerns for adopting educational innovation (Hall, 1979; Hall & Rutherford, 1976), Wisniewski and Alper (1991) described a complex socio-political process involved in securing full inclusion for students with severe disabilities. Recognition and acceptance of the developmental process involves examination of the developmental milestones that lend themselves to qualitative evaluation. These developmental milestones include: *awareness* of the innovation, seeking additional *information*, clarifying one's *role*, and considering the *management* issues that come with implementing the innovation on a trial basis. Later, concerns focus upon the innovation's *consequences* and *collaboration* with others that come with formal adoption of the educational innovation. Acceptance for the concerns one may have for adopting an educational innovation is an important aspect of the evaluation plan. Not all participants will readily accept the change. Consultee and consultants may be at developmentally different stages. The evaluation plan must address where the participants are developmentally with respect to the consultation plan and make use of this feedback in structuring consultation activities.

In summary, initial contact with the consultant will focus upon design and execution of the evaluation plan. Participants will have preferences for the type of information gathered. For some, data-based approaches that quantify pre/post comparisons are important and relevant indices. For others, qualitative assessment of the developmental process assessing consumer satisfaction or the developmental readiness to accept change are more relevant indices. With an understanding of the important decisions to be made, the consultant will need to identify decision-makers as well as the type of data that evaluate the outcomes of important decisions.

SUMMARY

Our concept of a free and appropriate public education for students with disabilities continues to change. This change is in response to our understanding of current best practices. Special education service delivery systems are experiencing extraordinary growth. In addition, philosophical and data-based approaches to providing special education services have increased the scope of services available. Consultation services offer options to address these challenges. Consultation services also provide school, family, and parental strategies to effect systems change.

In this chapter, several consultation models were discussed. The models provide potential solutions for these educational challenges. In addition, this chapter examined the procedural sequence involved in the consultation process. Consultation is a triadic relationship between consultant and consultee for the purpose of furthering the educational welfare of all students. It is a problem-solving process. This process includes developing relationships, gathering information, specifying goals, designing and implementing the intervention plan, and evaluating program outcomes. After the goal has been reached, the consultant helps the consultee develop a plan to monitor the plan's continued growth and maintenance.

We have addressed the importance of communication, an essential and necessary ingredient for interpersonal effectiveness in the consultation process. Effective communication influences the quality of the interpersonal relationships established. Communication aids in identifying issues of concern. Communication aids in gathering information that leads to specifying goals. Communication also helps the consultant and consultee to define, design, develop, and evaluate the intervention plan. Finally, communication is essential when resistance or conflict is present. Persistent barriers to educational interventions continue to limit those services that enable students with disabilities to acquire skills for adult life. Effective communication is one essential element to bring about systems change.

Consultation and the Consultative Process

1. Consultation is a process that involves collaborative efforts among family and a variety of school and community-based personnel.

2. The purpose of consultation is to resolve issues or concerns on behalf of students with special needs. It is a problem-solving process.

3. The process is interdisciplinary, involving individuals who have varying backgrounds, experiences, service interests, and resources for solving problems or issues of mutual concern.

4. Consultation is a technology for change.

5. In order to resolve problems or issues of concern, various consultation models have been employed. These include: mental health consultation, medical consultation, program consultation, behavioral consultation, process/organizational consultation, and advocacy consultation.

6. These consultation models provide consultants with specific guidelines to design, develop, implement, and evaluate change strategies.

7. Consultation is collaborative. Its members have varying abilities, roles, responsibilities, but *equal* status and power.

Consultative and Advocacy Relationships

8. Consultation is first and foremost a helping relationship that involves interpersonal skills.

9. During the consultation process, interpersonal relationships are established and an analysis of issues begins.

Communication

10. Communication skills are a critical aspect necessary to gathering information, defining goals, and developing a plan of action.

11. In the exchange of information, consultant and consultee create and deliver messages that are intended to lead to a mutual understanding of the issue at hand.

12. In this dialogue, various sources of interference may disrupt the process.

13. Eliminating distractions, arranging the setting, and attending to the speaker are skills that help facilitate the communication process.

14. Facilitative, influencing, and summarization are sending skills that may be employed in order to maintain an active conversation.

15. Confrontational, interpretation, and directional messages are communication strategies intended to lead to inter- or intrapersonal growth and behavioral change.

Information Gathering

16. Interviews and formal and informal assessment techniques are procedures for gathering information.

Designing an Intervention Plan

17. In designing an intervention plan, the consultee and consultant will draw upon their personal resources and expertise to develop the plan. One's contribution may be developed and structured around the various models of consultation.

Identifying and Defining Goals

18. The process of identifying and establishing goals may be facilitated by the use of the critical incidence technique.

19. A variety of consultation models are intended to bring about the desired changes as specified in the plan.

20. Mental health consultation focuses upon preventing and remediating of a wide range of mental health problems or facilitating positive social-emotional development and welfare experienced by individuals or groups.

21. Clinical consultation focuses upon providing the specialized experience and knowledge of an expert to resolve particular issues or problems.

22. Program consultation focuses upon instructional or programmatic change. In this model, the consultee-consultant design, develop, and implement innovative educational programs.

23. Behavioral consultation focuses upon the application of social learning principles to modify behavior in school, home, and community settings.

24. Process or organizational consultation focuses upon modifying interpersonal interactions among group members.

25. Advocacy consultation focuses upon those strategies that are intended to provide needed services.

Developing and Implementing the Plan

26. The goal of the consultation process is to bring about change in human or organizational behavior. The plan is intended to provide the vehicle for this change. Consultation models provide the knowledge and structure to develop solutions. Implementing this plan will depend upon the culture that exists for bringing about change.

Resistance and Conflict Resolution

27. There are persistent and powerful barriers to educational change. These barriers continue to limit consultation services.

Evaluating the Plan

28. Both quantitative and qualitative assessment procedures are available to provide formative and summative feedback on the efficacy of the consultation plan.

REFERENCES

Benes, K. M., Gutkin, T. B., & Kramer, J. J. (1991). "Micro-analysis of consultant and consultee verbal and nonverbal behaviors." *Journal of Educational and Psychological Consultation, 2*, 133–149.

Berenson, B. G., & Mitchell, K. M. (1974). *Confrontation for better of worse!* Amherst, MA: Human Resource Development Press.

Bergan, J. R. (1977). *Behavioral consultation.* Columbus: Merrill.

Berne, E. (1964). *Games people play: The psychology of human relationships.* New York: Grove Press.

Biklen, D. (1976). "Advocacy comes of age." *Exceptional Children, 42*(6), 308–13.

Bindman, A. J. (1959). "Mental health consultation: Theory and practice." *Journal of Consulting Psychology, 23*, 473–482.

Brann, P., Loughlin, S., & Kimball W. H. (1991). "Guidelines for cooperative teaching between general and special teachers." *Journal of Educational and Psychological Consultation, 2*, 197–200.

Brehm, S. S., & Brehm, J. W. (1981). *Psychological resistance.* New York: Academic Press.

Caplan, G. (1970). *The theory and practice of mental health consultation.* New York: Basic Books.

Carberry, H., Waxman, B., & McKain, D. (1981). "An in-service workshop model for regular class teachers concerning mainstreaming of the learning disabled child." *Journal of Learning Disabilities, 14*(1), 26–28.

Chester M. A., & Arnstein, F. (1970). "The school consultant: Change agent or defender of the status quo?" *Integrated Education, 8*(4), 19–25.

Chester, M. A., & Lohman, J. E. (1971). "Changing schools through student advocacy," in R. A. Schmuch & M. B. Miles (Eds.), *Organization development in schools.* Palo Alto, CA: National Press Books.

Cipani, E. (1985). "The three phases of behavioral consultation: Objectives, intervention, and quality assurance." *Teacher Education and Special Education, 8*(3), 144–152.

Conoley, J. C., & Conoley, C. W. (1982). *School consultation.* New York: Pergamon Press.

Davis, J. M., & Sandoval, J. (1991). "A pragmatic framework for systems-oriented consultation." *Journal of Educational and Psychological Consultation, 2*, 201–216.

Dinkmeyer, D., & McKay, G. D. (1973). *Raising a responsible child: Practical steps to successful family relationships.* New York: Simon & Schuster.

DiSalvo, V. S., Nikkel, E., & Monroe, C. (1989). "Theory and practice: A field investigation and identification of group members' perceptions of problems facing natural work groups." *Small Group Behavior, 20*(4), 551–567.

Elksnin, L. K., & Elksnin, N. (1989). "Collaborative consultation: Improving parent-teacher communication." *Academic Therapy, 24*(3), 261–269.

Erin, J. N. (1988). "The teacher-consultant: The teacher of visually handicapped students and collaborative consultation." *Education of the Visually Handicapped, 20*(2), 57–63.

Fine, M. J., Grantham, V. L., & Wright, J. G. (1979). "Personal variables that facilitate or impede consultation." *Psychology in the Schools, 16*, 533–539.

Flanagan, J. C. (1954). "The Critical Incident Technique." *Psychological Bulletin, 51*, 327–328.

Friend, M. (1984). "Consultation skills for resource teachers." *Learning Disability Quarterly, 7*, 246–250.

Friend, M., & Bauwens, J. (1988). "Managing resistance: An essential consulting skill for learning disabilities teachers." *Journal of Learning Learning Disabilities, 21*(9), 556–561.

Fullan, M. (1982). *The meaning of educational change.* New York: Teachers College Press.

Gallessich, J. (1982). *The profession and practice of consultation: A handbook for consultants, trainers of consultants, and consumers of consultation services.* San Francisco: Jossey-Bass.

Givens-Ogle, L., Christ, B. A., & Idol, L. (1991). "Collaborative consultation: The San Juan Unified School District Project." *Journal of Educational and Psychological Consultation, 2*, 267–284.

Gresham, F. M. (1991). "Moving beyond statistical significance in reporting consultation outcome research." *Journal of Educational and Psychological Consultation, 2,* 1–13.

Hall, C. W., & Richman, B. O. (1985). "Consultation with parents of handicapped children." *The Exceptional Child, 31*(3), 185–191.

Hall, G. E. (1979). "The concerns-based approach to facilitating change." *Educational Horizons, 57*(4), 202–208.

Hall, G. E., & Rutherford, W. R. (1976). "Concerns of teachers about implementing team teaching." *Educational Leadership, 34,* 226–233.

Hannah, M. E., & Midlarsky, E. (1987). "Siblings of the handicapped: Maladjustment and its prevention." *Techniques, 3*(3), 188–195.

Harris, A. M., & Cancelli, A. A. (1991). "Teachers as volunteer consultees: Enthusiastic, willing, or resistant participants?" *Journal of Educational and Psychological Consultation, 2,* 217–238.

Havelock, R. G. (1973). *The change agent's guide to innovation in education.* Englewood Cliffs: Educational Technology Publications.

Heron, T. E., & Swanson, P. N. (1991). "Establishing a consultant assistance team: A four-step "Bottom-Up" Procedure." *Journal of Educational and Psychological Consultation, 2,* 95–98.

Hyatt, S. P., Tingstrom, D. H., & Edwards, R. (1991). "Jargon usage in intervention presentation during consultation: Demonstration of a facilitative effect." *Journal of Educational and Psychological Consultation, 2,* 49–58.

Idol-Maestas, L., & Ritter, S. (1985). "A follow-up study of resource/consulting teachers: Factors that facilitate and inhibit teacher consultation." *Teacher Education and Special Education, 8*(3), 121–131.

Iverson, A., & Lee, S. W. (1991). "The effect of behavioral consultation on educational recommendations: A single case experimental design." *Journal of Educational and Psychological Consultation, 2,* 249–266.

Jerrell, J. M., & Jerrell, S. L. (1981). "Organizational consultation in school systems," in J. C. Conoley (Ed.), *Consultation in the schools.* New York: Academic Press.

Johnson, L. J., Pugach, M. C., & Hammitte, D. J. (1988). "Barriers to effective special education

consultation." *Remedial and Special Education, 9*(6), 41–47.

Kratochwill, T. R. (1991). "Defining constructs in consultation research: An important agenda in the 1990s." *Journal of Educational and Psychological Consultation, 2,* 291–294.

Kazdin, A. (1977). "Assessing the clinical or applied significance of behavior change through social validation." *Behavior Modification, 1,* 427–452.

Kiesler, C. A., Collins, B. E., & Miller, N. (1969). *Attitude change.* New York: Wiley.

Knoff, H. M. (1985). "Discipline in the schools: An inservice and consultation program for education staffs." *School Counselor, 32*(3), 211–218.

Kurpius, D. J. (1991). "Why collaborative consultation fails: A matrix for consideration." *Journal of Educational and Psychological Consultation, 2,* 193–195.

Lange, J. I. (1980). *A model of communication in process consultation* (ERIC Service Reproduction Service Number ED196076).

Margolis, H. (1986). "Resolving differences with angry people." *Urban Review, 18*(2), 125–136.

Margolis, H., & Brannigan, G. G. (1986). "Relating to angry parents." *Academic Therapy, 21*(3), 343–346.

Martens, B., Deery, K. S., & Gherardi, J. P. (1991). "An experimental analysis of reflected affect versus reflected content in consultative interactions." *Journal of Educational and Psychological Consultation, 2,* 117–132.

McClure, S. W., & Lindsey, J. D. (1984). "A road to "somewhere" for parents of severely handicapped children." *Pointer, 29*(1), 32–37.

McKellar, N. A. (1991). "Enhancing the IEP process through consultation." *Journal of Educational and Psychological Consultation, 2,* 175–187.

Medway, F. J., & Forman, S. G. (1980). "Psychologists' and teachers' reactions to mental health and behavioral school consultation." *Journal of School Psychology, 18*(4), 338–348.

Meyer, L., & Janney, R. (1989). "User-friendly measures of meaningful outcomes: Evaluating behavioral interventions." *Journal of the Association for Persons with Severe Handicaps, 14*(4), 263–270.

Meyers, J. (1981). "Mental health consultation," in J. C. Conoley (Ed.), *Consultation in the schools: Theory, research, procedures.* New York: Academic Press.

Mowder, B. A., Willis, W. G., & Wilderstrom, A. H. (1986). "Consultation and handicapped preschoolers: Priorities, goals, and models." *Psychology in the Schools, 23*(4), 373–379.

Paolucci-Whitcomb, P., & Nevin, A. (1985). "Preparing consulting teachers through a collaborative approach between university faculty and field-based consulting teachers." *Teacher Education and Special Education, 8*(3), 132–143.

Parsons, R. D., & Meyers, J. (1984). *Developing consulting skills.* San Francisco: Jossey-Bass.

Piersal, W. C., & Guthin, J. B. (1983). "Resistance to school-based consultation: A behavioral analysis of the problem." *Psychology in the Schools, 20,* 311–320.

Polsgrove, L., & McNeil, M. (1989). "The consultation process: Research and practice." *Remedial and Special Education, 10*(1), 6–13, 20.

Power, T. J., & Bartholomew, K. L. (1985). "Getting caught in the middle: A case study in family-school system consultation." *School Psychology Review, 14*(2), 222–229.

Pugach, M. C., & Johnson, L. J. (1988). "Rethinking the relationship between consultation and collaborative problems-solving." *Focus on Exceptional Children, 21*(4), 1–8.

Reisberg, L., & Wolf, R. (1986). "Developing a consulting program in special education: Implementation and interventions." *Focus on Exceptional Children, 19*(3), 1–15.

Rhodes, W. C., & Smith, C. R. (1980). "Beyond theory and practice: Implications in programming for children with emotional disabilities and responses." *Behavioral Disorders, 5*(4), 254–77.

Rocha, R. M. (1983). "Educating the handicapped—The need for close cooperation between parents and administrators." *NASSP Bulletin, 67*(466), 92–97.

Rogers, C. R. (1961). *On becoming a person.* Boston: Houghton-Mifflin.

Rogers, C. R. (1969). *Freedom to learn.* Columbus, Ohio: Charles E. Merrill.

Rosenfield, S. (1985). "Teacher acceptance of behavioral principles." *Teacher Education and Special Education, 8*(3), 153–158.

Rubin, S., & Morrison, G. S. (1985). "Getting home visits off to a good start: Guidelines for teachers." *Techniques, 1*(5), 355–363.

Salend, S. J., & Salend, S. (1984). "Consulting with the regular teacher: Guidelines for special educators." *Pointer, 28*(3), 25–28.

Sarason, S. B. (1971). *The culture of the school and the problems of change.* Boston: Allyn and Bacon.

Schein, E. H. (1969). *Process consultation: Its role in organization development.* Reading, MA: Addison-Wesley.

Schubert, M. A., Landers, M. F., Curtin, T. E., Anderson, T. E., & Curtis, V. (1984). "Communication: One key to mainstreaming success." *Exceptional Children, 31*(1), 46–53.

Seligson, M. (1987). "Don't fire that staff member yet." *Child Care Information Exchange, 53,* 33–36.

Sheridan, S. M., & Elliott, S. (1991). "Behavioral consultation as a process for linking the assessment and treatment of social skills." *Journal of Educational and Psychological Consultation, 2,* 151–173.

Skinner, M. E. (1991). "Facilitating parental participation during individualized education program conferences." *Journal of Educational and Psychological Consultation, 2,* 285–289.

Tharp, R. G., & Wetzel, R. J. (1969). *Behavior modification in the natural environment.* New York: Academic Press.

Warren, D. E., & Goldsberry, L. F. (1982). "Developing teachers collaboration through colleague consultation." *Texas Tech Journal of Education, 9*(2), 101–109.

Westby, C. E. (1990). "Ethnographic interviewing: Asking the right questions to the right people in the right ways." *Journal of Childhood Communication Disorders, 13*(1), 101–111.

Wisniewski, L. A., & Alper, S. (1991). *Developing integrated educational settings for students with severe disabilities: Guidelines for systems change* (Manuscript submitted for publication).

Witt, J. C. (1986). "Teachers' resistance to the use of school-based consultations." *Journal of School Psychology, 24,* 37–44.

Witt, J. C., Erchul, W. P., McKee, W. T., Pardue, M. M., & Wickstrom, K. F. (1991). "Conversational control in school-based consultation: The relationship between consultant and consultee topic determination and consultation outcome." *Journal of Educational and Psychological Consultation, 2,* 101–116.

Zwald, L., & Gresham, F. M. (1982). "Behavioral consultation in a secondary class: Using DRL to decrease negative verbal interactions." *School Psychology Review, 11*(4), 428–432.

9

MODELS AND METHODS OF ADVOCACY

Cynthia N. Schloss
*Missouri Protection and
Advocacy Services*

Donna Jayne
University of Missouri-Columbia

Chapter Objectives

After completing this chapter, you will be able to:

1. Identify models of advocacy ranging from formal to informal
2. Describe the function of each model
3. Describe the methods and general guidelines of each model
4. Highlight trends and issues in the advocacy movement
5. Discuss the transition and interaction between individual and organizational advocacy methods and models

Key Terms and Phrases

adversarial
case advocacy
citizen advocacy
class advocacy
collectivity
consumerism
contextualization
dynamic process
empowerment
external advocacy

family advocacy
formal advocacy
informal advocacy
internal advocacy
legal advocacy
person-to-person advocacy
policymakers
self-advocacy
systems advocacy

INTRODUCTION

The purpose of this chapter is to acquaint the reader with models and methods of advocacy through the discussion of four major topics. The first topic, formats of advocacy, includes definitions of systems and legal advocacy. The methods and practices included in each format are described.

The second topic, methods of advocacy, includes a description of the circle of advocacy, and an overview of formal and informal methods. Included in the discussion of each method are definitions, strengths and weaknesses, and examples. Informal advocacy is discussed in terms of the family, self-advocacy, citizen, and person-to-person approaches.

The third topic is the dynamic process of advocacy. The attempt to gain power through formation of large organizations is contrasted with the maintenance of a focus on individual needs.

The fourth topic includes the trends and issues currently of concern in the practice of advocacy. The consumerism movement is explored, and common concerns of consumers addressed. The role of professionals in advocacy is discussed within the principles of contextualization, empowerment, and collectivity. Finally, suggestions are offered through which policymakers can better meet the financial, legal, and advocacy needs of the consumer.

FORMATS OF ADVOCACY

Advocacy is typically described through one of two formats: systems and legal. *Systems advocacy* is promoted to change policies and practices affecting all persons in a certain group or class. This may be promoted through informal and formal discussions with agencies/organizations where change is requested. This may even consist of efforts to change federal, state, or local law. An excellent example is the passing of the Americans with Disabilities Act in 1990. Numerous individuals who advocate for the rights of individuals, as well as those persons with disabilities, expressed their concerns about discrimination in the work place. Court cases were filed, proactive discussions occurred, and the need for a change in the federal law was apparent. Advocates began organizing, and through their efforts new legislation was developed and passed in congress. Benefits of the law are outlined in Chapter 2.

Some activities can be more effectively accomplished by non-legal methods. Educators, social workers, parents, and individuals with disabilities can assist persons or groups in investigating reasonable alternative resolutions to needs and concerns. They can assist in determining the issues, assess the concerns and issues of the parties involved, and then carry out proactive discussions through effective mediation techniques. Historically, advocacy has been directed by a legal model, but it is now becoming more effective through non-legal methods.

Legal advocacy involves direct intervention conducted by an advocate who has been trained with a legal perspective. More emphasis is based on the law, and advocacy methods are more adversarial. Legal advocacy can focus on individual case situations on behalf of an individual. It may also include action taken on behalf of a group according to the group's expressed wishes. This is referred to as class advocacy. Case and class legal advocacy methods have been noted to be highly effective in establishing law and precedence in programming services for persons with disabilities. For example, parents of a public school student request extended school year programming as afforded by federal law. The state in which they reside does not provide it. Parents are told that fiscal resources for such programming are not available and therefore, can not be written into the individualized education plan. Through legal advocacy methods, the parents pursue extended school year programming and continue their pursuit through the court system. The parent's case on behalf of their child prevails, and the child is afforded the programming. The case sets a precedent, and extended school year programming could be considered as available in the state to all individuals whose individualized education plan prescribes it. Box 9-1 illustrates this case.

BOX 9-1 • Litigation in Education: A True Story

The situation began when the Vahles removed their son from what they, based on regression and other factors, felt to be an inappropriate occupational therapy (OT) program on March 21, 1989. After repeated, unsuccessful attempts over a three week period to cause the school to hold an IEP meeting to discuss and change their son's OT program, on April 11, 1989, the Vahles placed their son in what they felt to be an appropriate program for his special OT needs.

On June 9, 1989, the school finally agreed with the Vahles that the private program in which they had placed their son was, in fact appropriate. Prior to that time, the school continually stated that it felt the child's prior program was still appropriate and requested that the Vahles place their son back into that program. At the June 9 meeting, the Vahles asked to be reimbursed in the amount of $861.00, which covered the costs of their son's private OT services from April 11 to June 9, 1989.

The school refused and the Vahles requested a due process hearing on the issue of reimbursement. The hearing officer ruled in favor of the Vahles and ordered the school to reimburse the Vahles $861.00. The school appealed into Federal District Court and the Vahles counterclaimed for attorneys' fees for both the administrative and district court levels. After briefing and oral argument, Judge Battey affirmed the order of the hearing officer and also awarded attorneys' fees for both the district court and administrative levels.

The school then appealed on the issues of reimbursement and attorneys' fees to the Eighth Circuit Court of Appeals. Briefing was completed this past summer, and oral argument was held in St. Paul on December 13, 1990. (South Dakota Advocacy Services, 1991, p. 1)

The Court's Analysis was summarized as follows: "We affirm the order of the district court directing the School District to reimburse the Vahles $861 for the cost of the outside OT program for Darin. We also affirm the award for attorneys' fees and expenses." (p. 2)

METHODS OF ADVOCACY

There are two underlying methods of advocacy in an organization or community: formal and informal methods. Formal advocacy, also known as internal advocacy, is a method that works from inside the organization or community and receives direct support from the organization or community. Examples would include ombudsman, employees, and advisory councils. External advocacy, also known as informal advocacy, receives support from outside the organization or community and operates independently from their supporting groups. These might include community support groups, legal entities, and protection and advocacy programs. In any system there are pros and cons. Table 9-1 notes the most obvious for both internal and external advocacy formats.

The process of advocacy varies with the individual and community. Both systems and legal advocacy are involved, but the extent to which each is used differs. To best understand this process, you might wish to envision it as a "circle of advocacy" as noted in Figure 9-1 below.

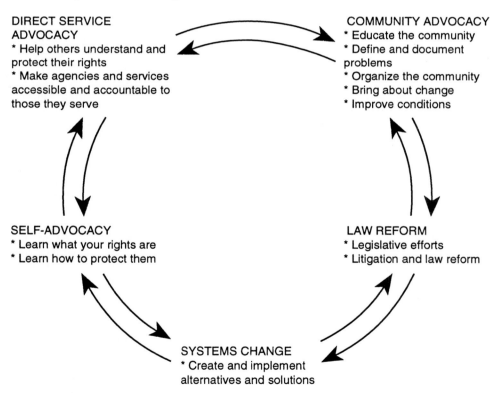

DIRECT SERVICE ADVOCACY
* Help others understand and protect their rights
* Make agencies and services accessible and accountable to those they serve

COMMUNITY ADVOCACY
* Educate the community
* Define and document problems
* Organize the community
* Bring about change
* Improve conditions

SELF-ADVOCACY
* Learn what your rights are
* Learn how to protect them

LAW REFORM
* Legislative efforts
* Litigation and law reform

SYSTEMS CHANGE
* Create and implement alternatives and solutions

FIGURE 9-1 • Circle of Advocacy

Note: From "Mental Health Advocacy Training Kit, Introduction to Mental Health Advocacy" by National Paralegal Institute, 1980, Washington, D.C.: National Paralegal Institute.

TABLE 9-1 • External and Internal Positions of Advocates/Ombudsmen

External*	Internal*
Pros:	***Pros:***
1. Independent—not related to treatment services and providers. No conflicts of interests. Impartial 2. Can form coalitions—easier to collaborate with other systems 3. Can resort to force, intimidation, coercion 4. Serves as mediator between client and systems 5. Can cut through bureaucratic red tape—not constrained by system, more freedom 6. Innovative and creative—can experiment with problem solving.	1. Easy access to clients and records 2. Easy access to service providers and policies. Easier to gain information 3. Relatively stable financial base 4. Institutional sanction for office 5. Negotiation skills rather than confrontation used 6. Accountable to the system
Cons:	***Cons:***
1. Limited access to environments or programs in which clients are served; structural barriers 2. Information difficult to obtain—frequently reported second-hand; may be faulty or misleading 3. Often view system as "all bad" 4. Financially unstable—obtaining funds can diffuse and hinder advocacy efforts 5. Temporary leadership—attrition rate high; part-time staff; volunteer staff 6. Become so involved in fighting the system that clients can be forgotten or ignored 7. Frequently not accountable to persons in system which they are advocating	1. Given the size, complexity and generally unresponsive nature of bureaucracies it is unlikely that an individual would be successful in moving the system alone. In order to move system you would need a larger group to feed into. System inertia. 2. Advocate could be manipulated by the system when system maintenance or staff interest conflicts with clients' needs. 3. Risk of losing job always present. 4. Clients distrustful of workers—perceive them as part of the establishment 5. Clients may be the recipients of unpleasant repercussions—privileges taken away because complained.
*Supported externally—operated on a human service delivery system from the outside	*Supported internally—works from inside the system and supported by that system

Note: From "Mental Health Advocacy Training Kit, Introduction to Mental Health Advocacy" by National Paralegal Institute, 1980, Washington, D.C.: National Paralegal Institute.

In this model there are two circles, one encompassed in the other, representing the different possible directions that an advocate may take. Five different advocacy methods are noted. One method is direct service advocacy in which the advocate or advocacy organization helps others understand and protect their rights. In a second method, self-advocacy, an individual learns his or her rights and how to protect those rights. Systems change, a third alternative, includes the creation and implementation of alternatives and solutions. A fourth method, law reform, includes legislative efforts, and litigation and law reform. Community advocacy, the final alternative, is typified by efforts to educate the community, define and document problems, organize the community, bring about change, and improve conditions. It may also switch directions as appropriate. For example, members of a community organization would like to see more supported living opportunities in their community. They define and document the problems, educate the community, and then discuss the issues with the local provider (direct service advocacy). The provider agrees with the concept and notes that there are few interested individuals. Consumers of these services inform the provider and discuss why the concept is important to them (self-advocacy) and propose a plan. The provider agrees and implements the plan in the next year (systems change). A local legislator is contacted by the consumer and invited to tour supported living programs. The legislator is impressed and introduces a bill to provide a tax benefit to organizations who develop supportive living programs and it passes into law (law reform). The community is excited and advocacy continues.

The above description is idealistic in nature, and the reader must realize that the described process may take years to evolve. Advocacy systems, whether internal or external, are typically classified as formal or informal. We will discuss each of these approaches.

Formal Advocacy Models

An advocate in a formal model is paid by the system in which he or she works. Typically "formal advocates" contend that the system needs reform and renewal, and this can be accomplished most effectively by activity within the system (Neufeld, 1980). Advocates are committed to identifying individuals whose rights and needs are not being met by the agency or system, and activity is geared toward changing the system to meet the client's needs and rights.

Advocates as a rule should not be the employees of the facility in which they work. Generally a much preferred arrangement is to separate the advocacy function from the provider of program or service. What is good for the provider is not necessarily good for the person who receives the service or programming. In true advocacy, the commitment to the individual takes primacy over the commitment to the employer when the two interests compete with one another. If an advocate chooses not to promote the best interest of a client and instead promotes the system, he or she ceases to be an advocate (Neufeld, 1980).

When the advocate can resist being co-opted by the system, strong advantages in formal advocacy appear. These might include: knowledge of the system, program data, investigation reports, and financial support. With such information, an advocate might be able to access services for his or her client in a faster and more effective fashion. Table 9-2 includes a listing of questions that an internal advocate might ask when promoting change within a system or agency.

TABLE 9-2 • Questions to Ask to Promote Change

The questions below can be used as a guide to promote change.

1. What is the problem? Identify your issues carefully. Prioritize them. Document the problem thoroughly. Double check your information.

2. Who is affected by the problem? How is each person you listed affected by the problem? Who benefits from continuation of the problem? Is someone's prestige or economic welfare being fed by the continuation of the problem?

3. When did the problem start? Has it been a continuous problem? Is it worse at certain times? What started the problem, made it worse or caused you to notice the problem?

4. What kinds of changes would solve the problem? How will you know when the problem is solved?

5. By what date should the problem begin to be resolved? How long should this process take?

6. What has been done to address the problem so far? What happened as a result of this? Should this be confirmed or does something else need to be tried?

7. Are there laws and regulations which relate to the problem at hand? Know and be able to refer to the ethical standards of your professional association.

After you have answered each of these questions develop a plan of action. Report the problem to your immediate supervisor or internal agency mechanism that will aid you in promoting change. Review your findings and plan with your contact focusing on issues and not on personalities involved.

Informal Advocacy

The term informal advocacy does not imply lack of organization or the absence of an effort to form and participate in a power structure. Also referred to as "external advocacy," informal advocacy implies support from private resources outside the human service system for individuals or groups not accountable to the system in which they are advocating (National Paralegal Institute, 1980). Informal, or external, advocacy for needed services and self-determination has both advantages and disadvantages. Informal advocates, because they are not answerable to the system, have often been viewed as confrontational and threatening in their promotion of system dismantling. In addition to placing themselves, or being placed, in adversarial positions, informal advocates are likely to have limited access to service environments or programs making it difficult to obtain accurate data and records. This can create credibility problems for groups and individuals.

Independence however, in spite of its accompanying problems, is also one of the main advantages of informal advocacy. Because efforts are not related to treatment services and providers, there are fewer conflicts of interest, and greater impartiality can be maintained. Lack of formal structure can ease the formation of coalitions without the push for unity being weakened by the system. In Table 9-3, seven steps are listed to promote avoidance of confrontational situations when working with agencies.

TABLE 9-3 • Steps to Avoid Confrontational Situations

How to avoid confrontational situations:

1. Establish a good rapport with the agency before any problems arise.
2. Always be prepared for meetings.
3. Always be certain you thoroughly understand the agency's proposals and the reasons behind them.
4. Be certain the agency understands your concerns.
5. Be sure to explore all possible solutions to the problems.
6. Identify any acceptable alternatives.
7. Seek assistance from outside sources.

Although informal advocates have been criticized for being confrontational, their freedom to use popular media and the courts has been responsible for major successes outlined in Chapter 2.

In a less adversarial position, informal advocates can serve as mediators between individuals and the system, and have greater freedom to cut through bureaucratic red tape. This freedom allows for a more innovative and creative approach to problem solving. Missouri Protection and Advocacy Services, a not-for-profit organization mandated by federal law, reported (1991) that a majority of complaints received from clients are corrected through non-litigious means focusing on mediation techniques. Table 9-4 identifies procedures for conducting a mediation activity with two groups who differ.

Informal advocacy can take a number of forms depending on the needs, abilities, and interests of the individuals involved. The methods and goals of a parent advocating for the rights of the family and the child who has a disability differ from those of an adult attempting to obtain and protect his or her own rights. Methods and goals would again differ for an individual interested in providing assistance for a friend or advocacy organization. We will discuss these methods and goals within the context of family advocacy, self-advocacy, citizen advocacy, and person-to-person advocacy.

Family Advocacy

Informal advocacy often begins when a child who is disabled is born into a family. In addition to coping with the initial emotional and physical crises facing the family, the same disability that impairs the functioning of a child may emotionally drain the whole family. Stresses are created that wear down strengths and resources (Cohen, Agosta, Cohen, and Warren, 1989). Demands and stresses may include: learning to implement and adjusting to the time demands of specialized care needs; time and travel for frequent medical consultations; locating and accessing needed services; dwindling financial resources; exclusion by professionals in decisions regarding the child; and lack of time for other children, spouse, and self.

Cohen et al. (1989), in a review of the literature, found that problems experienced by a particular family are related to a number of factors, including the

TABLE 9-4 • Procedures for Mediation

1. All mediations begin with a joint session that includes all parties.
2. Introductions are made and the mediator explains the process.
3. Confidentiality and informality are stressed.
4. Individual, family member, or advocate are invited to speak first to describe the issues and what they seek.
5. The representative of the agency then responds.
6. Others present are then asked to speak.
7. At the conclusion, the mediator reminds everyone that he or she will be speaking privately to both sides in separate sessions to work out an agreement.
8. Individual sessions with each party are then held.
9. Typically, this process leads to an agreement written by the mediator and reviewed by each side.
10. Both groups are brought together for a final joint session to sign the agreement.
11. If no agreement is reached, the mediator explains to the parents their appeal rights and provides a written list of outstanding issues.

seriousness of the family member's disability, family characteristics, specific parenting patterns, the family's capacity for coping with the problem, the presence of behavior problems, and the availability of community supports. Each of these factors will contribute to a family's ability and willingness to engage in advocacy for the family member who is disabled and for the family as a whole. Within the family structure, Hines (1986) recommends five important steps in developing a workable advocacy style.

1. *Problem analysis. Prioritize the problems facing the family and then analyze the problems requiring immediate attention.*
2. *Information gathering. Identify which agency has authority or responsibility for making the kinds of changes or providing the assistance needed.*
3. *Action planning. Develop a plan of action with the assistance of the person most directly associated with the problem.*
4. *Assertiveness. Improve interpersonal skills and develop an effective style of assertiveness.*
5. *Follow-up. Monitor all parties and agencies involved to assure the implementation of promised services and changes.*

Comprehensive family advocacy should include long-term, short-term, and ongoing goals. Long-term goals should be reviewed to gain a long-term perspective of the child's life and the programming that is necessary to achieve those goals. Short-term goals are needed to deal with immediate family needs for emotional support and adjustment to advance towards the long-term goals for the child. Ongoing goals are needed to ensure access to programs to minimize the effects of the disabling condition on the long-term goals. Turnbull and Shaffer (1986) identify family needs that can be translated into short-term, ongoing, and long-term goals. These are listed in Table 9-5.

Ultimately, the goal of family advocacy can be viewed as the normalization of the parenting period. The end product of effective family advocacy should be the transition of the member with a disability to self-advocacy supported by citizen advocacy.

TABLE 9-5 • Family Needs Translated Into Goals

Short-term

- Identify and meet the financial, legal, and advocacy needs of all family members.
- Access financial support that enables families to provide care for the individual with a disability in the home as contrasted to hospitals and institutions.
- Identify and develop access to medical, legal, financial, and personal supports to aid in times of crisis.
- Obtain non-stigmatizing financial assistance to meet needs in all areas of family life. Eligibility criteria for this assistance should consider income, number of dependents, and excess cost related to the disability.
- Obtain advocacy services to insure the protection of legal rights to all family members.

Ongoing

- Identify and operationalize the advocacy strengths of family members.
- Access financial assistance/planning services, legal, and advocacy services that enhance dignity for family members, are tailored to individual needs, coordinated across all stages of the family life-cycle, and exist within integrated community programs and settings.
- Protect the legal rights of the individual with a disability across all stages of the life-cycle.
- Access information on state-of-the-art practices related to financial assistance/planning services, legal, and advocacy services.
- Receive updates on benefit changes.
- Access services that help insure a positive future for the individual with a disability.

Long-term

- Create opportunities for the member with a disability to contribute to the economic assets of the family.
- Become knowledgeable about guardianship laws.
- Insure that the individual with a disability is provided with an educational program to expand decision-making capacity to the greatest extent possible.
- Identify the advocacy strengths of the individual with a disability. Provide support and encouragement to increase advocacy effectiveness across the life-cycle.
- Work to improve the system by encouraging professionals such as lawyers, trust officers, financial planners, and insurance adjusters to develop expertise in disability issues to increase their effectiveness in responding to family needs.
- Advocate for systems that are least stigmatizing, most cost-effective, and that most enhance the independence of the individual with a disability.

DISCUSSION GENERATOR 9-1 • Internal/Formal Advocacy

Often times we fit a client or student to an existing service or program. We ask "What services/programs are available?" and place a person in the one which comes closest to meeting his or her needs. Instead we need to be "client driven" and determine the person's needs prior to developing the program.

You are a member of an advisory council for an agency that provides services to persons with mental retardation. How would you advocate for a change to promote the agency becoming "client driven"?

Self-advocacy

Self-advocacy is in part consciousness-raising, an assertiveness-training program, and a springboard to direct consumer involvement (Herr, 1983). Self-advocacy groups such as People First and Partners in Policy Making stress training in the rights and responsibilities of adulthood. Singer and Apolloni (1981) characterize self-advocacy as the most basic form of self-assertion to protect or gain rights. They point out that even people with substantial disabilities can be taught rudimentary ways to communicate their needs and preferences.

A self-advocacy group is described by Rhoades, Browning, and Thorin (1986) as a common reference group that provides an opportunity for volunteer participation. These groups emphasize the power of members to assist one another rather than depending entirely on professionals. This experience enables members to develop a sense of empowerment and competence within a peer group that understands their problems. Peer group identification facilitates communication among persons who have experienced the same problem and societal reactions to that problem. It enhances socialization opportunities, promotes social learning of coping strategies developed by peers, allows new members to emulate veterans, and allows veterans to receive reinforcement from new members.

An important aspect of self-help groups is the role of the professional or non-peer participant (Rhoades, et al., 1986). Leadership in the group is reserved for the members who share a common condition or problem, while the professional performs three specific functions to enhance their efforts: (a) provide assistance in the formation of new self-help groups; (b) serve as a catalyst or facilitator, particularly while a group is being formed; and (c) serve as a resource person.

"Real supporters of self-advocacy know that a self-advocate is . . . working to empower people with disabilities" (Effective Self-Advocacy, 1990, p.3). To be realistic, the expectation that a person will be able to make choices should begin early in life, and opportunities furnished to make choices. Rogers (1988) provides an example of self-advocacy found in Box 9-2.

The steps involved in Box 9-2 are similar to those suggested for family advocacy (Rogers, 1988, Apolloni, 1984).

BOX 9-2 • Development of Self-Advocacy Skills

Joe, a patient in an inpatient unit, would like to see his grounds privileges increased. The trainer explains to Joe what his rights are and the proper procedures to follow in attaining his goal. Joe is assisted in strategy planning, e.g. "Do you go to the top of the facility administration first or do you work your way up from the bottom? Should you negotiate? How do you negotiate? The trainer may assist Joe in developing skills needed in successful self-advocacy, such as listening or assertiveness skills. Rather than going to the service provider on Joe's behalf, the trainer helps Joe develop the capability to speak for himself.

---

1. *Clarification.* To establish credibility, one must narrow down and focus on attainable goals.
2. *Organizational component.* Once an individual understands what he or she would like to accomplish, they will need to organize their case and establish goals.
3. *Presenting the case.* The individual will engage in the system to seek the desired change.
4. *Evaluation.* Having taking action, the individual needs to evaluate what was accomplished.

Apolloni (1984) suggests viewing self-advocacy as a cycle, an ongoing learning process:

> *There is no end to the process of self-advocacy. Self-advocates must reassess their needs and the services available to meet their needs on an ongoing basis. Each stage in a person's development potentially means new needs, new decision-makers to influence, and new follow-up visits. Being a truly effective self-advocate is not an easy task! It demands tenacity and perseverance . . . Irritants make pearls. (p.4)*

An interview on self-advocacy is found in Box 9-3.

Citizen Advocacy

Citizen advocacy works as much to change community attitudes as to improve living conditions for individuals. It derives its power from the fact that advocates are drawn from the very community which must take responsibility for the people with disabilities who live within it. Any status attendant on a citizen advocacy organization is derived from acceptance as an element of the community rather than a legal mandate (Ward, 1986).

Ward (1986) cited the definition of Wolfensberger and Zauha (1973) who describe a citizen advocate as:

a mature, competent citizen volunteer representing, as if they were his own, the interests of another citizen who is impaired in his instrumental competency . . . or who has major expressive (emotional) needs which are unmet and which are likely to remain unmet without special intervention . . . a friend who telephones and visits, who sends mail and gifts, and who perhaps invites his protégé into his home for visits . . . (p.91).

BOX 9-3 • Interview on Self-Advocacy

Beth is a born advocate, both for herself and others. She is thirty-two years old and has cerebral palsy. She works in the benchwork program of a not-for-profit private agency where she performs data entry using a head stick for typing.

Through her self-advocacy efforts Beth referred herself to a supported living program and now shares a home with Ann, her housemate and friend. When interviewed she was busy directing the planting of her first vegetable garden.

Beth tells her story:

I lived at home with my folks and my two brothers until I was fourteen. Then I moved to a residential facility about one hundred miles away from home. Boy, it was hard because I never was away from home before. Saying goodbye was the hardest part of moving. I talk to my parents on the phone now and then, and I see them fairly often.

I had never shared a room before and having a roommate was hard until we got to know each other. We got to be very good friends. She was a handicapped girl and couldn't talk at all. So I taught her how to talk with her eyes. I taught her "look up" for yes, and "look down" for no. I helped her a lot. We were together for a long time. When she went home it was hard to say goodbye. She lives in another state and we never see each other.

I decided I wanted my own home, and when I joined People First last year they got me going. I wrote a letter saying I would like to refer myself to supported living. It took a long time to find a house, but I found it. My case worker took me to meet Ann. We had lunch together to talk and got to know each other. Now we're housemates. My folks helped me move in and her folks helped her.

A long time ago when I first talked about having my own home my mom said, "Who will take care of you, who can you call?" That went on and on for a long time. Suddenly my parents changed their minds. I think they knew I could do it. They think I can do what I set my mind to and so do I.

The biggest problem in becoming more independent was convincing people I could do it. The hardest people to convince are the people in agencies. Because I'm handicapped, they don't know what I can do for myself once I set my mind to it.

The worst thing about how nonhandicapped people treat people who are handicapped is the way they look at you. Sometimes they don't consider how a handicapped person feels. I used to get my feelings hurt a lot when I lived at the learning center. That made me realize I had to move on. Everyday when I got home from work I immediately had to do my program (physical therapy) so I could do what I wanted to do in the evening. They wouldn't let me relax. Now when I get home I relax and talk to people.

Advocacy means doing things on your own. To become a self-advocate, talk to people and start planning things on your own. Write postcards and letters and tell people how you feel.

The most exciting thing that has happened to me through advocacy was moving into my house. Right now my house is number one.

This relationship is arranged and supported by a small citizen advocacy office which is completely independent of any organization or government agency providing services to persons with disabilities. A small staff of perhaps two people matches an advocate with a protégé who is disabled, conducts training programs and provides support to advocates in dealing with particular issues and problems. The staff will not attempt to control the relationship, or place limits on the issues that are to be taken up on the protégé's behalf. The advocate's primary loyalty is to the person on whose behalf advocacy occurs, not to the citizen advocacy office.

Snellen (1979) points out the importance of the protégé concept in citizen advocacy. "The term protégé implies a growth potential, a friend, a partner concept not altogether implied by the term client or by the traditional guardianship systems" (p.372). Within this concept the role of the advocate can take several forms. Practical guidance can be offered through advice, instruction, and practice in daily activities with the intent of increasing the independence of the protégé. The role of the friend provides the opportunity to offer emotional reinforcement by providing attention and affection, letting the protégé know that someone cares.

The essence of citizen advocacy is the relationship between the two people involved. It is as much concerned with satisfying emotional needs as solving practical problems. As this relationship develops, the advocate's family and friends become involved, and the protégé gradually becomes more involved with the advocate's network of friends, relatives, co-workers, and associates in the community.

While the advocate lacks any legal power, this is seen as a strength of the program because it also means that the advocate is a volunteer and owes allegiance to no one but the person served. The citizen advocate does not have a professional reputation to consider or a job to protect.

The citizen advocate also gains power as a non-professional and as a non-relative. The non-professional has no preconceived notions and feels no need to justify in professional terms any claims made about the person served. Perceptions of dealing with problems are not colored by training or experience which have taught the "right way" to approach a problem. The citizen advocate is more likely to state what he or she sees as a reasonable solution, and then perhaps challenge involved professionals to justify their disagreements. As non-relatives, citizen advocates provide a fresh view of problems and are less likely to become victims of intimidation. Relatives who have advocated for a person for years may accept second-rate services, be exhausted from years of struggle and chronic sorrow and grief. They may be fearful of confronting care providers who may say "take her home," if pushed too far.

Citizen advocacy does have inefficiencies. The extent to which an individual's problems are addressed and solved will depend on the individual advocate and the advocate/protégé relationship. While this one-to-one relationship can be the strongest point in favor of citizen advocacy, a weakness is the fact that it has no carry-over to others who are disabled. A legal decision can be seen as a test case which can then be applied to everyone in a similar situation. A victory in citizen advocacy is more likely to come from an individual who may solve a problem in a round-about, unpredictable way, or by simply refusing to take "no" for an answer until the decision-maker is too worn down to resist.

Widrick, Hasazi, and Hasazi (1990) cite numerous studies suggesting potential benefits of the citizen advocate-protégé relationship for persons with intellectual disabilities. First, friendships with peers, service providers, and others are associated with better personal, social, and vocational adjustment (Gollay, Freedman, Wyngaarden, & Kurtz, 1978; Hasazi, Gordon, & Roe, 1985; Romer & Heller, 1983; Rosen, 1988). Second, the results of several studies suggest that the informal assistance and support of nondisabled adults may be particularly important to the successful community adjustment of adults with disabilities living in relatively independent residential settings (Edgerton, 1975; Edgerton & Bercovici, 1976; Floor, Rosen, Baxter, Horowitz, & Weber, 1971). Third, there is evidence that many persons with mental retardation encounter difficulties in establishing friendships, particularly with nondisabled persons other than service providers (Bercovici, 1986; Bjaanes & Butler, 1974; Landesman-Dwyer, 1981; Rhodes & Browning, 1977; Scheerenberger & Felsenthal, 1977).

Person-to-Person Advocacy

Successful independence for a person with a disability may be enhanced by a special friend who gives a little extra help in daily life. Generally these friends are neither relatives nor professional service providers. They are simply caring people who take a personal interest in helping a friend who has special needs. No formal training or knowledge is required to give time or attention in order to help a friend be more independent or feel less lonely. All that is required is the willingness to take the risk of getting to know someone who may, initially, seem different (Singer & Apolloni, 1981).

In the preceding sections we have discussed methods for gaining access to various power structures in order to identify and protect the human and legal rights of persons with disabilities. However, it would be inaccurate to conceptualize this process as proceeding only in the direction of organization. Advocacy is, in reality, a two-way street on which the gaining of power through organization is balanced with a focus on the needs of the individual. This balance forms the dynamic process of advocacy.

ADVOCACY AS A DYNAMIC PROCESS

An advocate must have sufficient power to access the system in order to meet an individual's advocacy needs. In an effort to gain this power, the advocate typically joins a local group with goals matching his or her own. This group is part of a local coalition which, in turn, is a member of a regional network. The regional network is a part of a multi-state organization that, with like entities, participates in a national advocacy effort to access funds, bring about systems changes, and influence legislation.

This multi-layered advocacy effort must access a multi-layered human service system that Neufeld (1980) likens to a huge onion. "No matter how many layers are stripped away, there always seems to be another layer . . . a person attempting to strip away the bureaucratic layers is likely to be driven to tears before an accountable agent is found." (National Paralegal Institute, 1980).

Within such complicated structures, advocacy groups as well as human service providers can lose sight of individual needs. Maintaining a focus on these needs requires a dynamic process—an ongoing effort in which individuals strive for power through organization, while organizations attempt to avoid depersonalization through individual contact.

A workshop held at the 114th Annual Conference of the American Association on Mental Retardation, May 30, 1990, offered guidelines for this process. Participants providing input included people with disabilities, and state and local leaders, paid staff, and volunteer helpers from self-advocacy groups. Refer to Table 9-6 for a concise description of the process.

Ideally, the dynamic process works in two directions simultaneously. As each individual member attempts to contribute to the effectiveness of the larger body, the system maintains a focus on, and attempts to meet the needs of, the individual.

Thus far we have discussed advocacy formats, methods, and dynamic process. Functions, practices, goals, and definitions have been identified. But we do not claim to have done anything other than present a picture of advocacy at one point in time.

The practice of advocacy for and by persons with disabilities is very much a work in progress. At any given point in time, methods and goals will be influenced by a variety of issues including (but not limited to) societal norms and attitudes, the political climate, availability of funding, economic conditions, and scientific and medical knowledge. Because all of these issues affect the quality of life experienced by persons with disability, they in turn affect the practice of advocacy.

We will now discuss three trends and issues currently affecting advocacy. The discussion addresses consumerism, the role of professionals in consumerism, and the role of policymakers in consumerism.

CONSUMERISM

The growth of self-advocacy has been accompanied by a growing awareness among persons with disabilities of their status as consumers. Modeling their efforts on successful self-help and consumer organizations such as Alcoholics Anonymous

---

DISCUSSION GENERATOR 9-2 • Dynamic Process

Provide an example of a large organization or system (i.e., university, law enforcement agency, governmental agency, service provider, insurance company) losing touch with individual needs. Discuss ways in which this could be remedied.

TABLE 9-6 • Aids for the Dynamic Process

Individuals

- Becoming politically active
- Defining their own positions
- Forming or joining groups for change
- Involving community leaders in their lives and in their issues
- Influencing the way the media presents people with disabilities
- Participating in disability service system councils, boards, task forces, and committees
- Reaching out into the community for help

Groups

- Providing members with information about what local, state, and federal governments do, how elections work, how to vote, and how to get involved with a political party
- Making sure that local voting places are accessible and that people who have trouble reading have the help they need to vote
- Holding an annual legislative rally to help members learn how the legislature works while presenting issues to their legislators
- Giving members a better chance to educate their local legislators by meeting with them before the legislative session begins or before elections
- Developing a written legislative program, agreed to by members, to give a focus to legislative meetings and other lobbying work
- Providing members with information on legislators' voting record, new laws or regulations, and other groups' proposals

Coalitions

- Bringing different groups of people together to work for change on an issue they each believe is important
- Providing each chapter with more power
- Giving members a chance to develop leadership skills
- Helping members become comfortable working outside their own group
- Assuring that all members provide input in decision-making
- Fostering positive attitudes among members with dissimilar problems or disabilities

Service Providers

- Asking members of advocacy groups and coalitions to serve on councils, boards, task forces, advisory groups, and committees
- Maintaining a focus on the needs of the individuals served rather than the needs of the agency

Boards and Committees

- Providing mentorships to help develop leadership skills
- Keeping absent members up to date
- Accommodating individual communication methods such as signing, braille, tapes, etc.
- Providing a facilitator to help members understand difficult issues.

and Ralph Nader's group, these individuals view themselves as purchasers of human services. They accept the right and responsibility to hold providers accountable for the quality and appropriateness of their services.

The consumer movement is not limited to any disability sector. It is taking place among persons with a wide variety of disabilities, and these groups share a number of common concerns:

1. Stigma
2. The right to refuse treatment versus the right to receive treatment
3. Involuntary administration of medication
4. Involuntary commitment and outpatient commitment
5. Use and/or overuse of E.C.T.
6. Affirmative action
7. An integrated human services delivery system
8. Treatment carried out in the least restrictive environment
9. Adequate supports to remain involved in the community and to achieve autonomy
10. Housing assistance
11. Insurance coverage
12. Financial disincentives

The consumer movement reserves the leadership role in advocacy for those persons having disabilities. An equally important supportive role is assigned to professionals in various human service fields. A discussion of that role follows.

The Role of Professionals in Consumerism

Rose (1987) considers three principles vital in the role of professionals in today's consumer movement.

Contextualization
Professionals need to be aware of the belief that consumers know themselves better than the professionals do, and therefore have expertise to contribute to a dialogue. Consumers should be assisted to express, elaborate, externalize, and reflect on feelings, and better understand themselves in the context of daily life.

Empowerment
Professionals need to develop a process of dialogue through which consumers are supported in the generation of a range of possibilities appropriate to their needs. The consumer remains the center of all decisions regarding his or her life. It is the responsibility of the professional to question critically, elicit relevant information, and make the consumer comfortable with the assistance process.

Collectivity
The focus on this principle is on the social basis of identity. It is designed to reduce the negative feelings produced by viewing one's self as defective or unproductive. While the professional helps consumers improve their view, efforts are also made to develop social supports. Specific need areas such as housing, employment, and recreation are addressed as well as emotional needs.

Just as professionals can offer support directly in advocacy efforts, policymakers can indirectly offer support through appropriate decision making. A discussion of this role follows.

The Role of the Policymakers in Consumerism

To better meet the financial, legal and advocacy needs of the consumer with a disability, Turnbull and Shaffer (1986) suggest that policymakers:

1. Enact federal legislation to shift major funding streams away from residential institutions and to community and family support programs

2. Replicate successful family support programs in every state that provide financial subsidies to enable families to meet the needs of their member with a disability in the home and community setting

3. Eliminate all policy incentives that favor out-of-home care, and provide policy incentives that support families so that they can remain intact

4. Expand resources to Protection and Advocacy agencies to insure that all families have access to legal and other advocacy services

5. Monitor and enforce the implementation of the Rehabilitation Act

6. Support augmented funding of the Rehabilitation Act and retention of the rights and provisions contained therein

7. Protect the current and prospective Social Security benefit levels and eligibility for persons with disabilities under the Social Security Act

8. Strengthen and implement fully the home and community-based waivers of the Medicaid program

9. Provide a non-age restricted personal tax exemption for any family with a member with a disability

10. Establish model state statutes for limited guardianship and encourage state implementation

11. Establish criteria for determining eligibility of families for financial assistance based on a combination of factors including income, number of dependents, and the excess cost related to the disability

12. Implement, monitor, and evaluate interagency agreements to insure the provision of coordinated and comprehensive transportation to meet financial planning/assistance, legal, and advocacy needs

SUMMARY

Advocates promote the development and existence of rights, services, and resources of individuals. Advocacy is historically viewed as progressing from care provided by family, relatives and friends to governmental and social programs. Methods vary depending on the qualifications, values, skills and abilities, and resources of the advocate.

Advocacy is typically described by systems and legal formats. Systems advocacy is promoted to change policies and practices affecting all persons in a certain group or class. In legal advocacy, direct intervention is usually conducted by an advocate who has been trained with a legal per-

spective. Two underlying methods to advocacy are found in each format: formal and informal methods. Formal advocacy or internal advocacy, works from inside the organization or community and receives direct support from the organization or community. Informal advocacy or external advocacy, works from outside the organization or community and receives support from outside sources.

Formal advocacy proponents contend that the system needs reform and renewal and can be accomplished by activity within the system. Advocates, as a rule, should not be employed by the system in which they work. Strong advocates who can resist being co-opted by the system might be able to access services for their clients in a faster and more effective manner.

Informal advocacy proponents have often been viewed as confrontational and threatening because they are not answerable to the system. Independence is a main advantage over formal advocacy as well as fewer conflicts of interest and maintenance of impartiality. Informal advocates are likely to have limited access to service programs and environments making it difficult to obtain data and records, creating possible credibility problems for groups and individuals. Informal advocacy has not only relied on adversarial methods but has found mediation techniques to be quite effective. Informal advocacy groups have taken many shapes and forms including: family advocacy, self-advocacy, citizen advocacy, and person-to-person advocacy. Each of these groups were described in the preceding pages.

Three major trends and issues have been noted in the chapter: consumerism, the role of professionals in consumerism, and the role of the policy makers in consumerism. A growing awareness among persons with disabilities of their status as consumers has become quite apparent. Consumers accept the right and responsibility to hold providers accountable for the quality and appropriateness of their services. The consumer movement is not limited to mental health issues and occurs among persons with a wide variety of disabilities noting their concerns.

In this chapter we have described various models of formal and informal advocacy. Choice of a particular method is determined by the needs and abilities of those involved. The end result of an advocacy effort will be determined in large part by the interpersonal skills of the advocate. Chapter 10 addresses the systems change approach in advocacy.

Formats of Advocacy

1. Advocacy is typically described between one of two formats: systems and legal.

2. Systems advocacy is promoted to change policies and practices affecting all persons in a certain group or class.

3. Legal advocacy involves direct intervention conducted by an advocate who has been trained with a legal perspective.

Methods of Advocacy

4. Formal advocacy, also known as internal advocacy, is a method that works from inside the organization and/or community.

5. Informal advocacy, also known as external advocacy, operates independently from the organization and/or community.

6. An advocate in a formal model is paid by the system in which he or she works.

7. When the advocate can resist being co-opted by the system, strong advantages appear including: knowledge of system, program data, and investigation reports.

8. Informal advocates have often been viewed as confrontational, adversarial, and threatening to service providers.

9. Family advocacy can be viewed as the normalization of the parenting period.

10. Self-advocacy programs highlight the training of rights and responsibilities in adulthood and is viewed as the most basic form of self-assertion.

11. Citizen advocacy derives its power from advocates drawn from the community that must take responsibility for the persons with disabilities who live within it.

12. Successful independence may be enhanced by a friend who gives assistance in daily life through person-to-person advocacy.

Advocacy as a Dynamic Process

13. Advocacy, as a dynamic process, attempts to contribute to the effectiveness of the system as well as the needs of the individual.

Consumerism

14. The consumer movement reserves the leadership role in advocacy for those persons with disabilities.

15. Contextualization, empowerment, and collectivity are three principles vital in the role of professionals.

16. Policymakers provide legislative assistance to persons with disabilities in meeting their financial, legal, and advocacy needs.

REFERENCES

Apolloni, T. (1984, November). "Self-advocacy: How to be a winner." *National Information Center for Handicapped Children and Youth Newsletter*, 1–4.

Bercovici, S. M. (1986). *Barriers to normalization—the restrictive management of retarded persons*. Baltimore: University Park Press.

Bjaanes, A., & Butler, E. W. (1974). "Environmental variation in community care facilities for mentally retarded persons." *American Journal of Mental Deficiency, 78,* 429–439.

Cohen, S., Agosta, J., Cohen, J., & Warren, R. (1989). "Supporting families of children with severe disabilities." *Journal of the Association for Persons with Severe Handicaps, 14*(2), 155–162.

Edgerton, R. B. (1975). *The cloak of competence: Stigma in the lives of the mentally retarded.* Berkeley: University of California Press.

Edgerton, R. B., & Bercovici, S. (1976). "The cloak of competence: Ten years later." *American Journal of Mental Deficiency, 80,* 485–497.

Effective self advocacy: Empowering people with disabilities to speak for themselves, Report No. 90-4, 1990. Research and Training Center on Community Living, University of Minnesota.

Floor, L., Rosen, M., Baxter, D., Horowitz, J., & Weber, C. (1971). "Sociosexual problems in mentally handicapped females." *Training School Bulletins, 68,* 106–112.

Gollay, E., Freedman, R., Wyngaarden, M., & Kurtz, N. R. (1978). *Coming back.* Cambridge: Abt Books.

Hasazi, S. B., Gordon, L. R., & Roe, C. A. (1985). "Factors associated with the employment status of handicapped youth exiting high school from 1979 to 1983." *Exceptional Children, 51,* 455–469.

Herr, S. (1983). *Rights and advocacy for retarded people.* Toronto: Lexington.

Hines, M. (1986). "A practical guide to advocacy," in *Lifetime Planning Manual, 1984–85.* Lansing, MI: Michigan State Department of Mental Health. (ERIC Document Reproduction Service No. ED 266 831).

Landesman-Dwyer, S. (1981). "Living in the community." *American Journal of Mental Deficiency, 86,* 223–234.

Missouri Protection and Advocacy Services (1991, June). "Annual reports reflect MoP&AS activities." *Alliance,* 4–5.

National Paralegal Institute (1980). *Mental health advocacy training kit, introduction to mental health advocacy.* Washington, DC: National Paralegal Institute.

Neufeld, G. R. (1980). "Advocacy and the human service delivery system," in *Mental health advocacy training kit, introduction to mental health advocacy.* Washington, DC: National Paralegal Institute.

Rhoades, C., & Browning, P. (1977). "Normalization at what price?" *Mental Retardation, 15,* 20–26.

Rhoades, C., Browning, P., & Thorin, E. (1986). "Self-help advocacy movement: A promising peer-support system for people with mental disabilities." *Rehabilitation Literature,* 47 (1–2), 2–7.

Rogers, J. (1988). *Individual advocacy.* Philadelphia, PA: National Mental Health Consumers' Association.

Romer, D., & Heller, T. (1983). "Social adaptation of mentally retarded adults in community settings, a social-ecological approach." *Applied Research in Mental Retardation, 4,* 303–314.

Rose, S. (1987). "Advocacy/empowerment: An approach to clinical practice for social work." *Journal of Sociology and Social Welfare,* 41–51.

Rosen, J. W. (1988). *Community integration and adjustment of mentally retarded adults: Rela-*

tionships among residential setting, community-based activity, social support, and residential satisfaction (Unpublished doctoral dissertation, University of Vermont).

Scheerenberger, R. C., & Felsenthal, D. (1977). "Community settings for mentally retarded persons: Satisfaction and activities." *Mental Retardation, 15,* 3–7.

Singer, G., & Apolloni, T. (1981). *Successful living: Understanding Californians with special developmental needs.* Sacramento: California State Council on Developmental Disabilities.

Snellen, D. (1979). *Mental retardation: Nature, needs, and advocacy.* Boston: Allyn and Bacon.

South Dakota Advocacy Services (1991, April). "Eighth circuit court of appeals affirms special education decision." *South Dakota Report,* 1–2.

Turnbull, A., & Shaffer, H. (1986). Family state-of-the-art conference: A summary of conference proceedings. Washington, DC: Georgetown University Child Developmental Center, pp. 27–37.

Ward, J. (1986). "Citizen advocacy: Its legal context." *Australia and New Zealand Journal of Developmental Disabilities,* 12(2), 91–96.

Widrick, G., Hasazi, J., & Hasazi, S. (1990). "Citizen advocacy relationships: Advocate, protege, and relationship characteristics and satisfaction ratings." *The Journal of the Association for Persons with Severe Handicaps,* 15(3), 170–176.

Wolfenberger, W., & Zauha, H., Eds. (1973). *Citizen advocacy and protective services for the impaired and handicapped.* Canada: Macdonald-Downie.

10

A SYSTEMS CHANGE APPROACH
TO ADVOCACY

Diane Lea Ryndak
State University College at Buffalo

Chapter Objectives

After completing this chapter, you will be able to:

1. Define systems change
2. Describe how teachers and family members can create systems change through advocacy
3. Describe key roles played in the change process
4. Define the concepts of order, plasticity, and interchangeability in relation to roles played in the change process
5. Describe a model of systems change, including:
   (a) initial steps taken prior to the change process; and (b) the change process

Key Terms and Phrases

adversary
ally
bottom-up strategies
change agent (internal and external)
change initiator (internal and external)
cooperative
discrepancy analysis
inservice

interchangeability
order
plasticity
power sources
stakeholder
systems change
technical assistance
top-down strategies

INTRODUCTION

Since the beginning of educational programs for students with disabilities, teachers, and families have consistently advocated for effective services. This advocacy has led to a number of positive changes in relation to education, including: the passage of legislation (Americans with Disabilities Act, 1991; Education for All Handicapped Children Act, 1975); the development and adoption of meaningful curriculum content (Horner, Meyer & Fredericks, 1986; Sailor et al., 1986; Snell, 1987); and placement of students with disabilities with their non-disabled same-age peers (Laski, 1985; Stainback & Stainback, 1985).

These changes would not have been possible if an individual had not identified an essential need that was unmet for a student and committed themselves to advocating for change. While such changes have occurred at national, state, and local levels as a result of legislative mandates, litigation outcomes, and policy changes (Clark & Astuto, 1986; Hamre-Nietupski, Nietupski & Maurer, 1990; Williams et al., 1986), a number of changes less broad in scope occur every day. These changes may occur when a teacher, family member, or administrator looks critically at current educational services, finds something lacking, and becomes an advocate for program improvements (Aspinwall & Gibbs, 1989; Freeman, 1991; Rosenberg, Tesolowski & Stein, 1983).

Any individual is a potential advocate. Initial attention of teachers and family members who are potential advocates frequently is on students rather than services, identifying whether students' needs are being met through the services provided. The need for advocacy for students may be evident in a number of ways. For instance, a student may demonstrate: (a) lack of anticipated progress during a school year, or across years; (b) varying levels of knowledge across settings; (c) inconsistent growth compared with other students who have similar needs; or (d) increases of inappropriate behaviors in the school, in the community, or at home. Regardless of the way in which the need for advocacy is evident for one student, an advocate recognizes that other students with disabilities may experience the same difficulties. Consequently, the focus of advocacy may go beyond one student to impact a group of students.

Teachers and family members also may identify discrepancies that exist between the educational services provided and those currently accepted as best practices (Arick, Falco & Brazeau, 1989). Such discrepancies may be inherent to a district's services and operational procedures. Such discrepancies may be caused by the following:

1. Interpretation and implementation of the district's mission and philosophy statements for students with disabilities
2. The district's procedures for determining placement of a student in the least restrictive environment
3. Procedures for determining content of students' individualized education programs

4. Policies and procedures surrounding the delivery of educational and related services
5. Instructional procedures utilized in classes, the school, and the community
6. Roles of family members, general and special education teachers, related services personnel, school psychologists, and administrators in the educational program.

It should be noted that *change is a process that is completed by individuals* (Bollington & Hopkins, 1989; Hord, Rutherford, Huling-Austin & Hall, 1987). Therefore, the purpose of this chapter is to describe: (a) the roles that teachers and family members may play when advocating for changes in educational services; and (b) how a systems change approach to advocacy may effect services for all students with disabilities.

KEY ROLES PLAYED IN THE CHANGE PROCESS

Numerous individuals are involved in systems change, and it is critical for teachers and family members to understand the various roles they play in relation to the desired change. Karasoff (1991) refers to individuals who are affected by change as *stakeholders*. During the change process, it is possible for several stakeholders to act in similar roles, as well as for one stakeholder to act in a number of different roles (Knoop, 1987). Possible roles are briefly described in the following sections.

Students with Disabilities

While not necessarily being an active member in the systems change process (McDonnell & Hardman, 1989), *students with disabilities* are the focal point of the systems change approach to advocacy presented in this chapter. Students with disabilities are critical to this systems change approach in at least three ways. In this approach all systems change efforts: (a) are begun because of students' unmet needs; (b) continue until those needs are met to the satisfaction of all stakeholders; and (c) are evaluated for effectiveness, as well as effect, in reference to those needs.

Change Initiator

The *change initiator* is the individual who first identifies an unmet need and resolves to effect change until that need is met. Change initiators may be internal or external to the school system. Internal change initiators may include school board members (Knoop, 1987; McDonnell & Hardman, 1989), teachers (Freeman, 1991; McDonnell & Hardman, 1989), administrators (Dobbs, Primm & Primm, 1991; McDonnell & Hardman, 1989; Nietupski, Hamre-Nietupski, Houselog, Donder & Anderson, 1988), family members (Beach Center on Families and Disabilities, 1990; Goldberg & Kuriloff, 1991; McDonnell & Hardman, 1989), related services personnel (McDonnell & Hardman, 1989), or other school building personnel (McDonnell & Hardman, 1989). While family members are not always seen as such, they are indeed part of the educational process, and therefore are internal to the system. As such, they may function very effectively as change initiators.

External change initiators may include parent advocates (Beach Center on Families and Disabilities, 1990; Goldberg & Kuriloff, 1991; McDonnell & Hardman, 1989), teacher trainers (Freeman, 1991), experts in specific fields (Powers, 1986), or local citizens (McDonnell & Hardman, 1989). State departments of education (Hamre-Nietupski, Nietupski & Maurer, 1990), state or federally funded projects, professional associations (TASH, 1987), and family advocacy groups, may also function as change initiators. These individuals or organizations may effect change by identifying discrepancies between the educational services provided and current best practices. While external change initiators may not be able to directly change a school system, they may disseminate information and create interest, leading internal agents to create change.

Power Sources

Power sources are individuals with the capacity to effect change in either a positive or negative manner. Of immediate concern are those power sources who are: (a) most respected in the building or district; (b) most immediately affected by the proposed change; or (c) most powerful in influencing the opinions of others.

School board members, superintendents, building principals, and special education administrators are the most easily identified power sources. However, these individuals may not be the power sources of immediate concern. Frequently, essential power sources are individuals who are overlooked, or not considered to be in a role of authority. For example, a teacher may attempt to better meet the needs of students with severe disabilities by maximizing their interactions with non-disabled peers during lunchtime. Before progressing, there are a number of potential power sources who may effect the teacher's success, including:

1. Administrators
2. Teachers of the nondisabled students
3. Some nondisabled students
4. Parents of either the students with or without disabilities
5. The cafeteria workers
6. The maintenance workers
7. Paraprofessionals in either class
8. The students' educational team members
9. Other professionals or volunteers in the cafeteria at the same time

Each potential power source may be identified as being an ally, a cooperative, or an adversary. An *ally* actively assists in producing the desired change, while an *adversary* actively hinders change efforts. A *cooperative*, on the other hand, neither actively assists nor actively hinders those efforts. Rather, a cooperative usually takes a "wait and see" position, allowing the change to occur and then independently evaluating the merit of the change.

Change Agents

Change agents are individuals who actually conduct the activities through which the desired change will occur. Such activities focus on: (a) sharing information related to the content of, and reasons for, the desired change; (b) providing assistance that allows the change to occur; and (c) providing training required to effectively implement the change. Change agents may again be internal or external to a school system, with any number of change agents required to complete the change process.

Order, Plasticity, and Interchangeability

Key to understanding the roles that stakeholders play in the systems change process are the concepts of (a) order; (b) plasticity; and (c) interchangeability. *Order* refers to the primary, secondary, and tertiary roles individuals play during the change process, and the relationship of that role to others playing the same role. For instance, the primary change initiator is the individual who begins the change process. As the change process progresses, other individuals may become change initiators, but will act as such in a secondary manner; that is, their activities as change initiators follow the lead of the primary change initiator. Primary, secondary, and tertiary players can exist for all roles in the change process.

Plasticity refers to the possibility of stakeholders changing roles during the change process. For instance, change initiators and allies provide information, training, and assistance to other stakeholders aiming for role changes from (a) adversary to cooperative; (b) cooperative to ally; and (c) ally to change agent or change initiator. Figure 10-1 demonstrates how the primary change initiator (CI #1) can identify an ally (Ally #1) who may change roles and become a secondary change initiator (CI #2). Both CI #1 and CI #2 may then identify two more allies (Ally #3 and Ally #4) who may also change roles and become secondary or tertiary change initiators (CI #3 and CI #4). In this fashion, the efforts required to produce change is spread across a number of individuals and the base of support for the change is broadened (Knoop, 1987). If systems change activities are not successful, however, role changes may occur in the other direction (for example, ally to cooperative; cooperative to adversary), leading to disintegration of the base of support for change.

Interchangeability refers to stakeholders periodically changing roles with each other on a temporary basis. Most notably this can be observed between change initiators and allies, as each takes the lead during various aspects of the change process. Given this view of the roles played by stakeholders in the change process, a systems change approach to advocacy is presented in the remainder of the chapter.

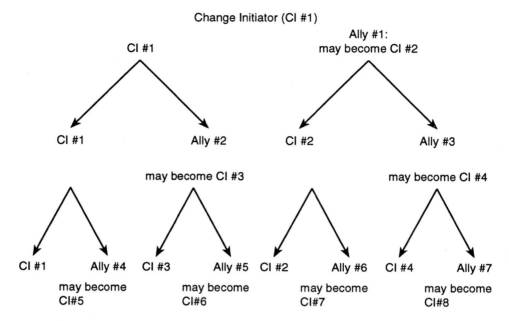

Change Initiator (CI #1)

FIGURE 10-1 • **Flowchart of developing roles for systems change process, starting with the primary change initiator who identifies his first ally. The ally may choose to become a secondary change initiator, leading to both the primary and secondary change initiators broadening the base of support for the proposed change by identifying additional allies and potential change initiators.**

A SYSTEMS CHANGE APPROACH

There are a number of approaches for describing changes that occur within a school system. These approaches focus on different aspects of the system, such as the: (a) degree to which the district's graduates with disabilities succeed in adult life; (b) type and quality of instructional strategies and programs used in the educational process; and (c) performance of various members of the service delivery system (for example, teachers, paraprofessionals, psychologists, related services personnel, administrators). The approach to advocating for systems change presented in this chapter focuses on a combination of these aspects, by identifying needs of students with disabilities that are unmet by their service provider (Ryndak,

Doyle, Pagels, Oubre & Schooley, 1989). See Box 10-1 for a summary of the steps in this model.

Change can occur using either top-down or bottom-up strategies (Hord, Rutherford, Huling-Austin & Hall, 1987). For educational programs, top-down strategies would be utilized by district administrators (Knoop, 1987; Spiegel-McGill, 1991), and bottom-up strategies by teachers and family members (Robison & Robison, 1991). Both have been effective in producing changes in educational services for students with disabilities.

Initial Steps Taken Prior to Effecting Change

Several steps must be taken to "set the stage" before a teacher or family member can effect change in services. By definition, the *responsibility* for the completion of initial steps will be with the change initiator. In addition, the change initiator will actually *complete* the initial steps. For later steps, however, *responsibility* for completion will be shared between the change initiator and allies, while the actual activities will be *completed* by change agents.

Initial Step 1: Identify an Unmet Need of a Student with Disabilities

When identifying problems that have arisen in educational services, teachers and family members may observe a number of situations. First, a student may not demonstrate the amount of growth anticipated during a specified period of the academic year. Second, the individualized education programs for a student across two or more years may look very similar, indicating the lack of anticipated progress in areas of need across time. Third, the amount and type of growth demonstrated

---

BOX 10-1 • A Systems Change Model

Initial Steps

1. Identify an unmet need of a student with disabilities
2. Conduct a discrepancy analysis
3. Commit to meeting the student's need
4. Consider time factors
5. Identify power sources and their roles

The Change Process

1. Work with allies
2. Work with cooperatives and adversaries

3. Plan formal training and technical assistance
4. Provide training and technical assistance
5. Implement the change
6. Evaluate the effect of the change

Steps in one systems change model, identified in two sets of steps; one set including steps completed by a potential change initiator prior to the change process actually beginning, and one set including steps of the change process itself.

by a student in one environment may not match the growth demonstrated in other environments. Fourth, the amount and type of growth demonstrated by a student may not correlate with the amount of growth demonstrated by similar students. Fifth, the frequency or type of inappropriate behaviors demonstrated by a student either at home, in school, or in the community may increase. Any of these situations should act as a trigger for a detailed analysis of the educational services being provided.

Besides these student-centered triggers, new information about best educational practices is available to teachers and family members through professional journals and conferences (Knoop, 1987). Such information should also prompt advocates to look critically at services and identify any need that is unmet.

Initial Step 2: Conduct a Discrepancy Analysis

After identifying an unmet need, the teacher or family member may complete a discrepancy analysis. Through this process, further information is gathered, assisting in the identification of the problem (Arick, Falco & Brazeau, 1989). Through this analysis, every aspect of the educational services provided should be reviewed. To complete a discrepancy analysis, the teacher or family member simply compares the educational services provided to current best practices for students with similar needs. Several tools that identify current best educational practices exist to assist in this review (Kleinert, Smith & Hudson, 1990; Meyer, 1987; Ryndak, Doyle, & Pagels, 1989; Vermont Department of Education, 1990).

The completion of a discrepancy analysis will produce three desired outcomes. First, the results allow the teacher or family member to identify discrepancies between the educational services provided and those consistent with current best practices. The discrepancies identified should lead to a clear definition of the systemic variables resulting in the student's unmet need. The teacher or family member can hypothesize which systemic variables should be changed to allow the student's need to be met. In changing a systemic variable, all current and future students with disabilities may benefit, however, the effect of the change efforts would be observed first in the educational services provided for the identified student with the unmet need.

The second outcome is more effective communication. As the teacher or family member discusses the hypothesized effect of the proposed change with other stakeholders, the discrepancy analysis provides a common ground for communication about best practices.

The third outcome is a basis for systematic change in services. As the change process progresses, a discrepancy analysis tool may be used to plan how and when changes will be implemented across different components of educational services, as well as to record the completion of change efforts across those components.

Initial Step 3: Commit to Meeting the Student's Need

Up to this point in the process, the teacher or family member has been only a *potential* change initiator. No steps have been completed that will directly produce change. The time has come, however, for the potential change initiator to decide whether he actually will commit to creating change for the benefit of a student with disabilities. If made, the commitment must include working toward that desired change until the student's need is met. Without this level of commitment, the change process may either never begin or never lead to change that positively impacts a student's unmet need.

For teachers, this is one of many times throughout the change process when their professional and personal ethics are questioned. Some changes are relatively easy for a teacher to implement. Such changes usually "fit in with" existing policies and procedures, and, therefore, do not "threaten" the main philosophical position of a district. An example is the modification of a community-based instruction program in a district already committed to this approach.

Other changes, however, may not be as easily implemented. For instance, the same teacher may believe firmly that students need community-based instruction, but may work in a district that has either never considered the need for community-based instruction or rejected the practice. Does the teacher work toward developing a community-based instructional program, or ignore the students' needs, allowing existing policies and procedures to dictate actions?

The issue becomes even more complex when that teacher is either new to a district or not tenured. Such a decision will have broad ramifications for: (a) the identified student with an unmet need; (b) future students with similar needs; (c) the teacher's life in that district; (d) the teacher's self-respect; and (e) the teacher's personal reputation. This also is true when a family member, administrator, or other stakeholder acts as the change initiator.

Although this is only one of the times when the potential change initiator must decide whether to take actions until a student's need is met, the question for each of these key decision times remains the same. Is the student's need important enough to commit the time and energy required to create change? Is the need important enough to risk possible adverse personal effects? At each decision time, the potential change initiator, in essence, is defining the future for both himself and students.

Initial Step 4: Consider Time Factors

It is often easy to identify numerous reasons for delaying action. In the case of initiating change in educational services, it is easy to rationalize! For example, it's easy to say:

1. "This is a busy time of year. I'll wait until things slow down or somebody else notices the unmet need."
2. "My administrators like things the way they are. I don't want them to dislike me or my performance, so I'll wait until they change buildings or retire."

This list could be endless! The only important factor to consider is student-centered time. Students with disabilities are identified because they have difficulty acquiring, maintaining, and generalizing information. Because of this, they will learn less information at a slower rate than their nondisabled peers, with the amount of information learned across time decreasing for students with more severe disabilities. Since there are a predetermined number of years during which students with disabilities receive educational services, it is critical that their time not be wasted. Too frequently teachers and family members hear from districts "We'll do that next year," or "Give us some time to develop that." The question that a change initiator should constantly ask is *what can I do **now** to either create the desired change, or set the stage for that change to happen as quickly as possible?* According to Ryndak et al. (1989) **"The time is always right"** to begin change in educational services to benefit students, especially students with disabilities. The amount and type of change will vary, however, depending upon the variables in each situation.

Initial Step 5: Identify Power Sources and Their Roles

The last step to be completed before progressing to the actual change process is to identify power sources who are in positions to positively or negatively effect change efforts, and the roles they will probably play initially in the process (Knoop, 1987). Since at least one student with unmet needs has already been identified and a change initiator has committed to effecting change, there is no need to identify others to play these two roles at the moment.

There are two ways to proceed when identifying the relevant power sources and their roles. First, make a list of the stakeholders perceived to be potential power sources in relation to the desired change. Indicate which of these individuals is definitely an ally, cooperative, or adversary in relation to the forthcoming change efforts. Remember, an ally will actively assist in producing the desired change; an adversary will actively hinder efforts; and a cooperative will usually take a "wait and see" position, allowing the change to occur and then independently evaluating the merit of the change.

The second way to identify relevant power sources is to list all of the stakeholders who either are knowledgeable already about the content of the desired change, or have initiated or supported changes that have benefited students. Again, indicate which of these is definitely an ally, cooperative, or adversary. The change initiator now has two lists of potential power sources, with a strongly anticipated role for at least some of the stakeholders on each list.

It is critical at this time to verify that the anticipated roles are indeed the roles that each power source will play. The only way to verify this is to present some information to each of the stakeholders and judge their response as either consistent or inconsistent with their anticipated roles. The lists should be modified based upon this new information. The change initiator also must decide whether to complete the same procedure with each stakeholder for whom a role was not easily identified. Two deciding factors influencing this decision may be: (a) how immediately each stakeholder could assist or hinder the change efforts; and (b) how directly each stakeholder would be involved in the change. For stakeholders considered not to be immediately influential or directly involved, the change initiator may only keep track of the information made available to them, as well as the ally that made the information available. This will help determine when to reconsider the potential role of these stakeholders.

A change initiator must anticipate when a power source is about to take a stand as an ally, a cooperative, or an adversary. Before that occurs, that power source must have the best information possible upon which to base their decision. It is easier to gain an ally or cooperative before they have taken a stand as an adversary.

Finally, stakeholders should be identified who: (a) are internal to the district; and (b) can and will act as change agents for the desired change. Internal change agents must be knowledgeable about the content of the desired change, able to effectively share that knowledge with others, in a position that allows them to share that knowledge with others, and respected within the district. When a change agent is part of the system, the proposed change usually is more easily accepted. In addition to being less threatening, internal change agents are less costly and less cumbersome to use than external change agents. Internal change agents, therefore, should be used whenever possible to complete the activities that will create the change. If internal change agents are not available, however, change agents who are external to the district should be identified.

Once power sources and their anticipated roles are identified, the actual change process can be initiated. To obtain the most change for the largest number of students as quickly as possible, periodically review the lists of stakeholders, adding or subtracting names as their role(s) at that time are verified. Remember plasticity and interchangeability! The role(s) that a stakeholder plays at one point in the change process may not be the role they play throughout the process. Roles change as individuals obtain new information and form new opinions.

The Change Process

This systems change approach to advocacy has six steps in the actual change process. These steps incorporate planning activities that will facilitate changes, completing those activities to prepare for the implementation of changes, implementing changes, and evaluating the effect of those changes.

Change Process Step 1: Work with Allies

To ensure that all allies are working cooperatively, there must be open discussion about: (a) the identified unmet need of the student with disabilities; (b) the content of the desired change; and (c) the ways in which the change would help the district more fully meet the needs of all students with disabilities. This should result in a clear definition of purpose, scope, and outcomes expected from change efforts (Knoop, 1987).

Once consensus is reached on these, an action plan should be developed, including both: (a) specific objectives, detailing what will be different when the change efforts are completed and the identified need is met; and (b) a set of activities to be completed for each objective, leading to the understanding, acceptance, and implementation of the desired change (Knoop, 1987). See Box 10-2 for examples of activities. As agreement is reached on each activity, identify the ally that will be responsible for the completion of that activity and the timeframe in which the activity will be completed. Careful consideration should be given to which ally completes which activity. Some activities, for example, are best **not** completed by teachers as employees of the district. Other activities may **not** be completed by family members without creating an adversarial situation.

An action plan with such detail will allow allies to work in a collaborative manner, keeping each activity in the agreed upon sequence. This will decrease duplication of activities, gaps in activities, and completion of activities that counteract the positive effects of other activities. By tracking the completion of activities, it can also be established whether stakeholders anticipated to be allies are actually acting as allies. In addition, key times will become evident throughout the change process for reviewing the list of power sources and verifying their current role.

Change Process Step 2: Work with Cooperatives and Adversaries

Working with cooperatives and adversaries is quite different from working with allies. While allies generally share your level of knowledge related to the desired change or work together to obtain new information, the same cannot be assumed for cooperatives and adversaries. The allies' task is to facilitate both their acquisition of information related to the content of the desired change and the completion of activities that promote the desired change (Knoop, 1987).

The goal is to provide enough information so that cooperatives who are close to being allies become more and more supportive, until they become allies. The same is applied to adversaries. It is possible that when provided enough accurate and credible information on the content of the change, adversaries will become less certain that the change will not result in positive effects, and begin to act as cooperatives. While this type of evolution cannot be expected for every cooperative and adversary, the fewer individuals who hinder the change process and the more

---

BOX 10-2 • Potential Activities for Action Plans

1. Identify resources currently available
   a. Materials
   b. Funding
   c. Support
   d. Expertise
   e. Knowledge of conferences or workshops
   f. Knowledge of internal and external support services
2. Identify potential resources that already exist
3. Identify additional resources required
4. Obtain use of currently available, potential, and additional resources required
5. Disseminate information through:
   a. Written materials
   b. Meetings
   c. Presentations
   d. Inservice sessions
   e. Workshops
   f. Conferences
   g. Technical assistance
6. Solicit support and commitment from internal and external people (power sources, change agents)

Examples of activities to be identified by a change initiator and his allies that potentially will lead to meeting established objectives of systems change efforts.

individuals who assist in the change process, the easier it will be to create the desired change.

Change Process Step 3: Plan Formal Training and Technical Assistance

In most systems change efforts, not all of the stakeholders will be reachable through informal dissemination efforts. To reach all of the stakeholders of the change both inservice sessions and technical assistance activities should be planned. Inservice sessions, where information is presented to large groups of stakeholders, are more effective when they include simulated use of the information presented (Thousand, Nevin-Parta, & Fox, 1987). In contrast, technical assistance refers to one-to-one consultation with the implementers of the new information in the actual settings in which they are expected to use the new information. It verifies that implementers of the change actually can use the new information by: (a) observing how the new information is used; and (b) providing feedback to the implementers, with strategies for improving their use of it. In comparison to inservice sessions, technical assistance activities tend to be ongoing, with long-term support provided to implementers until the change has been implemented consistently across all students (Thousand, Nevin-Parta, & Fox, 1987).

Any number of combinations of inservice sessions and technical assistance activities are possible. The appropriate combination must be determined by the stakeholders responsible for the implementation of the change. In most situations, this combination is determined by program administrators, who also bear the cost of these activities. Systems change efforts are most successful, however, when administrators work in conjunction with the change initiator, allies, and stakeholders (Thousand, Nevin-Parta, & Fox, 1987). This ensures the inclusion of: (a) all relevant new information in the training activities; (b) all stakeholders in an appropriate combination of training activities; and (c) all stakeholders in determining the change process.

Change Process Step 4: Provide Training and Technical Assistance

Plans for providing inservice sessions to all stakeholders and technical assistance to all implementers must be implemented diligently. As each training activity is completed, evaluate the effect of the activity and determine whether the next scheduled activity will meet the current needs of the stakeholders and implementers (Thousand, Nevin-Parta, & Fox, 1987). If so, then the planned activities can continue. If not, additional or alternate activities should be identified.

Change Process Step 5: Implement the Change

Once inservice activities have been completed, the actual change should be implemented (Knoop, 1987). Implementation of the change will occur at a different time in the change process for every situation. In some situations, allies will be ready to implement the desired change almost immediately, while in other situations it may take several months or years. How quickly the change can be implemented will depend on several variables, such as: (a) how novel the change is to the district; (b) how much opposition to the change exists; (c) how difficult the change will be to implement; and (d) how many people are involved in implementing the change.

Whenever the change is actually implemented, it is essential that the implementation occurs in a systematic and planned manner and that technical assistance activities also occur throughout the implementation of the change. In this way, change agents can ensure that those responsible for long-term implementation of the change have both the knowledge and resources required to successfully institutionalize the change. For example, let's return to the teacher who is implementing a new community-based instructional program. Before implementing the program, that teacher must be fully aware of all aspects of community-based instruction. How does it differ from classroom- or building-based instruction? What safety precautions must be taken in the community? What about liability for transportation or in case of an accident during instruction in the community? What additional resources are needed to implement community-based instruction for one student; two students; five students? Are those resources available?

Once aware of all the relevant aspects of the change and comfortable with the district's responses to questions related to the change, those teachers and their supervisors must secure any additional resources that are required. For our example, these might include: (a) paraprofessional, peer, and/or volunteer support; (b) coverage for the students not involved in the community-based instruction; (c) funds required for community-based activities; (d) public or school district transportation; and (e) additional training.

Once both the knowledge and resources required for successful implementation are acquired, the change can actually be implemented. Initially the change may only be implemented for one or two students, with a timeline and plan in place for full implementation across all students. The point is to prepare adequately, begin carefully, and plan systematically for full implementation (Knoop, 1987).

Change Process Step 6: Evaluate the Effect of the Change

Remembering the focus on an unmet need of a student with disabilities, it is essential to determine the effect of the change on that need. Since the change potentially will effect a number of students with disabilities with the same unmet need, evaluation must encompass a representative sample that includes students with a variety of characteristics. Such an evaluation will determine whether by meeting the unmet need of one student, the district has met the same needs of other students with similar needs, and has not inadvertently created a situation where needs that were previously met are no longer met.

If the change has not been beneficial for students, another review of the situation is necessary, and the stakeholders must decide the next course of action. Are more information, time and/or resources needed to appropriately implement the change? Does the manner in which the change has been conceptualized or implemented need to be modified? Is there an alternate way to meet the need of the student? In all of these cases, additional change efforts will be required.

Once satisfied that the change has been beneficial for students, however, the change initiator's role in this cycle of advocacy for systems change is complete. The next cycle of systems change efforts will begin when another advocate identifies an additional unmet need.

SUMMARY

In this chapter, we have described a systems change approach to advocating for services to meet the needs of students with disabilities. A model of systems change was presented including steps to be taken before and during the change process. Key roles played in the change process were also detailed. In the next chapter, we address specific strategies used to produce change.

Introduction

1. Besides advocating for state and federal changes, teachers and family members can create meaningful change in educational services on a smaller scale every day through advocacy.

2. Advocacy for change is frequently initiated when a student has a need that is not being met adequately, or when a discrepancy exists between the educational services provided and current best practices.

3. Change is a process completed by individuals.

Key Roles Played in the Change Process

4. Identifying the various roles played by each stakeholder during systems change efforts allows the change initiator and allies to minimize opposition to the change and maximize cooperation.

5. Various stakeholders may play the same role, with secondary and tertiary players following the lead of the primary players in that role.

6. Any stakeholder can change roles throughout the change process.

7. Stakeholders may periodically exchange roles with each other on a temporary basis.

A Systems Change Approach

8. Changes that occur within a school system may be described in a number of ways. This approach to advocating for systems change focuses on identifying needs of students with disabilities that are met by their service provider.

9. Change has effectively been produced in educational services using both top-down strategies and bottom-up strategies.

10. As advocates, teachers and family members can act as change initiators, who complete several initial steps. These steps begin with clearly identifying an unmet need for at least one student. This may lead to conducting a discrepancy analysis between the educational services provided and current best practices.

11. The advocate consciously decides whether or not to commit to creating change to meet the student's unmet need. They must consider both their ethical position and the effect the change (or lack of change) will have on that student, other students, and themselves.

12. The time is always right either to create change, or set the stage for change to happen as quickly as possible.

13. The committed advocate, now a change initiator, identifies the role(s) initially anticipated for each stakeholder that may effect change efforts either positively or negatively. Correctly identifying roles will minimize opposition to the change and maximize cooperation.

14. The change initiator works closely with allies, cooperatives, and adversaries, planning activities that will facilitate the acceptance, understanding, and implementation of the desired change.

15. Formal inservice training sessions and technical assistance activities should be planned, implemented, and evaluated to determine whether the objectives of the activity were met. Pursuant activities are conducted or modified as needed.

16. After sufficient inservice sessions and technical assistance activities have been completed across stakeholders, the change is implemented.

17. An evaluation is completed on the effect the change has had on: (a) the unmet need of the identified student; (b) the unmet needs of similar students; and (c) previously met needs of all students.

REFERENCES

American with Disabilities Act, 1991.

Arick, J., Falco, R., & Brazeau, K. (1989). "Prioritizing inservice needs for educators of students with severe handicaps in heterogeneous integrated settings." *Education and Training in Mental Retardation, 24*(4), 371–380.

Aspinwall, K. & Gibbs, B. (1989). "Schools as learning organizations: Seven critical steps." *Educational Change and Development, 4*(7).

Beach Center on Families and Disabilities (1990). "Parent to parent national survey." *Exceptional Parent, 20*(7).

Bollington, R. & Hopkins, D. (1989). "School based review—as a strategy for the implementation of teacher appraisal and school improvement." *Educational Change and Development, 8*(17).

Clark, D. L. & Astuto, T. A. (1986). "The significance and permanence of changes in federal education policy." *Educational Researcher, 15*(8), 4–13.

Dobbs, R. F., Primm, E. B., & Primm, B. (1991). "Mediation: A common sense approach for resolving conflicts in education." *Focus on Exceptional Children, 24*(2), 1–11.

Education for All Handicapped Children Act (P.L. 94-142). (1975). 20 U.S.C. Sections 1401, *et seq.* (1982).

Freeman, A. (1991). "Being transformative in special educational needs." *Educational Change and Development, 11*(2), 15–19.

Goldberg, S. S. & Kuriloff, P. J. (1991). "Evaluating the fairness of special education hearings." *Exceptional Children, 57*(6), 546–555.

Hamre-Nietupski, S., Nietupski, J., & Maurer, S. (1990). "A comprehensive state education agency plan to promote the integration of students with moderate/severe handicaps."

Journal of The Association for Persons with Severe Handicaps, 15(2), 106–113.

Hord, S. M., Rutherford, W. L., Huling-Austin, L., & Hall, G. E. (1987). *Taking charge of change.* Alexandria, VA: Association for Supervision and Curriculum Development.

Horner, R. H., Meyer, L. H., & Fredericks, H. D. B. (1986). *Education of learners with severe handicaps: Exemplary service strategies.* Baltimore, MD: Paul H. Brookes.

Karasoff, P. (1991, Winter). "Systems Change: Critical activities." *TASH Newsletter,* pp. 7, 10.

Kleinert, H., Smith, & Hudson (1990). *Quality program indicators for students with moderate and severe handicaps.* Frankfort, KY: State Department of Education.

Knoop, R. (1987). "Bringing about change." *Education Canada,* Spring.

Laski, F. G. (1985). "Judicial address of education for students with severe mental retardation: From access to schools to state of the art," in D. Bricker and J. Filler, Eds., *Severe mental retardation: Theory into practice.* Reston, VA: Council for Exceptional Children, pp. 36–48.

McDonnell, A. P. & Hardman, M. L. (1989). "The desegregation of America's special schools: Strategies for change." *The Journal of The Association for Persons with Severe Handicaps, 14*(1), 68–74.

Meyer, L. H. (1987). *Program quality indicators (PQI): A checklist of most promising practices in educational programs for students with severe disabilities* (Available from The Association for Persons with Severe Disabilities, 7010 Roosevelt Way N.E., Seattle, WA 98115).

Nietupski, J., Hamre-Nietupski, S., Houselog, M., Donder, D. J., & Anderson, R. J. (1988). "Proactive administrative strategies for implementing community-based programs for students with moderate/severe disabilities." *Education and Training in Mental Retardation, 23*(2), 138–146.

Powers, M. D. (1986). "Promoting community-based services: Implications for program design, implementation, and public policy." *The Journal of The Association for Persons with Severe Handicaps, 11*(4), 309–315.

Robison, A. Q. & Robison, G. A. (1991). "Integration—don't take it for granted." *Exceptional Parent, 21*(6).

Rosenberg H., Tesolowski, D. G., & Stein, R. J. (1983). "Advocacy: Education's professional responsibility to handicapped citizens." *Education and Training of the Mentally Retarded, 18*(4), 266–270.

Ryndak, D. L., Doyle, M. B., & Pagels, M. (1989). *Program component checklist* (Available from D. L. Ryndak, Exceptional Education Department, State University College, Buffalo, New York 14222).

Ryndak, D. L., Doyle, M. B., Pagels, M., Oubre, J., & Schooley, R. (1989, December). *School-district initiated systems change—How to make it happen* (Paper presented at the meeting of The Association for Persons with Severe Handicaps, San Francisco, CA).

Sailor, W., Halvorsen, A., Anderson, J., Goetz, L., Gee, K., Doering, K., & Hunt, P. (1986). "Community intensive instruction," in R. H. Horner, L. H. Meyer, & H. D. B. Fredericks, Eds., *Education of learners with severe handicaps: Exemplary service strategies*. Baltimore, MD: Paul H. Brookes, pp. 251–288.

Snell, M. E. (Ed.). (1987). *Systematic instruction for persons with severe handicaps*, 3rd ed. Columbus, OH: Charles E. Merrill.

Spiegel-McGill, P. (1991). "Integration of children with special educational needs in the public schools: A district-wide mission." *The Forum, 17*(1), 11–12.

Stainback, S. & Stainback, W. (1985). *Integration of students with severe handicaps into regular schools*. Reston, VA: Council for Exceptional Children.

TASH (1987). "Deinstitutionalization policy." *TASH Newsletter, 13*(February), 4.

Thousand, J., Nevin-Parta, A., & Fox, W. L. (1987). "Inservice training to support the education of learners with severe handicaps in their local public schools." *Teacher Education and Special Education, 10*(1), 4–13.

Vermont Department of Education (1990, September). *Best practice guidelines for meeting the needs of all students in local schools (draft)*. Montpelier, VT: State Department of Education.

Williams, W., Fox, W., Christie, L., Thousand, J., Conn-Powers, M., Carmichel, L., Vogelsberg, R. T., & Hull, M. (1986). "Community integration in Vermont." *Journal of The Association for Persons with Severe Handicaps, 11*, 294–299.

11

STRATEGIES FOR ADVOCATING THROUGH SYSTEMS CHANGE

Diane Lea Ryndak

State University College at Buffalo

Chapter Objectives

After completing this chapter, you will be able to:

1. Describe key variables that affect the effectiveness of systems change efforts
2. Describe how change may be initiated by a district, family member, or a teacher
3. Describe a teacher's role in the change process, regardless of the initiator
4. Describe how the change process can be monitored to ensure that change happens
5. Describe how to measure the effects of change on short- and long-term performance of students
6. Describe how to measure teachers' and family members' level of satisfaction related to educational services provided before and after change has occurred

Key Terms and Phrases

attitudes and values
district-initiated change
measuring effect of change
monitoring the change process
ongoing professional growth

outcomes-based orientation
parent-initiated change
stages of concern
teacher-initiated change

INTRODUCTION

Chapter 10 presented a systems change approach to advocating changes in educational services for students with disabilities. This approach incorporates the roles of various stakeholders in relation to change and specific steps to be completed, both prior to initiating change and throughout the change process. The purpose of this chapter is to describe: (a) key variables that determine the extent to which systems change efforts are effective; (b) strategies for initiating systems change; (c) a teacher's role in the change process; (d) procedures for monitoring the change process; and (e) methods for evaluating the effects of change on students, family members, and school personnel.

KEY VARIABLES IN SYSTEMS CHANGE EFFORTS

Changing the manner in which a district operates is a complex undertaking (Villa & Thousand, 1992). It requires the cooperation and collaboration of a number of stakeholders, all of whom are different in respect to several variables. Each variable can affect whether systems change efforts will be successful.

Attitudes and Values

Stakeholders respond to changes being advocated based on attitudes and values they have formed through prior experiences and knowledge (Hanline & Halvorsen, 1989; Stainback, Stainback & Stainback, 1988; Villa & Thousand, 1992). For example, stakeholders' knowledge of, and experience with, students with disabilities will determine their beliefs about students' potential and the role that education plays in developing that potential. Many attempts to improve educational services for students with severe disabilities are met with comments by stakeholders that reflect attitudes and values about the students, their value to and role in society, and their right to equal access to effective educational services.

To deal with such attitudinal and value-based difficulties, teachers and family members advocating for change can provide information that counterbalances prior misinformation. In addition, stakeholders may be encouraged to become involved in the experiences and needs of a student with disabilities. This allows stakeholders to identify, along with a student, the potential effects of the proposed change on that student, and the effects that the actual change eventually does have on that student (Villa & Thousand, 1992).

Other attitudes and values that have no relation to students with disabilities may also influence the degree to which advocacy for systems change is effective. For example, regardless of who initiates change, some stakeholders may respond negatively because: (a) the idea for change was not their own; (b) they had been influential in establishing the component of educational services for which change is proposed; or (c) they see the change as a statement that they currently are not providing the best services for students (Villa & Thousand, 1992).

In all of these cases, the stakeholder is a power source and must be identified as such prior to initiating the change process. Teachers and family members may want to recruit these stakeholders as allies early in the change process, assisting them in understanding the need for change and sharing ownership in the change efforts.

Acquisition of Technical Knowledge

A second variable that is key during systems change efforts is technical knowledge (Villa & Thousand, 1992). Stakeholders responsible for implementing the change must either have, or be willing to acquire, the technical knowledge required to implement the change. It is essential that the change initiator and allies identify the technical knowledge held by stakeholders and future implementors, and the technical knowledge that must be acquired prior to implementation (Villa & Thousand, 1992). With this information, formal inservice sessions and technical assistance activities can be planned.

To do so, the change initiator and allies must include district administrative personnel. While change can be initiated from the bottom, without administrative support no change effort can ultimately be effective. It must be verified, therefore, that there is support for such activities within the administration. If not, teachers and family members can complete a number of activities to facilitate administrative support.

Outcomes-Based Orientation

A third variable critical for effective systems change efforts is a pervasive concern about outcomes (Rainforth, York, & Macdonald, 1992). During change, it is easy to become engrossed in the change activities themselves, and lose sight of the reason change is occurring. This systems change approach to advocacy has the outcome-based orientation of meeting an unmet need for at least one student, while attempting to meet the same need for other students with similar needs. These outcomes will not be seen, however, until change has been implemented.

A concern for outcomes that is pervasive throughout a district is evident if the district has an outcome-based orientation across activities, such as student evaluation, personnel training, and program evaluation. When evident, an outcome-based orientation leads to several questions after any activity: (a) what were the desired outcomes of this activity; (b) have those outcomes been realized; and (c) if not, what other activities should be completed to try to achieve the desired outcome (Villa & Thousand, 1992)? This orientation will ensure that change efforts will continue until the desired outcome has been achieved.

Ongoing Professional Growth

A fourth variable that is key to effective systems change efforts is the extent to which a district emphasizes ongoing professional growth (Rainforth, York, & Macdonald, 1992). This emphasis gives stakeholders two major advantages: (a) stakeholders are more prepared mentally for change; (b) stakeholders have a better understanding of how best educational practices change over time. When stakeholders are consistently aware of changes in best practices, change in their services becomes less threatening and is personalized much less frequently. Thus, the more stakeholders are involved in ongoing professional growth activities, the more prepared they are to understand, accept, and implement changes.

FACILITATING CHANGE IN A DISTRICT

Systems change in a district is a complex process, with many stakeholders involved with any change in educational services. In the following sections, we will discuss: (a) the importance of involving all stakeholders in the change process from the beginning; (b) examples of the change process when initiated by a district, parent, or teacher; and (c) the role of the teacher in facilitating change, regardless of the initiator.

Facilitating Change at All Levels

It is impossible to implement change at one level within an educational program without affecting other levels (Villa & Thousand, 1992). For example, if a teacher wants to implement a community-based instructional program for students with disabilities, it is impossible for the teacher to modify the classroom's daily schedule without simultaneously modifying such components as the: (a) role of paraprofessionals in the provision of services both in the school and in the community; (b) role of therapists during instruction; (c) procedures used to identify appropriate IEP content; (d) acceptance of community-based curriculum content on IEPs; and (e) administrative policies on transportation and the provision of educational services off the school premises. A teacher must address each of these areas for his or her proposed change to be implemented successfully.

To ensure that barriers to implementation of changes are minimized throughout the change process, allies identify all stakeholders who will be influential in the change process, as well as the activities that must occur in order for those stakeholders to have the knowledge they require (Villa & Thousand, 1992) to support and/or implement the change (see Chapter 10 for detailed information). The more that key stakeholders are involved in planning and conducting change activities and in implementing the actual change, the more support for the change they can demonstrate (American Association of School Administrators, 1988). These representatives should be the stakeholders most likely to be power sources. As such, they would be the key stakeholders for a change initiator to keep informed and to recruit as an ally or cooperative.

In planning and conducting change activities, schedule activities so that each set of stakeholders has access to the information at every step of the process (Villa & Thousand, 1992). If one set of stakeholders is more advanced in their knowledge about the change, it would be easy for a member of that set to move ahead with implementation of the change without considering the effect of their actions on the other sets.

For example, let's return again to our teacher who wants to implement a community-based instructional program. It may be possible for this teacher to independently gain the information he or she personally needs to both implement the program and provide necessary training for paraprofessionals. If, however, the teacher chooses to implement the change without considering other stakeholders, any number of situations may occur. For instance, parents may complain because their children are no longer receiving the educational services to which they are accustomed. Administrators or related services personnel may complain when they are not able to locate the students, teacher, or paraprofessionals in the classroom. Administrators may stop the community-based instruction because of liability concerns, lack of understanding of the relevance of community-based instruction for students with disabilities, or concern over role definitions and union intervention.

Any of these responses leads to stressful situations, leaving negative impressions about the change and those involved. Such impressions can be avoided if effective change activities are planned and implemented simultaneously across sets of stakeholders. To describe how this may occur, strategies to initiate change, for use by stakeholders in different roles, are described below.

District-Initiated Change

One source from which change can be initiated within educational services is the district, itself, through the school board, superintendent, district administrators, or building administrators (Bollington & Hopkins, 1989; Clayton, 1991; McDonnell & Hardman, 1989; McGregor, Janssen, Larsen & Tillery, 1986; Spiegel-McGill, 1991; Stainback, Stainback & Stainback, 1988; Winfield, 1991). Since the district is the provider of services, and any systemic change will be reflected in those services, educational change occurs most easily when it is initiated by the district. Even so, district change initiators and allies must carefully plan and implement activities that lead to acceptance of the proposed change by all stakeholders. In addition, strategies must be developed for how change will both begin within and permeate throughout the system. The following sections include strategies for use by districts to facilitate change, and the role that teachers play in those change efforts.

Strategies for Providing Information, Assistance, and Training

While there are a number of ways in which districts can facilitate change in their services, the majority of directors of statewide systems change grants strongly supported two strategies: (a) encouraging ownership of the proposed change by involving as many stakeholders as possible (Ryndak & Militello, 1992); and (b) starting change on a small scale, but systematically expanding implementation across the district (California Research Institute, 1990; Villa & Thousand, 1992).

To facilitate district change, one district (Ryndak & Doyle, 1991) used several change strategies and activities. Box 11-1 describes these in relation to the district's unmet student needs, and how stakeholders' roles changed during their change process.

BOX 11-1 • **District-Initiated Change—multiple roles played by specific stakeholders and strategies used to produce change during change efforts initiated by an actual school district**

Need

Students with mild, moderate and severe disabilities lack opportunities to interact with nondisabled peers of the same age throughout the day, resulting in stigma, low self-esteem, and poor social interactions skills.

INITIAL ROLE	FUTURE ADDITIONAL ROLES
Change Initiator	
Director of Special Education	Change agent
Allies	
Teachers of students with disabilities	Change agents
Speech therapist	Change agent
Cooperatives	
Assistant superintendent	Ally and change agent
One elementary building principal	Ally and change agent
Middle school principal	
Middle school assistant principal	Ally and change agent
Some regular education teachers in elementary and middle schools	Allies and change agents
Adversaries	
Teachers' union president	Cooperative
Some related services personnel	Cooperatives and allies
One elementary principal	Cooperative
Change Agents	
Consultant in the area of integrated special education	
Consultant in the area of integrated related services	
Consultant in the area of systems change strategies	

Strategies

1. Encouraged ownership at building and classroom levels.
2. Provided inservice and technical assistance activities for the acquisition of new knowledge.
3. Administratively supported implementation efforts first with the students with severe disabilities, then replicated changes with students with mild disabilities.
4. Implemented changes in one school, then replicated the changes in other schools.
5. Supported the building of networks across implementors.
6. Facilitated collaboration.

Activities

1. Provided inservice to faculty, staff, and parents.
2. Provided technical assistance to immediate implementors of the change.
3. Blended inservice and technical assistance for this change with other district-wide change efforts (e.g., outcomes-based education).
4. Established a district-wide Advisory Board.

Note that when taken in isolation, each activity is only one piece of a large plan for implementation of districtwide change. Since this plan addressed the needs of professionals, para-professionals, parents, administrators, school staff, and students, only through a carefully planned series of activities could the district provide, in a timely manner, enough information, assistance and training for all stakeholders (Villa & Thousand, 1992).

Role of the Teacher in Facilitating District-Initiated Change

There are a number of roles that a teacher can play when their district initiates change. Assuming that a teacher both supports the proposed change and will be effected immediately by the change, that teacher may choose to volunteer services for relevant activities, such as: (a) participation on an advisory board and task forces; (b) procurement of materials for dissemination of information; (c) identification of external resources for change agents; and (d) participation in inservice sessions and technical assistance activities. Which role is played will depend upon the degree to which the teacher wants to be associated with the actual change process, as compared with implementation of the proposed change.

Parent-Initiated Change

Parents of students with disabilities are another source from which systemic change can be initiated (Beach Center on Families and Disabilities, 1990; Hanline & Halvorsen, 1989; McDonnell & Hardman, 1989; Robison & Robison, 1991). Since parents do not directly implement changes within a district, it may be more difficult for them to effect changes. Preferably, parent-initiated change efforts should incorporate collaboration with district personnel (Hamre-Nietupski et al., 1988). Unfortunately, however, efforts to be collaborative are not always successful, and parents may resort to more formal procedures for convincing districts to change their services (Dobbs, Primm & Primm, 1991; Goldberg & Kuriloff, 1991; Prasse, 1986; Robison & Robison, 1991; Ryndak & Militello, 1992).

Regardless of the manner in which parents convince district personnel that a change is needed in services, once the decision to change is made, it is critical that parents work collaboratively with the district to bring about that change (Rainforth, York, & Macdonald, 1992). As when change is initiated by the district, the change initiators (that is, parents) and their allies must carefully plan and implement activities that will lead to widespread acceptance of the change and develop a strategy that spreads that change throughout the system. The following sections include strategies for use by parents to facilitate change, and the role that teachers play in those change efforts.

Strategies for Providing Information, Assistance, and Training

Parents agree with the two concepts identified by the directors of statewide systems change projects previously discussed; that is, encouraging stakeholders' ownership of the proposed change, starting on a small scale (California Research Institute,

1990; Rainforth, York, & Macdonald, 1992; Villa & Thousand, 1992). Differences exist, however, in how parents can put these concepts into practice.

For instance, it is not possible for parents to conduct either planning, training, or implementation activities for district personnel. Since parents are usually seen as external to the educational system (Hamre-Nietupski et al., 1988; Villa & Thousand, 1992), they must "sell" their idea for change to the educational system. To accomplish this, one set of parents distributed information about a proposed change to as many stakeholders as possible. They held personal conversations with stakeholders, shared videotapes, distributed literature, and facilitated networking with those already implementing the change in other districts (see Box 11-2).

In doing so, the parents actually were attempting to sell their idea to at least one stakeholder internal to their district. They hoped that this stakeholder would then advocate for the change. This transferred ownership to an internal stakeholder, making the change process easier. When parents are successful at transferring ownership, an internal stakeholder can proceed with district-initiated change activities, such as those already discussed.

When parents have been unable to sell their idea for change, they have resorted to their legal rights as parents of a child with disabilities and begun due process procedures (Robison & Robison, 1991; Ryndak & Militello, 1992). While not the most desirable method of effecting change because of the adversarial nature of the relationships that develop between parents and school personnel, it has proven to be effective when other strategies fail.

Role of the Teacher in Facilitating Parent-Initiated Change

As with district-initiated change, there are a number of roles a teacher can play when parents initiate change. Assuming that a teacher involved in the services provided for the parents' child will be affected immediately by the change and supports the change, the teacher may obtain information offered by the parents and become an internal change initiator. The teacher's role then is to continue to sell the change to the district, especially in relation to the child of the parents who provided the information. Activities used by teachers to facilitate change are included in the teacher-initiated change section below. While a teacher engages in these activities, many parents will continue to share information with school board members and administrators; thus, information is being disseminated from two sources to different levels of stakeholders in the district.

In this role, a teacher functions as an ally and secondary change initiator. Once sufficient information is obtained to implement, or teach others to implement the change, the teacher then acts in the role of change agent. As with district-initiated change, a teacher may or may not accept these roles, depending upon the degree to which he wants to be associated with the change process, in comparison with being involved only in the implementation of the change. With parent-initiated change, however, a teacher accepts an added risk with any of these roles because of the adversarial relationship that could develop with his employer (Rock, Geiger, & Hood, 1992).

BOX 11-2 • Parent-Initiated Change—multiple roles played by specific stakeholders and strategies used to produce change during change efforts initiated by actual parents of a student with moderate disabilities

Need

Sixteen year old female student, exhibiting inappropriate behaviors in the self-contained special education room in which she received services, required consistent opportunities throughout the day to (a) interact appropriately with her non-disabled same-age peers, and (b) get exposure to age-appropriate curriculum content.

INITIAL ROLE	FUTURE ADDITIONAL ROLES
Change Initiator	
Parents	Change agent
Allies	
Other parents	Change agents
One school psychologist	
Lawyer for the parents	
Cooperatives	
Building principal	Ally
Some regular education teachers	Allies and change agents
Guidance counselor	
Adversaries	
Superintendent	
Director of Special Education	Cooperative
Coordinator of Special Education	Cooperative
Some regular education teachers	Cooperatives and allies
Change Agents	
Consultant in integrated special education	

Strategies

1. Shared information on integration with special education administration, the child's educational team, building principal, superintendent, and school board members.
2. Completed an independent educational evaluation focused on discrepancies with current best educational practices.
3. Initiated a due process hearing to change services from self-contained settings to integrated settings (i.e., regular class settings with same-age peers).
4. Once integrated services were established for one student, the change was extended so that it affected other students with similar needs. This resulted in integrated services for a handful of students in Year 1, ten students in Year 2, forty students in Year 3, and plans for further development of integrated services in the ensuing years.

Teacher-Initiated Change

A third source from which systemic change can be initiated within educational services includes teachers (McDonnell & Hardman, 1989; Rock, Geiger & Hood, 1992; Rosenberg, Tesolowski & Stein, 1983; Wershing, Gaylord-Ross & Gaylord-Ross, 1986). While teachers are internal to a district and are the implementors of proposed changes, it could be as difficult for them to effect change as for parents. The more highly a teacher is respected, and the more closely related the change is to his or her area of expertise, the easier it is for that teacher to recruit allies and cooperatives for the change process.

Since teachers do not have a formal mechanism for challenging a district, allies and cooperatives must be recruited through collegial and collaborative efforts. As when change is initiated by a district, the change initiator (that is, a teacher) and allies must plan and implement activities that lead to widespread acceptance of the change. They must also develop a strategy to begin change, and to spread that change throughout the system. The following sections contain strategies for teachers to use facilitate change, and their role in those change efforts.

Strategies for Providing Information, Assistance, and Training

There are a number of ways in which a teacher can facilitate change in educational services. As with parents, teachers have found it helpful to address the issue of ownership of the proposed change (Rainforth, York, & Macdonald, 1992), and start on a small scale (Villa & Thousand, 1992).

A teacher will frequently identify colleagues to assist in meeting the unmet need of a student (Hamre-Nietupski et al., 1988; Wershing, Gaylord-Ross & Gaylord-Ross, 1986). Colleagues may be teachers of students without disabilities of the same age, teachers of specific academic content, or other building staff, but all have some formal connection to the proposed change, are approachable about new educational ideas, and are power sources. As such, it is probable that colleagues' comments to other stakeholders will be credible. Frequently, teacher-initiated changes will appear to be test-cases, reflecting the attitude of "Let's try something new for Amanda, and see if it more fully meets her needs" (Villa & Thousand, 1992).

If done in isolation, such test-cases are interesting, but seldom lead to long-term or widespread implementation of change. To facilitate both long-term and widespread implementation, therefore, teachers who are advocates view test-cases as one component of a change process, and must develop other activities that address the varying needs of stakeholders. When compared with activities completed by districts, however, their activities will be less formal. For instance, when sharing literature or videotapes on the change, the topic first may be discussed informally with a colleague, and then the information provided later with reference to the informal discussion (for example, "You seemed interested in *the topic*, so I thought you might like to see this"). While appearing to be casual, such interactions actually must be thought out carefully so that they systematically build the knowledge base of stakeholders and lead to more widespread support for, and ownership of, the proposed change. Through a series of activities, a teacher can provide information to stakeholders in a nonthreatening manner.

Once support has been fostered, change can be implemented on a small scale. As the positive effects of change become evident to implementers and their perceptions are shared, implementation inevitably will spread to other students with similar unmet needs. Box 11-3 describes an unmet need identified by one teacher, strategies that teacher used to promote change in students' educational services, and how roles changed for various stakeholders throughout the change process.

Role of the Teacher in Facilitating Change

When functioning as change initiator, a teacher attempts to identify allies and cooperatives early in the change process, so that ownership of the change is shared with as broad a base of support as possible. Once a support base exists and change is implemented on a small scale, a teacher usually will continue in the role of change agent as he or she assists in spreading information to additional stakeholders and implementing the change for other students. Now, however, that information includes the effect that the change has had on their student's unmet need.

MONITORING THE CHANGE PROCESS FOR SUCCESS

Monitoring the change process is not easy. Any one activity in that process may have an infinite number of effects on stakeholders, either singly or collectively (Villa & Thousand, 1992). For instance, the distribution of written information about the proposed change may cause a reaction not only from stakeholders who received the material, but also from those who saw or heard about the material from others. In addition, each stakeholder's reaction may be different.

When monitoring the change process, change initiators and allies must be able to "read" the reactions of every stakeholder. Upon reading those reactions, change initiators and allies must respond immediately to any questions, concerns, or needs for further information (Villa & Thousand, 1992), even if their response is only an acknowledgment of a concern and a commitment to prepare to address that concern.

Hord, Rutherford, Huling-Austin, and Hall (1987) refer to six stages of concern experienced by those experiencing change, and group these under three dimensions. When concern is focused on the *self*, a stakeholder may not be aware of any concern, or may be concerned about either obtaining information or identifying the effect the change will have on him, personally. When concern is focused on the *task*, a stakeholder may be concerned about how the change effects his preparation or management time. Finally, when concern is focused on the *impact* of the change, a stakeholder may be concerned with the effect on unmet student needs, his ability to correlate their efforts with those of other stakeholders, or additional change that may be more beneficial for the student. When monitoring the change

BOX 11-3 • **Teacher-Initiated Change—description of multiple roles played by specific stakeholders, and strategies used to produce change, during change efforts initiated by an actual teacher of students with multiple disabilities**

Need

Students with multiple disabilities placed in a self-contained room in an elementary school have no consistent opportunities to interact with nondisabled peers of the same age.

INITIAL ROLE	FUTURE ADDITIONAL ROLES
Change Initiator	
Teachers of students with multiple disabilities	Change agent
Allies	
Speech therapist	Change agent
Paraprofessionals	
Some regular education teachers	Change agents
Chair of special education	Change agent
Cooperatives	
Building principal	Ally and cooperative
Parents of students with multiple disabilities	Allies
Some regular education teachers	Allies and change agents
Teachers of special subject areas (e.g., art, music, P.E.)	Allies and change agents
Occupational therapist	Ally and change agent
Physical therapist	Ally
Cafeteria workers	Allies
Custodians	Allies
Office staff	Allies
Adversaries	
Some regular education teachers	Either cooperatives or allies
Change Agents	
Consultant in integrated services for students with multiple disabilities	

Strategies

1. Integrated 1–2 students for one hour per day, then expanded to 50% of the school day by the end of year 1. Expanded to 100% of the day for entire "class" of students with multiple disabilities at the beginning of the second academic year.
2. Provided informal inservice on integrated services to faculty and staff from the school, parents, and administration.

Eventually provided formal inservice sessions.

3. Provided on-going technical assistance to stakeholders immediately involved in the integrated services.
4. Expanded integrated services from the one class of students to all of the students with disabilities in the school, and then to all of the students with disabilities in the district.

process, it is helpful to identify which stage of concern stakeholders are demonstrating. By doing so, the change initiator, allies, and change agents can provide information and support directed to alleviate their immediate concerns.

MEASURING THE EFFECT OF CHANGE

Beyond monitoring the change process itself, advocates who are change initiators, allies, and change agents are interested in the effect of that change (Villa & Thousand, 1992). The effect of any change will be evident both in attitudes expressed by stakeholders and changes in outcomes experienced by students. Effects may include the: (a) student's immediate and long-term performance; (b) level of satisfaction with that performance as expressed by family members and stakeholders; and (c) level of satisfaction with the implementation of the change as expressed by family members and stakeholders (Villa & Thousand, 1992).

Student's Immediate Performance

When looking at effects of a change in educational services, stakeholders initially observe changes in a student's performance in relation to the unmet need. The effect will be discerned by comparing the student's performance before the change occurred with his performance after the change occurred. Through this comparison, advocates may determine whether the unmet need has been met. If not, additional changes may be necessary. If the comparison indicates negative changes for the student, then the change should be reassessed. This reassessment should consider: (a) whether the proposed change has been implemented appropriately and completely; (b) if so, whether the change was ill-conceived to meet the student need; and (c) whether an alternate change would be more effective in meeting the student need.

Students' Long-Term Performance

Once students' immediate performances indicate their unmet need has been addressed through change, advocates should evaluate the effect of that change on students' long-term performance. This evaluation may focus on the differences in students' performances after one, two, and three years, or on performances after exiting educational services.

For example, after modifying their educational services for students with severe disabilities to incorporate opportunities to interact with non-disabled peers in school and in the community, the Madison Public Schools evaluated the relative effectiveness of the two types of services by determining the extent to which their graduates participated in work, home life, and recreation with nondisabled adults (Brown et al., 1986). Once it determined that the integrated educational services were more effective in fostering the outcomes desired for their graduates (living, working, and recreating with nondisabled adults in the community for a majority of time), the district also conducted a cost-benefit analysis, comparing the two types of services (Piuma, 1989). While advocates need not complete so extensive an evaluation of long-term effects of change, they must be concerned with whether the change has positively affected students on a long-term basis. This can be determined only by comparing students' long-term performances with the performances of similar students whose educational services did not incorporate the change.

Parents' Level of Satisfaction

An advocate is concerned with stakeholders' perceptions of both the change process and the effect of the change. As consumers of educational services, parents are powerful when they relay information about a district to other parents, districts, and board members. Since they have the power to spread either positive or negative impressions, and since they are valued members of the educational process, it is critical to determine how satisfied they are with the change.

Their level of satisfaction may differ in relation to the change process itself (that is, how change was facilitated and their role in the process), versus the effect the change has had on either their child or other students with and without disabilities. Advocates may do a comparison of parents' perceptions of either the: student for whom the change was implemented, comparing her performance before and after the change occurred; or students who completed the program before and after the change was implemented.

The information obtained will be valuable for advocates when determining how well they included parents in the change process, and the extent to which parents see the same effects of the change as advocates. This information should be incorporated into the next change process in which that advocate participates.

Stakeholders' Level of Satisfaction

As with parents, important information can be obtained by determining the degree to which stakeholders are satisfied with both the change process and the effects of the change. With stakeholders, however, the information will assist in determining the extent to which the change may be expected to be inherent in the district's future operating procedures. For example, if stakeholders have negative impressions of the change process, believe the change did not address an unmet student need, or believe the amount of effort and turmoil involved in creating that change was not in balance with the effect achieved, those feelings may ferment over time. When this occurs, stakeholders may continue to work against change, even after it has been implemented. The issue may be ignored for a while, but at some point the discordant stakeholders may attempt to have the change reevaluated, with the intent of returning to previous methods of operating.

Monitoring stakeholders' level of satisfaction will alert advocates to possible sources of discord. Having this knowledge will allow advocates to continue efforts to solidify the position of the change in the system, and to deal with any residual feelings in a proactive manner. One method of addressing residual feelings is to assist the discordant stakeholder in achieving a different change they believe to be important and not in conflict with the change that has just occurred. While not always the answer, it will help reaffirm that stakeholder's position in district politics.

SUMMARY

Key variables that determine the effectiveness of change, along with specific strategies for initiating systems change were discussed in this chapter. Teachers' roles and procedures for monitoring and evaluating the effects of change were also described. It was pointed out that consumer satisfaction and the effect of change determine the degree to which the change will be assimilated throughout an entire system.

Introduction

1. The purpose of this chapter is to describe: (a) key variables that determine the extent to which systems change efforts are effective; (b) strategies for initiating systems change; (c) a teacher's role in the change process; (d) procedures for monitoring the change process; and (e) methods for evaluating the effects of change.

Key Variables in Systems Change Efforts

2. Each stakeholder is different in respect to a number of variables that can effect change efforts.

3. Stakeholders respond to change based on their attitudes and values.

4. Teachers and family members can provide stakeholders information that counterbalances prior misinformation.

5. Teachers and family members can encourage stakeholders to become involved with a student, in relation to the change.

6. Teachers and family members can assist power sources in understanding the need for change and sharing ownership in change efforts.

7. Stakeholders must either have the technical knowledge required to implement a change, or acquire that knowledge through inservice sessions and technical assistance activities.

8. Administrative support is required to plan and conduct formal inservice sessions and technical assistance activities.

9. If administrative support for change does not exist, teachers and family members can complete activities to facilitate that support.

10. Focusing on the outcome of change ensures that change efforts will continue until the original purpose for creating change is accomplished.

11. By emphasizing ongoing professional growth a district has established two advantages for stakeholders. First, stakeholders are more prepared mentally for change; second, stakeholders have a better understanding of how best educational practices change over time.

Facilitating Change in a District

12. Change implemented at one level of a system affects stakeholders at other levels.

13. Stakeholders at all levels need to understand, accept, and implement change simultaneously; therefore, change activities must simultaneously address stakeholders at all levels.

14. Changes in educational services occur most easily when initiated by a district.

15. Two strategies for facilitating district-initiated change are: (a) encouraging ownership of the change by involving as many stakeholders as possible; and (b) starting change on a small scale and expanding implementation after initial success.

16. During district-initiated change, a teacher decides which role(s) to play. To facilitate change, a teacher may assist in change activities.

17. It is more difficult for parents to initiate change than for districts. Working in a collaborative manner is preferable, but efforts at parent-initiated change often are successful only after formal due process procedures.

18. Since parents may not conduct systems change activities directly, they must "sell" their idea for change to stakeholders. These stakeholders may then advocate for systems change.

19. Upon receiving information on a change proposed by parents, a teacher may choose to become a secondary change initiator. By doing so, that teacher accepts the risk of developing an adversarial relationship with the district.

20. Initiating change as a teacher may be as difficult as for parents. Teachers initiating change will identify allies and conduct numerous informal activities to build a solid base of support.

21. Teachers frequently use a 'test-case' to demonstrate the validity of proposed change.

Monitoring the Change Process for Success

22. While monitoring the change process, the change initiator and allies respond immediately to stakeholders' questions, concerns, and needs for additional information.

23. Stakeholders progress through several stages of concern, including concern for self, the task, and the impact of the change.

Measuring the Effect of Change

24. Advocates for systems change must be concerned about the effects of that change on stakeholders.

25. The effect of change should first be evident when comparing the targeted student's performances before and after the change. If the change is negative, advocates should re-assess the change.

26. One, two, or three years after the change, the effect of the change should be measured by comparing the performances of students before and after the change, or by comparing the performance of students involved in the change with the performance of students receiving other services.

27. The degree to which parents, as consumers of educational services, are satisfied with both the change process and the effect of the change is of interest to advocates because of their potential influence on the opinions of stakeholders.

28. The degree to which stakeholders are satisfied with the change process and the effect of the change will determine the extent to which the change may be assimilated throughout the system.

REFERENCES

American Association of School Administrators (1988). *Adversaries for school leaders*. Arlington, VA: American Association of School Administrators.

Beach Center on Families and Disabilities (1990). "Parent to parent national survey." *Exceptional Parent, 20*(7).

Bollington, R. & Hopkins, D. (1989). "School based review—As a strategy for the implementation of teacher appraisal and school improvement." *Educational Change and Development, 10*(1), 8–17.

Brown, L., Shiraga, B., Ford, A., Nisbet, J., VanDeventer, P., Sweet, M., York, J., & Loomis, R. (1986). "Teaching severely handicapped students to perform meaningful work in nonsheltered vocational environments," in R. J. Morris and B. Blatt, Eds., *Special education: Research and trends*. Elmsford, NY: Pergamon Press.

California Research Institute (1990). *Meeting of the Directors of Statewide Systems Change Grant*. San Francisco: San Francisco State University.

Clayton, C. E. (1991). Chapter 1 Evaluation: Progress, problems, and possibilities. *Educa-

tional Evaluation and Policy Analysis, 13(4), 345–352.

Dobbs, R. F., Primm, E. B., & Primm, B. (1991). "Mediation: A common sense approach for resolving conflicts in education." *Focus on Exceptional Children, 24*(2).

Goldberg, S. S. & Kuriloff, P. J. (1991). "Evaluating the fairness of special education hearings." *Exceptional Children, 57*(6), 546–555.

Hamre-Nietupski, S., Krajewski, L., Nietupski, J., Ostercamp, D., Sensor, K., & Opheim, B. (1988). "Parent/professional partnerships in advocacy: Developing integrated options within resistive systems." *Journal of The Association for Persons with Severe Handicaps, 13*(4), 251–259.

Hanline, M. F. & Halvorsen, A. (1989). "Parent perceptions of the integration transition process: Overcoming artificial barriers." *Exceptional Children, 55*(6), 487–492.

Hord, S. M., Rutherford, W. L., Huling-Austin, L., & Hall, G. E. (1987). *Taking charge of change.* Alexandria, VA: Association for Supervision and Curriculum Development.

McDonnell, A. P. & Hardman, M. L. (1989). "The desegregation of America's special schools: Strategies for change." *The Journal of the Association for Persons with Severe Handicaps, 14*(1), 68–74.

McGregor, G., Janssen, C. M., Larsen, L. A., & Tillery, W. L. (1986). "Philadelphia's urban model project: A system-wide effort to integrate students with severe handicaps." *The Journal of The Association for Persons with Severe Handicaps, 11*(1), 61–67.

Piuma, M. F. (1989). *Benefits and costs of integrating students with severe disabilities into regular public school programs: A study summary of money well spent.* San Francisco, CA: San Francisco State University, Department of Special Education.

Prasse, D. P. (1986). "Litigation and special education: An introduction." *Exceptional Children, 52*(4), 311–312.

Rainforth, B., York, J., & Macdonald, C. (1992). *Collaborative teams for students with severe disabilities: Integrating therapy and educa-*

tional services. Baltimore, MD: Paul H. Brookes.

Robison, A. Q. & Robison, G. A. (1991). "Integration—Don't take it for granted." *Exceptional Parent, 21*(6).

Rock, S. L., Geiger, W. L., & Hood, G. (1992). "CEC's standards for professional practice in advocacy: Members' attitudes and activities." *Exceptional Children, 58*(6), 541–547.

Rosenberg, H., Tesolowski, D. G., & Stein, R. J. (1983). "Advocacy: Education's professional responsibility to handicapped citizens." *Education and Training of the Mentally Retarded, 18*(4), 266–270.

Ryndak, D. L. & Doyle, M. B. (1991). *Severe handicaps technical assistance project: Second year report* (Available from D.L. Ryndak, Exceptional Education Department, State University College, Buffalo, New York 14222).

Ryndak, D. L. & Militello, N. (1992). *Getting an integrated educational program for your child: Common steps taken by parents* (Manuscript submitted for publication).

Spiegel-McGill, P. (1991). "Integration of children with special educational needs in the public schools: A district-wide mission." *The Forum, 17*(1), 11–12.

Stainback, G. H., Stainback, W. C., & Stainback, S. B. (1988). "Superintendents' attitudes toward integration." *Education and Training in Mental Retardation, 23*(2), 92–96.

Villa, R. A. & Thousand, J. S. (1992). "Restructuring public school systems: Strategies for organizational change and progress," in R. A. Villa, J. S. Thousand, W. Stainback & S. Stainback (Eds.), *Restructuring for caring and effective education: An administrative guide to creating heterogeneous schools.* Baltimore, MD: Paul H. Brookes, pp.109–137.

Wershing, A., Gaylord-Ross, C., & Gaylord-Ross, R. (1986). "Implementing a community-based vocational training model: A process for systems change." *Education and Training of the Mentally Retarded, 21*(2), 130–137.

Winfield, L. F. (1991). "Lessons from the field: Case studies of evolving schoolwide projects." *Educational Evaluation and Policy Analysis, 13*(4), 353–362.

12

ETHICAL ISSUES RELATING TO FAMILIES OF PERSONS WITH DISABILITIES

Patrick J. Schloss
University of Missouri-Columbia

Joan G. Henley
University of Missouri-Columbia

Chapter Objectives

After completing this chapter, you will be able to:

1. Discuss elements of the Constitution of the United States that serve as a foundation for the ethical treatment of persons with disabilities
2. Differentiate between positive presumption and negative presumption as related to the rights of people with disabilities
3. Identify sources of ethical standards for professional treatment of persons with disabilities and their families
4. Describe implications of prominent legislation and litigation for professional ethics
5. Discuss the provisions of standards and codes of major professional organizations as related to the ethical behavior of professionals
6. Describe general principles of naturalism, religious ethics, moral relativism, humanistic reciprocity, duty-based ethics, utilitarianism, and causalism as applied to the ethical behavior of service providers and their families
7. Establish personal professional standards for ethical conduct based on litigation, legislation, ethical guidelines from professional organizations, and philosophical principles
8. Apply professional standards for ethical conduct to daily problems relating to the education and treatment of persons with disabilities

Key Terms and Phrases

assurance of privacy	moral relativism
Buckley Amendment/Family	naturalism
Rights and Privacy Act of 1974	negative presumption
causalism	nondiscriminatory assessment
Code of Ethics	and treatment
Council for Exceptional Children	positive presumption
due process	religious ethics
duty-based ethics	situation ethics
humanistic reciprocity	surrogate parent
impartial hearing	type A information
inalienable rights	type B information
independent consultant	type C information
informed consent	utilitarianism

We noted in the second chapter that, throughout recorded history, moral imperatives have guided advocacy efforts on behalf of persons with disabilities. Efforts of ethically guided parents and practitioners have resulted in a strong social conviction. This conviction has supported equal opportunity for all individuals with disabilities. Though still debated (see Aloia, 1984), the current status of educational and social service is the direct result of these foundations.

We also noted that ideas and activities viewed as morally responsible at one point in history may be viewed as being harsh and abusive in another. During the survival era, for example, failing to practice eugenics resulted in a hardship to able family members. Consequently, infanticide was considered to be ethical and moral while engaging in extraordinary care to preserve the life of a person with disabilities was considered to be immoral. Conversely, we currently hold to a moral, standard that regardless of cost, all individuals with disabilities should be provided equal protection under the Constitution of the United States.

The moral standards of advocates for individuals with disabilities have been manifested in the rights they have sought to assure. Certain basic rights cherished by all Americans have clearly been identified as critical human rights goals for individuals with disabilities. As members of the general society value privacy, so are individuals with disabilities assured privacy. As society values equal access to government sponsored programs, so are individuals with disabilities assured access to programs. As general society values protection from inhumane treatment, so do we assure individuals with disabilities protection from unjust adversity.

Other, more subjective or personal rights have produced disagreement within society. Does an individual with disabilities have the right to extraordinary care that may result in accelerated cognitive development? Conversely, should more modest educational services be provided that are less costly to the general society, but are effective only in sustaining marginal progress? What decisions are made when the rights of one individual are in conflict with the rights of another? Can the right of an aggressive youth to a free and appropriate public education be suspended if it is in conflict with another child's right to be protected from the child's potentially harmful conduct?

It is important that professionals and family members be aware of the ethical foundations through which basic human rights are accorded individuals with disabilities. All professionals and family members should be aware of assurances to ethical treatment provided through our legal process. Equally important, professionals and family members should recognize the ethical standards from which they address the more subjective or personal issues. This chapter will address both topics. We will review basic ethical standards imposed by Federal law. Then we will consider the ethical standards developed and disseminated by professional organizations. Next, we will consider general ethical standards that have been debated throughout history. Finally, we will present a process model for forming ethical judgments.

ETHICAL TREATMENT UNDER LAW

The Constitution of the United States guarantees individuals "certain inalienable rights." The rights of life, liberty, and the pursuit of happiness are assured to all individuals unless there is sufficient evidence to support the revocation of rights. Cobb (1973) refers to this standard as *positive presumption.* One is presumed to be protected under the constitution unless mitigating factors are disclosed. Unfortunately, the presence of a disability may alter social perceptions and introduce a *negative presumption* in which an individual is assumed not to have rights until he or she is proven worthy. It is important to emphasize that negative presumption violates constitutional and social standards for citizens of this country. Under due process of law, professionals must hold to an ethical standard that all citizens are entitled to constitutional guarantees without the presumption of eligibility.

Because of the potential for negative presumption, family members, professionals, and advocates have sought to further clarify constitutional guarantees. Their action is noted in case law and legislation. We will describe several of the basic rights articulated by the courts and legislature. These rights prescribe, in part, ethical conduct of service providers.

Ethical Responsibility to Assure Privacy

Individuals with disabilities have been particularly vulnerable to breaches in confidentiality. The presence of handicapping conditions and extra services required often produces the need for more extensive recordkeeping. The use of multiple service providers (for example, vocational rehabilitation, family services, education, medical, and so on) often prompts the sharing of records. The potential impact of diagnosis and treatment plans often encourages extensive data collection in order to justify the results of an appraisal. Finally, family members' passionate interest in seeking a favorable diagnosis and optimistic prognosis may result in the documentation of misleading information (Abeson, 1976).

These conditions serve to highlight the ethical responsibility of professionals to ensure the confidentiality of information kept in educational records. In 1974 Congress passed the Buckley Amendment of Public Law 93-380 (Family Rights and Privacy Act of 1974). This legislation mandates practices that ensure the ethical treatment of personal information.

The Buckley Amendment identifies three types of information likely to be contained in students' educational records. Type A information is essential for the accurate diagnosis, classification, and placement of the child or youth. Type B information is important for the health and safety of the learner. This may include information on medical treatment, allergies, or dietary restrictions. Type C information is anecdotal and unverified. If not verified, it must be removed from a student's educational record.

The Buckley Amendment also has ethical implications for the release of educational records. Under the amendment, family members must provide written consent prior to a record being shared with an outside individual or agency (including media). This provision ensures that family members are aware of all individuals or agencies that have access to educational records. Family members can prevent the release of information if they believe that knowledge of the information may be detrimental to the child or youth (Fanning, 1977; Pasanella and Volkmor, 1977).

Ethical Responsibility of Providing Access to Information

A related ethical responsibility of professionals involves the free access to educational records maintained by schools and other agencies. Family members have historically been denied access to their child or youth's educational records. These records provide basic assessment information used to make critical educational decisions. As a result, family members have been unable to determine the basis upon which educational decisions are made. Further, absent the necessary information, family members were unable to confirm or challenge the appropriateness of important educational decisions. Another issue involved the extent of data collection efforts. Family members were typically not informed of what information was being collected and stored in a student's educational record. Additionally, they were not informed of the purpose for which information was being collected. Compounding the problem, there was generally no mechanism for systematically purging records that were no longer educationally relevant.

The Buckley Amendment provides an ethical standard requiring that schools notify family members prior to collecting formal diagnostic information. Family members must be informed of the procedures used to collect data and the purpose for which data are collected. Family members must also be informed of their right to review educational records within 45 days of their request. They are also entitled to have a person of their choosing review and evaluate their child's records. If requested, the school must provide a qualified professional to explain the record contents to family members. In addition, copies of educational records must be made available if requested by family members. Finally, the Buckley Amendment includes due process provisions if family members and school personnel disagree on the necessity of particular records being maintained or the appropriateness of their distribution (Goldberg, 1982).

Ethical Responsibility of Nondiscriminatory Assessment and Treatment

Numerous examples of discrimination based on culturally biased assessment and treatment have been reported over the past few decades. In many cases, children and youth from culturally diverse backgrounds were identified and placed in special programs as if they were disabled. Actual deficiencies, however, simply resulted from bias against the cultural norms of the family in the assessment instrument and its interpretation. Timed tests, for example, favor a competitive culture. Many children from Native American backgrounds are encouraged to work slowly and methodically. Many scales use items that favor the dominant suburban middle class culture. Asking about the origin of dairy products favors suburban and rural students over children from inner city backgrounds. Finally, the mere presentation of items in written English is biased against students from families in which Spanish is the dominant language.

The major problem of culturally biased assessment is the resulting overrepresentation of minority students in special education programs. Family members and advocates have sought relief from the court system to reduce or eliminate overrepresentation that results from cultural bias. A series of cases including *Diana* v. *State Board of Education* (1970), *Ruiz* v. *State Board of Education* (1970), and *Larry P.* v. *Riles* (1972) were filed on behalf of minority children and youth. The results of these cases establish the ethical standards by which assessment and placement of students from minority backgrounds must occur.

The first standard is that professionals administer tests in the native or dominant language of the student. Tests outside of the student's native language should not be interpreted with reference to a dissimilar, but favored, norm group. The second standard is that intelligence tests, or other measures that are inherently culturally "loaded," should not be used as a sole source of information when making a diagnosis or placement (Sage & Burrello, 1986). Daily school work, reports from family members, and other data should be used to supplement or replace these data. Finally, test developers should strive to construct and validate tests that are as culturally free or culturally fair as possible. At minimum, the possibility of cultural bias should be discussed in test manuals, and individual student reports should acknowledge error that may result from cultural bias.

Ethical Responsibility to Provide Due Process

Throughout American history, individuals with disabilities have often been denied the right of procedural due process under the Constitution of the United States. The Fifth and Fourteenth Amendments stipulate that no person can be deprived of basic rights without due process of law. Despite this, we have been quick to deprive individuals with disabilities of basic liberty through mandatory confinement in substandard institutions. Within these settings, individuals with disabilities may have been deprived rights of association, property rights, and the right of free expression.

Turnbull, Strickland, and Brantley (1982) define due process as "a procedure that seeks to ensure the fairness of educational decisions and the accountability of both the professionals and parents in making these decisions. Due process can be viewed as a system of checks and balances concerning the identification, evaluation, and provision of services regarding handicapped students" (p. 10).

Public Law 94-142 includes provisions that mandate the revocation of rights only through due process of law. The due process provisions of Public Law 94-142 that have implications for the ethical conduct of educators are described as follows:

- Family members must be informed prior to the collection of diagnostic information that may result in special class placement. They must be informed of the purpose of data collection, as well as the possible outcomes based on the assessment findings.
- Family members must provide informed consent prior to their child or youth being assessed. They must also consent to changes in classification and placement.
- Family members must be provided the opportunity to employ an independent consultant to evaluate and possibly challenge educational decisions made by school district personnel.
- Family members must be provided the opportunity to have an impartial hearing when disputes arise.
- State agencies must appoint a surrogate parent when the child or youth is not represented by family members and is unable to advocate for himself or herself.

Family members of students with disabilities also have the right to be represented by an attorney through all due process matters. If the family prevails in a due process hearing, The Handicapped Children's Protection Act (P.L. 99-372) provides for reimbursement to family members by the educational agency.

The codes of ethics adopted and disseminated by many professional organizations further extend and clarify "rule-based" ethical standards. In many cases, they extend legal guides to specific problems commonly faced by the profession. Professional standards and codes will be discussed in the following section.

PROFESSIONAL STANDARDS AND CODES

Many professional organizations associated with the care and treatment of individuals with disabilities have articulated standards and codes of ethical conduct. These standards are generally based upon the philosophical and legal principles discussed in this chapter. In many cases, however, they include specific statements that reflect the unique mission of the organization. For this reason, it is important that professionals understand the codes and standards for ethical behavior advanced by their professional associations.

For special educators, the most visible and influential professional association is The Council for Exceptional Children. Their code of ethics (1983) is stated as follows:

> *We declare the following principles to be the Code of Ethics for educators of exceptional persons. Members of the special education profession are responsible for upholding and advancing these principles. Members of The Council for Exceptional Children agree to judge them in accordance with the spirit and provisions of this Code.*
>
> I. *Special education professionals are committed to developing the highest education and quality of life potential of exceptional individuals.*
> II. *Special education professionals promote and maintain a high level of competence and integrity in practicing their profession.*
> III. *Special education professionals engage in professional activities which benefit exceptional individuals, their families, other colleagues, students, or research subjects.*
> IV. *Special education professionals exercise objective professional judgment in the practice of their profession.*
> V. *Special education professionals strive to advance their knowledge and skills regarding the education of exceptional individuals.*
> VI. *Special education professionals work within the standards and policies of the profession.*
> VII. *Special education professionals seek to uphold and improve where necessary the laws, regulations, and policies governing the delivery of special education and related services and the practice of their profession.*
> VIII. *Special education professionals do not condone or participate in unethical or illegal acts, nor violate professional standards adopted by the Delegate Assembly of CEC.*

More detailed professional standards for ethical conduct have been advanced by *The American Personnel and Guidance Association* and the *American Psychological Association*. Common themes within the professional standards of these associations include the following: responsibility to the profession; competence; professional relationships; appropriate representation of credentials and abilities; protection of the client; confidentiality; appropriate use of assessment instruments and findings; administrative conduct; protection of human subjects; and professional development (refer to Hummel, Talbutt, and Alexander, 1985, for a complete review).

GENERAL ETHICAL STANDARDS

We noted earlier that all ethical standards are not addressed specifically by law or professional organizations. Only as problems become chronic and pervasive across society, do they receive the attention of higher courts, the legislature, or professional groups. Problems that are unique to an individual family or that are of a personal nature must be addressed through the individual ethics of professionals.

Much has been written over the centuries about personal values, morals, and ethics. Standards have been based on individual principles of fair practice as well as broad-based canons of personal ethics. While this writing does not apply specifically to professional ethics, one can generalize from broad personal ethics to those that have a direct impact on education. We will review general moral principles that apply to service providers and families. Those that are particularly relevant are *naturalism, religious ethics, moral relativism, humanistic reciprocity, duty-based ethics, utilitarianism,* and *causalism.* These will be discussed separately.

Naturalism

Greek scholars including Socrates, Plato, and Aristotle laid the foundation for the modern philosophy of ethics. Their strongest influence is recognized in the writings of St. Thomas Aquinas, David Hume, Aldous Huxley, and contemporary philosophers. Each writer emphasizes the importance of natural order. Central to this order is the human capacity for intelligent action. The ability to reason and deduce solutions to novel situations is unique to our species. This feature establishes the basis from which all human ethics are founded (McInereny, 1982).

The fulfilled life, as defined by Greek scholars, is based on insight, reason and intellectual responding. According to Greek scholars, intellect is the source of our personal happiness as well as the happiness of others (Norman, 1983). Professionals are ethically compelled to fully develop their knowledge and skills in the chosen discipline. Ethical treatment of individuals with disabilities and their families can only occur when the professional avails himself or herself of all available professional information. Ethical judgments must be based on this information.

An element of Greek philosophy that is particularly relevant to questions of ethics in professional life involves the practice of moderation. Greek philosophers believed that to be happy, and promote the happiness of others, one must behave in a reasonable, and thoughtful manner. The *Golden Mean* stipulates that ethical behavior is void of extremes in judgment and action. Based on this standard, our decisions and actions on behalf of families and students with disabilities are considered ethical if we are moderate and thoughtful in our decisions and responses.

Religious Ethics

Basic Judeo-Christian Doctrine follows from one's knowledge of an omnipotent and omniscient God. Hebrew Scriptures emphasize that there is no distinction between religion and ethics. This is also consistent with the ethics of Islam in which no act is ethical or meritorious unless dedicated to Allah. In both cases, the principles of faith passed down through religious traditions and scriptures establish patterns of ethical conduct.

Judeo-Christian Doctrine emphasizes that we are made in the "image and likeness of God" and that all ethical conduct emulates the behavior of the merciful and loving God (VanWyk, 1990). Jews and Christians strive to understand God and follow his example through their interactions with others. Jews accomplish this by reading the works of prophets while Christians also study the life of Jesus. As noted above, Islamic tradition stresses the importance of actions taken on behalf of the supreme being, Allah. No action, regardless of the importance to the individual or others, is ethical unless it is conducted for the eventual benefit of Allah.

The Ten Commandments also serve as a foundation for the Judeo-Christian ethic. The first and most important commandment is to love God. This is consistently interpreted in both Jewish and Christian teachings as the act of emulating God. The second commandment is to love others as yourself. This commandment is popularized as the *Golden Rule*—"Do unto others as you would have them do to you." The teachings of Mohammed, the central prophet of Islam, parallel those of the Jewish and Christian faiths. Professionals are encouraged to engage in standards of conduct that reflect the manner in which they would hope to be treated by other professionals. As we hope to be treated with compassion by others, so we should strive to treat others with compassion. We trust that physicians, attorneys, accountants, and others will perform services for us in a responsible and competent manner. Consequently, we strive to serve our students and their families in a competent and responsible manner. We value the ability to interact freely with other professionals and expect that our wishes will influence final decisions. Therefore, we encourage the free exchange of information with our students and their families. We consider their views when reaching final decisions.

Moral Relativism

The moral relative position is often advocated by anthropologists such as Ruth Benedict. The position holds that the ethical value of an action is based on social standards (Ladd, 1973). If people in this country hold to a value that it is proper to work on Sunday, then it is morally correct to work on Sunday. In Italy, where people generally reserve Sunday for religious and social observances, it is morally incorrect to work. In effect, the term "ethically and morally right" is synonymous with "approved by society."

The legal foundation previously described early in this chapter suggests the social foundation for a moral relativistic view of efforts on behalf of persons with disabilities. Further, the professional codes of ethics, described later, highlight socially relativistic standards. These two sources indicate what the broader society and the more specific culture of professional groups accept as appropriate on behalf of individuals with disabilities. Professionals who follow these social standards may be described as being ethical from within the framework of cultural relativism.

Humanistic Reciprocity

Carl Rogers and other contemporary authors extend the Judeo-Christian ethic to a secular humanistic view. Humanistic reciprocity emphasizes the need for empathy and the unconditional acceptance of others. Advocates argue that all human beings share the same need to be loved, respected, and fulfilled. Empathy toward others allows us to recognize that as these needs are clear in our lives, they are equally important in the lives of others (Rogers, 1961). Reciprocity assures our obligation to satisfy these needs in others. In general, ethical conduct is judged by the extent to which an action assists another individual in gaining love, respect, and fulfillment.

Professionals practice humanistic reciprocity by recognizing the need for love, respect, and fulfillment of students and their families. In general, the disposition of professionals should be viewed as nonjudgmental and unconditionally accepting. Encouraging family members to participate fully in the educational process is based on a recognition of the need for respect. Benevolent decisions that provide for the comfort and safety of the student and family are based on the need for love. Finally, decisions that encourage the full intellectual, social, and vocational growth of the student and family is based on the need for fulfillment.

Duty-based Ethics

Immanuel Kant proposed that the major problem of moral traditions in American and European cultures is not deciding what is ethically responsible, rather it is doing one's duty when it conflicts with natural inclinations. In addressing this issue, he acknowledges that religious ethics were basically correct, but lacking an overriding principle of "exceptionless doctrine."

The categorical imperative was proposed by Immanuel Kant to address this shortcoming, and is basic to all moral behavior. It is the principle to which all other ethical principles must conform (VanWyk, 1990). Based on the categorical imperative, an action is ethical and moral to the extent that it can be applied to all humans. A rule that requires exception for individuals or classes of people cannot be ethical. Also, the arbitrary, discriminatory, or pejorative treatment of an individual or class of individuals based on irrelevant events is not ethical. In general, the categorical imperative emphasizes the equal treatment of all people given similar conditions.

The implications for Kant's views in special education services should be clear. Ethical treatment is rule governed. The rules should be applied equally to all individuals regardless of disability, race, socioeconomic status, sex, or age. Only substantive changes in conditions can yield changes in treatment under the rule.

Kant would concur that professionals are responsible for providing free and appropriate public education to all students. Any departure that is not based on a substantial change in condition would violate the categorical imperative. He would agree that family members have the right to be represented by an attorney and to employ a specialist to offer second opinions relating to the nature of educational services as schools exercise these rights. In short, any practice of professionals toward students or family members in a specific situation should be appropriate for other students and family members in similar situations. Also actions of school personnel in a given situation should be appropriate for family members in similar situations.

Utilitarianism by Rule and Act

Rule utilitarianism shares the exceptionless nature of the categorical imperative. Beyond this, however, a universal rule is judged to be ethical if it effects the greatest good for the greatest number of people. Act utilitarianism allows for individual judgments in specific situations. Again, however, an individual act is judged to be ethical if the act produces the greatest amount of good for all concerned. The classical writing of Bentham (1823) defines utilitarianism in the following manner:

> *By the principle of utility is meant that principle which approves or disapproves of every action whatsoever, according to the tendency which it appears to have to augment or diminish the happiness of the party whose interest is in question; or . . . (the action's ability to) promote or to oppose that happiness. (p. 365)*

Utilitarianism requires that we judge the effects of our rules or actions on people. We must be able to identify all people that are effected by our rules or actions. We must also discern varying levels of positive or negative outcomes. Ethical insight from a utilitarianism perspective results from weighing the positive to negative value of an outcome and the pervasiveness across people of the effect (Norman, 1983).

Professionals following a utilitarian perspective must determine if their rules or actions serve the greatest good for those they serve. When conflicting judgments occur, the judgment selected should be the one that passes the test of the greatest good. For example, an administrator may be required to judge if the district engage in public school based educational programs or center based programs for individuals with severe disabilities. He or she must be able to identify positive outcomes associated with each decision. Further, he or she must judge the extent to which these benefits are shared across people. The decision that produces the greatest good for the largest number of families, students, professionals, and other citizens, with be the ethical decision.

Causalism

This philosophy judges an action to be ethical based on its impact on the broader society. Actions that have a positive effect on the general welfare of society are viewed as being ethical. Those that have a negative impact are unethical. The production and sale of alcohol can be considered unethical as the overall effect on society is negative as judged by associated crime, domestic violence, automobile fatalities, health risks, and so on. Medical research may be viewed as being ethical because the general effect on society is the prolongation of life and reduction of suffering.

This perspective calls on professionals to judge the effects of their decisions on the greater good of society. For a particular student, do skills acquired though a functional skills curriculum produce greater good for society when contrasted with basic skills? Does a state educational agency's decision to provide early intervention services serve the greater good of citizens in the state over delaying services until first grade?

INTEGRATING ETHICAL THEORIES

The preceding ethical positions have both common and conflicting elements. Conflicting elements must be resolved through the values of the individual professional as shaped by litigation, legislation, and the ethical guidelines for professional organizations. Recognition of the common elements may provide the greatest utility in developing a set of personal standards for ethical conduct. They are highlighted as follows:

- Ethical professional behavior is rooted in knowledge of the discipline. Professional insight and an intellectual perspective on the problems of students with disabilities must underlie ethical judgments and actions.
- Ethical professional behavior may be categorized as being moderate. Given extremes of possible judgments or actions, a thoughtful approach is likely to fall within the middle range.
- Ethical professional conduct generally reflects judgments or actions toward students and their families that would be selected regardless of relationship, social status, or other variables. The most critical test may be whether the professionals would form the same judgment or pursue the same course of action if they or their family members were the recipient.
- Ethical professional conduct is accepting and nonjudgmental when rejection and adverse judgment serve no therapeutic purpose.
- Ethical professional conduct can be generalized to all individuals under similar conditions. Arbitrary, discriminating, or pejorative treatment based on race, social status, sex, disabling condition, or other variables not directly related to the judgment or action violates ethical standards.
- Ethical professional conduct results from the careful study of possible outcomes and a recognition that the judgment or action will produce the most favorable outcome for the largest number of people.
- Ethical professional conduct reflects the interests of the individual as well as the broader society.

A PLAN OF PROFESSIONAL ETHICS

To this point in the chapter, we have made few moral judgments. Rather, we have provided an overview of standards from which these judgments can be made. It should also be clear that these standards are often conflicting and subjective. For example, one can adopt a personal ethic based on hedonistic utilitarianism. Such a position would allow one to advocate for any action that advances the greatest pleasure for the greatest number of people. This standard would be at odds with the golden rule of treating others as you would wish to be treated.

Beyond major issues addressed by the courts, legislature, or significant professional associations, we recognize the sanctity of the individual in reaching ethical judgments. However, we hold strongly to the view of Thomas Aquinas that ethical judgments must be made through thoughtful and intelligent deliberation. As sentient beings, we must understand, communicate, act on, evaluate, and revise our ethical standards with expanding experience. The final section of this chapter provides a process approach to professional ethics. We highlight the major questions raised by professionals concerned for their ethical conduct. We also identify major considerations within each question.

Upon What Ethical Standards Do I Form Judgments?

We suggest that preservice professionals develop ethical standards in advance of specific problems. This approach is the most thoughtful and planful. It can be contrasted with the practice of "situation ethics" in which standards are developed in response to individual events.

A priori standards avoid lost objectivity resulting from being personally enmeshed in an ethical dilemma. To illustrate, we may possess a personal ethic indicating that it is wrong to give incorrect or incomplete information to administrators about our professional activity. Situations in which not divulging all information is appropriate may be defined in advance (for example, when it violates client confidentiality, when the information is not relevant to the administrator, and so on). Conversely, we may wait until an ethical dilemma occurs and establish a specific solution. In the case of a priori standards we are less likely to yield to "temptations" of the current situation. Our emotional reactions toward the problem and solution do not adversely influence our ethics when decisions are thought out in advance of a specific problem.

The first standard from which decisions may be based is legislation and litigation. We have no question about the general ethics of providing services for individuals with disabilities, confidentiality, due process, and so on. These questions are prescribed by law and we recognize that practicing outside of just laws is inherently unethical. It is important to note that one can ethically work toward revising a law that is not viewed as proper. We advocate upholding the law by our actions until the law is changed.

The next standard may be that suggested by our professional organizations. A substantial amount of thought by the most knowledgeable and experienced members of the profession has gone into developing and ratifying these standards. Further, when we represent ourselves within the professional organization, we communicate that we abide by the organization's standards.

Finally, given the failure of the two preceding standards to provide insight and resolution for specific ethical problems, we invoke our own philosophy of ethics. The preceding summary of major positions may assist in clarifying personal standards for moral behavior. One may hold strictly to a single moral doctrine, or form a personal perspective based on several of the positions.

What Are the Objective Facts in a Specific Case?

We have established a clear standard for professional ethics that guides action in individual situations. The sentient professional, however, still must identify how the specific problem relates to our ethical standards. This process begins with the identification of objective facts in the case. A thorough study of all aspects of the problem should be conducted. This study begins with an analysis of objective facts. Who is being affected by a given decision? What are the real effects of the decision? Over what period of time? What alternatives are available? What are the impediments to using the alternatives?

Is Additional Information Needed?

The analysis of objective facts often results in additional unanswered questions. The professional should recognize the need to obtain necessary information and outside sources for this information should be solicited. As emphasized above, the only standard of personal ethics that we impose is that of the naturalists—professional ethics must be based on thoughtful and intelligent insight.

What Are the Functional and Ethical Issues?

Any situation that poses an ethical dilemma can be studied from two perspectives. The first includes functional aspects of the dilemma. Functional aspects may be viewed as matters of expedience, convenience, or utility. With reference to assessing a minority student, functional questions may include the time and place of assessment or the availability of an examiner and testing materials.

The second perspective involves the ethical issues. These may include questions of whether the results of assessment will accurately reflect the child's competence or offer increased participation in the mainstream of society.

It is important that we consider both ethical and functional issues. In most cases, functional issues may be difficult to resolve, but trivial to the future of the participants. Conversely, ethical issues are often easily resolved (if ethical standards are ignored), but critical to the future of the child. It may be difficult to schedule an examination, but the actual time the examination occurs is not consequential to the future of the child. Whether or not the test should be given may be easily decided (outside of ethical constraints), but the outcome may be critical to the future adjustment of the child.

How Will My Judgment and Actions Affect Others?

Professional decisions seldom affect only the individual making the decision. It is important that we consider all individuals that are affected by our decisions. It is at this level of concern that we are likely to identify values conflicts that have ethical implications.

The most direct and obvious individual affected by our professional judgment is the student. It is important that we consider his or her wishes regardless of age or capability. Almost of equal importance are the interests of family members. Family members' input is particularly essential when age, developmental, cognitive, or communication limitations restrict the child or youth's ability to fully participate in decision-making. In this case, we assume that family members may be the principle advocate.

As emphasized repeatedly, family members should be well informed of all issues and possible solutions. They should also be provided an expedient channel through which their opinions may be known. Finally, their ideas should be considered carefully by all professionals.

Other individuals that may be affected by the solution include professionals providing services, administrators responsible for schedule and finances, other students, and so on. The extent to which these individuals are effected by the action should dictate, in part, the weight given their input. Individuals that are only marginally influenced by the decision or action may provide minimal input. Individuals who are influenced substantially should actively contribute to the decision.

It is important to note that basic ethical standards cited above suggest that we act to effect the greatest good for all concerned. It is also important that we treat others as we would wish to be treated. Consequently, informed participation by all affected is essential to arriving at ethical decisions. From a purely pragmatic standpoint, many professionals recognize that solutions not popular with those affected are often doomed to failure through nonsupport or sabotage. The chances of a successful outcome can be enhanced by providing information and soliciting support from all concerned.

Can I Accommodate Their Views and Act Ethically?

Unfortunately, the decisions faced by special education professionals are not always universally supported. We have encouraged professionals to consider input from all affected parties with the greatest weight given to those affected the greatest. In most cases, this will be the student and his or her family members. Accommodation of the views of others may be a foundation of ethical action (particularly if the golden rule and utilitarian standards are adopted).

On occasion, however, the wishes of others may yield an unethical solution. For example, an administrator may request that a child not be identified as behaviorally disordered because the school district does not have appropriately certified staff. Though the administrator is affected by the solution, his or her desires are contrary to the ethical conduct of the professional. Similarly, a family member may request the termination of special education services because having a child in special classes is embarrassing. The professional may recognize the importance of these services for the child or youth and note that not having services would severely limit the child's adult adjustment.

The professional must determine if the interests of others will produce an unethical solution. When it does, he or she must begin negotiations to arrive at a mutually agreeable and ethical outcome. When informal discussions fail to yield an acceptable conclusion, he or she may use a more formal "due process" mechanism. An impartial hearing may be requested when the conflict is with family members. The involvement of higher administrative authorities (such as superintendent, school board, office of civil rights, labor relations board, and so on) may be requested when the conflict is between professionals and/or administrators.

What Is My Final Course of Action?

Action should occur only after collecting all necessary information and engaging in substantial and thoughtful deliberation. As emphasized repeatedly, the professional should weigh all facts against a priori ethical standards. Special weight should be given to guarantees of the Constitution of The United States, subsequent litigation and legislation, the standards of professional organizations, and historical standards of ethics.

Does My Action Have the Desired Functional Outcome?

A functional outcome is the practical effect that our action has on the student or family. The anticipated functional outcome of a decision to place a student in a self-contained class may be to improve self-concept and academic achievement. The anticipated functional outcome of a decision to administer an intelligence test is the acquisition of information about the student's learning and behavioral characteristics.

We must assume that all professional judgments and actions are made with the expectation that specific functional outcomes will be achieved. From a practical standpoint, we continually judge the relative merits of interventions when initial plans are developed. Once implemented, we seek to confirm that our hypothesized effect was achieved. This knowledge helps us to refine future interventions.

Does My Action Have the Desired Ethical Outcome?

An action is judged to be ethical if it conforms to a priori standards for professional ethics. If we espouse the golden rule as a guiding ethic, an action is judged to be ethical if it actually results in an outcome that we would choose for ourselves. Following act utilitarianism as a guiding ethic, we would judge an action to be ethical if it actually results in an outcome that serves the greatest good for the largest number of people.

We have emphasized that all professional judgments and actions be guided by a strong sense of professional ethics. We must continually judge the extent to which our judgments and actions actually conform to our ethical standards. This knowledge helps us to refine our ethical or moral positions.

How Are My Ethical Standards Influenced by the Outcome?

We have continually emphasized the importance of thoughtful judgments as a basis of ethical action. The naturalist position advanced in this chapter states that all ethical behavior is based on knowledge. Many sources of information may serve as a foundation for professional behavior. None, however, is more salient and relevant than actual experience.

We encourage each professional to evaluate the outcome of major professional actions with reference to the ethical standards from which the action was initiated. A professional espousing the act utilitarian ethic should decide if a specific action did, in fact, result in the greatest good for the greatest number of people. A professional who bases actions on the golden rule must determine if the professional conduct resulted in effects that she or he would find desirable under similar circumstances.

The answers to these questions will influence future ethical decisions. One would not expect a person's ethical standards and judgments to change if past outcomes are consistent with initial expectations. When outcomes are not consistent with initial expectations, we expect subsequent changes in ethical judgments made under similar circumstances.

In short, this final step in our process approach to reaching ethical judgments produces a return to the initial step. The outcome of an evaluation of ethical professional judgment signals a possible revision of a priori ethical standards that underlie future judgments. All professional experiences serve as a foundation for ethical standards that support future experiences.

SUMMARY

We have provided an overview of standards for arriving at ethical professional judgments and actions. Four major elements were described as being essential to the ethical conduct of professionals. Collectively, they serve as a foundation for all moral conduct in work with students and their families.

First, it is important that professionals be aware of litigation and legislation that establishes the rights of students with disabilities and their family members. Findings of these cases and provisions of the laws are based on the Constitution of The United States that guarantees life, liberty, and the pursuit of happiness, as well as equal protection (and opportunity) under law. Also, it is important that professionals adhere to the philosophy of *positive presumption*. All individuals with disabilities are entitled to protections under the constitution unless mitigating factors are demonstrated.

Second, it is important that professionals be aware of the standards for ethical conduct promulgated by professional organizations that they represent. Members of the Council for Exceptional Children, for example, should be familiar with its code of ethics. They should strive to adhere to these standards when applicable to professional action.

Third, professionals should be aware of ethical standards formulated and debated by philosophers over the centuries. These standards include naturalism, religious ethics, moral relativism, humanistic reciprocity, duty-based ethics, utilitarianism, and causalism. These philosophical positions should serve as a foundation for the formation of personal and professional ethics. They should be considered whenever one is faced with unique or personal decisions.

We conclude by again emphasizing that there is no universally agreed upon ethic for working with students and their families. Beyond litigation and legislation (which even in itself is a source of moral debate and controversy), few standards are unequivocal. In fact, some widely held ethical standards may yield opposing solutions. The golden rule, for example, may suggest that extraordinary services be provided a student because we would wish the same for our child or youth. A utilitarianism standard, however, may suggest withholding the services because they would detract from resources available to the greater good of the general school population.

We believe that these differences are resolved, in part, by encouraging the consideration of a process approach to developing, evaluating, and refining professional ethics. The approach that we describe is based on the naturalism view that all ethical conduct results from thoughtful deliberation and consideration of all relevant facts. Given the careful consideration of moral conduct and outcomes, we believe that the majority of professionals will engage in conduct fitting the norms of society and the expectations of students and family members.

Ethical Treatment Under the Law

1. Persons with disabilities should be protected by the standard of "positive presumption." This standard indicates that they are entitled to the rights articulated in the constitution unless mitigating factors support the need to restrict liberties.

2. The Buckley Amendment of Public Law 93-380 (Family Rights and Privacy Act of 1974) protects the right of family members to free access to educational records. It further supports the privacy of individuals with disabilities by restricting the access of others to these records.

3. Numerous court cases have addressed the importance of nondiscriminatory assessment and treatment. Tests must be administered in the native or dominant language of the student. Culturally "loaded" tests should not be used as a sole source of information, and test developers are encouraged to produce culture free or culture fair instruments.

4. Public Law 94-142 ensures that students with disabilities and their families are accorded due process under law. Specific due process rights include: Notifying family members prior to collection of diagnostic information; requesting informed consent from family members prior to assessment, classification, or placement; permitting the use of an independent consultant to evaluate educational decisions; arranging an impartial hearing when disputes arise; and providing a surrogate parent when a child or youth is not represented by a family member.

Professional Standards and Codes

5. Professional organizations including the Council for Exceptional Children, the American Personnel and Guidance Association, and the American Psychological Association have outlined standards for ethical professional conduct. These codes typically emphasize a commitment to competence, integrity, objectivity, and professionalism.

General Ethical Standards

6. Not all ethical standards that govern professional conduct are specified in the law. Individual professionals must have a personal code of ethics that guides their behavior.

7. Ethical standards that may apply to professional judgments include: Naturalism, religious ethics, moral relativism, humanistic reciprocity, duty-based ethics, utilitarianism, and causalism. These ethical standards include the following elements:

Naturalism—The human capacity for intelligent action distinguishes us from all other life. Ethical behavior results from the full development and use of knowledge and skills. Also, ethical behavior avoids extremes in judgment and action.

Religious ethics—Ethical behavior is indistinguishable from religious behavior. Ethical behavior results from understanding and following the teachings of a superior being. Ethical insights result from studying religious writings. Finally, a common tenet of most religious ethics is the golden rule, "Doing to others as you would wish them to do to you."

Moral relativism—The ethical value of an action is based on social standards. "Ethical behavior" is synonymous with "socially accepted behavior."

Humanistic reciprocity—Ethics are based on a standard of empathy and unconditional acceptance of others. Ethical behavior is judged by the extent to which it enables others to gain love, respect, and fulfillment.

Duty-based ethics—The categorical imperative is an overriding ethical standard. It emphasizes that an action is ethical to the extent that it can be applied to all individuals. In short, the categorical imperative requires equal treatment for all individuals.

Act and rule utilitarianism—An act or rule is considered to be ethical if it advances the greatest good for the greatest number of people.

Causalism—Actions that have a positive effect on the general welfare of society are considered to be ethical. Those that have a negative impact are unethical.

Integrating Ethical Theories

8. The preceding ethical standards possess both common and conflicting elements. Common elements include an emphasis on: knowledge and skill in the discipline, moderation in judgments and action, respect for human diversity, the treatment of others as we would like to be treated, the absence of critical judgment when judgment serves little therapeutic purpose, generalizability of conduct to all people, assessing the benefit to the greatest number of people, and support for the interests of the individual as well as the broader society.

A Plan of Professional Ethics

9. Each professional must establish a personal plan for ethical conduct. Such a plan may involve answering the following questions:

Upon what ethical standards do I form judgments?

What are the objective facts in a specific case?

Is additional information needed to arrive at a judgment?

What are the functional and ethical issues?

How will my judgment and actions affect others?

Can I accommodate the views of others and still act ethically?

What is my final course of action?

Does my action have the desired functional outcome?

Does my action have the desired ethical outcome?

How are my ethical standards influenced by the outcome?

REFERENCES

Aloia, G. F. (1984). "A decade of deterioration: The treatment of handicapped infants." *New Oxford Review, 51,* 18–21.

Abeson, A. (1976). "Confidentiality and record keeping," in F. Weintraub, A. Abeson, J. Ballard, & M. LaVor, Eds. *BLIC policy and the education of exceptional children.* Reston, VA: Council for Exceptional Children.

Bentham, J. (1823). *An introduction to the principles of morals and legislation.* London, 1789. Reprinted in *Ethical theories,* A. I. Melden, ed. Englewood Cliffs, NJ: Prentice-Hall, 1967.

Cobb, H. (1973). "Citizen advocacy and the rights of the handicapped," in W. Wolfensberger & H. Zauha, Eds. *Citizen advocacy and protective services for the impaired and handicapped* (Canada: Macdonald-Downie), pp. 149–161.

Council for Exceptional Children. (1983). Code of ethics and standards for professional practise. *Exceptional Children, 50(3),* 205–218.

Diana v. *State Board of Education,* C-70-37, RFP District of Northern California (1970).

Fanning, P. (1977). "The new relationship between parents and schools." *Focus on Exceptional Children, 9,* 1–10.

Goldberg, S. (1982). *Special education law: A guide for parents, advocates, and educators.* New York: Plenum.

Hummel, D. L., Talbutt, L. C., & Alexander, M. D. (1985). *Law and ethics in counseling.* New York: Van Nostrand.

Ladd, J. (1973). *Ethical relativism.* Belmont, CA: Wadsworth.

Larry P. v. *Riles,* 343 F. Supp. 1306 (N.D. Calif. 1972).

McInereny, R. (1982). *Ethica Thomistica: The moral philosophy of Thomas Aquinas.* Washington, D.C.: Catholic University Press.

Norman, R. (1983). *The moral philosophers: An introduction to ethics.* New York: Oxford University Press.

Pasanella, A. L., & Volkmor, C. B. (1977). *To parents of children with special needs: A manual on parent involvement in educational programming* (Los Angeles: California Regional Resource Center).

Rogers, C. (1961). *On becoming a person.* Boston: Houghton-Mifflin.

Ruiz v. *State Board of Education.* C. A. No. 218294. Super. Ct. Sacramento, Calif, 1972.

Sage, D., & Burrello, L. (1986). *Policy and management in special education.* Englewood Cliffs, NJ: Prentice Hall.

Scheerberger, W., & Zauha, H. (1973). "Funding, governance and safeguards of citizen advocacy services," in W. Wolfensberger & H. Zauha, Eds. *Citizen advocacy and protective services for the impaired and handicapped.* Canada: Macdonald-Downie, pp. 149–161.

Turnbull, A. P., Strickland, B. B., & Brantley, J. C. (1982). *Developing and implementing individualized education programs.* Columbus, OH: Merrill.

VanWyk, R. N. (1990). *Introduction to ethics.* New York: St. Martin's Press.

13

RESOURCES FOR THE ADVOCATE

Cynthia N. Schloss
Missouri Protection and Advocacy Services

Chapter Objectives

After completing this chapter, you will be able to:

1. Identify and describe agency resources at the federal level
2. Identify and describe resources available from professional and consumer organizations
3. Identify and describe key acronyms and legal terms used in advocacy
4. Utilize available resources

Key Terms and Phrases

acronyms
Americans with Disabilities Act (ADA)
developmental disabilities
fair housing
independent living

organizations
resources
vocational rehabilitation
zero reject

INTRODUCTION

Numerous resources are available to advocates for persons with disabilities. Since the majority of the federal contribution to services for persons with disabilities is made directly to the states, and spending is determined by each state, it is impossible to identify agencies in each state or location. In view of this, we have outlined the general scope of federal support for services to individuals with disabilities. The reader may contact federal agencies who will then direct him or her to appropriate state agencies. States and localities providing services from their own resources will not be identified in this chapter. Local information and referral centers should be contacted for further information.

Organizations serving advocates and persons with disabilities as well as their family members may be an additional resource. Again, national organizations will be identified in this chapter and the reader is encouraged to contact national offices for state and local chapter information.

A major stumbling block for advocates is the use of acronyms. Commonly used acronyms are provided to aid the reader in interpreting information provided by national, state, and local agencies.

AGENCY RESOURCES

Additional resources may be needed when advocating for yourself or other individuals. Resources may result from federal and state law or federal governmental agencies available to persons who request them. These resources are usually free of charge. Figure 13-1 depicts a sample letter requesting additional information.

Contacts are also necessary for filing a complaint or grievance. Review Figure 13-2 for a sample letter of complaint. Another use of a resource is to ask assistance for direct intervention or legal representation. A sample letter is depicted in Figure 13-3. It is important to be concise and factual when requesting assistance. Be open and candid about all facts and circumstances surrounding the situation. Time and energy will be saved with a full and complete disclosure of all facts. A speedier solution is likely to be obtained. Refer to Figure 13-4 for procedures to use prior to seeking legal assistance.

Programs for Persons with Developmental Disabilities

The term *developmental disabilities* applies to persons with a mental or physical impairment that was manifested before their twenty-second birthday, that is likely to continue for an indefinite length of time, and results in substantial functional limitations in at least three areas of major life activity (Administration on Developmental Disabilities, 1991). Services vary across the country including diagnosis,

---

FIGURE 13-1 • Sample Letter—Requesting Information

```
                        925 Advocacy Lane
                  Civil Rights, Missouri 12345
                        August 1, 1993


U.S. Department of Housing and Urban Development
451 Seventh Street, SW, Room 5252
Washington, DC 20410


To Whom It May Concern:
   I am very interested in the development of group
homes in my city. Please send me information on
federal and state resources that might be available
for my use.
   I appreciate your assistance.

Sincerely,


Mary Protector
```

---

evaluation, and treatment of the handicapping condition, personal care, day care, and special living arrangements; training for jobs, education, and sheltered employment; recreation programs; social and legal services; information and referral to services; and transportation (Clearinghouse on Disability Information, 1989). Under the Developmental Disabilities Assistance and Bill of Rights Act, as amended by P.L. 100-146 and P.L. 101-496, states receive basic state grant monies for planning, administration, and services. State Developmental Disability Planning Councils coordinate these monies through comprehensive planning, coordination of resources, and development of programs to fill gaps in services. The law also provides a legal advocacy component in each state through a designated agency to promote the rights of persons with developmental disabilities. These agencies are known as "protection and advocacy" offices and assist persons with disabilities or their family members regarding information and referral, technical assistance, legislative information, advocacy intervention, and/or legal representation. Goals and objectives for each protection and advocacy agency vary depending on established priorities. University affiliated programs, or UAPs, are the third designated program under the Law. UAPs have been established to research and promote "state-of-the-art" practices in the field of developmental disabilities. At the national level, contact:

FIGURE 13-2 • **Sample Letter—Filing a Complaint**

```
                      925 Advocacy Lane
                 Civil Rights, Missouri 12345
                      August 1, 1993


Architectural and Transportation
Barriers Compliance Board
1111 18th Street, NW
Washington, DC 20036


Dear Compliance Specialist:
  I would like to file a complaint about the
inaccessibility of the new post office in Civil
Rights, Missouri. The post office is located at 678
West Main in Civil Rights and was built in 1990 with
federal monies.
  Doorways into the post office are not wide enough
for a person in a wheel chair to pass through.
  I would appreciate any assistance you could give to
remedy this situation. Thank you.

Sincerely,


John Stamp
```

1. Administration on Developmental Disabilities
   Department of Health and Human Services
   Room 329D, Humphrey Building
   Washington, D.C. 20201
2. National Association of Protection and Advocacy Systems
   900 Second Street, NE, Suite 211
   Washington, DC 20002
3. National Association of Developmental Disabilities Councils
   1234 Massachusetts Avenue, NW, Suite 103
   Washington, DC 20005
4. American Association of University Affiliated Programs
   8630 Fenton Street, Suite 410
   Silver Spring, MD 20910

FIGURE 13-3 • **Sample Letter—Requesting Assistance**

925 Advocacy Lane
Civil Rights, Missouri 12345
August 1, 1993

National Association of Protection
and Advocacy Systems
900 Second Street, NE, Suite 211
Washington, DC 20002

Dear Executive Director:
   I live in Civil Rights, Missouri, and need
assistance in obtaining a free and appropriate
education for my child. I have been told by my local
school district that my daughter should not attend
the same school as her friends because she is
disabled. My husband and I feel that it would be
appropriate.
   I would appreciate your direct assistance. I would
also appreciate you referring me to our state
advocacy agency.

Sincerely,

Concerned Parent

Education

Persons with disabilities have historically been denied appropriate education services at all levels. In recent years, services have rapidly improved and implementation of appropriate education services is the considered the norm. Federal courts have affirmed the "zero reject" concept. No child can be denied a public school education based on the severity of disability. Basic opportunities and protections are afforded to persons with disabilities and their family members.

Special education is specially designed instruction to meet the unique educational needs of persons with disabilities. The amount of special instruction varies with each person. Some need only minor environmental modifications or special equipment while others require special educational personnel. Finally, some students require related services or special instruction, modifications, special equip-

---

FIGURE 13-4 • Procedures to Follow Prior to Seeking Legal Assistance

Individuals should keep written records and notes of all actions taken prior to seeking legal assistance, including:

1. copies of all applications or contacts with any party, agency, or organization;
2. copies of all letters sent or received regarding the dispute;
3. written notation of all dealings regarding the dispute, including the names of the persons contacted;
4. all conversations held with an adverse party, agency, or organization regarding the dispute;
5. dates of all communications; and
6. a summary of any complaint against any party, agency, or organization involved.

(Missouri Protection and Advocacy Services, 1990, p. 167)

ment, and related services. The Individuals with Disabilities Education Act of 1990 (IDEA), an amendment to the Education for All Handicapped Act, P.L. 94-142, is the most recent federal legislation regarding special education. The Act guarantees four rights and two protections for each student and his or her parents, guardians, or surrogate parents. For each student with disabilities, the public education agency must provide:

1. A free appropriate public education
2. An education in the least restrictive environment
3. Related services
4. Fair assessment

The Act provides two protections through:

1. An individualized education program (IEP)
2. Due process procedures

The Act provides funds to each state and is an "entitlement" statute. In complying with IDEA, each state is required to submit a state compliance plan to the federal government for approval. This plan identifies the state's rules for the implementation of IDEA. To receive a copy of your state's compliance plan contact your state's department of education. For further information on IDEA or to file a complaint at the federal level, contact:

U. S. Department of Education
Office of Special Education Programs
330 "C" Street, SW, Mary Switzer Bldg.
Washington, DC 20202

Parent training centers have been developed across the United States, through federal funds, to provide assistance and training to parents on their child's and family's rights in the special education process. The location of the nearest parent training center can be obtained by contacting the state's department of education or the U.S. Department of Education.

The Family Educational Rights and Privacy Act (FERPA), P.L. 93-380, or Buckley Amendment gives parents of students under age 18, and students age 18 and over, the right to examine records kept in the student's personal file. More information on this right can be obtained by contacting the state Department of Education. Alternately, if you believe that a school is not in compliance with federal regulations regarding access to student records, a complaint can be filed by contacting:

Family Policy Compliance Office
U.S. Department of Education
400 Maryland Ave., SW
Washington, DC 20202-4605

The Carl Perkins Act of 1984, P.L. 98-524, as amended, requires vocational education programs accessible to all persons, including those with disabilities. School systems are required to tell persons with disabilities and their parents about vocational education programs by the time the student is 15 years old or in the ninth grade. For a copy of your state's annual plan or for more information regarding the Act contact your state's department of education or:

U.S. Department of Education
Office of Special Education Program
330 "C" Street, SW, Mary Switzer Bldg.
Washington, DC 20202

Vocational Rehabilitation Programs

All states have coordinated programs of vocational rehabilitation and independent living as required under the Vocational Rehabilitation Act of 1973, as amended, to assist persons with disabilities in becoming employable, independent, and integrated into the community (Clearinghouse on Disability Information, 1989). These goals are achieved by providing a wide range of services, financial assistance, and training. Each state's resources vary and are allocated according to guidelines of the state and input from vocational rehabilitation counselors and administrators, advocates, and persons with disabilities and their family members. A written individualized plan for rehabilitation and independent living is developed for every eligible individual by the individual and his or her rehabilitation counselor(s). The rehabilitation program may provide a variety of services including: medical examination and assistance; rehabilitation counseling; educational opportunities; financial assistance; and job training, referral, and placement. Although the federal government provides monies to the states, individual services are received at the state and local level.

In several states, a separate program has been established to deal specifically with persons who have visual impairments. Staff limit their caseloads to clients who are visually impaired or serve as consultants to regular rehabilitation counselors. Information on state rehabilitation agencies can be obtained by contacting:

U.S. Department of Education
Rehabilitation Services Administration
400 Maryland Ave., SW
Washington, DC 20202

Special emphasis on rehabilitation services for persons with hearing impairments has a special office at the federal office within the Rehabilitation Services Administration. Contact:

Rehabilitation Services Administration
Deafness and Communicative Disorders Branch
Mary Switzer Building, Room 3219
Washington, DC 20202-2736

Federal funds have been allocated to help support the Helen Keller National Center for Deaf and Blind Youth and Adults. The Center assists persons who are deaf and blind. Eligibility for the Center's program can be reviewed by contacting:

Helen Keller National Center
111 Middle Neck Road
Sands Point, NY 11050

Through the 1984 amendments to the Vocational Rehabilitation Act of 1973, mandated client assistance programs (CAP) were established in each state to assist individuals who are eligible or may be eligible for services under the Act and are having problems in securing services. Information and referral, technical assistance, legislative information, advocacy assistance, and/or legal representation is typically available through state CAPs. Information on state CAP programs can be obtained from Rehabitational Services Administration or:

National Association of Protection and Advocacy Systems
900 Second Street, NE, Suite 211
Washington, DC 20002

General Disability Rights Programs

In 1990, the United States Congress recognized that 43,000,000 Americans have one or more disabilities, and that society has historically isolated and discriminated against individuals with disabilities so that such persons are severely disadvantaged socially, vocationally, economically, and educationally (Missouri Protection and Advocacy Services, 1991). Congress declared that "the Nation's proper goals regarding individuals with disabilities are to assure equality of opportunity, full participation, independent living, and economic self-sufficiency for such individuals." Congress passed the Americans with Disabilities Act of 1990 (ADA) to eliminate discrimination against and expand opportunities for persons with disabilities in nearly all aspects of their lives. Requirements for implementation of the Act are noted in Figures 13-5, 13-6, and 13-7. For more information on ADA contact:

> U.S. Department of Justice, Civil Rights Division
> Coordination and Review Section
> P.O. Box 66118
> Washington, DC 20035-6118

Under the Architectural Barriers Act of 1968, certain public buildings constructed or financed by federal dollars after August 12, 1968, must be accessible to individuals with physical disabilities. This Act covers such buildings as federal courthouses, government office buildings, and national parks facilities. To request information regarding the Act or to file a violation, contact:

> Architectural and Transportation Barriers Compliance Board
> 1331 F Street, NW
> Washington, DC 20004-1107

Section 504 of the Rehabilitation Act of 1973 prohibits discrimination on the basis of handicap under any program or activity receiving federal financial assistance or under any program or activity conducted by any federal agency. If an individual feels an activity or program receiving federal funds is inaccessible, a written complaint should be sent to the Office for Civil Rights of the federal agency that provided the federal funds.

The Fair Housing Amendments Act of 1988 expands the coverage of the 1968 Civil Rights Act by adding its protections in the area of housing to persons with disabilities (Missouri Protection and Advocacy Services, 1991). The Amendments were described by Congress as a "clear pronouncement of a national commitment to end the unnecessary exclusion of persons with handicaps from the American mainstream." The Act covers nearly every type of housing and protects individuals with virtually all disabilities. For more information on details of the Act and your enforcement rights contact:

> U.S. Department of Housing and Urban Development
> 451 Seventh Street, SW, Room 5252
> Washington, DC 20410

FIGURE 13-5 • **Americans with Disabilities Act Requirements Fact Sheet**

Employment:

- Employers may not discriminate against an individual with a disability in hiring or promotion if the person is otherwise qualified for the job.
- Employers can ask about one's ability to perform a job, but cannot inquire if someone has a disability or subject a person to tests that tend to screen out people with disabilities.
- Employers will need to provide "reasonable accommodation" to individuals with disabilities. This includes steps such as job restructuring and modification of equipment.
- Employers do not need to provide accommodations that impose an "undue hardship" on business operations.

Who needs to comply:

- All employers with 25 or more employees must comply, effective July 26, 1992.
- All employers with 15–24 employees must comply, effective July 26, 1994.

Transportation:

- New public transit buses ordered after August 26, 1990, must be accessible to individuals with disabilities.
- Transit authorities must provide comparable para transit or other special transportation services to individuals with disabilities who cannot use fixed route bus services, unless an undue burden would result.
- Existing rail systems must have one accessible car per train by July 26, 1995.
- New rail cars ordered after August 26, 1990, must be accessible.
- New bus and train stations must be accessible.
- Key stations in rapid, light, and commuter rail systems must be made accessible by July 26, 1993, with extensions up to 20 years for commuter rail (30 years for rapid and light rail).
- All existing Amtrak stations must be accessible by July 26, 2010.

Public Accommodations:

- Private entities such as restaurants, hotels, and retail stores may not discriminate against individuals with disabilities, effective January 26, 1992.
- Auxiliary aids and services must be provided to individuals with vision or hearing impairments or other individuals with disabilities, unless an undue burden would result.
- Physical barriers in existing facilities must be removed, if removal is readily achievable. If not, alternative methods of providing the services must be offered, if they are readily achievable.
- All new construction and alterations of facilities must be accessible.

State and Local Government:

- State and local governments may not discriminate against qualified individuals with disabilities.
- All government facilities, services, and communications must be accessible consistent with the requirements of section 504 of the Rehabilitation Act of 1973.

Telecommunications:

- Companies offering telephone service to the general public must offer telephone relay services to individuals who use telecommunications devices for the deaf (TDD's) or similar devices.

Note: From *Americans with Disabilities Act Requirements Fact Sheet* by U.S. Department of Justice, 1991 (Washington, D.C.: U.S. Department of Justice).

FIGURE 13-6 • Americans with Disabilities Act Requirements in Public Accommodations Fact Sheet

General:

- Public accommodations such as restaurants, hotels, theaters, doctors' offices, pharmacies, retail stores, museums, libraries, parks, private schools, and day care centers, may not discriminate on the basis of disability. Private clubs and religious organizations are exempt.
- Reasonable changes in policies, practices, and procedures must be made to avoid discrimination.

Auxiliary Aids:

- Auxiliary aids and services must be provided to individuals with vision or hearing impairments or other individuals with disabilities, unless an undue burden would result.

Physical Barriers:

- Physical barriers in existing facilities must be removed, if removal is readily achievable. If not, alternative methods of providing the services must be offered, if they are readily achievable.
- All new construction in public accommodations, as well as in "commercial facilities" such as office buildings, must be accessible. Elevators are generally not required in buildings under three stories or with fewer than 3,000 square feet per floor, unless the building is a shopping center, mall, or a professional office of a health care provider.
- Alterations must be accessible. When alterations to primary function areas are made, an accessible path of travel to the altered area (and the bathrooms, telephones, and drinking fountains serving that area) must be provided to the extent that the added accessibility costs are not disproportionate to the overall cost of the alterations. Elevators are required as described above.
- Entities such as hotels that also offer transportation must generally provide equivalent transportation service to individuals with disabilities. New fixed-route vehicles capable of carrying more than 16 passengers must be accessible.

Remedies:

- Individuals may bring private lawsuits to obtain court orders to stop discrimination, but money damages cannot be awarded.
- Individuals can also file complaints with the Attorney General who may file suits to stop discrimination and obtain money damages and penalties.

Note: From *Americans with Disabilities Act Requirements in Public Accommodations Fact Sheet* by U.S. Department of Justice, 1991 (Washington, D.C.: U.S. Department of Justice).

FIGURE 13-7 • Americans with Disabilities Act Statutory Deadlines

I. Employment
   - The ADA requirements become effective on:
     July 26, 1992, for employees with 25 or more employees.
     July 26, 1994, for employers with 15–24 employees.

II. Public Accommodations
   - The ADA requirements become effective on:
     January 26, 1992, generally.
     August 26, 1990, for purchase or lease of new vehicles that are required to be accessible.
   - New facilities designed and constructed for first occupancy later than January 26, 1993, must be accessible.
   - Generally, lawsuits may not be filed until January 26, 1992. In addition, except with respect to new construction and alterations, no lawsuit may be filed until:
     July 26, 1992, against businesses with 25 or fewer employees and gross receipts of $1 million or less.
     January 26, 1993, against businesses with 10 or fewer employees and gross receipts of $500,000 or less.

III. Transportation
   A. Public bus systems
      - The ADA requirements become effective on:
        January 26, 1992, generally.
        August 26, 1990, for purchase or lease of new buses.

   B. Public rail systems—light, rapid, commuter, and intercity (Amtrak) rail
      - The ADA requirements become effective on:
        January 26, 1992, generally.
        August 26, 1990, for purchase or lease of new rail vehicles.
      - By July 26, 1995, one car per train accessibility must be achieved.
      - By July 26, 1993, existing key stations in rapid, light, and commuter rail systems must be made accessible with extensions of up to 20 years (30 years, in some cases, for rapid and light rail).

   C. Privately operated bus and van companies
      - The ADA requirements become effective on:
        January 26, 1992, generally.
        July 26, 1996 (July 26, 1997, for small providers for purchase of new over-the-road buses).
        August 26, 1990, for purchase or lease of certain new over-the-road buses

Note: From *Americans with Disabilities Act Requirements in Public Accommodations Fact Sheet* by U.S. Department of Justice, 1991 (Washington, D.C.: U.S. Department of Justice).

ORGANIZATIONS AND OTHER AGENCIES

Numerous resources are available through organizations serving advocates and persons with disabilities as well as their family members. Through federal and private monies and volunteer services, numerous agencies have been established to serve as a resource to advocates and persons with disabilities. Key national organizations and resources will be identified and briefly described as found in various publications available to persons with disabilities (Missouri Linc, 1987; Center for Psychiatric Rehabilitation, 1988; Clearinghouse on Disability Information, 1989; National Mental Health Association & National Mental Health Consumers' Association, 1989). Additional resources will also be identified.

Key Organizations and Resources

American Association of the Deaf/Blind (AADB)

A consumer organization that provides information on aids and devices. AADB publishes a magazine in braille with articles written by persons who are deaf/blind.

American Association of the Deaf/Blind
814 Thayer Avenue, Room 300
Silver Spring, MD 20910

American Association on Mental Deficiency (AAMD)

AAMD is a professional organization representing a variety of interests and disciplines dealing with many forms of developmental disabilities. AAMD promotes the highest standards of programming for persons with mental retardation, to facilitate cooperation among those working with persons who have mental retardation, and to educate the public to understand, accept, and respect persons with mental retardation.

American Association on Mental Deficiency
1719 Kalorama Road, NW
Washington, DC 20009

American Bar Association (ABA)

Professional organization of licensed attorneys with bar associations in each state. The Commission on the Mental and Physical Disability Law was established by ABA to help individuals who are mentally disabled to obtain adequate treatment in human environments, safeguard their basic rights, and to educate and mobilize the association to provide needed legal services. The Bar has additional segments focusing on the needs of the elderly, indigent, and disabled.

American Bar Association
Commission on Mental and
  Physical Disability Law
1800 M. Street, NW, Suite 200
Washington, DC 20036

American Foundation for the Blind (AFB)

Established to serve as the national partner of local services for persons who are visually impaired or blind. A newsletter is available at the present address.

American Foundation for the Blind
15 West 16th Street
New York, NY 10011

American Graham Bell Association for the Deaf (AGBA)

A publication and information center about deafness. Oral-deaf education is emphasized. Materials designed for parents, teachers, and oral-deaf adults are available by request.

> American Graham Bell Association
> for the Deaf
> 3417 Volta Place, NW
> Washington, DC 20007

National Technical Institute for the Deaf (NTID)

Provides a post secondary technological education to students with hearing impairments. NTID also serves as a resource to other education institutions enrolling students with hearing impairments. Resource materials can be obtained from the following address.

> Rochester Institute of Technology
> National Technical Institute for the Deaf
> Johnson Building, P.O. Box 9887
> Rochester, NY 14623-0887

The ARC (ARC—Formerly the Association for Retarded Citizens)

The goals of the Association are to prevent mental retardation, to find cures, and to assist persons with mental retardation in their daily lives. ARC works on state and local levels as well to communicate and interpret the needs of persons with mental retardation to the public and government agencies.

> The ARC
> 500 E. Border St., Suite 300
> Arlington, TX 76011

Learning Disabilities Association of America (LDA)

LDA is a national organization devoted to defining and finding solutions for the broad spectrum of learning programs.

> Learning Disabilities Association
> of America
> 4156 Library Road
> Pittsburgh, PA 15234

Autism Society of America

This national organization promotes appropriate services for persons with autism. Conferences are held annually for members and interested persons.

> Autism Society of America
> 8601 Georgia Ave., Suite 503
> Silver Spring, MD 20910

Council for Exceptional Children (CEC)

CEC is a national professional organization that provides information on behalf of its membership. Members include special education teachers and administrators, related services professionals, parents, and others who are concerned about improving the quality of life for persons with disabilities.

> Council for Exceptional Children
> 1920 Association Drive
> Reston, VA 22091

Foundation for Dignity

A non-profit corporation devoted to the promotion and maintenance of the dignity, civil rights, independence, and personal development for persons with mental or physical disabilities. Activities of the Foundation include: direct service, consultation, public and professional education, publications, and a disability advocacy database.

> Foundation for Dignity
> 37 S. 20th Street, Suite 601
> Philadelphia, PA 19103

Mental Health Law Project (MHLP)

MHLP is a public interest organization advocating for the rights of children and adults who are mentally disabled through litigation, policy advocacy, and education. Newsletter and publications are available from the following address:

Mental Health Law Project
2021 L Street, NW, Suite 800
Washington, DC 20036

Muscular Dystrophy Association (MDA)

MDA supports research into neuromuscular disorders. It also provides medical care and other direct services free to persons with muscular dystrophy through its clinics and local chapters. Sponsorship of self-help groups, information and referral, and publications are also available.

Muscular Dystrophy Association
3561 E. Sunrise
Tucson, Arizona 85718

National Alliance for the Mentally Ill (NAMI)

NAMI is a self-help organization of persons with mental illness, their families, and friends. The goals of NAMI are mutual support, education, and advocacy of persons with severe mental illness. State and local chapters are active across the United States.

National Alliance for the Mentally Ill
2101 Wilson Blvd., Suite 302
Arlington, VA 22201

National Association for the Visually Handicapped (NAVH)

This organization serves as an information and referral agency for all partially sighted persons. NAVH offers the use of a large assortment of materials for persons who are partially sighted, their families, and persons assisting them.

National Association for the
Visually Handicapped
22 West 21st Street
New York, NY 10010

National Easter Seal Society

The Easter Seal Society is the nation's largest and oldest voluntary health agency providing direct rehabilitation services to persons with disabilities. It provides services for the prevention and treatment of disabling conditions on a state and local basis.

National Easter Seal Society
70 East Lake Street
Chicago, IL 60601

National Federation of the Blind

This is the largest organization supporting the interests of persons with visual impairments in America. Chapters exist in each state. The Federation's purpose is the complete integration of persons who are blind into society on a basis of equality.

National Federation of the Blind
1800 Johnson Street
Baltimore, MD 21230

National Head Injury Foundation (NHIF)

NHIF is an advocacy group composed of families, friends, medical, and social service professionals concerned with the physical and emotional well-being of persons who have been head injured. NHIF serves as a clearinghouse for information and referral.

National Head Injury Foundation
1140 Connecticut Ave., NW, Suite 812
Washington, D.C. 20036

National Information Center for Children and Youth with Disabilities

The Center is a free information service to help parents, educators, providers, advocates, and others who are interested in the lives of persons with disabilities.

> National Information Center for Children
> and Youth with Disabilities
> P.O. Box 1492
> Washington, DC. 20013

National Library Services for the Blind and Physically Handicapped (NLS)

The National Library contains a collection of full-length braille and talking books and magazines produced for persons who are blind or have physical disabilities. Materials are available at no cost to persons who cannot hold, handle, or read conventional printed material. Cooperating network libraries are located across the United States.

> National Library Services for the
> Blind and Physically Handicapped
> Library of Congress
> Washington, DC 20542

National Mental Health Association (NMHA)

This is a citizen's volunteer advocacy organization concerned with all aspects of mental health and mental illness. Activities include advocating for social change, anti-stigma campaign, research activities, leadership in prevention, and public information.

> National Mental Health Association
> 1021 Prince Street
> Alexandria, VA 22314-2971

President's Committee on Employment of the Handicapped

The Committee serves in an advocacy and public awareness role in fostering job opportunities for persons with disabilities. The Americans with Disabilities Act of 1990 is a prime example of the Committee's efforts.

> President's Committee on Employment
> of the Handicapped
> 1111 20th Street, NW, Suite 636
> Washington, DC 20036-3470

SPECIALNET

This is a computer-based communication network created by the National Association of State Directors of Special Education (NAS-DSE) for state and local education personnel, college and university personnel, and other special education personnel. Bulletin boards contain information on a variety of special education topics.

> Special Net International
> 1350 New York Ave., NW, Suite 500
> Washington, DC 20005-4709

The Association for Persons with Severe Handicaps (TASH)

A membership organization involved in a range of issues related to living, working, and learning environments for persons with severe disabilities. A journal and newsletter are provided through memberships. Additional publications are available.

> The Association for Persons with
> Severe Handicaps
> 7010 Roosevelt Way, NE
> Seattle, WA 98115

United Cerebral Palsy Association (UCPA)

UCPA is a national direct service organization providing an array of services at each of its affiliate agencies. Services range from preschool to adult work programs. Publications are available by request.

> United Cerebral Palsy Association
> 1522 K Street, NW
> Washington, D.C. 20005

Key organizations and agencies were addressed in the previous section. Additional resources and addresses are now provided representing numerous disability groups. Again, only national and federal resources are provided and the reader is requested to make initial contacts at this level when local and state sources are unknown.

ADDITIONAL RESOURCES

- AFL-CIO
  Department of Community Services
  815 16th Street, NW
  Washington, DC 20007
- Academy of Child Psychiatry
  3615 Wisconsin Ave., NW
  Washington, DC 20016
- Alcohol & Drug Problems Association of
  North America
  444 N. Capitol Street, Suite 181
  Washington, DC 20001
- American Arbitration Association
  140 West 51st Street
  New York, NY 10020-1203
- American Association for Children's
  Residential Centers
  440 First Street, NW, #310
  Washington, DC 20001
- American Association for Counseling
  Development
  5999 Stevenson Ave.
  Alexandria, VA 22304
- American Council of Rural Special
  Education
  Western Washington University
  Miller Hall 359
  Bellingham, WA 98225
- American Hospital Association
  50 F Street, NW, Suite 1100
  Washington, DC 20001
- American Occupational Therapy
  Association
  1383 Piccard Drive
  P.O. Box 1725
  Rockville, MD 20849-1725

- American Physical Therapy Association
  1111 North Fairfax Street
  Alexandria, VA 22314-1488
- American Psychiatric Association
  1400 K Street, NW
  Washington, DC 20005
- American Psychological Association
  750 First Street, NE
  Washington, DC 20002
- American Speech-Language-Hearing
  Association
  10801 Rockville Pike
  Rockville, MD 20852
- Association for the Care of Children's
  Health
  7910 Woodmont Ave., #300
  Bethesda, MD 20814-3015
- Association for the Education and Rehabili-
  tation of the Blind & Visually Impaired
  206 N. Washington Street, Suite 320
  Alexandria, VA 22314
- Association of Psychiatric Outpatient
  Centers of America
  1925 E. Dublin-Granville Road
  Columbus, OH 43229-3517
- CASSP Technical Assistance Center
  Georgetown University
  2233 Wisconsin Ave., NW, Suite 215
  Washington, DC 20007
- Child Welfare League of America
  440 First Street, NW, #310
  Washington, DC 20001-2085
- Epilepsy Foundation of America
  4351 Garden City Drive
  Landover, MD 20785

- ERIC Clearinghouse on Handicapped and Gifted Children
  Council for Exceptional Children
  1920 Association Drive
  Reston, VA 22091-1589
- Family Service America
  1319 F Street, NW, #606
  Washington, DC 20004
- Federal Mediation and Conciliation Service
  2100 K Street, NW
  Washington, DC 20427
- Federation of Behavioral, Psychological, & Cognitive Science
  1200 17th Street, NW
  Washington, DC 20036
- Gallaudet University
  800 Florida Avenue, NE
  Washington, DC 20002
- Head Start
  ACF/ACYF
  Department of Health & Human Services
  P.O. Box 1182
  Washington, DC 20013
- Higher Education and Adult Training for People with Disabilities
  One Dupont Circle, NW, Suite 800
  Washington, DC 20036-1193
- Independent Living Research Utilization Project
  The Institute for Rehabilitation and Research
  2323 S. Shepherd, Suite 1000
  Houston, TX 77005
- International Association of Psychosocial Rehabilitation Services
  P.O. Box 278
  McLean, VA 22101
- March of Dimes Birth Defects Foundation
  1275 Mamaroneck Avenue
  White Plains, NY 10605
- Mediation Institute
  605 First Avenue, Suite 525
  Seattle, WA 98104

- National Association of the Deaf
  814 Thayer Avenue
  Silver Spring, MD 20910-4500
- National Association for Rights, Protection, and Advocacy
  4107 Legation Street, NW
  Washington, DC 20015
- National Association of Rehabilitation Facilities
  P.O. Box 17675
  Washington, DC 20041
- National Association of Private Psychiatric Hospitals
  1319 F Street, NW, Suite 1000
  Washington, DC 20004
- National Association of Social Workers
  7981 Eastern Avenue
  Silver Spring, MD 20910
- National Association of State Alcohol & Drug Abuse Directors
  444 N. Capitol Street, Suite 642
  Washington, DC 20001
- National Association of State Directors of Special Education
  1800 Diagonal Road, Suite 320
  Alexandria, VA 22314
- National Association of State Mental Health Program Directors
  1101 King Street, #160
  Alexandria, VA 22314
- National Center for Law & Deafness
  800 Florida Avenue, NE
  Washington, DC 20002
- National Clearinghouse for Professions in Special Education
  1800 Diagonal Road, Suite 320
  Alexandria, MD 22314
- National Down Syndrome Congress
  1800 Dempster Street
  Park Ridge, IL 60068-1146
- National Information Center on Deafness
  Gallaudet University
  800 Florida Avenue, NE
  Washington, DC 20002

- National Institute for Dispute Resolution
  1901 L Street, NW, Suite 600
  Washington, DC 20036
- National Legal Aid and Defender
  Association
  1625 K Street, NW, 8th Floor
  Washington, DC 20006
- National Mental Health Consumers'
  Association
  311 S. Juniper Street, Room 902
  Philadelphia, PA 19107
- National Rehabilitation Information
  Center
  8455 Colesville Road, Suite 935
  Silver Spring, MD 20910-3319
- National Spinal Cord Injury Association
  600 West Cummings Park, Suite 2000
  Woburn, MA 01801
- The Orton Dyslexia Society
  Chester Building, Suite 382
  8600 LaSalle Road
  Baltimore, MD 21204-6020
- Sibling Information Network
  The A.J. Pappanikou Center
  991 Main Street, Suite 3A
  East Hartford, CT 06108

- Sick Kids (need) Involved People
  c/o SKIP of New York
  990 Second Ave.
  New York, NY 10022
- Society of Professionals in Dispute
  Resolution
  1100 Connecticut Ave., NW, Suite 700
  Washington, DC 20036
- Special Olympics International
  1350 New York Avenue, NW
  Suite 500
  Washington, DC 20005-4709
- Spina Bifida Association of America
  1700 Rockville Pike, Suite 540
  Rockville, MD 20852
- Superintendent of Documents
  U.S. Government Printing Office
  Washington, DC 20402
- Trace Research and Development Center
  on Communication, Control, and
  Computer Access for Handicapped
  Individuals
  S-151 Waisman Center
  1500 Highland Avenue
  University of Wisconsin-Madison
  Madison, WI 53705

ACRONYMS

Acronyms are typically used by persons to save time in writing and speaking which is acceptable. In the next few pages, the author has noted the most commonly used acronyms in working with students with disabilities. The author recommends that the reader maintain a listing for their use. They may be necessary.

AAMD	American Association on Mental Deficiency
AAMR	American Association on Mental Retardation
AASA	American Association of School Administrators
ABE	Adult Basic Education
ABS	Adaptive Behavior Scale
ACMRDD	Accreditation Council for Services for Mentally Retarded and Other Developmentally Disabled Persons

ADA	Alcohol and Drug Abuse or Americans with Disabilities Act
ADD	Administration on Developmental Disabilities or Attention Deficit Disorder
AFDC	Aid to Families with Dependent Children
AFT	American Federation of Teachers
AG	Attorney General
AMI	Alliance for the Mentally Ill
ANSI	American National Standards Institute
ARC	The ARC
ARF	Association of Rehabilitation Facilities
ASA	Autism Society of America
ASHA	American Speech, Language, and Hearing Association
BD	Behavior Disordered
BIA	Bureau of Indian Affairs
CA	Chronological Age
CAP	Client Assistance Program
CARF	Commission on Accreditation of Rehabilitation Facilities
CASSP	Child and Adolescent Service System Project
CEC	Council for Exceptional Children
CF	Cystic Fibrosis
CMHC	Community Mental Health Center
CP	Cerebral Palsy or Community Placement
CRF	Community Residential Facility
CSPD	Comprehensive System of Personnel Development
DD	Developmentally Disabled
DSA	Down Syndrome Association
DSM III	Diagnostic and Statistical Manual of Mental Disorders
ECSE	Early Childhood Special Education
ECT	Electro Convulsive Therapy
ED	Education Department or Emotionally Disturbed
EEG	Electroencephalogram
EFA	Epilepsy Foundation of America
EHA	Education for All Handicapped Children Act
EMR/H	Educable Mentally Retarded/Handicapped
EPSDT	Early and Periodic Screening, Diagnosis and Treatment
ERIC	Educational Resources Information Center
ERT	Educational Resource Teacher
FAPE	Free Appropriate Public Education
FERPA	Family Educational Rights and Privacy Act
FY	Fiscal Year
HB	House Bill
HEATH	Higher Education And The Handicapped
HI	Hearing Impaired
HUD	Housing and Urban Development
ICF	Intermediate Care Facility

ICF-MR	Intermediate Care Facility for the Mentally Retarded
IDEA	Individuals with Disabilities Education Act
IEP	Individualized Educational Program
IHE	Institute of Higher Education
IHP	Individualized Habilitation Plan
IIP	Individualized Instructional Program
IMS	Instructional Management System
IPP	Individualized Program Plan
IQ	Intelligence Quotient
I&R	Information and Referral
ITP	Individualized Treatment Plan
IWRP	Individual Written Rehabilitation Plan
JCAH	Joint Commission of Hospitals
JTPA	Job Training Partnership Act
LD	Learning Disabilities
LDA	Learning Disabilities Association
LEA	Local Education Agency
LRE	Least Restrictive Environment
MD	Multi-Disciplinary or Muscular Dystrophy
MH	Mental Handicap
MHA	Mental Health Association
MI	Mentally Ill or Mental Illness
MR	Mentally Retarded
MSW	Masters of Social Work Degree
NADDC	National Association of Developmental Disabilities
NAPAS	National Association of Protection and Advocacy Systems
NAPRFMR	National Association of Private Residential Facilities for the Mentally Retarded
NASDSE	National Association of State Directors of Special Education
NASMRPD	National Association of State Mental Retardation Program Directors
NEA	National Education Association
NFDH	National Foundation of Dentistry for the Handicapped
NFP	Not-for-profit
NHIF	National Head Injury Foundation
NICHCY	National Information Center for Children and Youth with Disabilities
NIMH	National Institute for Mental Health
NMHCA	National Mental Health Consumers Association
NRA	National Rehabilitation Association
NSAC	National Society for Children and Adults with Autism
OCR	Office of Civil Rights
OH	Orthopedically Handicapped
OJT	On-the-Job Training
OSE	Office of Special Education
OSERS	Office of Special Education and Rehabilitative Services

OT	Occupational Therapy
P&A	Protection and Advocacy
PCEH	President's Committee on Employment of the Handicapped
PDR	Physician's Desk Reference
PKU	Phenylketonuria
PL	Public Law
POHI	Physically, Other Health Impaired
POS	Purchase Of Services
PT	Physical Therapy
PTA	Parent Teacher Association
PTO	Parent Teacher Organization
RCF	Residential Care Facility
R&D	Research and Development
RSA	Rehabilitation Services Administration
SB	Senate Bill
SEA	State Education Agency
SEP	Special Education Program
SH	Severely Handicapped
SNF	Skilled Nursing Facility
SPC	State Planning Council
SSA	Social Security Act or Administration
SSDI	Social Security Disability Insurance
SSI	Social Security Income
ST	Speech Therapist
TA	Technical Assistance
TASH	The Association for Persons with Severe Handicaps
TMR/H	Trainable Mentally Retarded/Handicapped
UAP	University Affiliated Program
UCPA	United Cerebral Palsy Association
VAC	Vocational Adjustment Counselor
VI	Visual Impairment
VR	Vocational Rehabilitation
VRE	Vocational Resource Educator

Summary

The purpose of this chapter was to provide the reader information on available resources for the advocate to use when promoting and reviewing disability issues. Key agencies and legislative provisions are described noting resources available to persons with disabilities, their family members, professionals, and other interested persons. Federal and national contacts were provided with suggested methods in obtaining information from state and local organizations and agencies. Suggested formats are provided to request information and materials, organization of documentation, and filing a complaint or grievance. Commonly used acronyms and definitions conclude the chapter.

Introduction

1. Numerous resources are available to advocates of persons with disabilities.

Agency Resources

2. Resources may result from federal and state law or federal governmental agencies available to persons who request them.

3. Under the Developmental Disabilities Assistance and Bill of Rights Act, states receive monies to provide information on planning, research and legal assistance concerning persons with developmental disabilities.

4. Numerous resources are available, as a result of federal legislation, to provide information on special education.

5. All states have coordinated programs for vocational rehabilitation and independent living assistance to assist persons with disabilities.

6. Congress has assured persons with disabilities equality of opportunity, full participation, independent living, and economic self-sufficiency.

Organization and Other Agencies

7. Numerous resources are available through organizations serving advocates and persons with disabilities as well as their family members.

8. Numerous acronyms are used by professionals to save time in writing and speaking.

REFERENCES

Administration on Developmental Disabilities (1991). *Visions of: Independence—productivity—integration for people with developmental disabilities.* Washington, DC: Administration on Developmental Disabilities.

Center for Psychiatric Rehabilitation (1988, May). *Community support network news.* Boston, MA: Center for Psychiatric Rehabilitation.

Clearinghouse on Disability Information (1989). *Pocket guide to federal help for individuals with disabilities.* Washington, DC: Clearinghouse on Disability Information.

Missouri Linc (1987). *Missouri transition guide: Procedures and resources.* Columbia, MO: Missouri Linc.

Missouri Protection and Advocacy Services (1991). *Legal rights for Missourians with disabilities.* Jefferson City, MO: Missouri Protection and Advocacy Services.

National Mental Health Association & National Mental Health Consumers' Association (1989). *Resource and training manual: Involving consumers and family members in protection and advocacy for mentally ill individuals systems.* Alexandria, Virginia: National Mental Health Association.

U.S. Department of Justice (1991). *Americans with disabilities act requirements fact sheet.* Washington, DC: U.S. Department of Justice.

U.S. Department of Justice (1991). *Americans with disabilities act requirements in public accommodations fact sheet.* Washington, DC: U.S. Department of Justice.

U.S. Department of Justice (1991). *Americans with disabilities act statutory deadlines.* Washington, DC: U.S. Department of Justice.

AUTHOR INDEX

SUBJECT INDEX